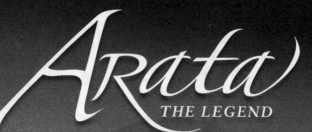

Arata THE LEGEND

CHARACTERS

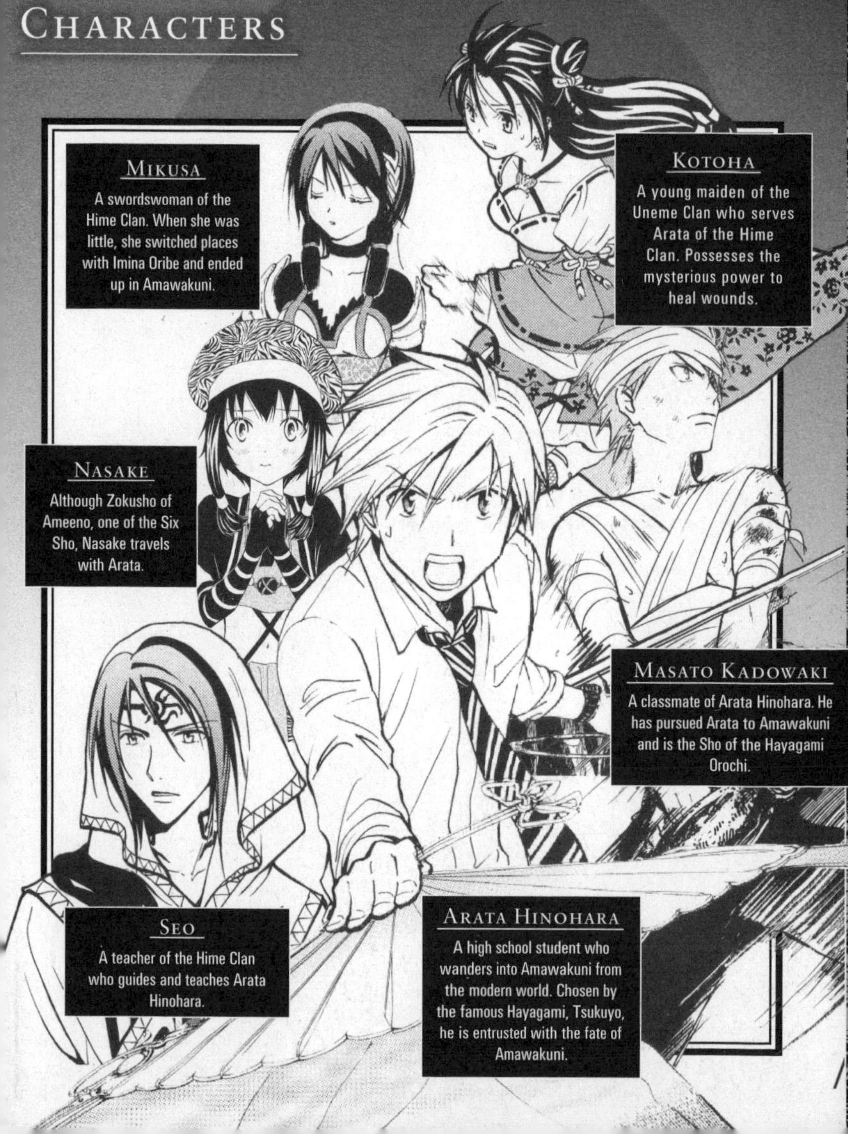

MIKUSA

A swordswoman of the Hime Clan. When she was little, she switched places with Imina Oribe and ended up in Amawakuni.

KOTOHA

A young maiden of the Uneme Clan who serves Arata of the Hime Clan. Possesses the mysterious power to heal wounds.

NASAKE

Although Zokusho of Ameeno, one of the Six Sho, Nasake travels with Arata.

MASATO KADOWAKI

A classmate of Arata Hinohara. He has pursued Arata to Amawakuni and is the Sho of the Hayagami Orochi.

SEO

A teacher of the Hime Clan who guides and teaches Arata Hinohara.

ARATA HINOHARA

A high school student who wanders into Amawakuni from the modern world. Chosen by the famous Hayagami, Tsukuyo, he is entrusted with the fate of Amawakuni.

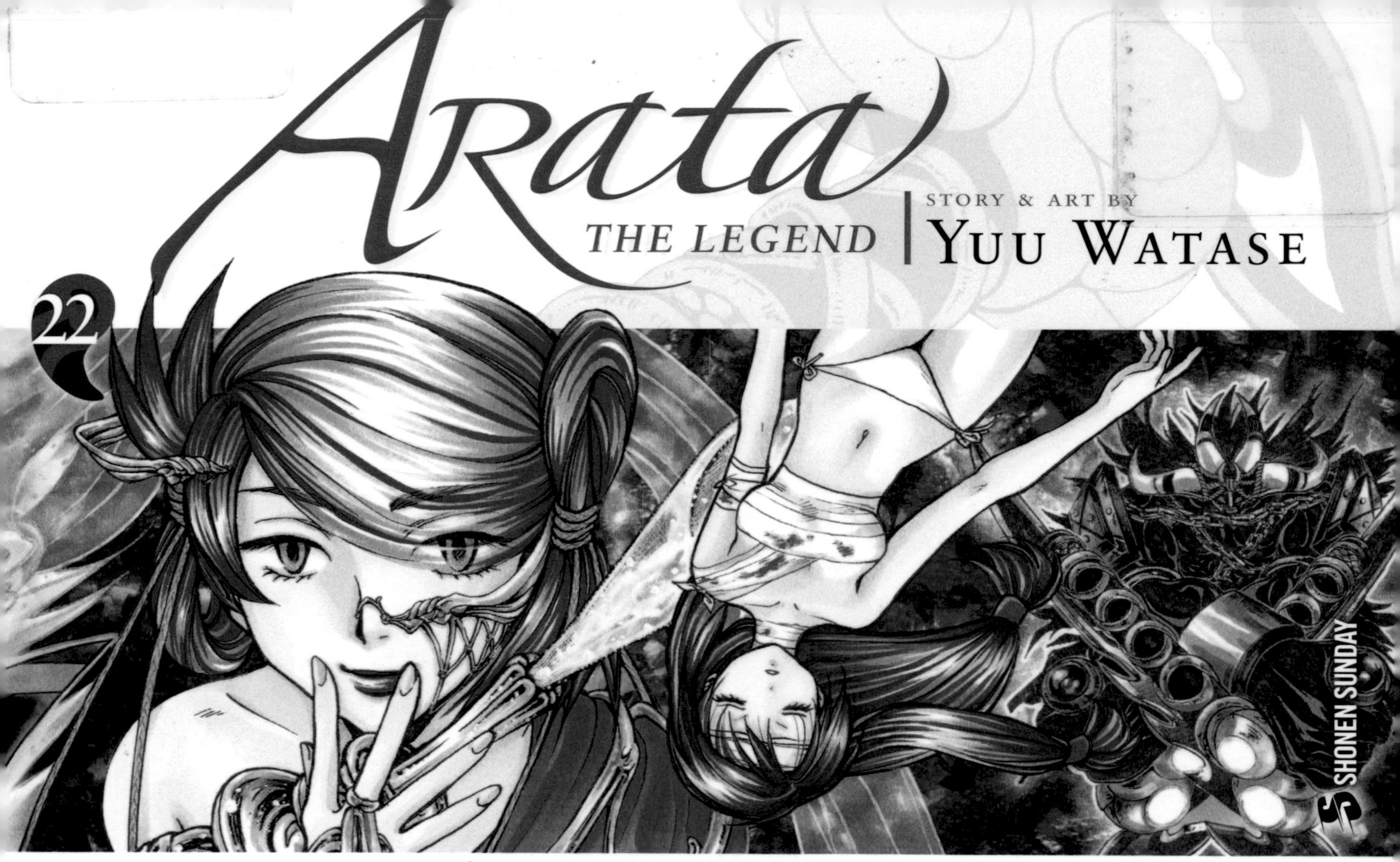
Arata
THE LEGEND
STORY & ART BY
YUU WATASE
22
SHONEN SUNDAY

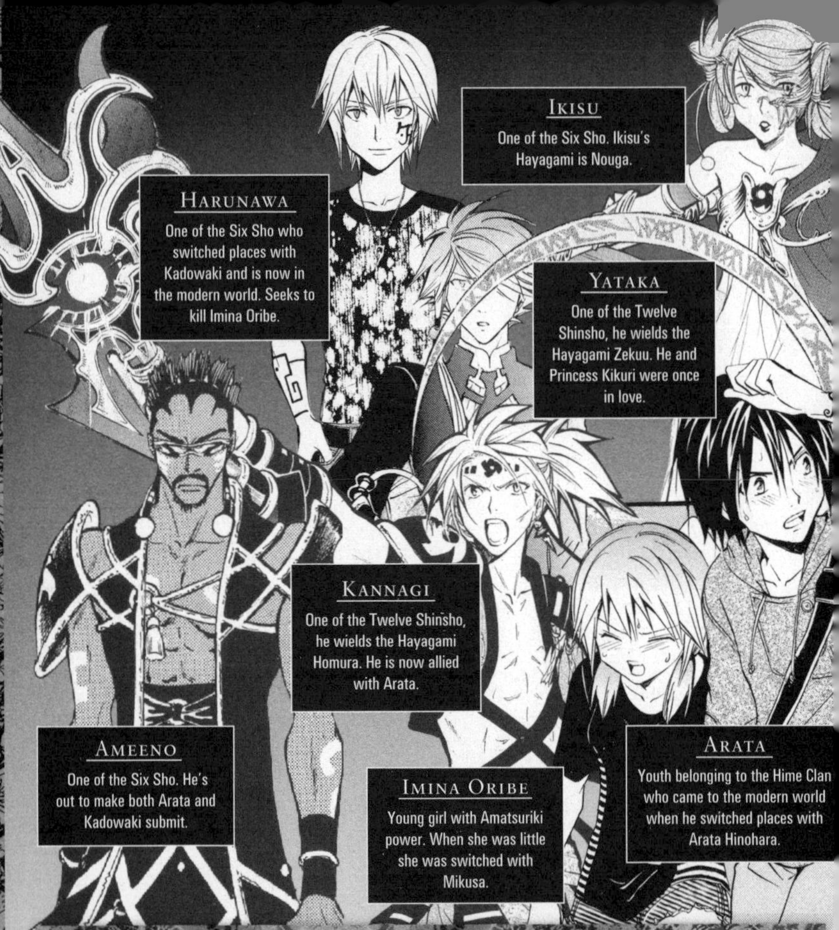
IKISU
One of the Six Sho. Ikisu's Hayagami is Nouga.
HARUNAWA
One of the Six Sho who switched places with Kadowaki and is now in the modern world. Seeks to kill Imina Oribe.
YATAKA
One of the Twelve Shinsho, he wields the Hayagami Zekuu. He and Princess Kikuri were once in love.
KANNAGI
One of the Twelve Shinsho, he wields the Hayagami Homura. He is now allied with Arata.
AMEENO
One of the Six Sho. He's out to make both Arata and Kadowaki submit.
IMINA ORIBE
Young girl with Amatsuriki power. When she was little she was switched with Mikusa.
ARATA
Youth belonging to the Hime Clan who came to the modern world when he switched places with Arata Hinohara.

The Story Thus Far

Arata Hinohara, finding himself in Amawakuni, a land in another dimension, is chosen as the successor to the legendary Hayagami Tsukuyo. In order to stop the fighting that ensued after Princess Kikuri's collapse, he continues his journey to make all the Sho submit and unify the Hayagami.

Kanate, who once journeyed with Arata, voluntarily submits to Arata's rival Kadowaki in order to give Arata and Kadowaki a chance to fight and perhaps settle matters between them. But Kadowaki unwisely lets Arata believe Kanate was made to submit by force. This so enrages Arata that he demonizes and winds up seriously injuring his companion Kotoha. Desperate to make amends, Arata and his mentor Seo enter the territory of Ikisu, one of Arata's enemies, to find someone who can heal Kotoha's wounds. But a complication arises when another enemy, Ameeno, shows up!

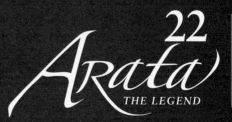

22

Arata

THE LEGEND

CONTENTS

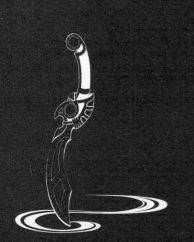

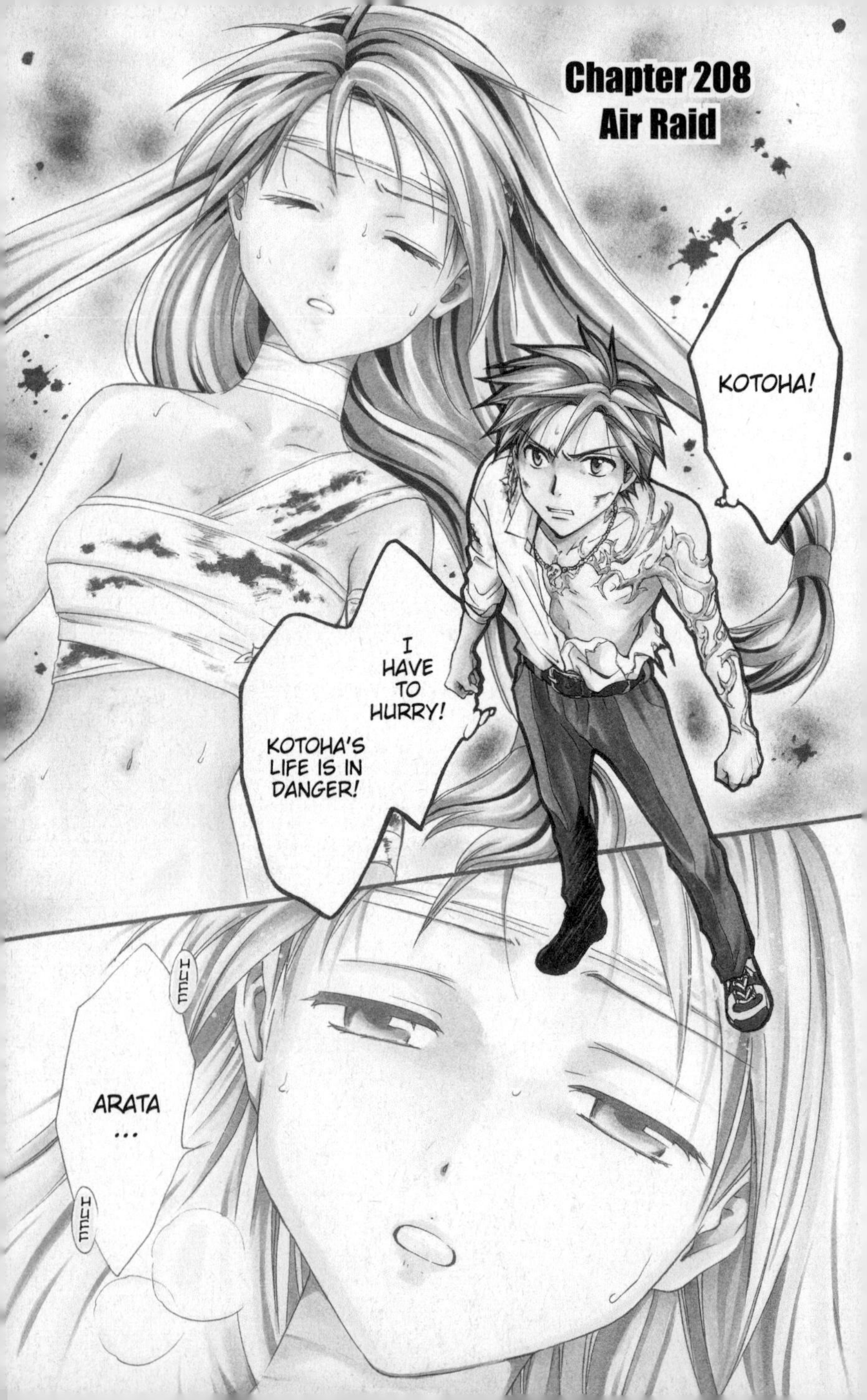
Chapter 208
Air Raid
KOTOHA!
I HAVE TO HURRY!
KOTOHA'S LIFE IS IN DANGER!
HUFF
ARATA...
HUFF

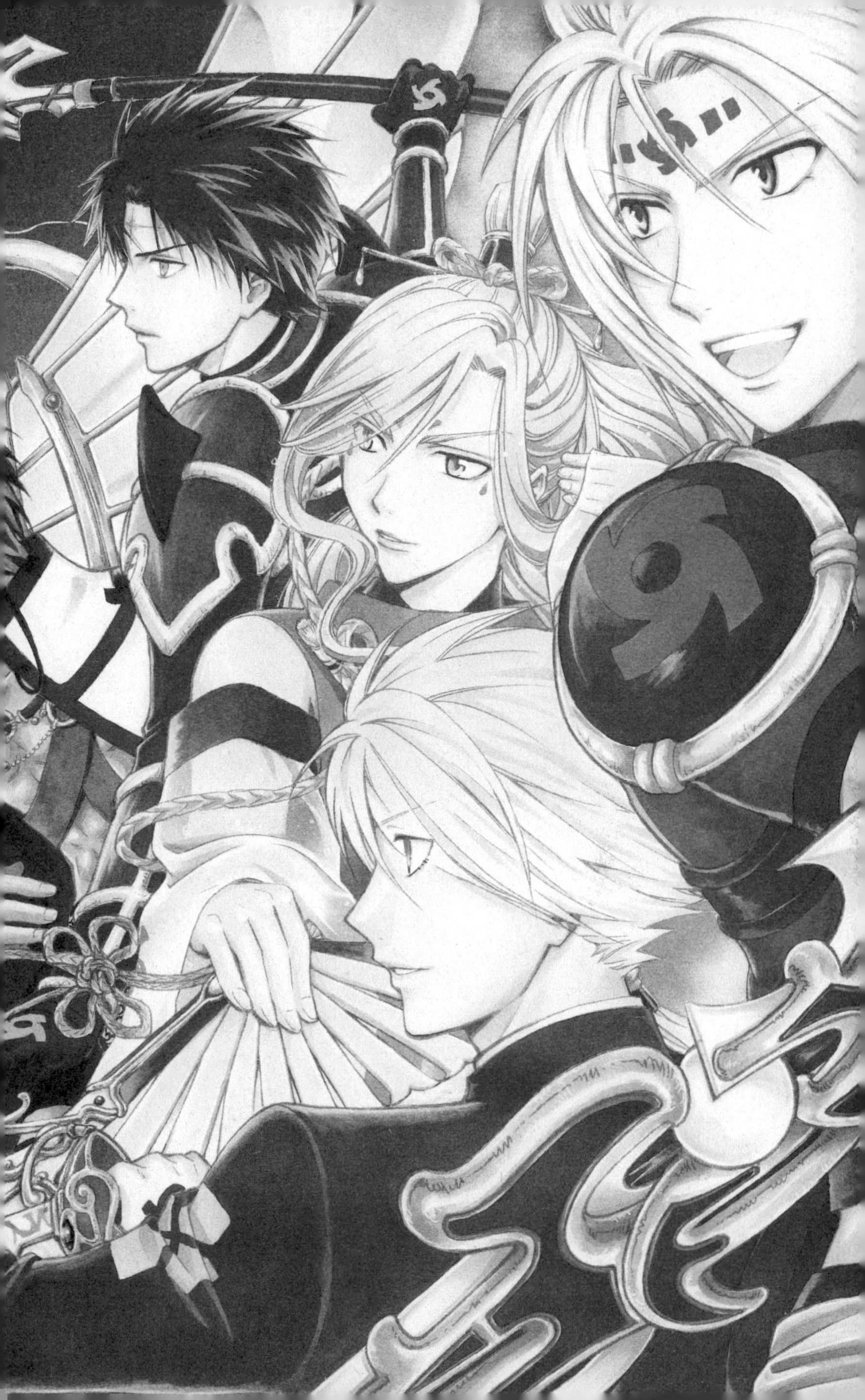

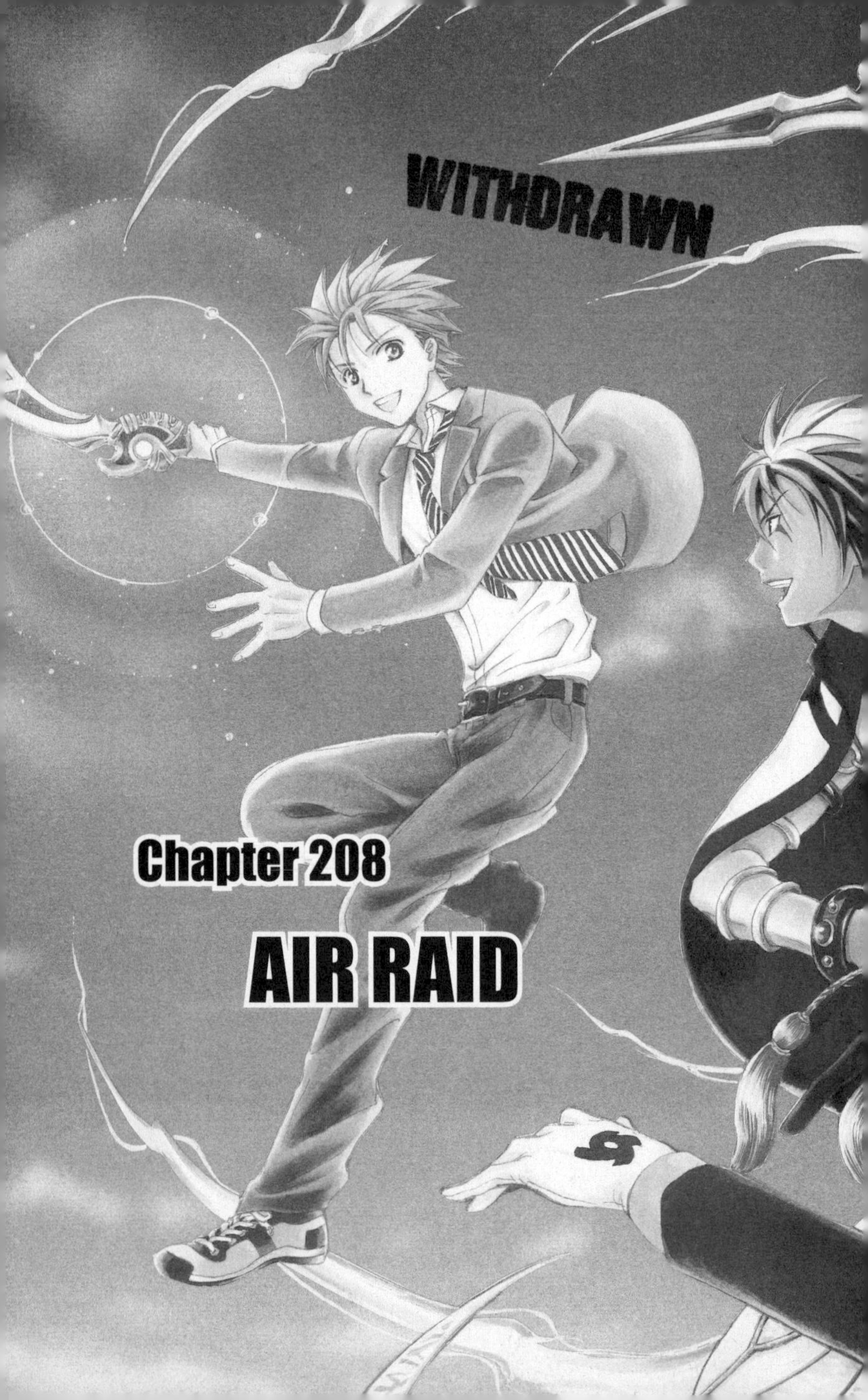
Chapter 208
AIR RAID

Arata
THE LEGEND

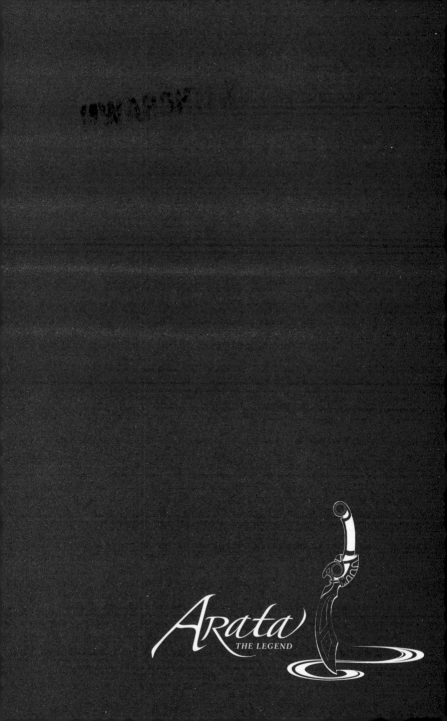

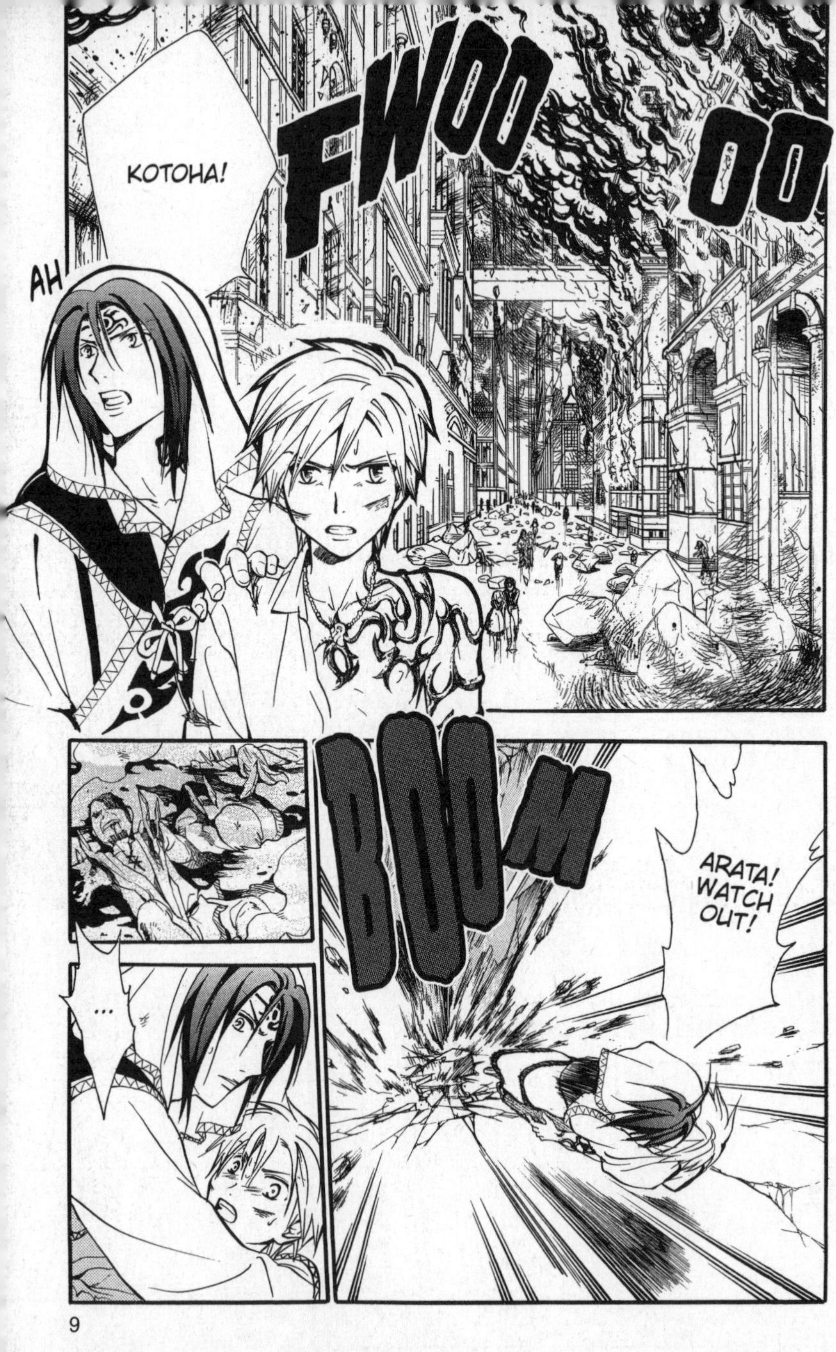
FWOOOO
KOTOHA!
AH
ARATA! WATCH OUT!
BOOM
...

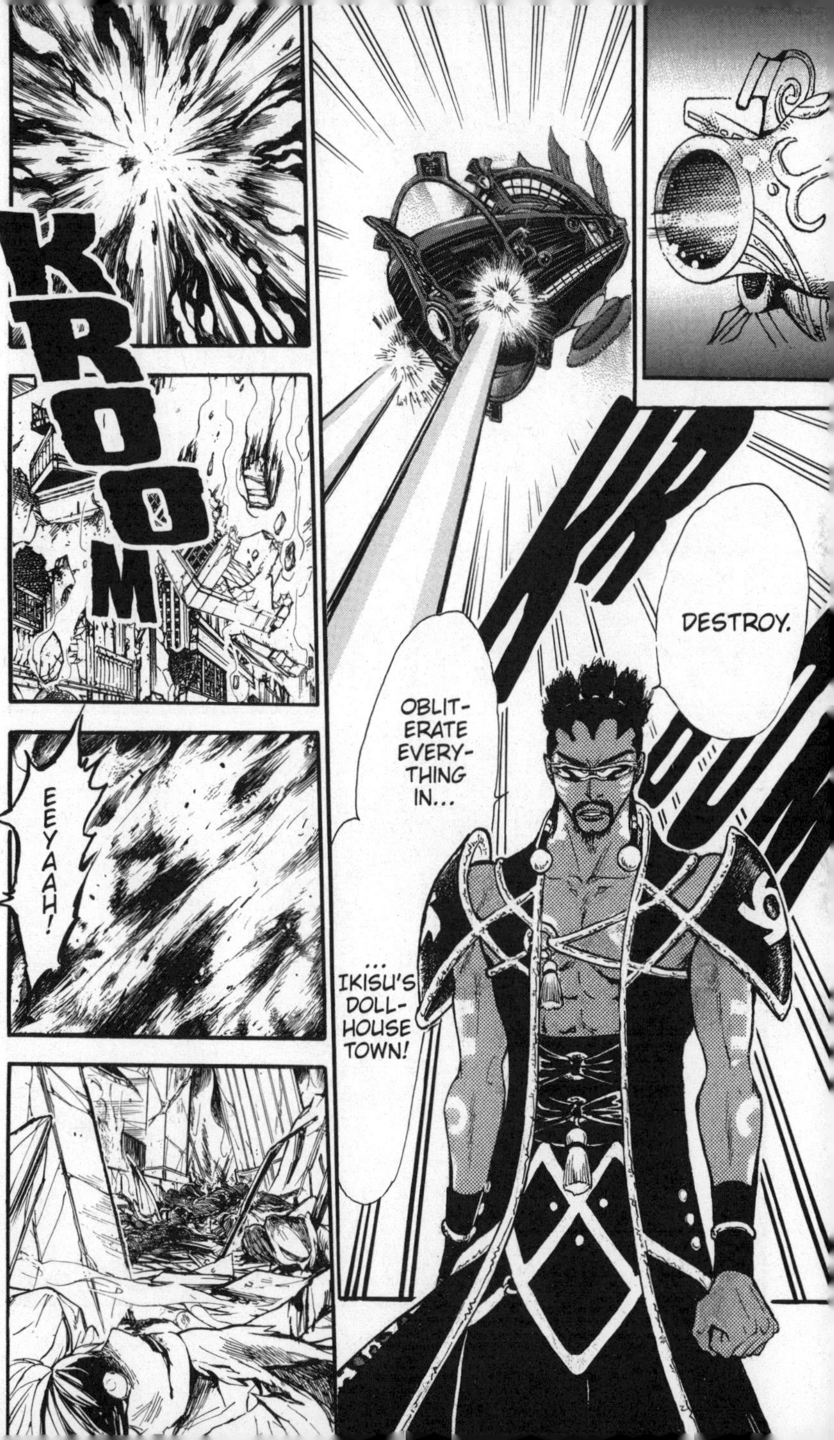
DESTROY.
OBLIT-
ERATE
EVERY-
THING
IN...
...IKISU'S
DOLL-
HOUSE
TOWN!
KROOM
EEYAAH!

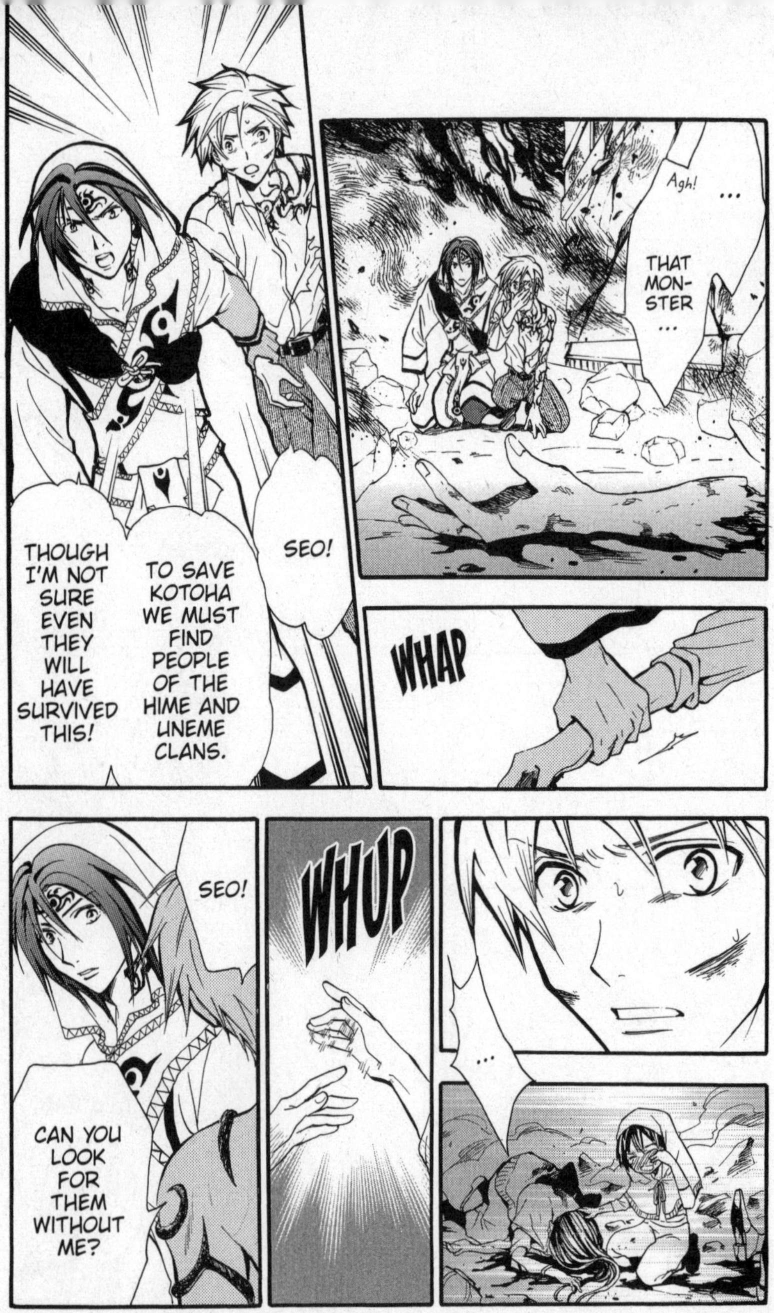
Agh!
...
THAT MONSTER ...
WHAP
SEO!
TO SAVE KOTOHA WE MUST FIND PEOPLE OF THE HIME AND UNEME CLANS.
THOUGH I'M NOT SURE EVEN THEY WILL HAVE SURVIVED THIS!
...
WHUP
SEO!
CAN YOU LOOK FOR THEM WITHOUT ME?

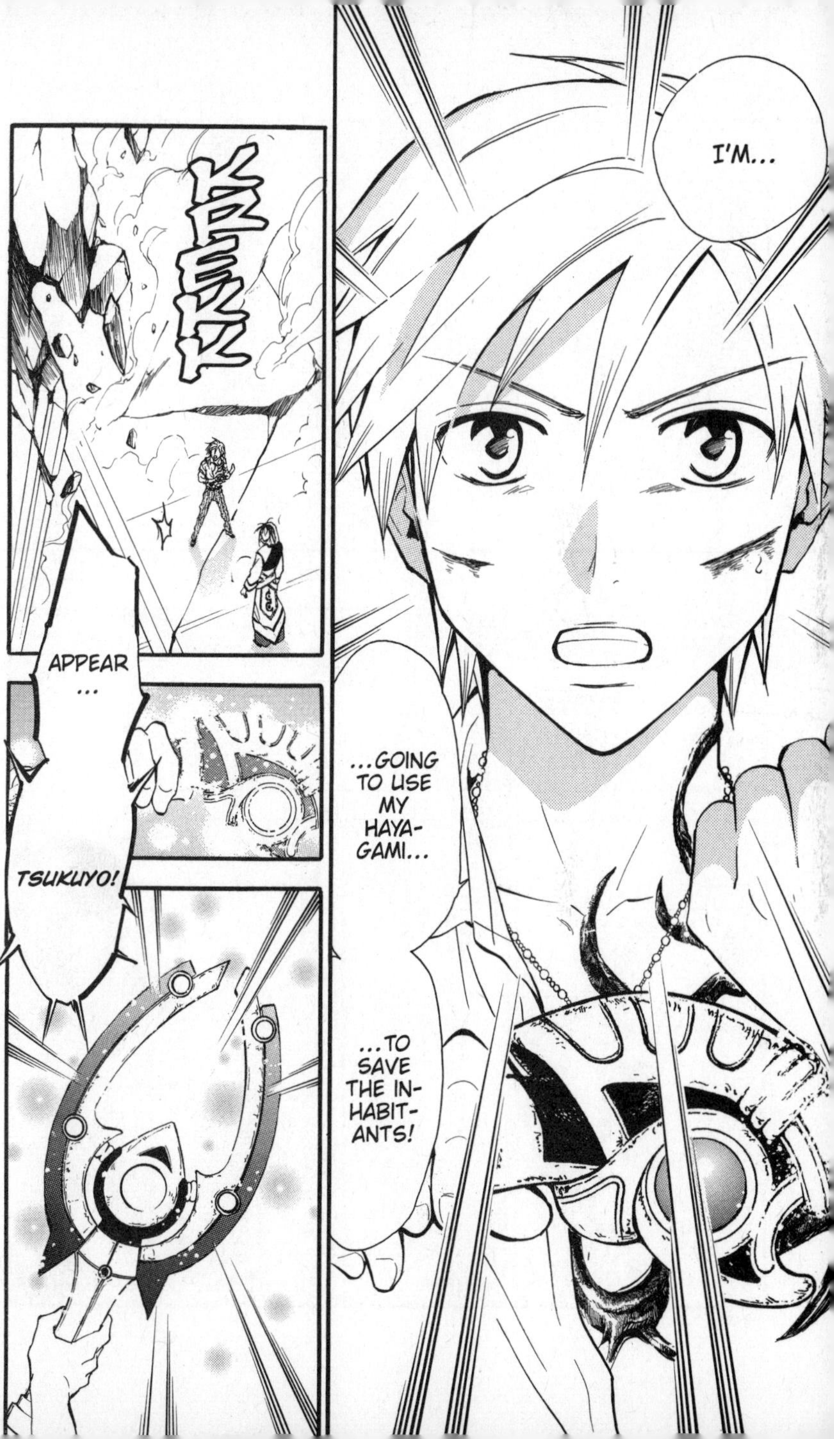
I'M...
...GOING TO USE MY HAYA-GAMI...
...TO SAVE THE IN-HABIT-ANTS!
APPEAR... TSUKUYO!

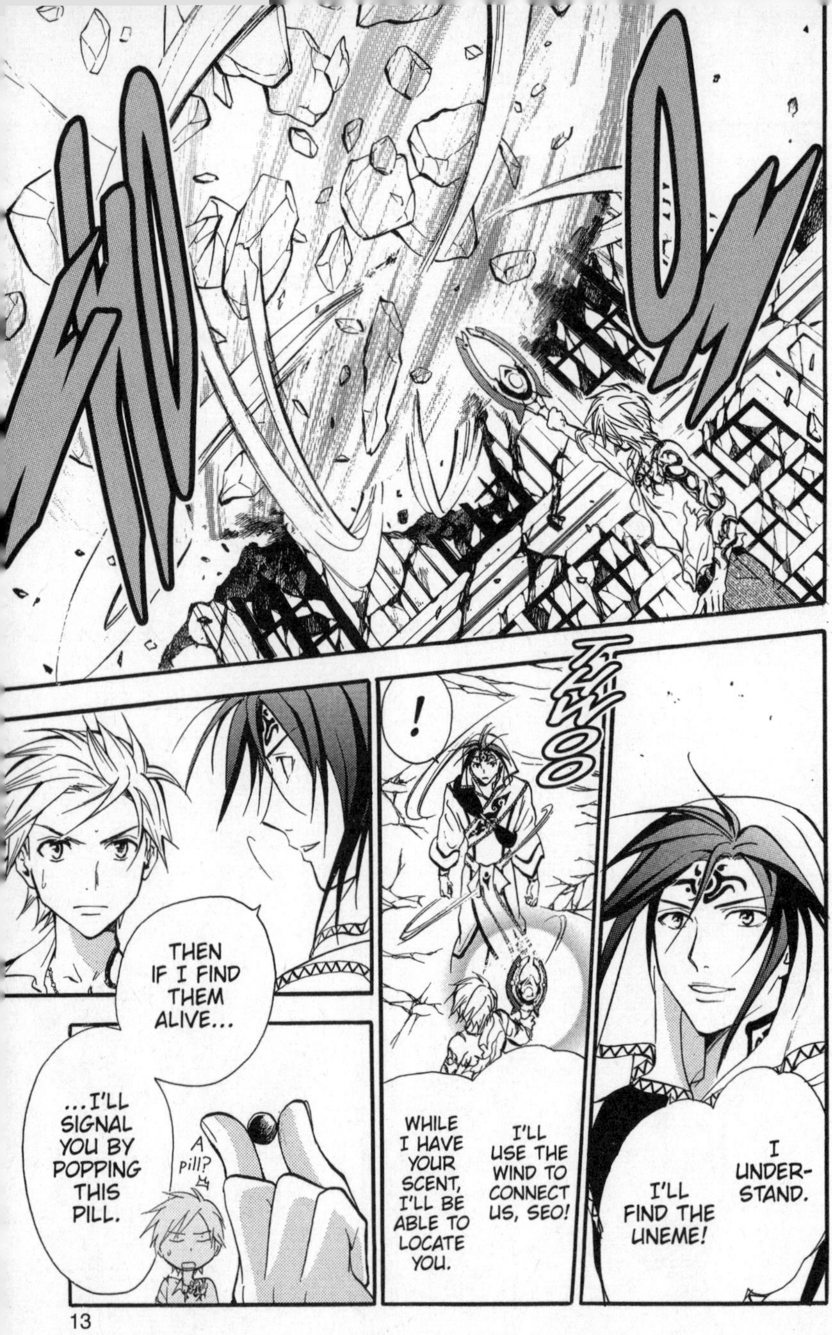
I UNDERSTAND.
I'LL FIND THE UNEME!
!
I'LL USE THE WIND TO CONNECT US, SEO!
WHILE I HAVE YOUR SCENT, I'LL BE ABLE TO LOCATE YOU.
THEN IF I FIND THEM ALIVE...
...I'LL SIGNAL YOU BY POPPING THIS PILL.
A pill?

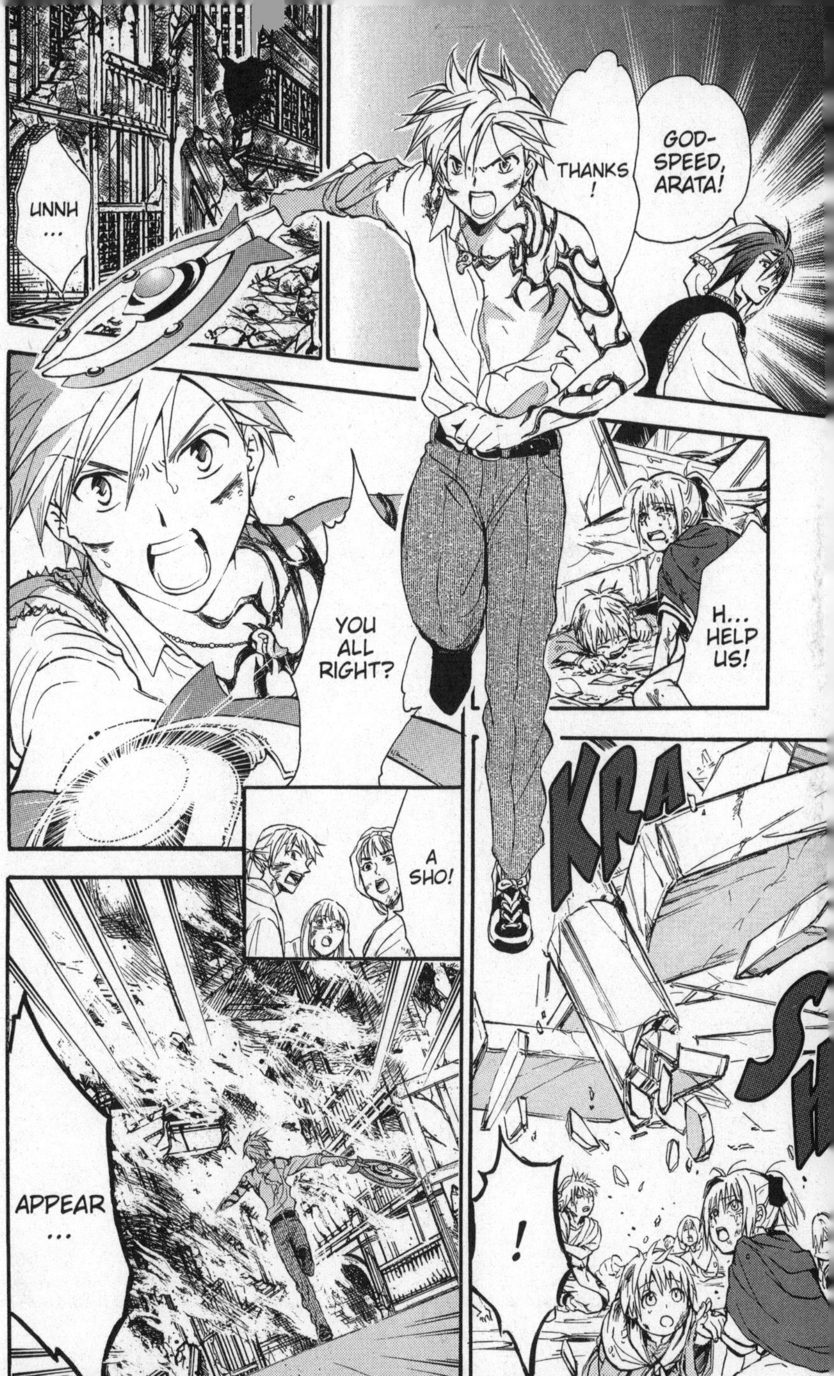
GOD-SPEED, ARATA!
THANKS!
UNNH...
H... HELP US!
YOU ALL RIGHT?
A SHO!
KRA
SH
!
APPEAR...

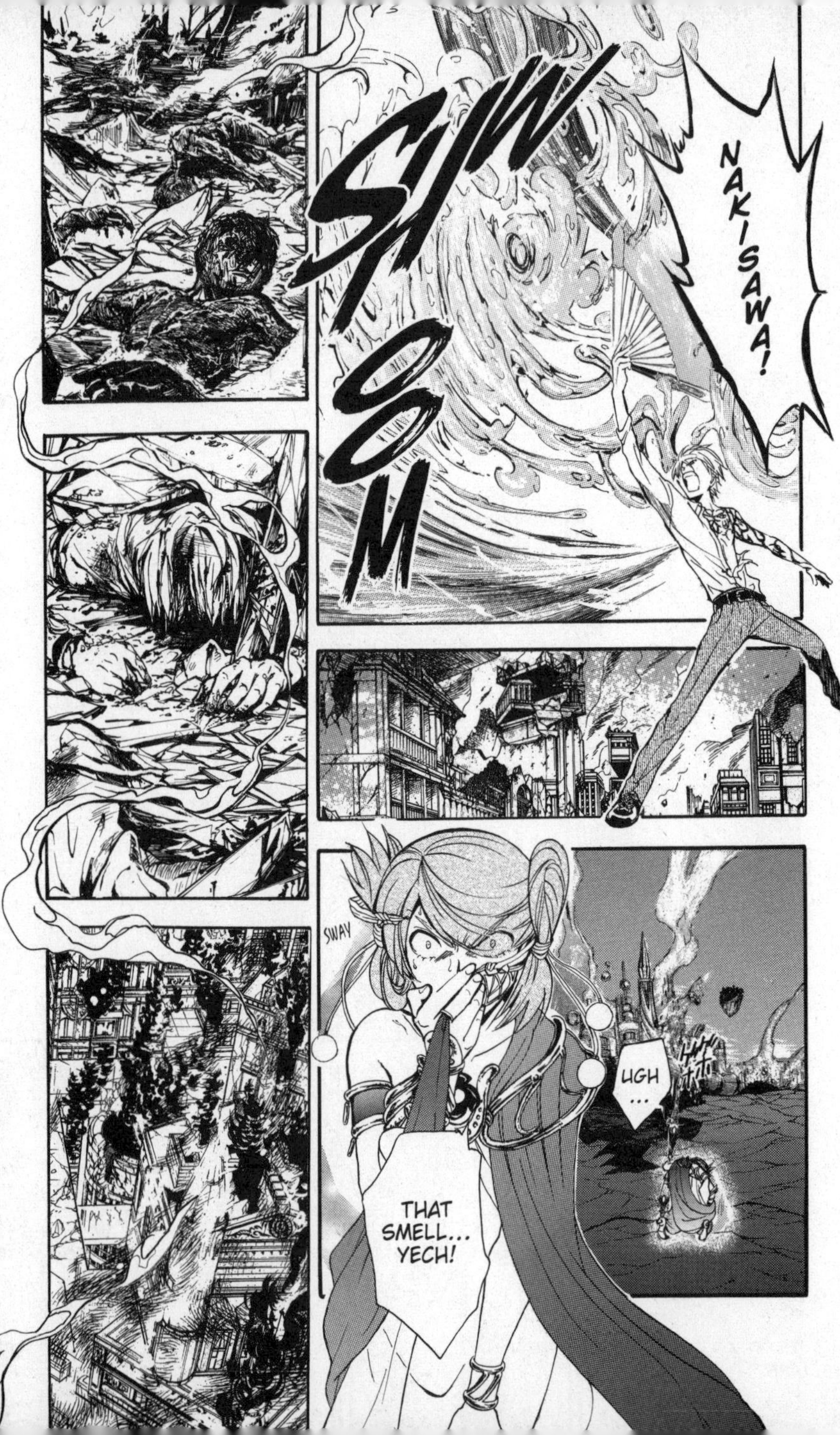
NAKISAWA!
SHWOOM
UGH...
SWAY
THAT SMELL... YECH!

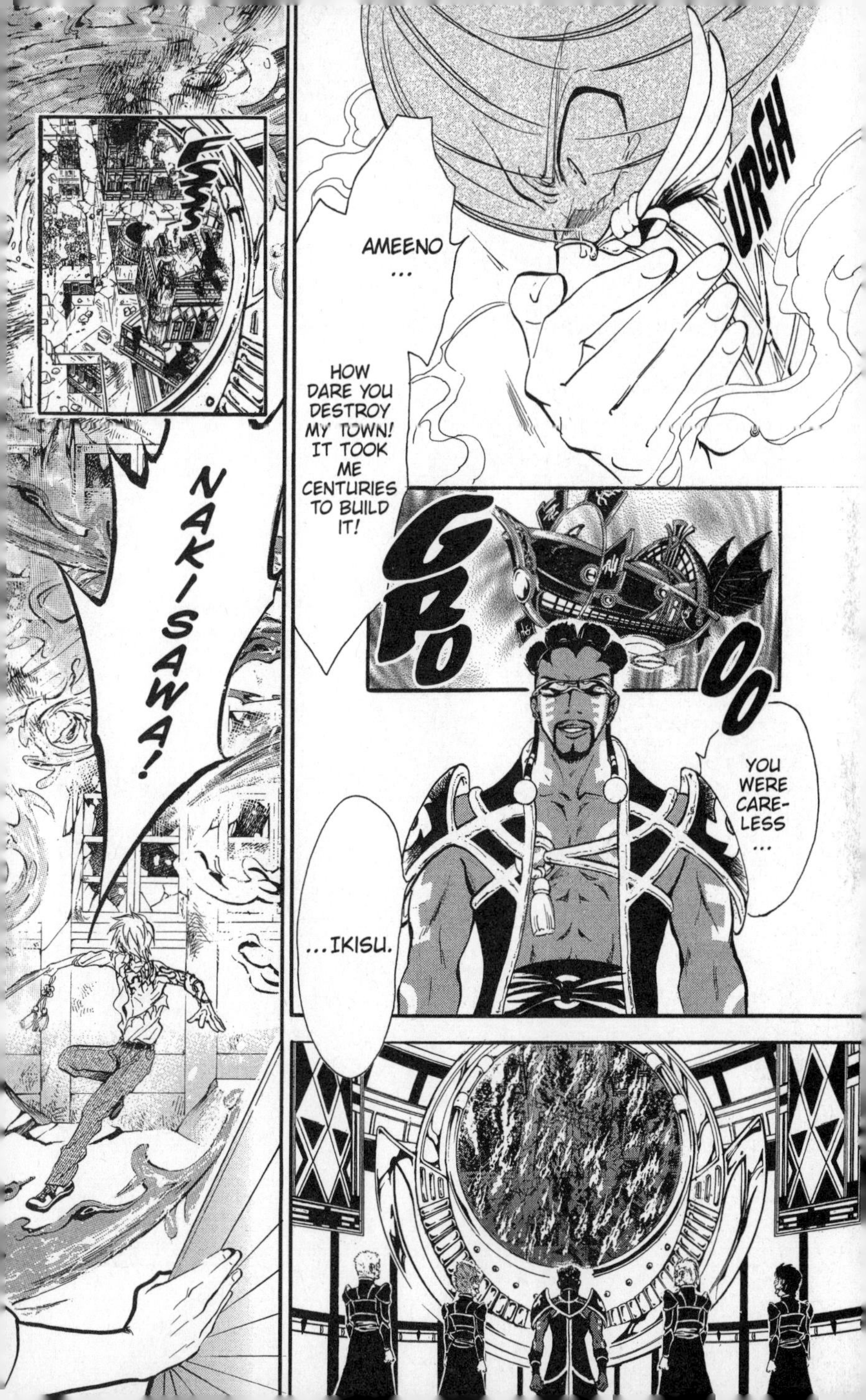
URGH
AMEENO...
HOW DARE YOU DESTROY MY TOWN! IT TOOK ME CENTURIES TO BUILD IT!
GBOOO
YOU WERE CARELESS...
...IKISU.
NAKISAWA!

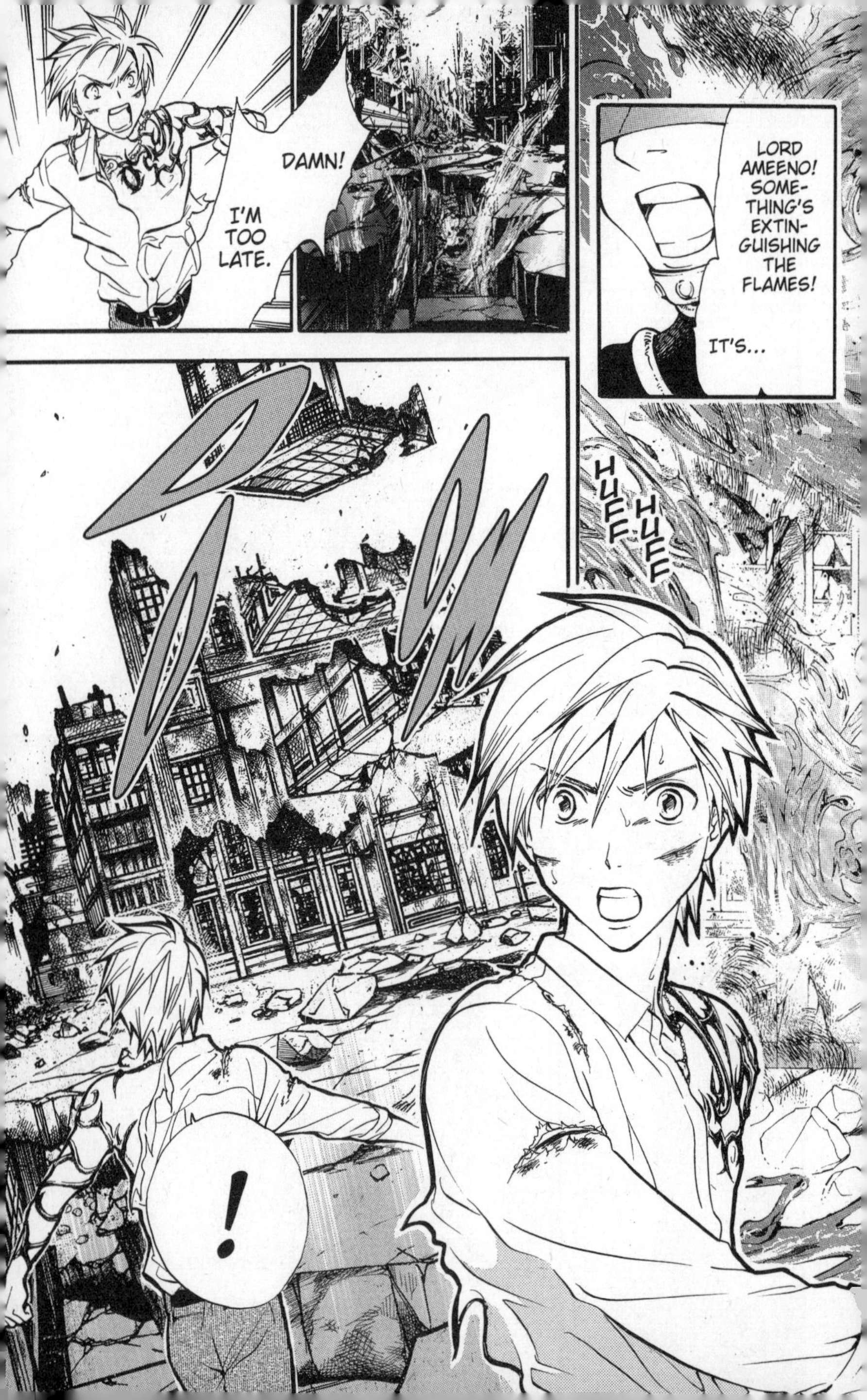
LORD AMEENO! SOME-THING'S EXTIN-GUISHING THE FLAMES!
IT'S...
DAMN!
I'M TOO LATE.
HUFF HUFF
!

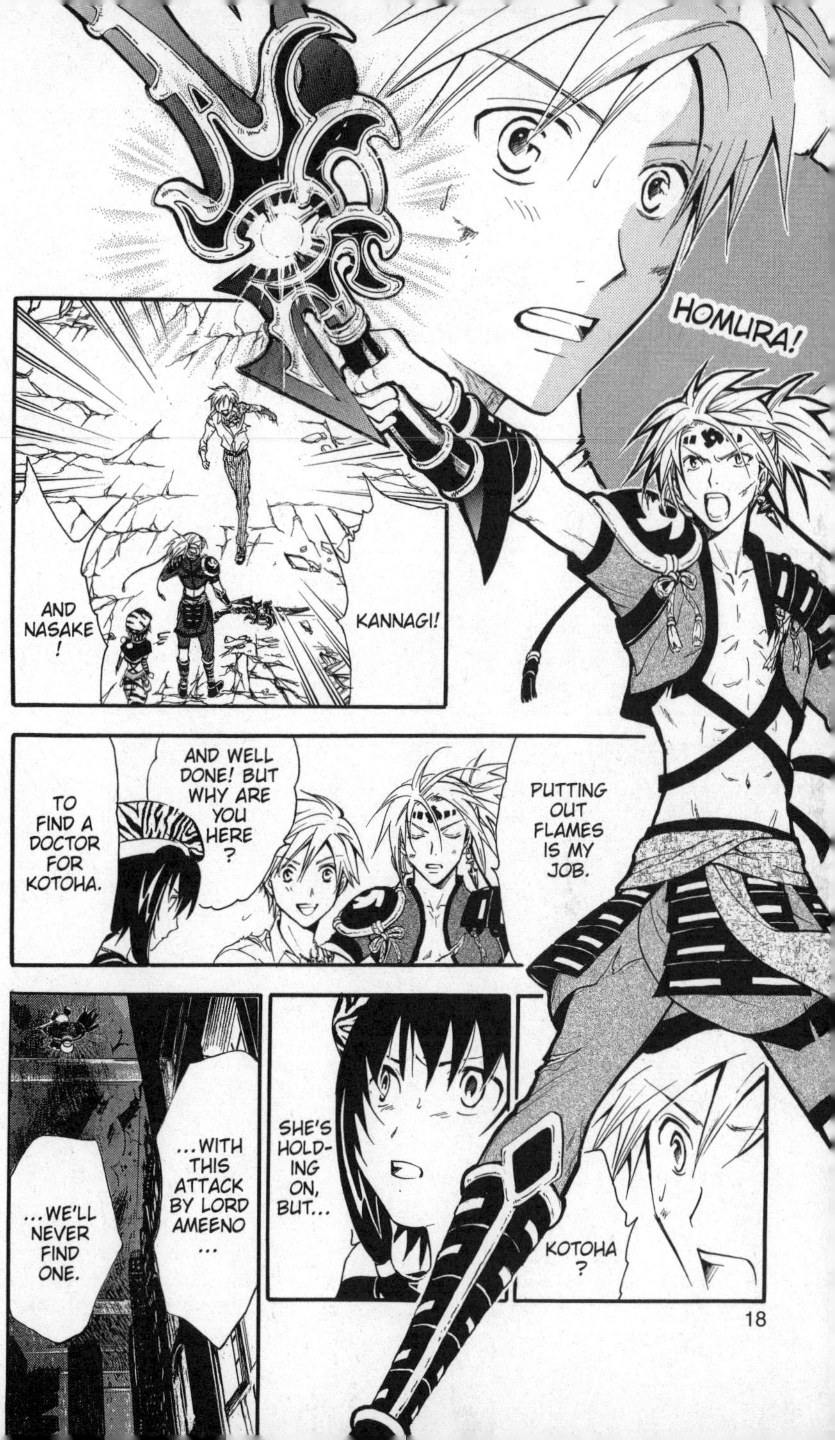
HOMURA!
KANNAGI!
AND NASAKE!
PUTTING OUT FLAMES IS MY JOB.
AND WELL DONE! BUT WHY ARE YOU HERE?
TO FIND A DOCTOR FOR KOTOHA.
KOTOHA?
SHE'S HOLD-ING ON, BUT...
...WITH THIS ATTACK BY LORD AMEENO...
...WE'LL NEVER FIND ONE.

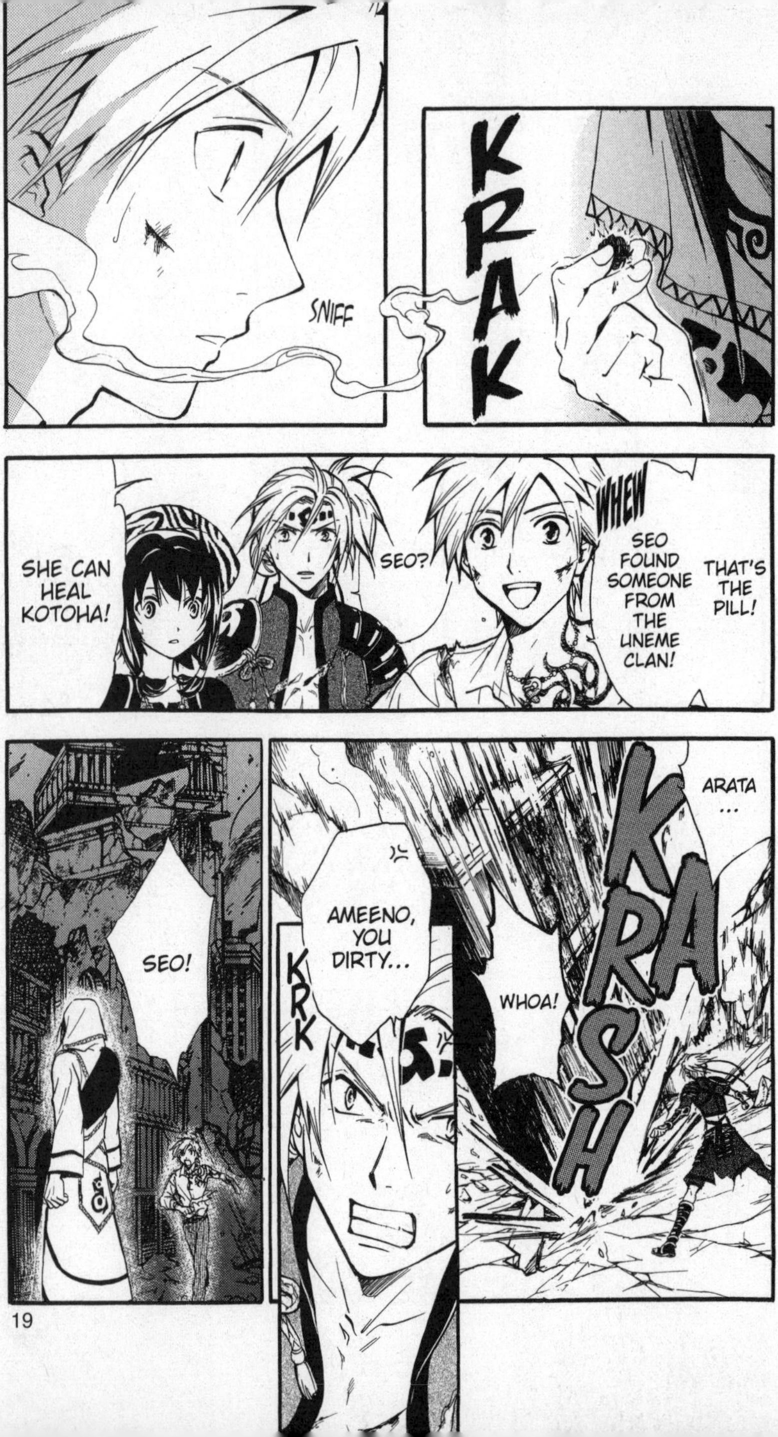
KRAK
SNIFF
THAT'S THE PILL!
WHEW
SEO FOUND SOMEONE FROM THE UNEME CLAN!
SEO?
SHE CAN HEAL KOTOHA!
ARATA ...
KRASH
WHOA!
AMEENO, YOU DIRTY...
KRK
SEO!

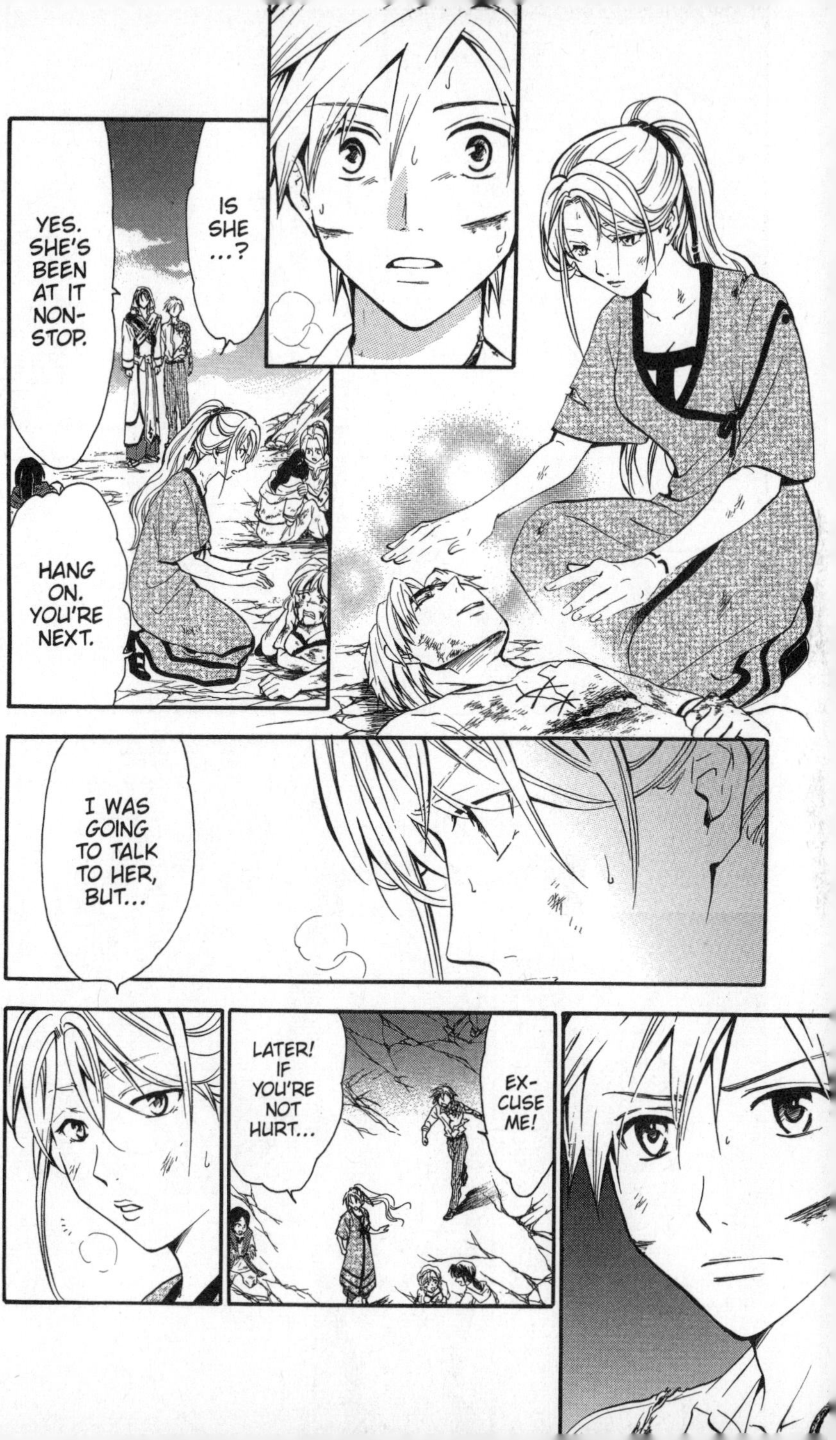
IS SHE ...?
YES. SHE'S BEEN AT IT NON-STOP.
HANG ON. YOU'RE NEXT.
I WAS GOING TO TALK TO HER, BUT...
EX-CUSE ME!
LATER! IF YOU'RE NOT HURT...

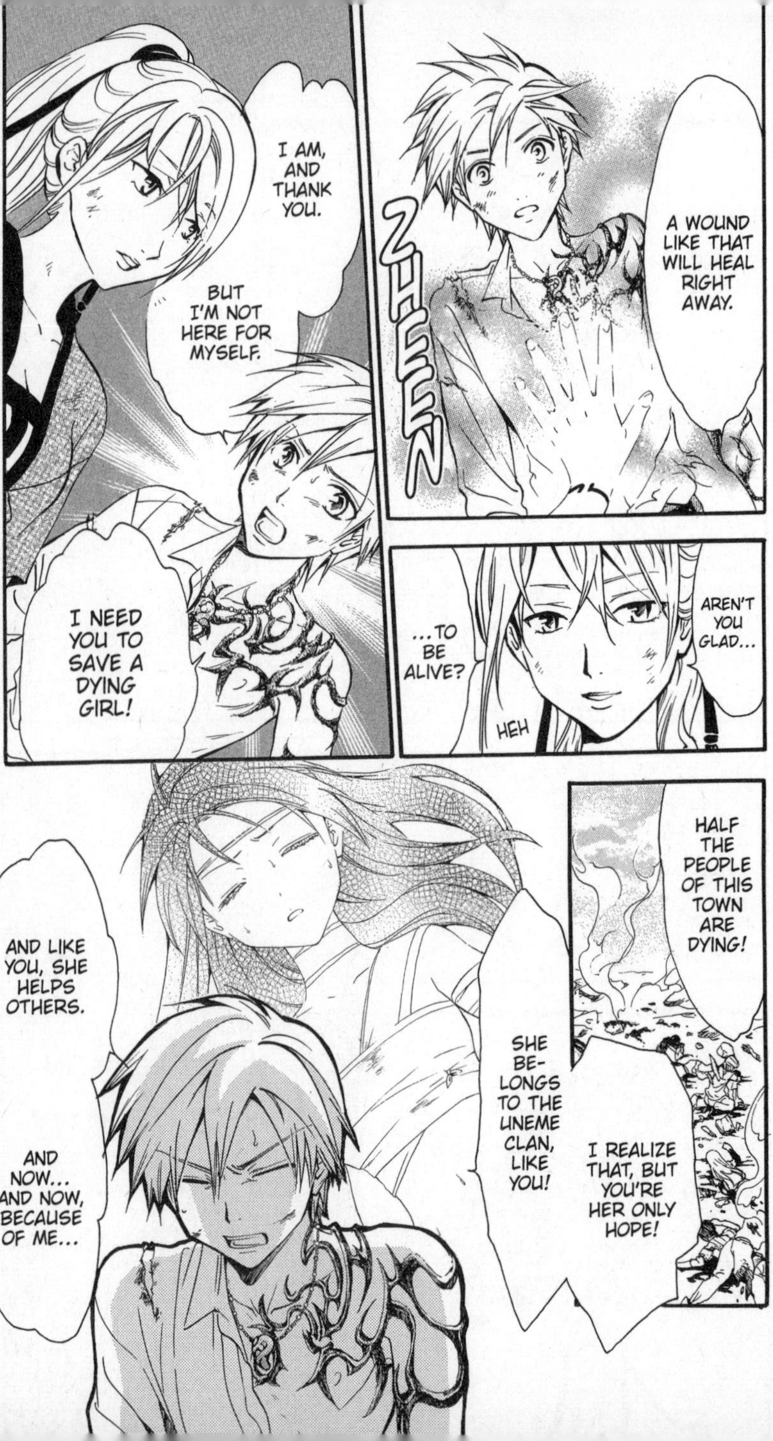
ZHEEN
A WOUND LIKE THAT WILL HEAL RIGHT AWAY.
AREN'T YOU GLAD...
...TO BE ALIVE?
HEH
I AM, AND THANK YOU.
BUT I'M NOT HERE FOR MYSELF.
I NEED YOU TO SAVE A DYING GIRL!
HALF THE PEOPLE OF THIS TOWN ARE DYING!
I REALIZE THAT, BUT YOU'RE HER ONLY HOPE!
SHE BE-LONGS TO THE UNEME CLAN, LIKE YOU!
AND LIKE YOU, SHE HELPS OTHERS.
AND NOW... AND NOW, BECAUSE OF ME...

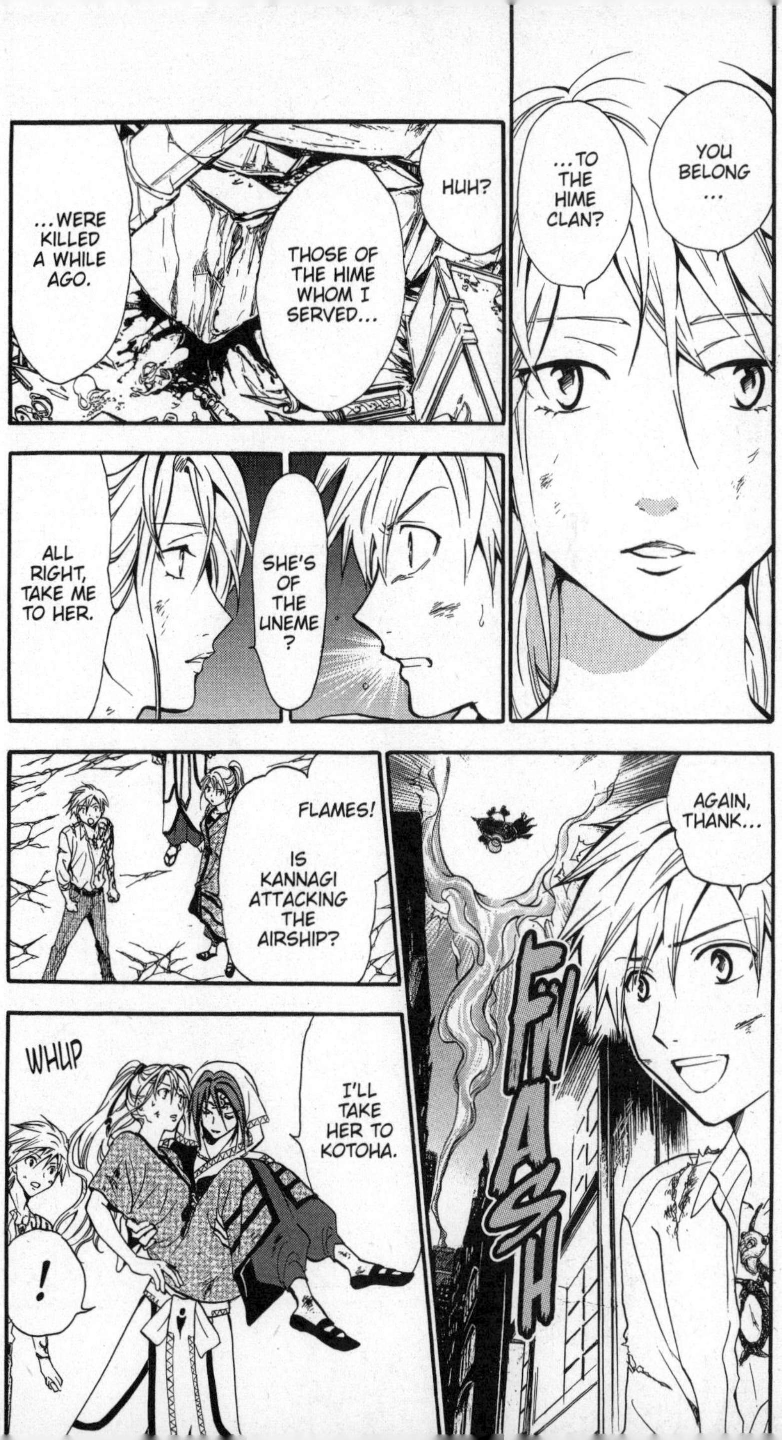
YOU BELONG...
...TO THE HIME CLAN?
HUH?
THOSE OF THE HIME WHOM I SERVED...
...WERE KILLED A WHILE AGO.
SHE'S OF THE UNEME?
ALL RIGHT, TAKE ME TO HER.
AGAIN, THANK...
FWASH
FLAMES!
IS KANNAGI ATTACKING THE AIRSHIP?
I'LL TAKE HER TO KOTOHA.
WHUP
!

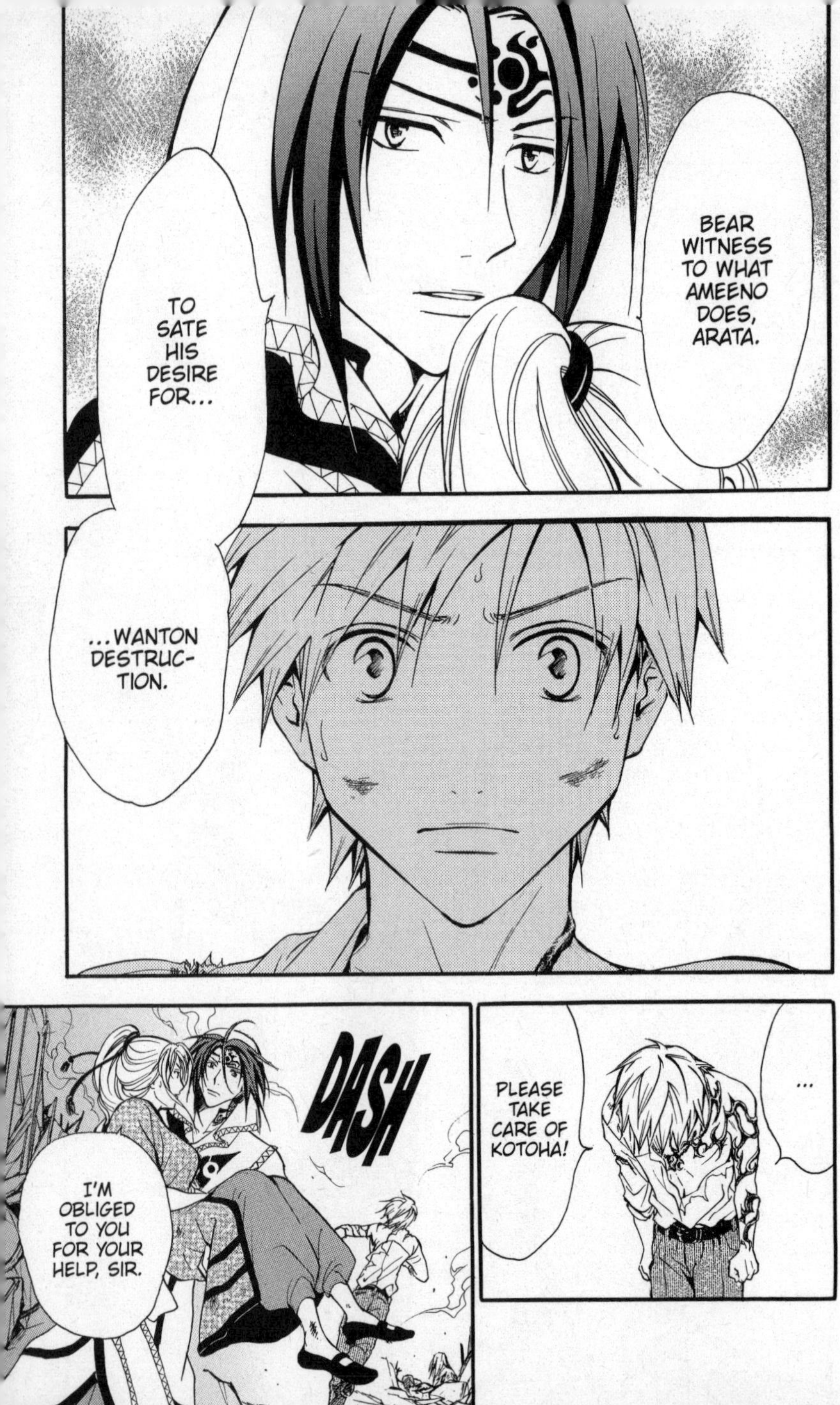
BEAR WITNESS TO WHAT AMEENO DOES, ARATA.
TO SATE HIS DESIRE FOR...
...WANTON DESTRUC-TION.
...
PLEASE TAKE CARE OF KOTOHA!
DASH
I'M OBLIGED TO YOU FOR YOUR HELP, SIR.

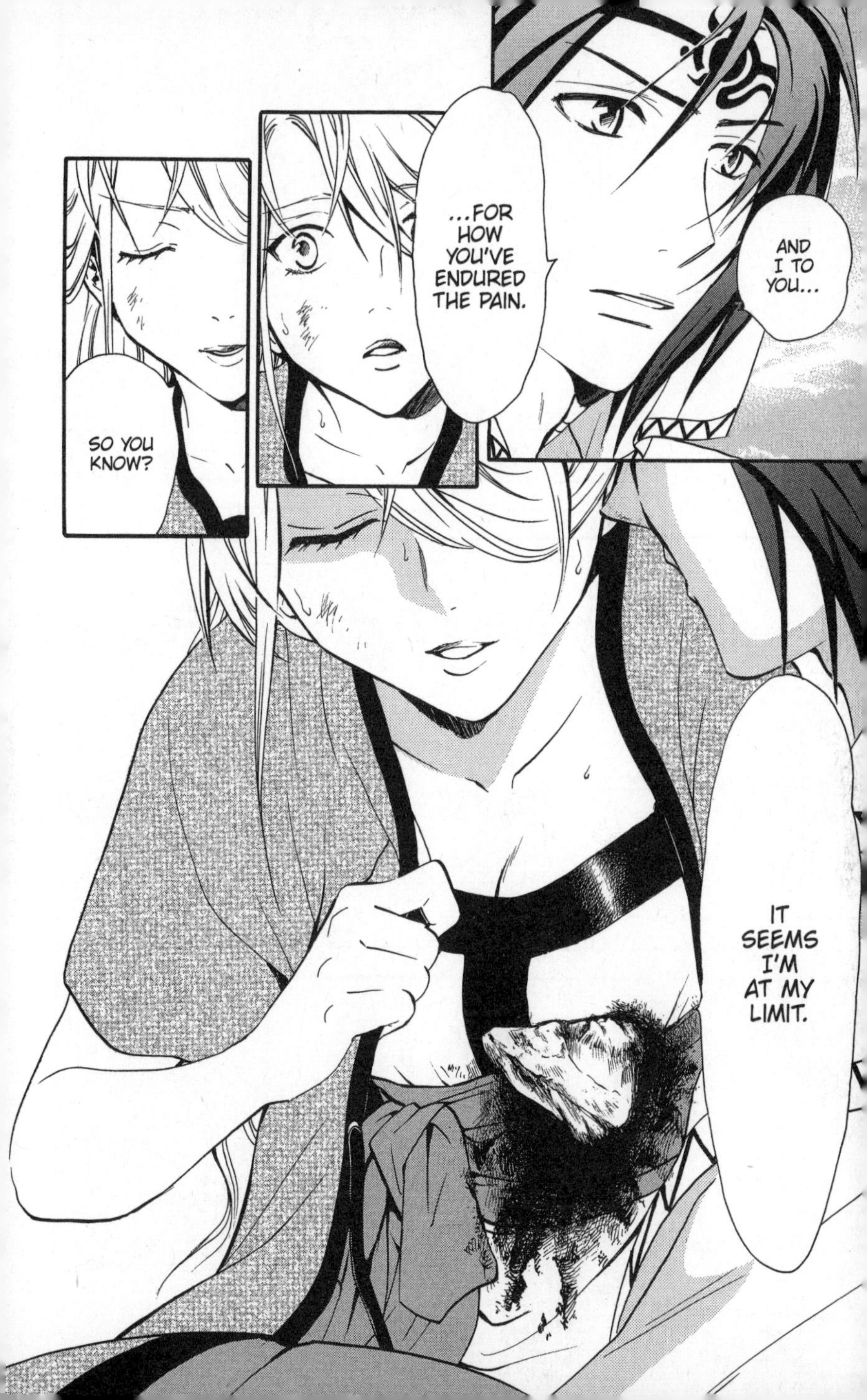
...FOR HOW YOU'VE ENDURED THE PAIN.
AND I TO YOU...
SO YOU KNOW?
IT SEEMS I'M AT MY LIMIT.

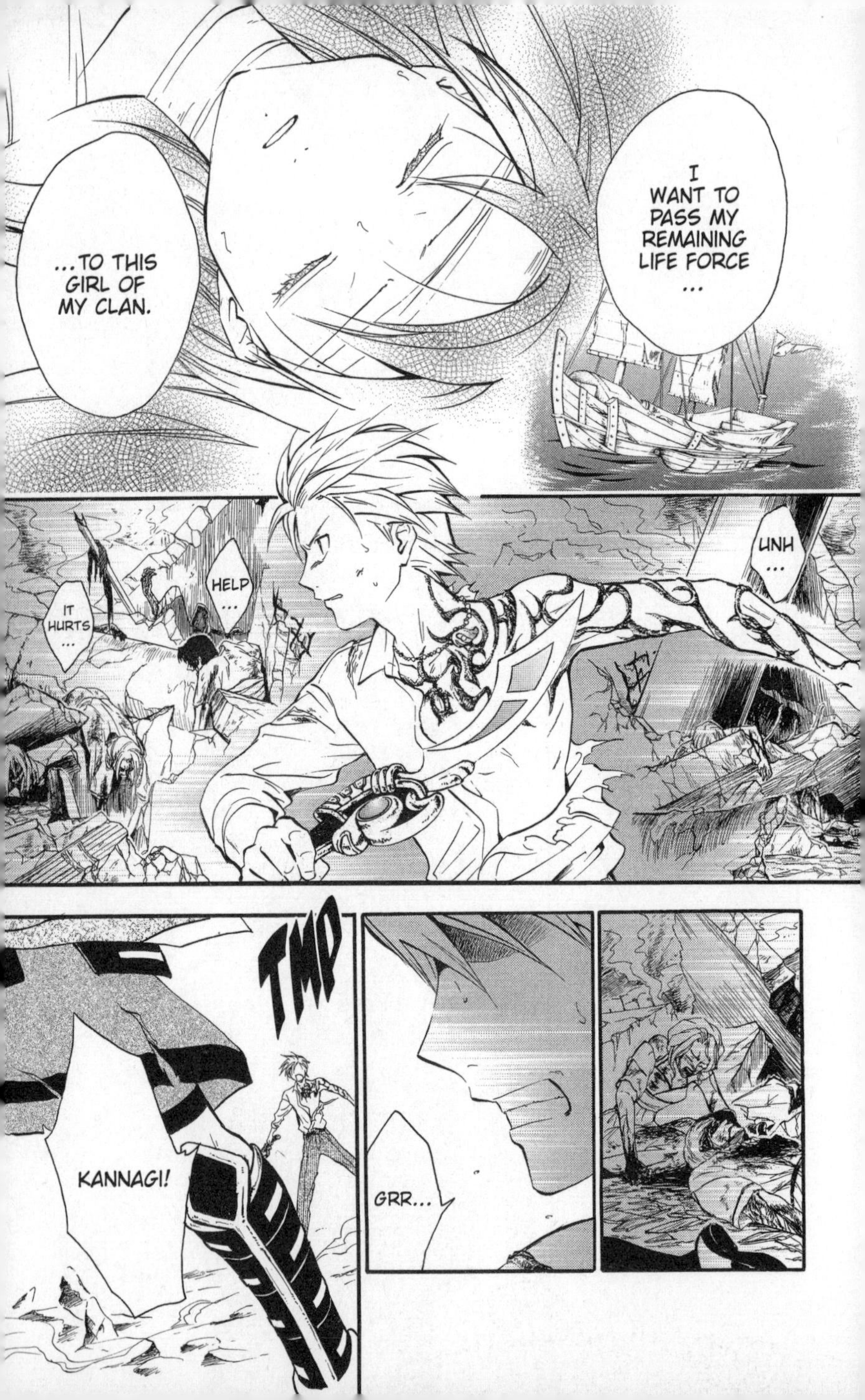
I WANT TO PASS MY REMAINING LIFE FORCE ...
...TO THIS GIRL OF MY CLAN.
UNH ...
HELP ...
IT HURTS ...
GRR...
TMP
KANNAGI!

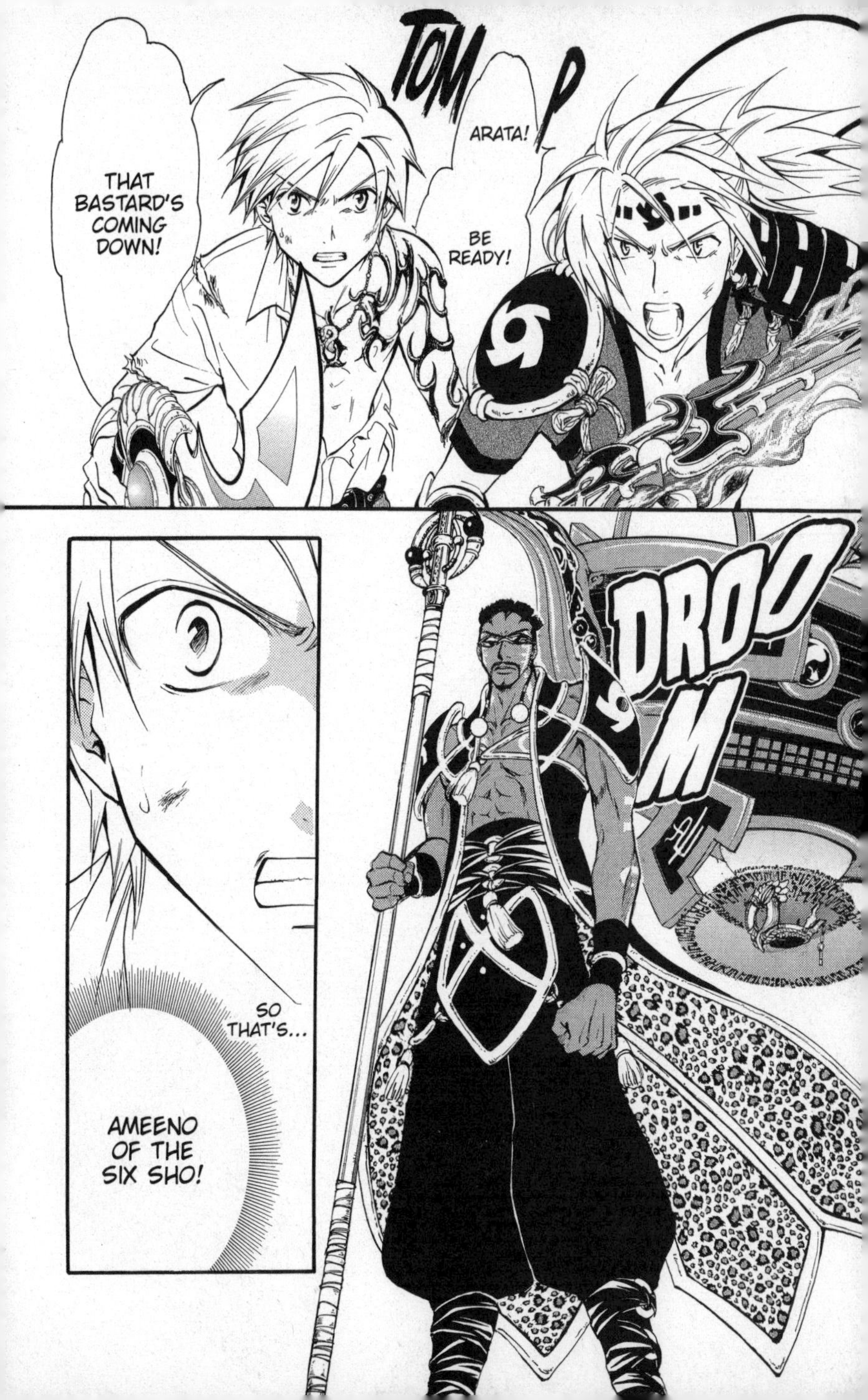
TOMP
ARATA!
BE READY!
THAT BASTARD'S COMING DOWN!
DROOM
SO THAT'S...
AMEENO OF THE SIX SHO!

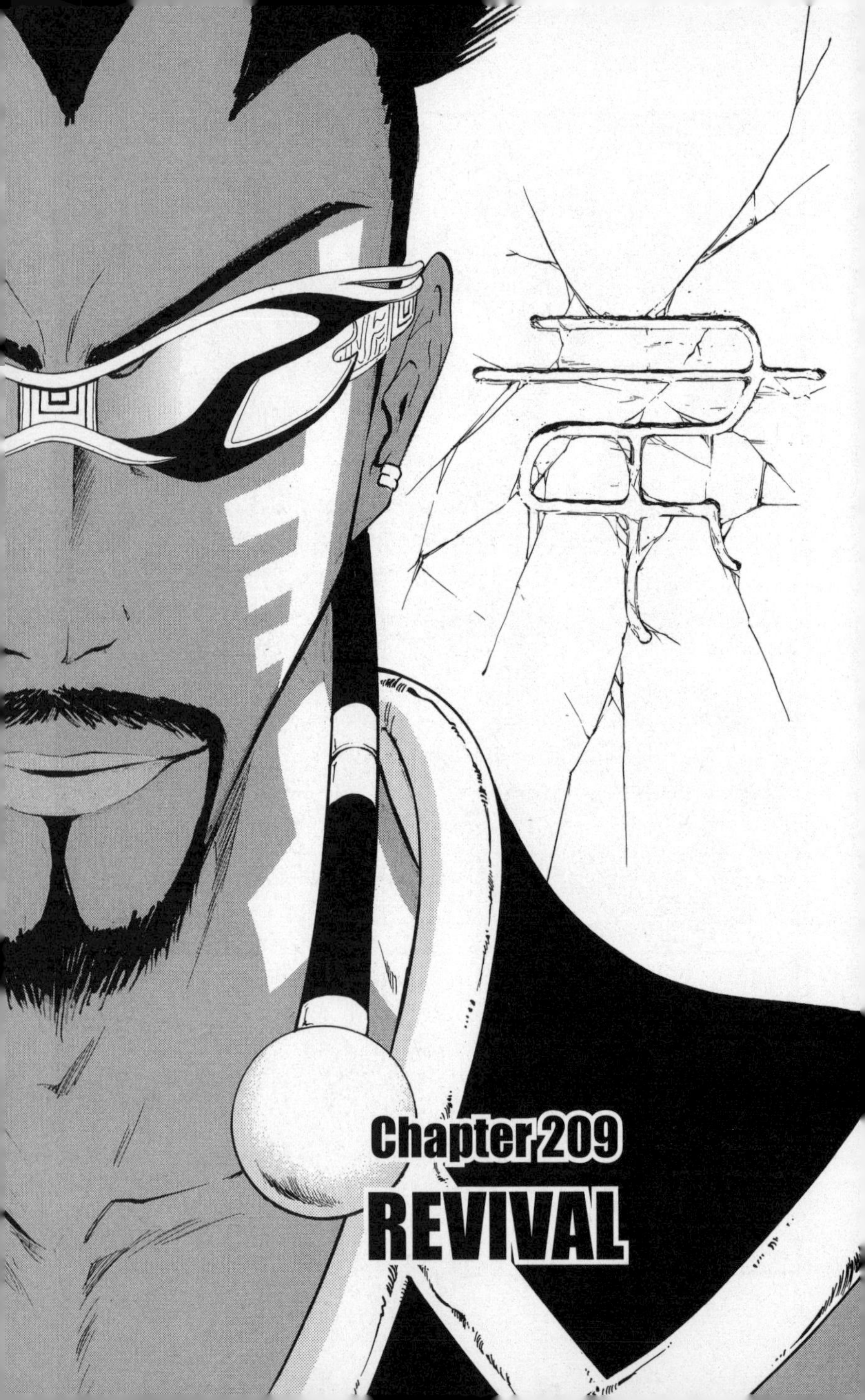
Chapter 209
REVIVAL

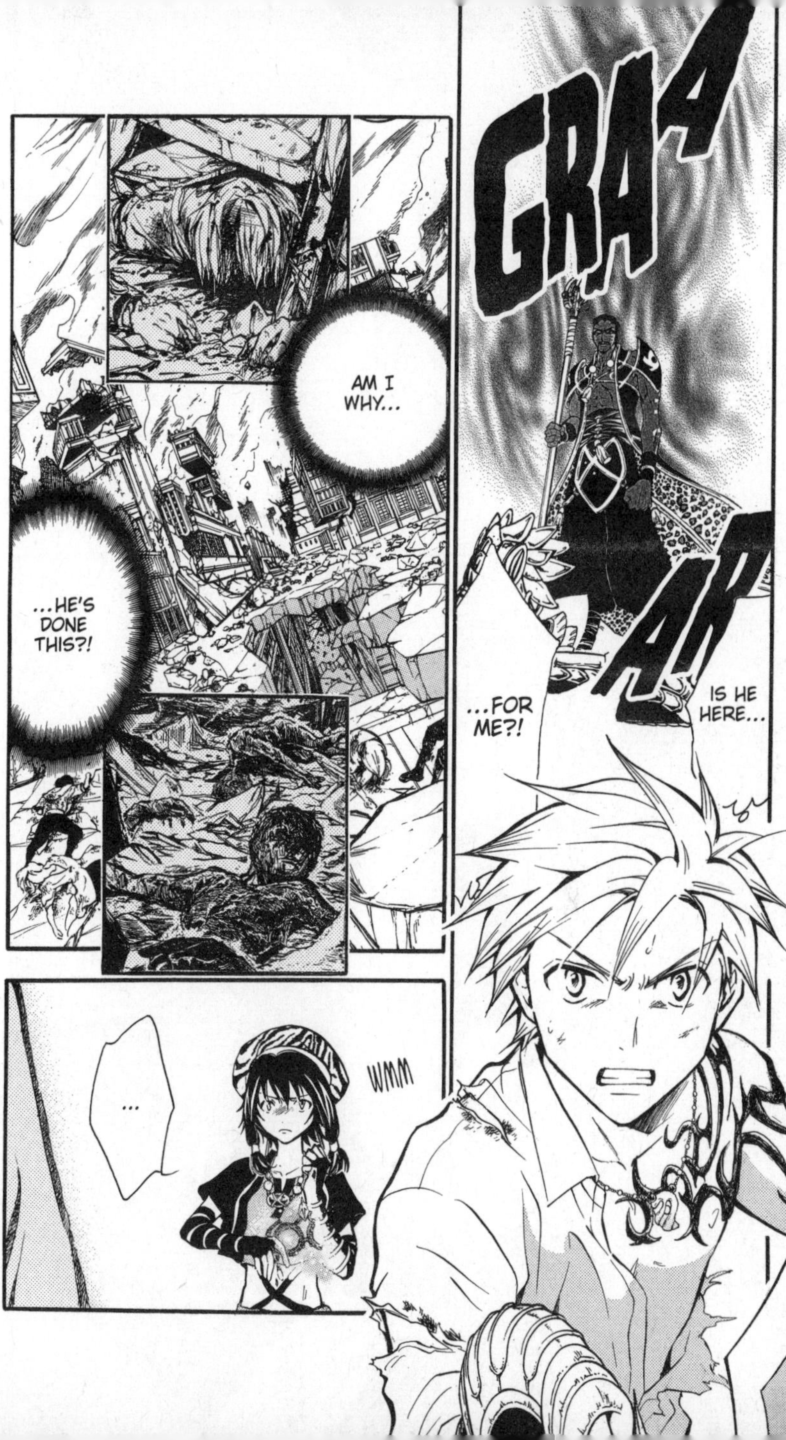

GRAA
AH
IS HE HERE...
...FOR ME?!
AM I WHY...
...HE'S DONE THIS?!
WMM
...

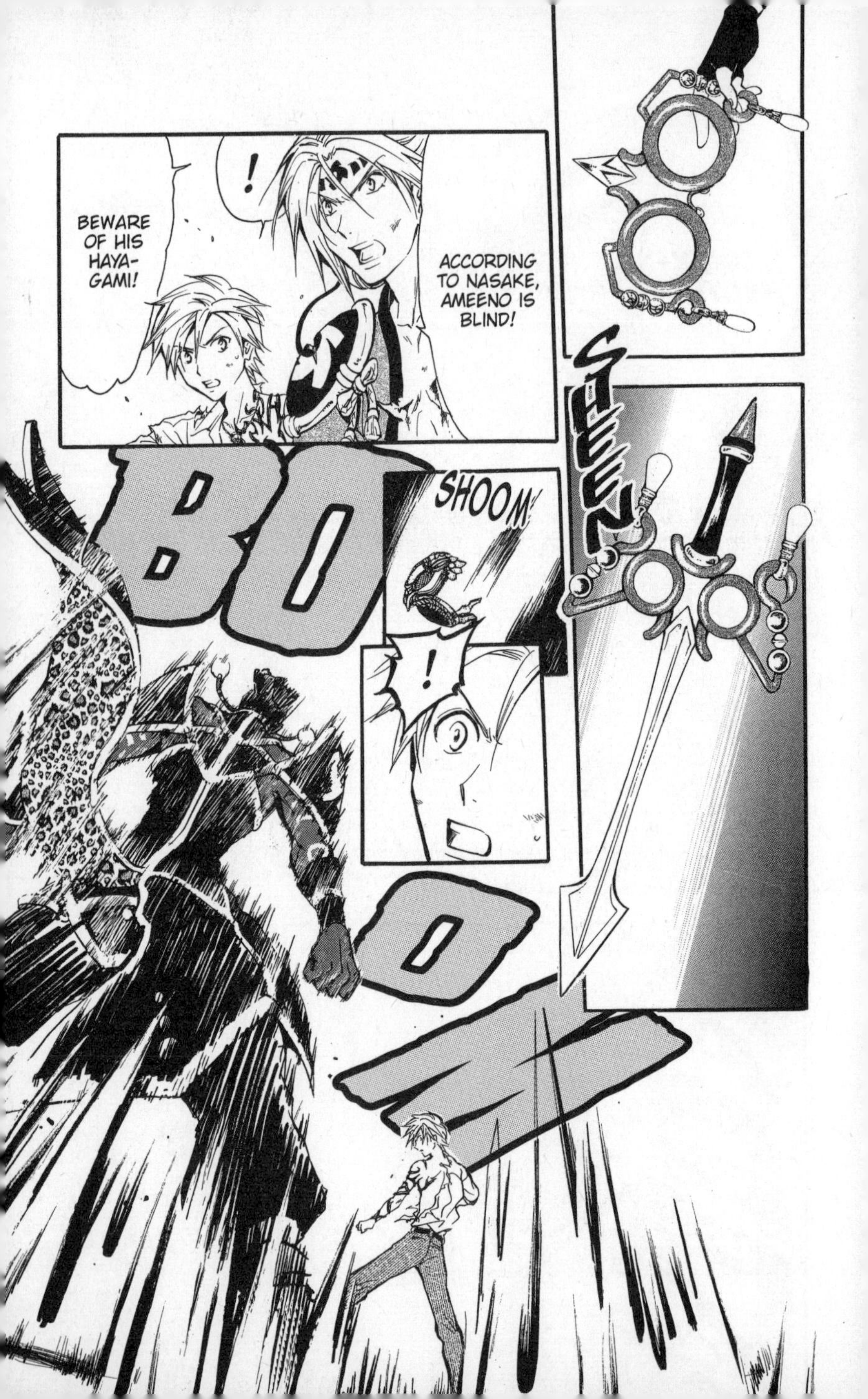

!
ACCORDING TO NASAKE, AMEENO IS BLIND!
BEWARE OF HIS HAYA-GAMI!
SHEEN
SHOOM
!
BOOM

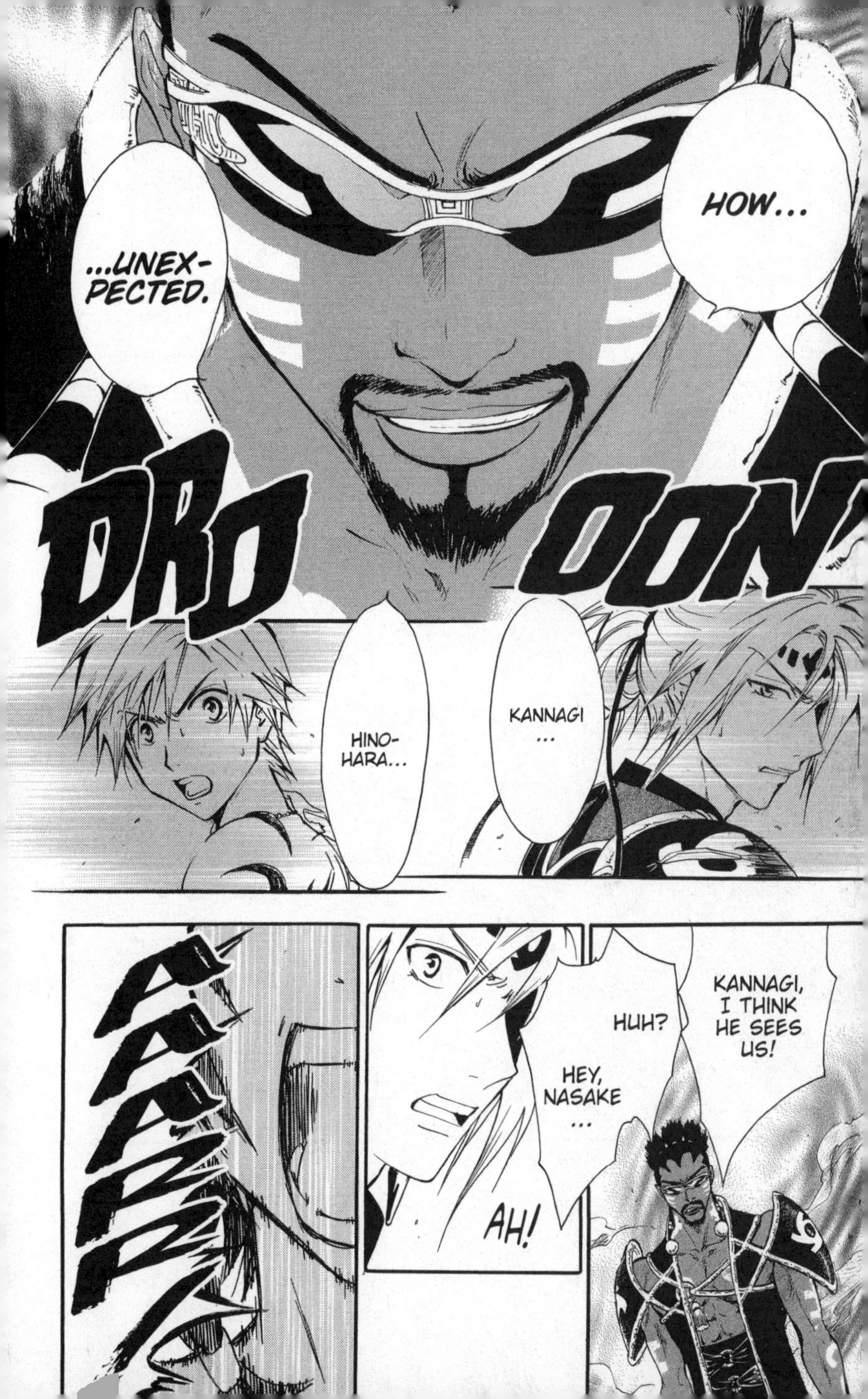
HOW...
...UNEX-PECTED.
DRO
OON
KANNAGI ...
HINO-HARA...
KANNAGI, I THINK HE SEES US!
HUH?
HEY, NASAKE ...
AH!

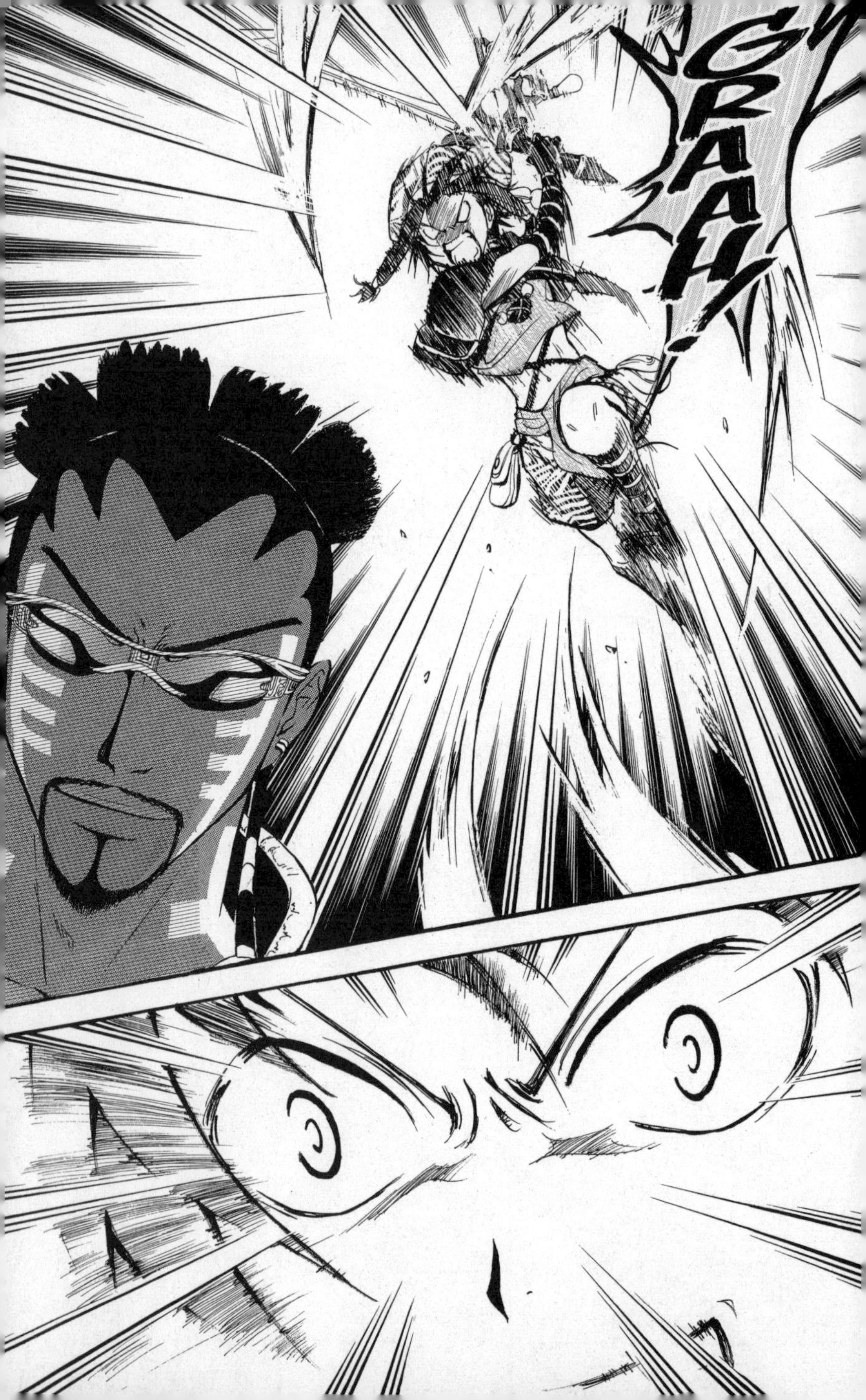
GWRAAH!!

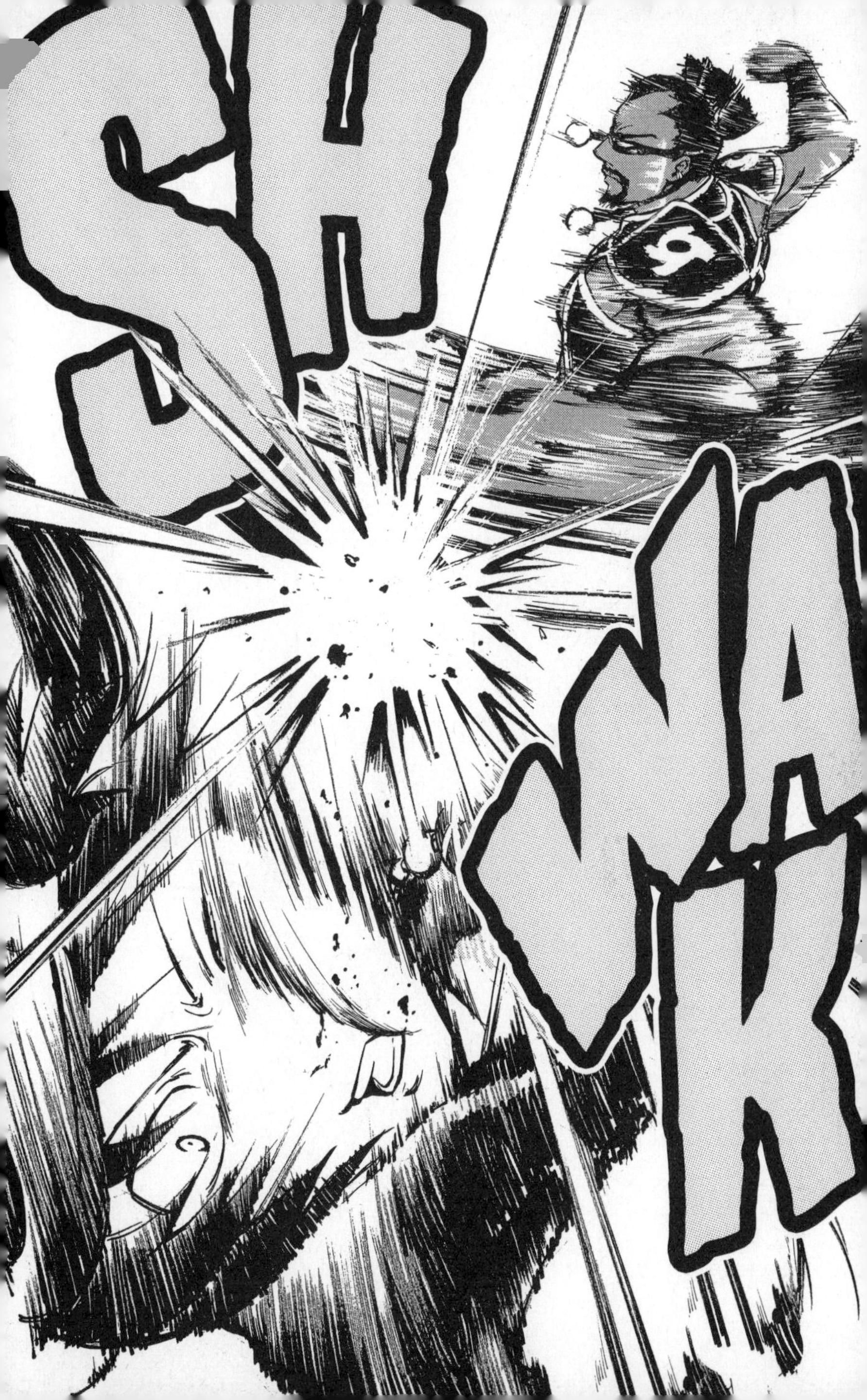
SHWAK

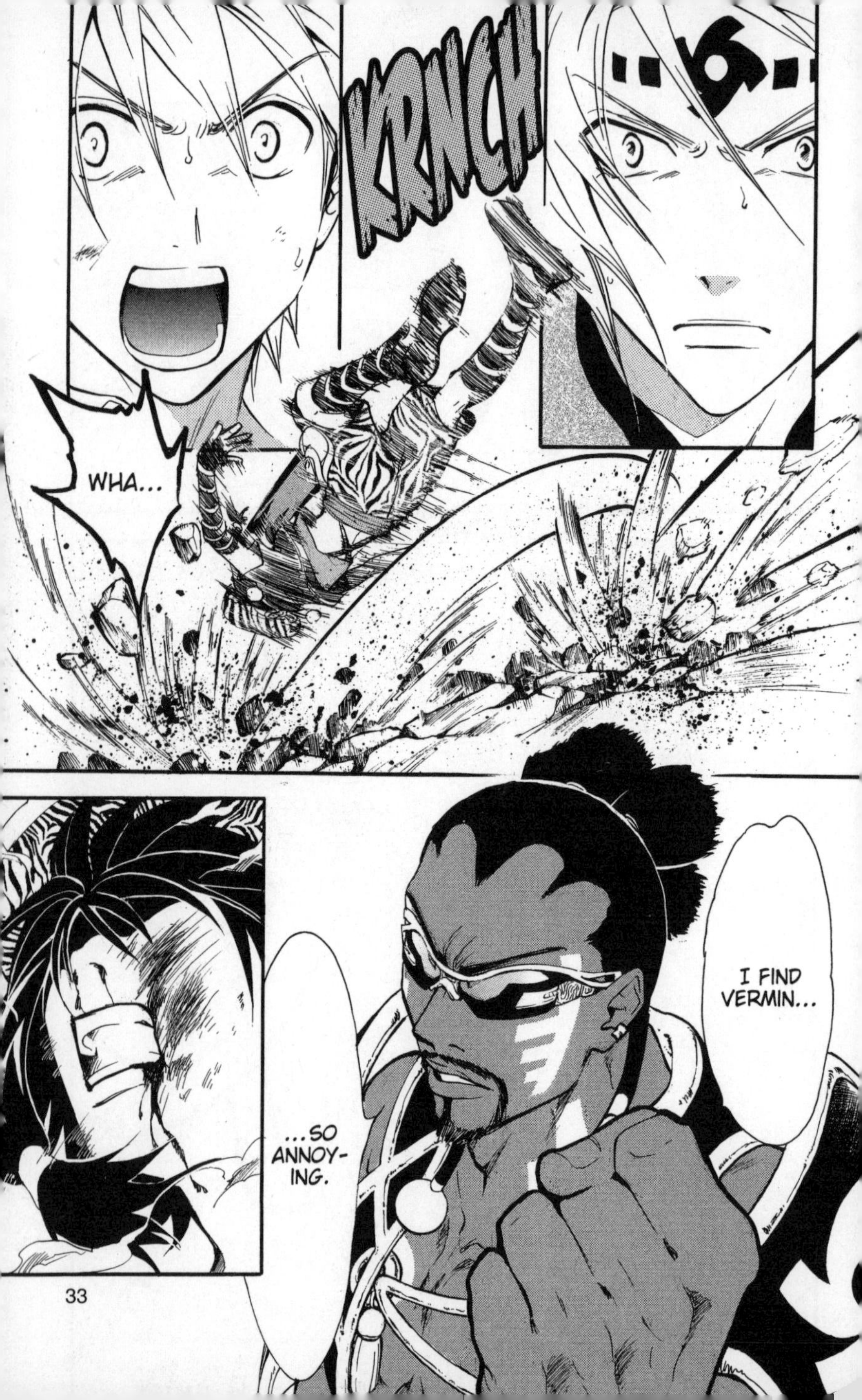
KRNCH
WHA...
I FIND VERMIN...
...SO ANNOY-ING.

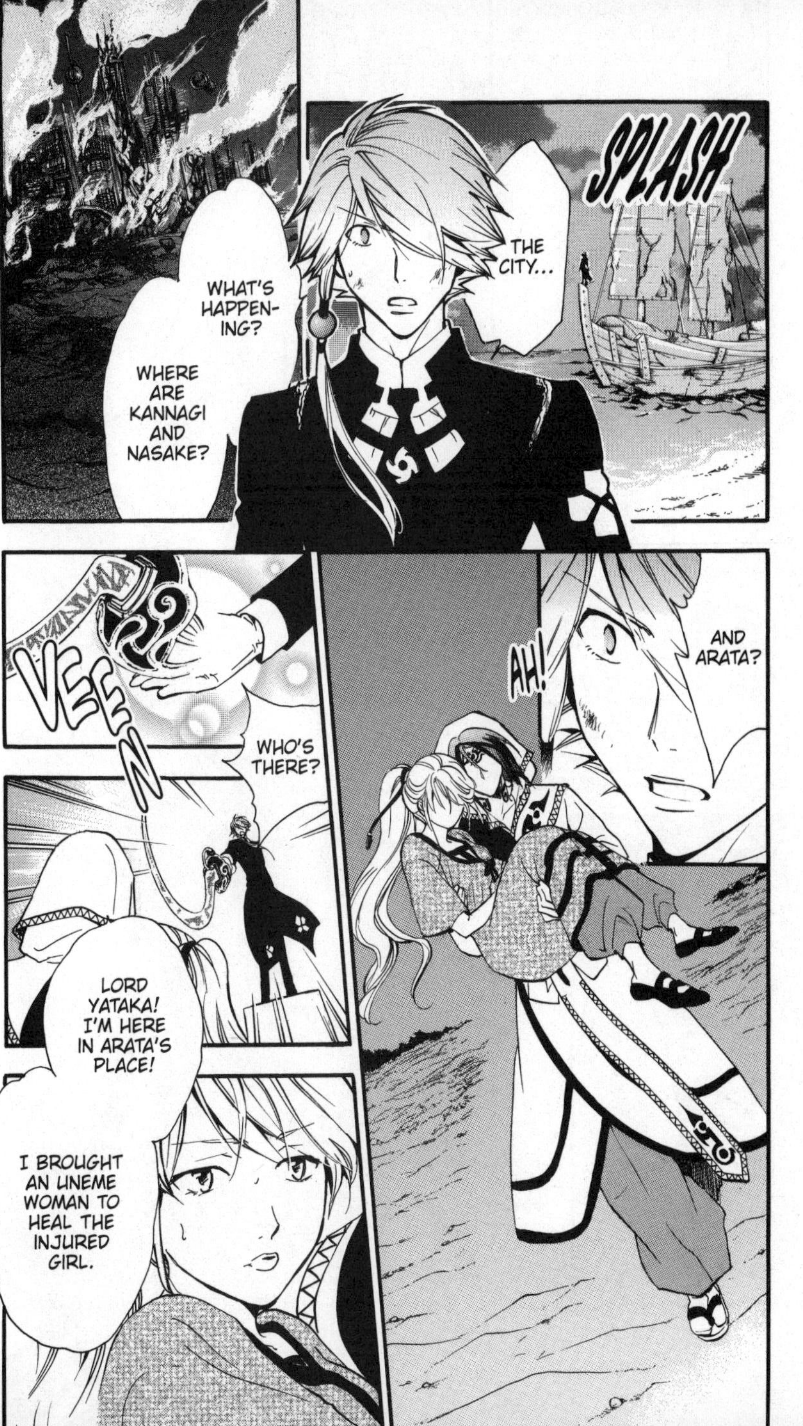
SPLASH
THE CITY...
WHAT'S HAPPENING?
WHERE ARE KANNAGI AND NASAKE?
AND ARATA?
AH!
VEEEN
WHO'S THERE?
LORD YATAKA! I'M HERE IN ARATA'S PLACE!
I BROUGHT AN UNEME WOMAN TO HEAL THE INJURED GIRL.

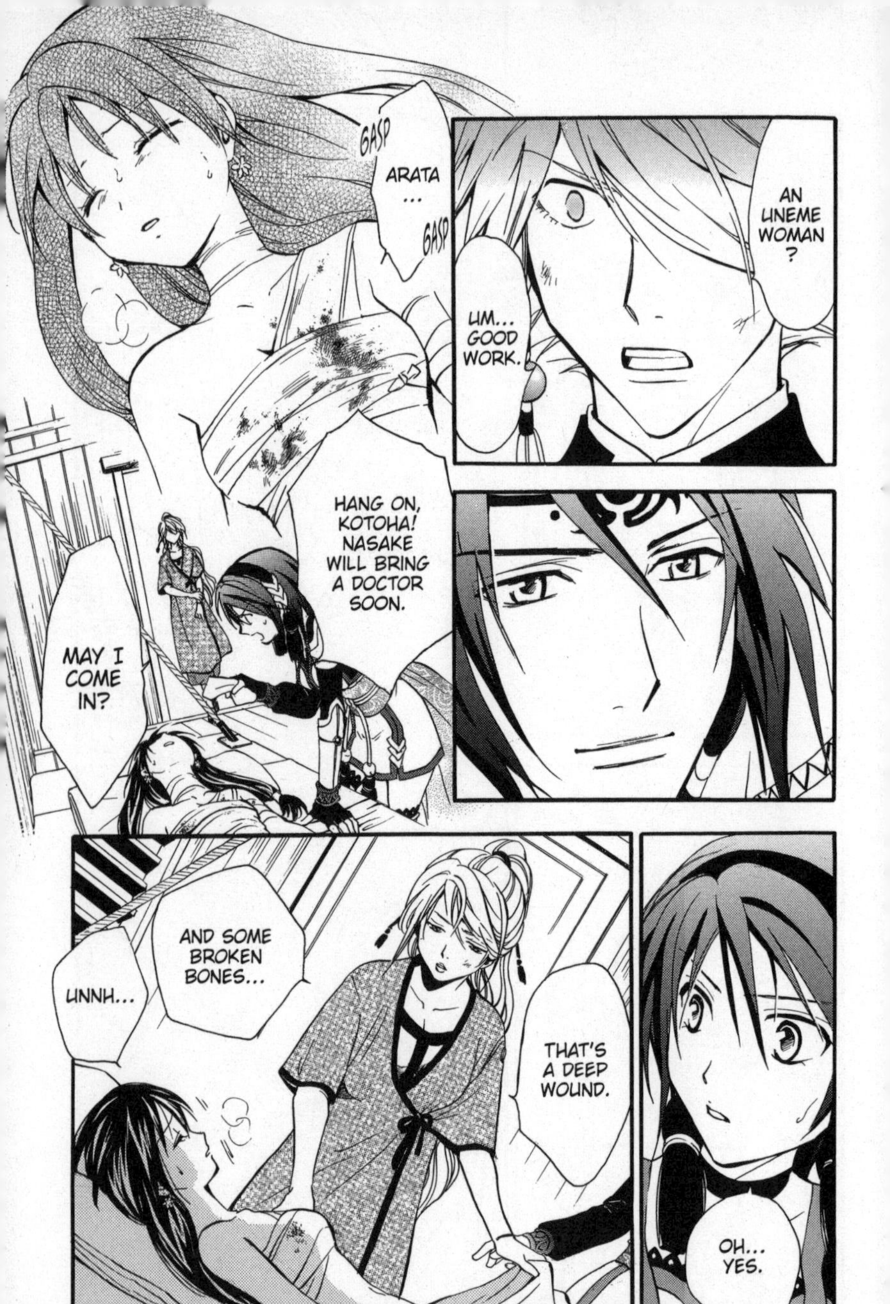
AN UNEME WOMAN?
UM... GOOD WORK.
GASP
ARATA...
GASP
HANG ON, KOTOHA! NASAKE WILL BRING A DOCTOR SOON.
MAY I COME IN?
OH... YES.
THAT'S A DEEP WOUND.
AND SOME BROKEN BONES...
UNNH...

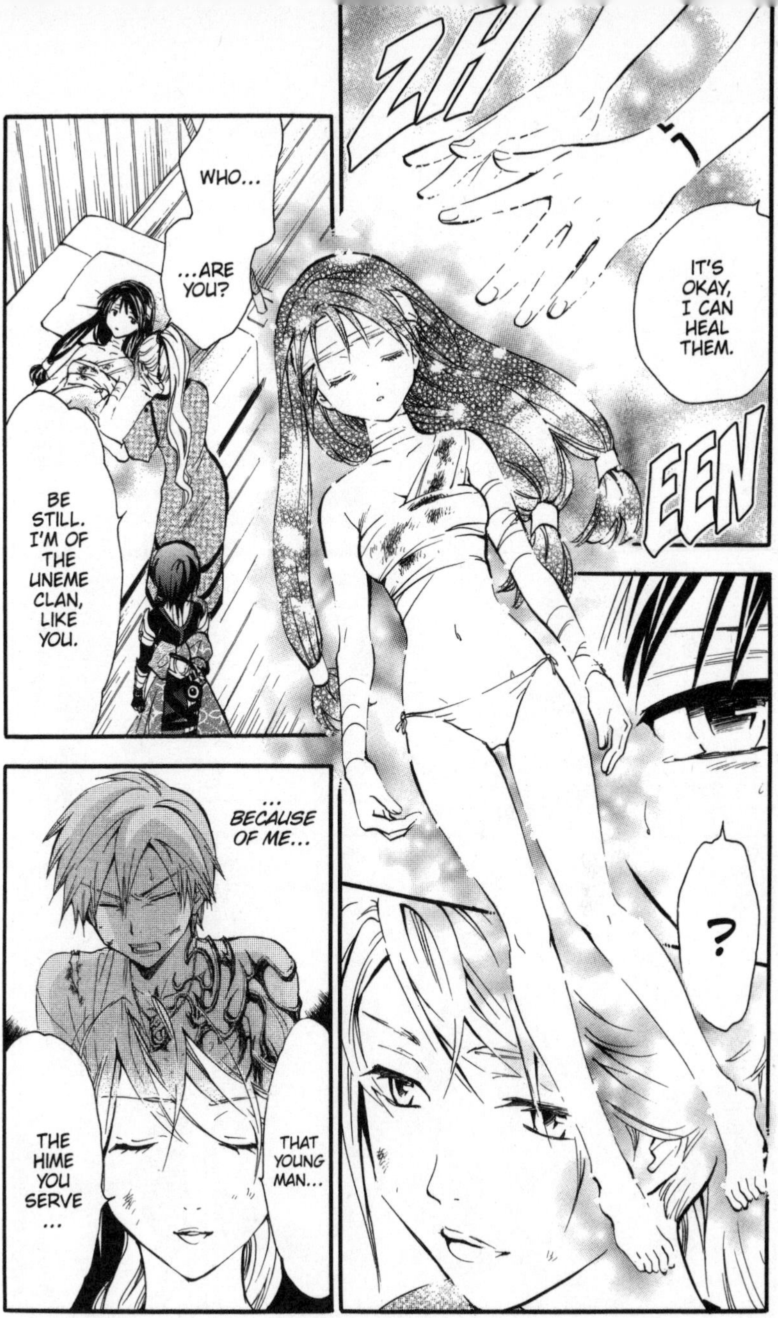
ZH
IT'S OKAY, I CAN HEAL THEM.
EEN
WHO...
...ARE YOU?
BE STILL. I'M OF THE UNEME CLAN, LIKE YOU.
?
...BECAUSE OF ME...
THAT YOUNG MAN...
THE HIME YOU SERVE...

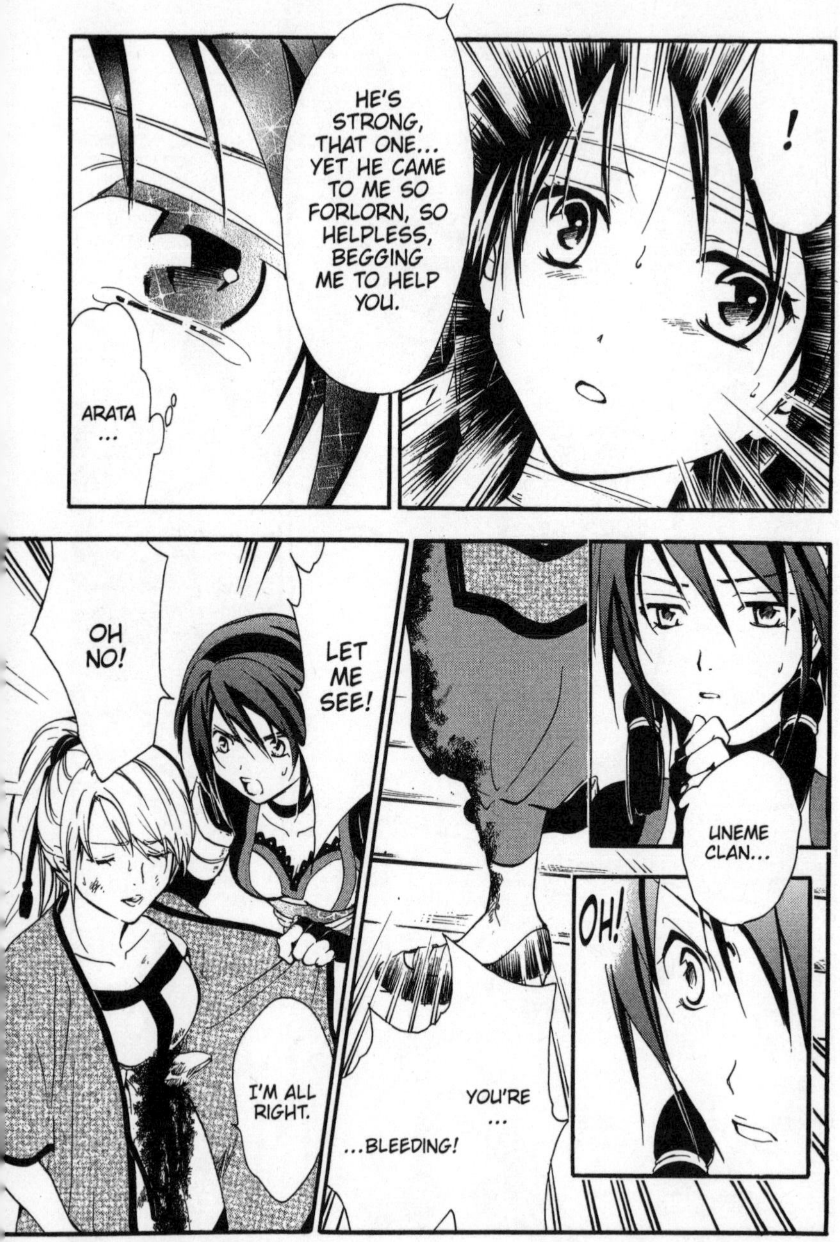
!
HE'S STRONG, THAT ONE... YET HE CAME TO ME SO FORLORN, SO HELPLESS, BEGGING ME TO HELP YOU.
ARATA ...
UNEME CLAN...
OH!
YOU'RE ...
...BLEEDING!
OH NO!
LET ME SEE!
I'M ALL RIGHT.

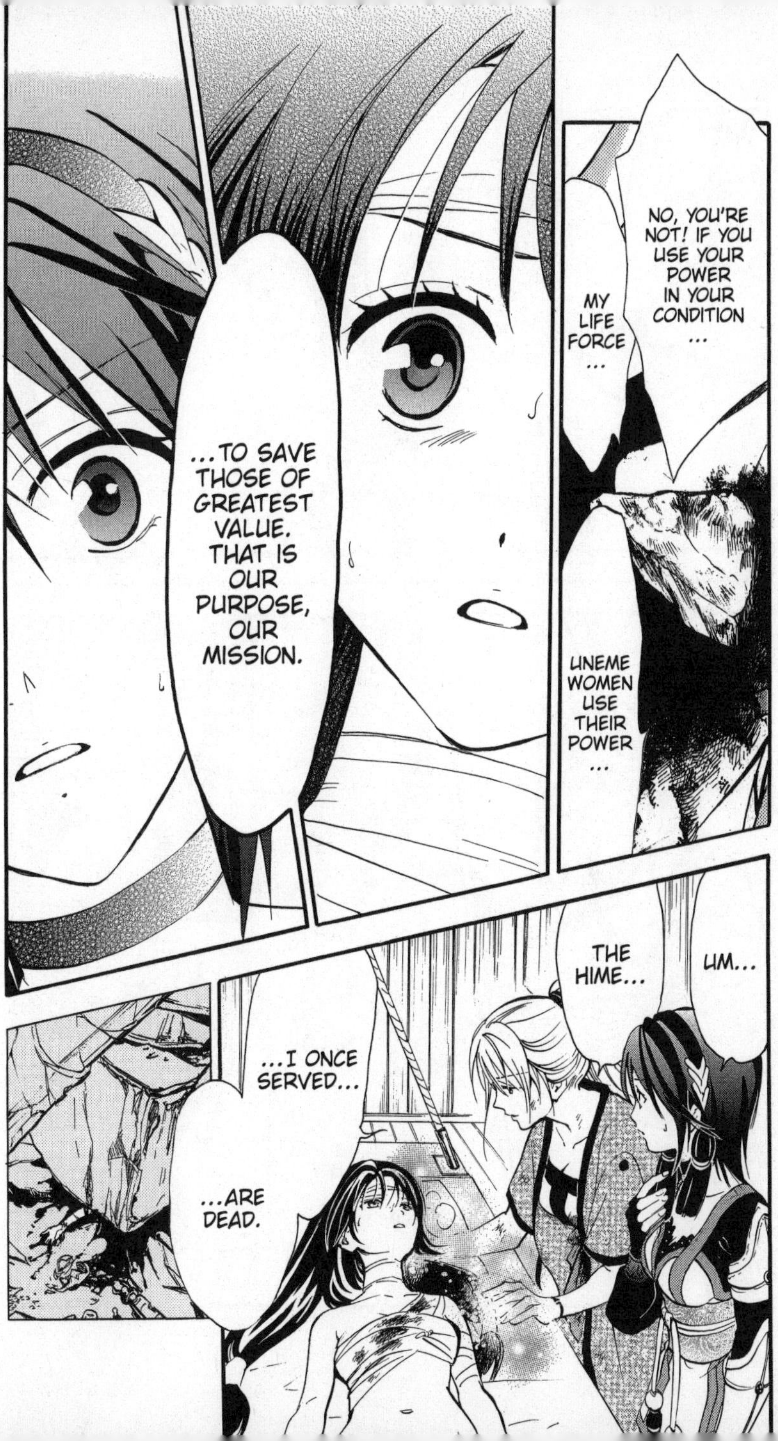
NO, YOU'RE NOT! IF YOU USE YOUR POWER IN YOUR CONDITION ...
MY LIFE FORCE ...
UNEME WOMEN USE THEIR POWER ...
...TO SAVE THOSE OF GREATEST VALUE. THAT IS OUR PURPOSE, OUR MISSION.
UM...
THE HIME...
...I ONCE SERVED...
...ARE DEAD.

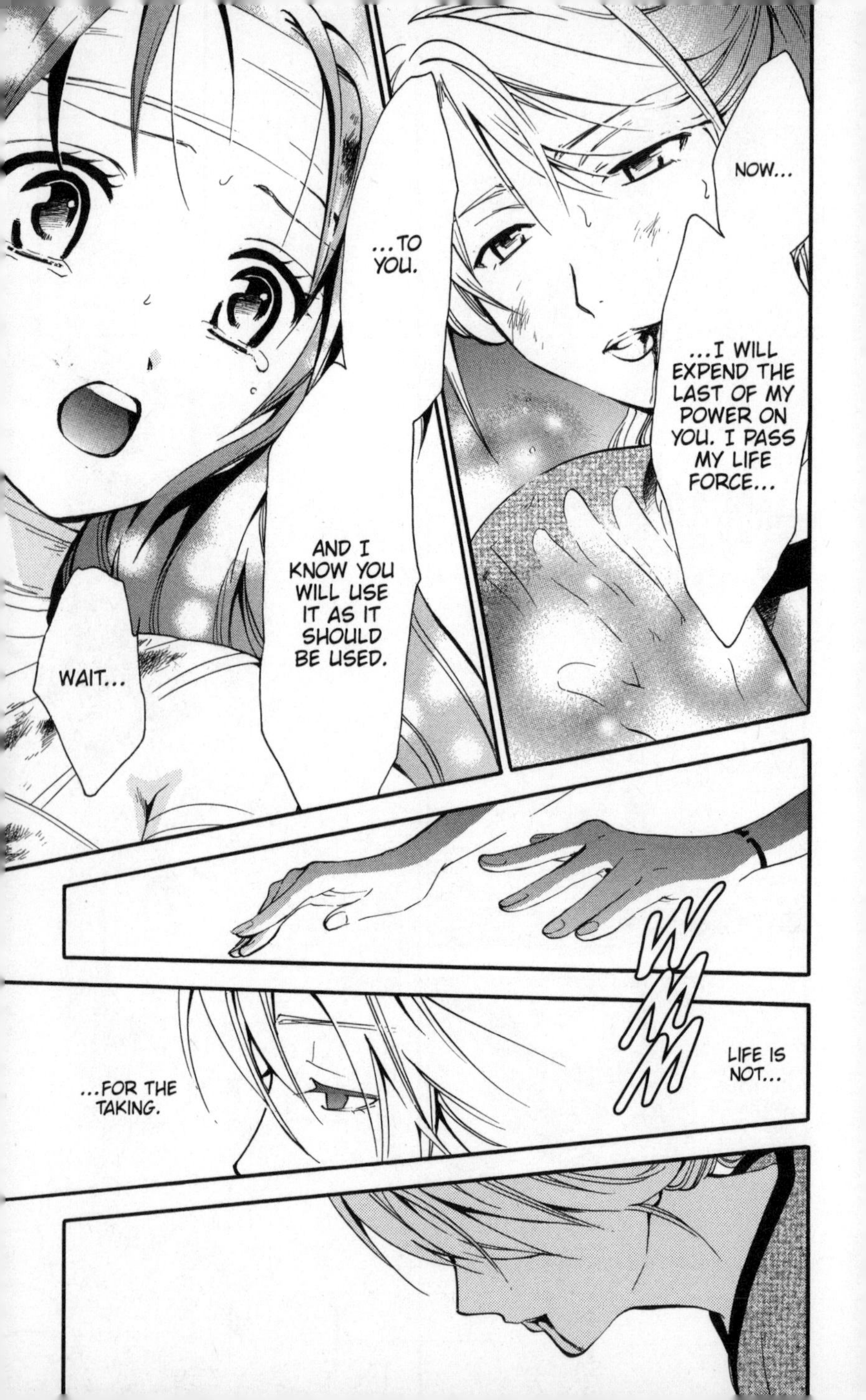
NOW...
...I WILL EXPEND THE LAST OF MY POWER ON YOU. I PASS MY LIFE FORCE...
...TO YOU.
AND I KNOW YOU WILL USE IT AS IT SHOULD BE USED.
WAIT...
LIFE IS NOT...
...FOR THE TAKING.

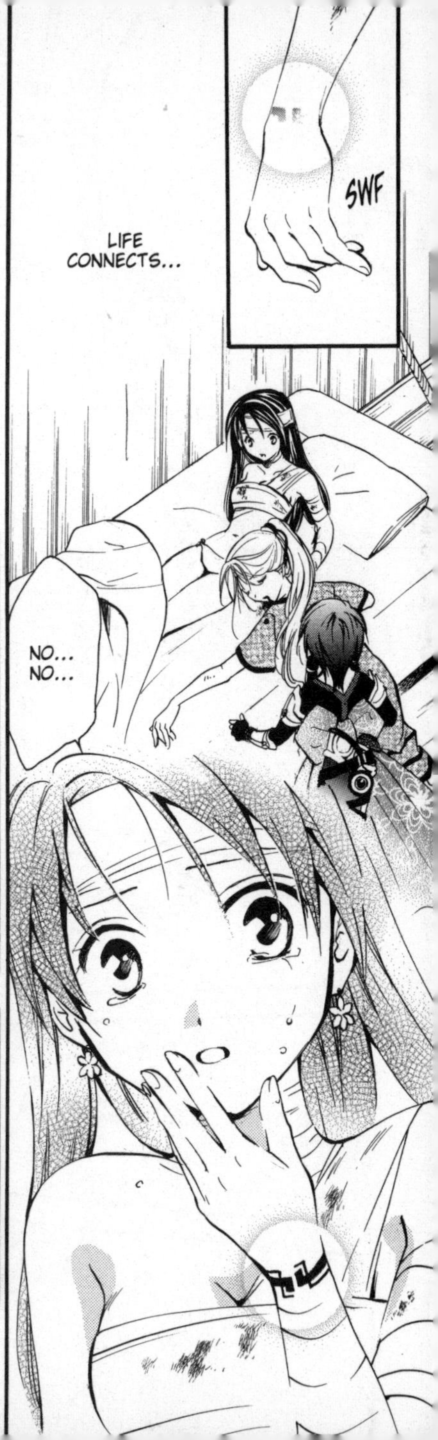
SWF
LIFE CONNECTS...
NO... NO...

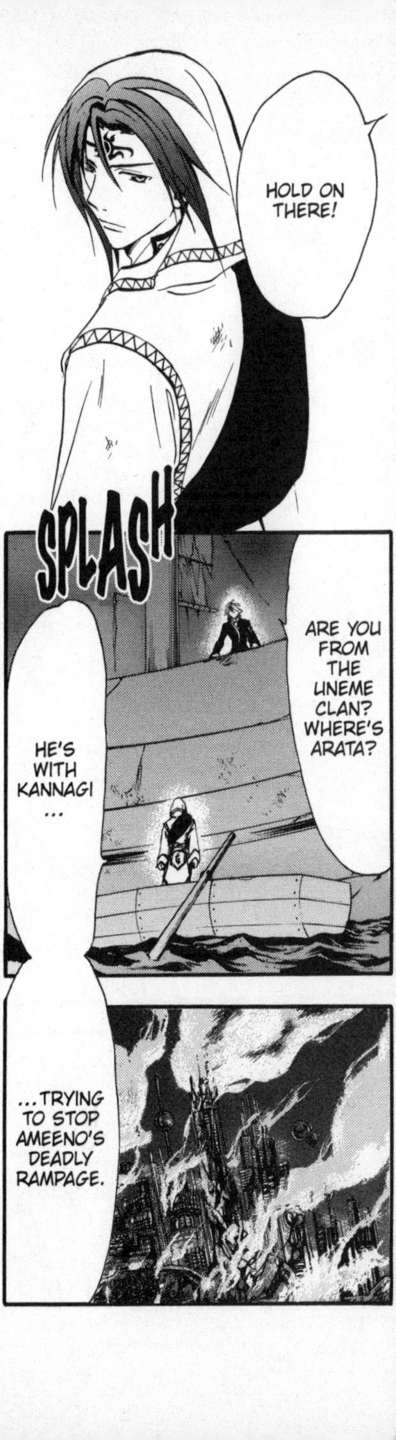
HOLD ON THERE!
SPLASH
ARE YOU FROM THE UNEME CLAN? WHERE'S ARATA?
HE'S WITH KANNAGI ...
...TRYING TO STOP AMEENO'S DEADLY RAMPAGE.

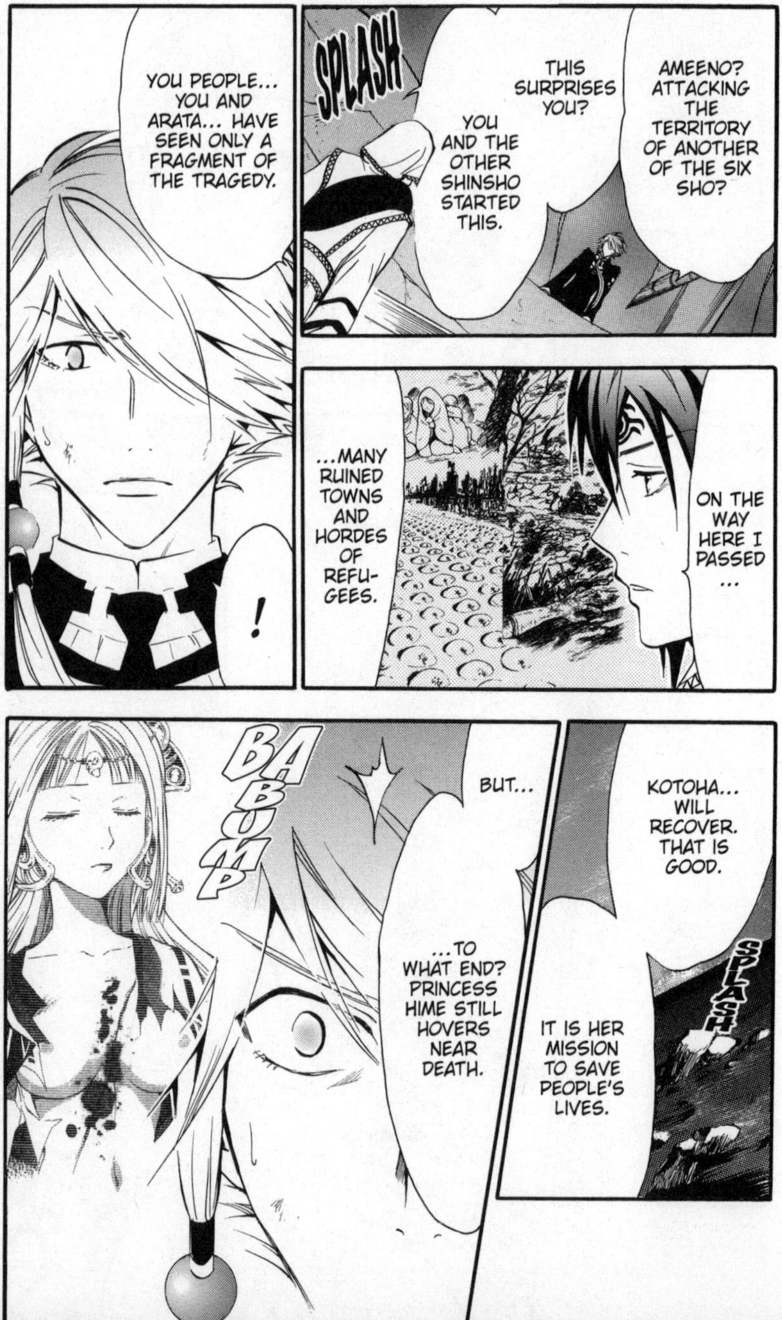
AMEENO? ATTACKING THE TERRITORY OF ANOTHER OF THE SIX SHO?
THIS SURPRISES YOU?
SPLASH
YOU AND THE OTHER SHINSHO STARTED THIS.
ON THE WAY HERE I PASSED...
...MANY RUINED TOWNS AND HORDES OF REFUGEES.
YOU PEOPLE... YOU AND ARATA... HAVE SEEN ONLY A FRAGMENT OF THE TRAGEDY.
!
KOTOHA... WILL RECOVER. THAT IS GOOD.
SPLASH
IT IS HER MISSION TO SAVE PEOPLE'S LIVES.
BUT...
BABUMP
...TO WHAT END? PRINCESS HIME STILL HOVERS NEAR DEATH.

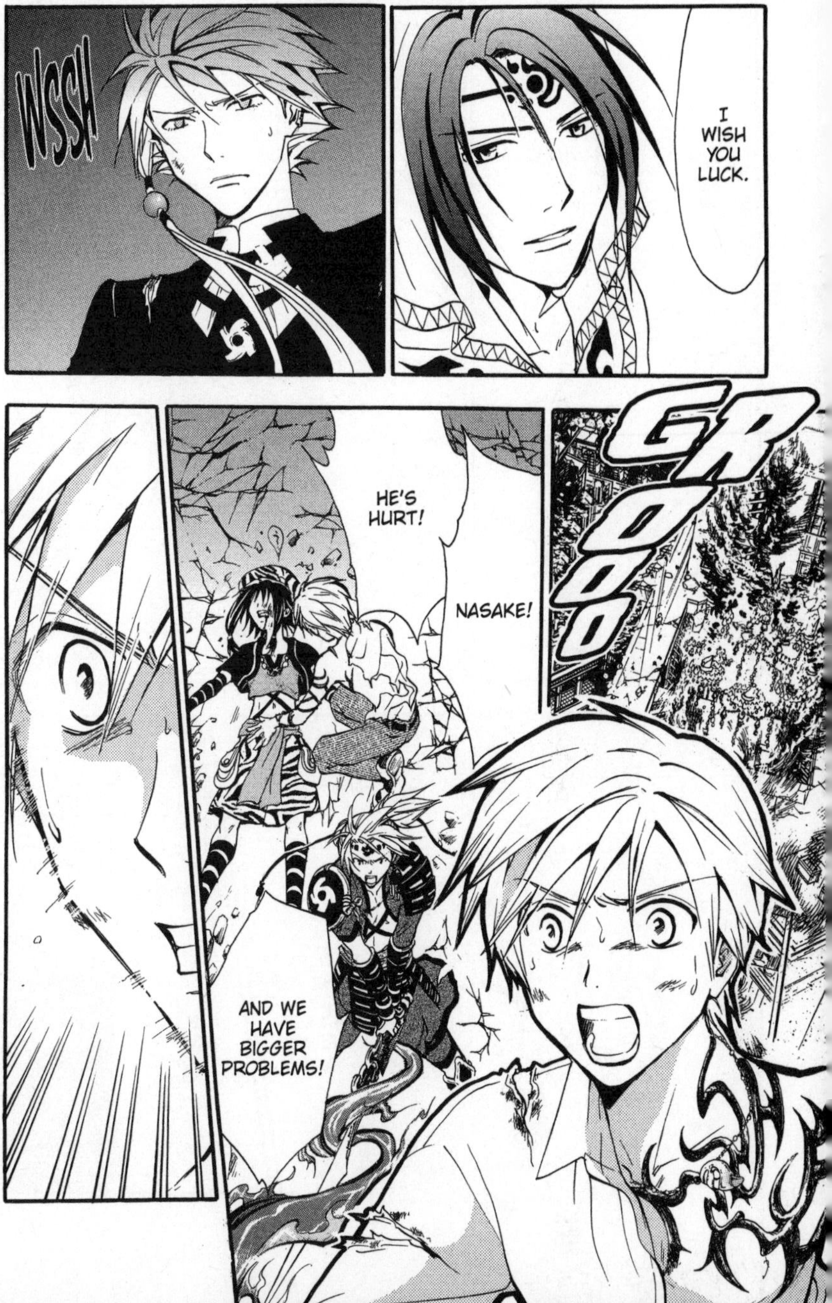
I WISH YOU LUCK.
WSSH
GROOO
NASAKE!
HE'S HURT!
AND WE HAVE BIGGER PROBLEMS!

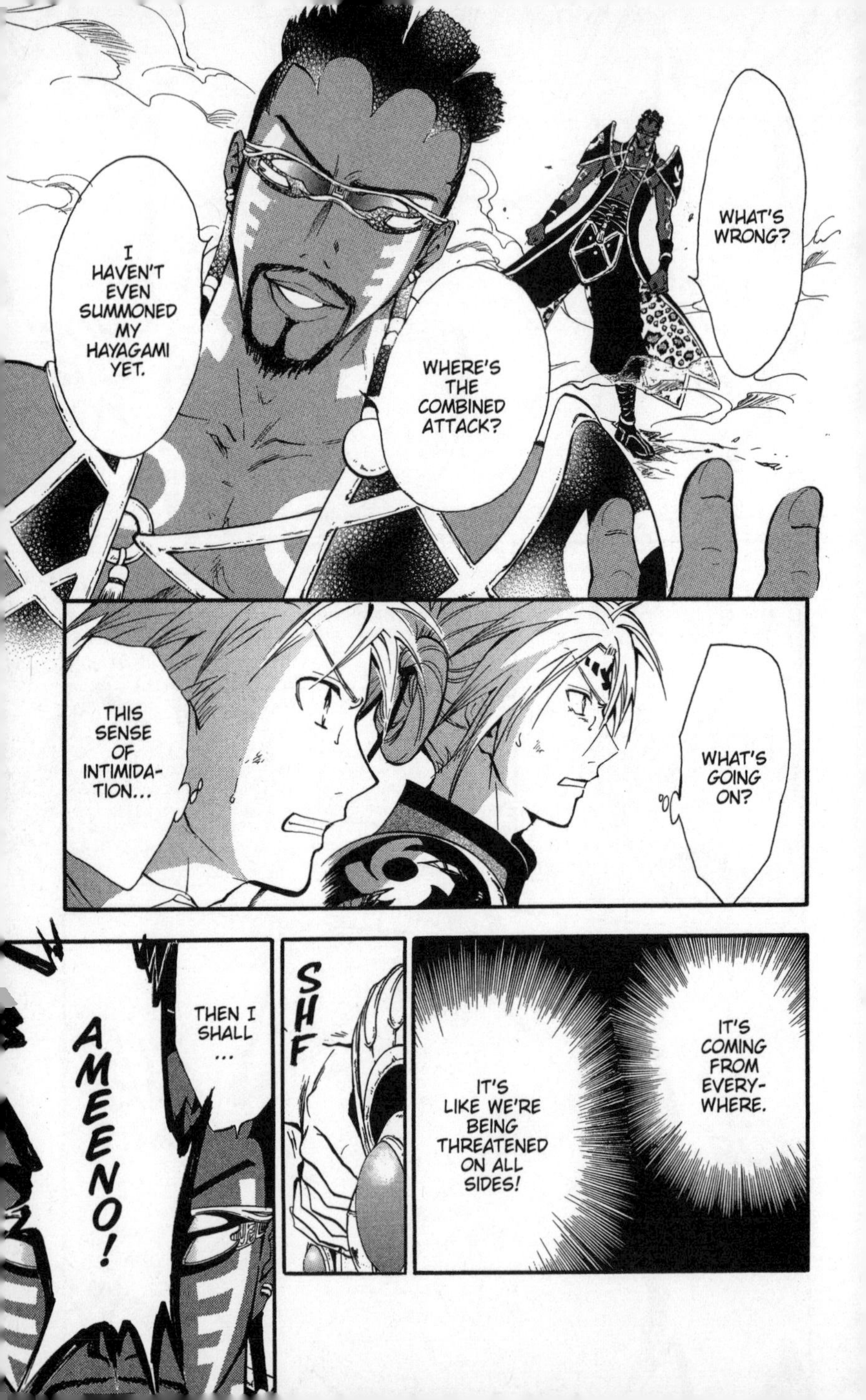
WHAT'S WRONG?
WHERE'S THE COMBINED ATTACK?
I HAVEN'T EVEN SUMMONED MY HAYAGAMI YET.
WHAT'S GOING ON?
THIS SENSE OF INTIMIDATION...
IT'S COMING FROM EVERYWHERE.
IT'S LIKE WE'RE BEING THREATENED ON ALL SIDES!
SHF
THEN I SHALL...
AMEENO!

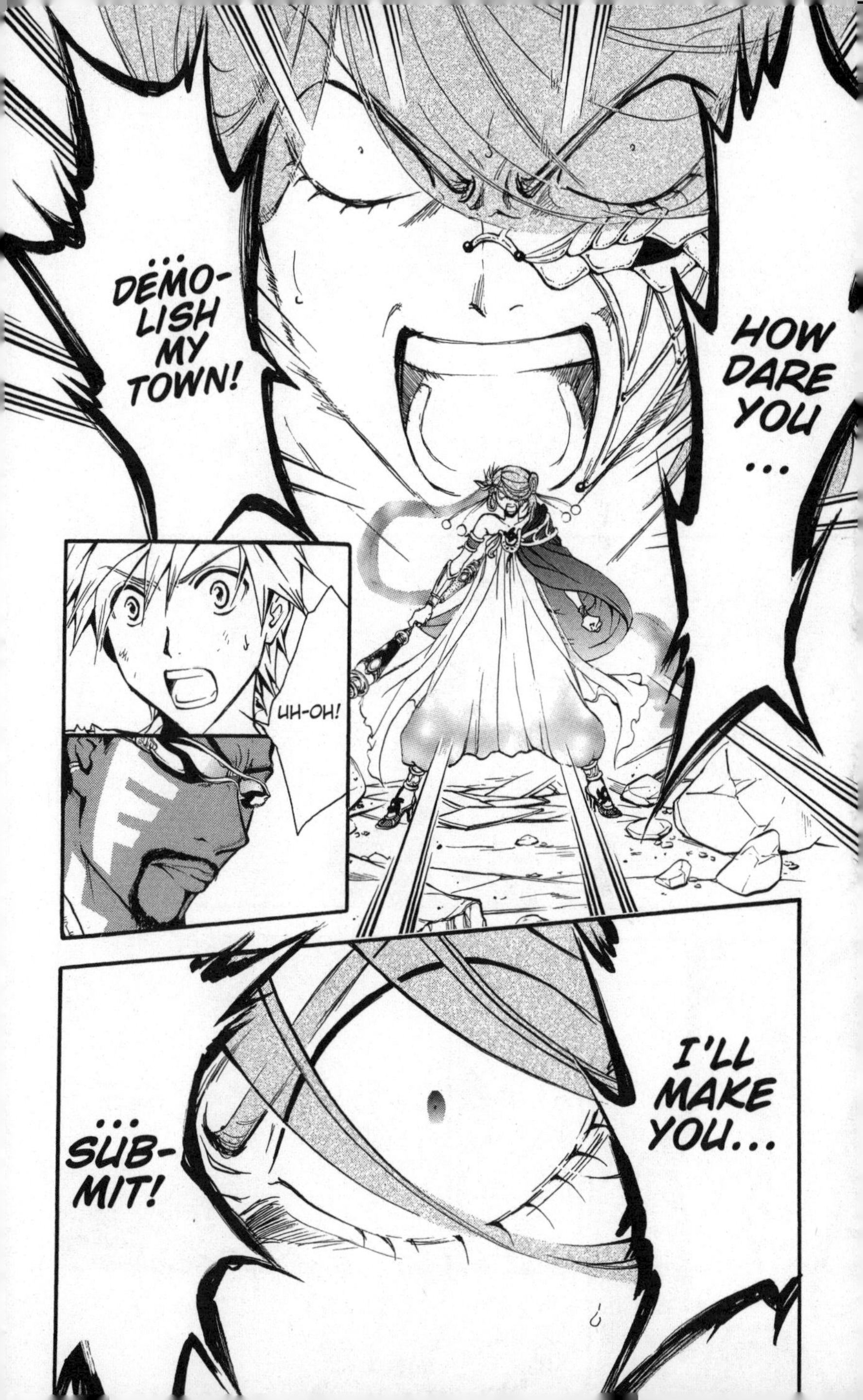
HOW DARE YOU...
...DËMO-LISH MY TOWN!
UH-OH!
I'LL MAKE YOU...
...SÜB-MIT!

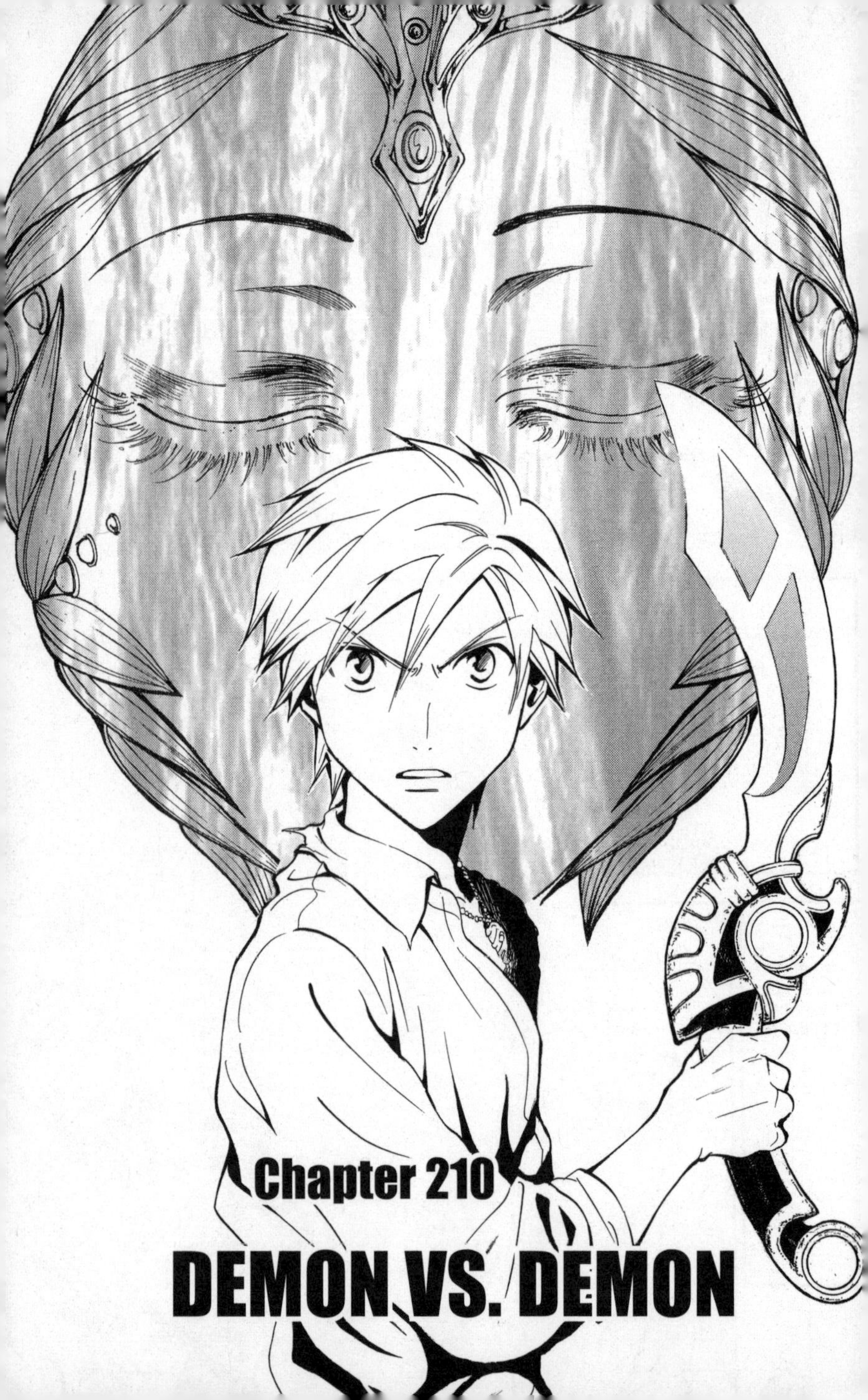
Chapter 210
DEMON VS. DEMON

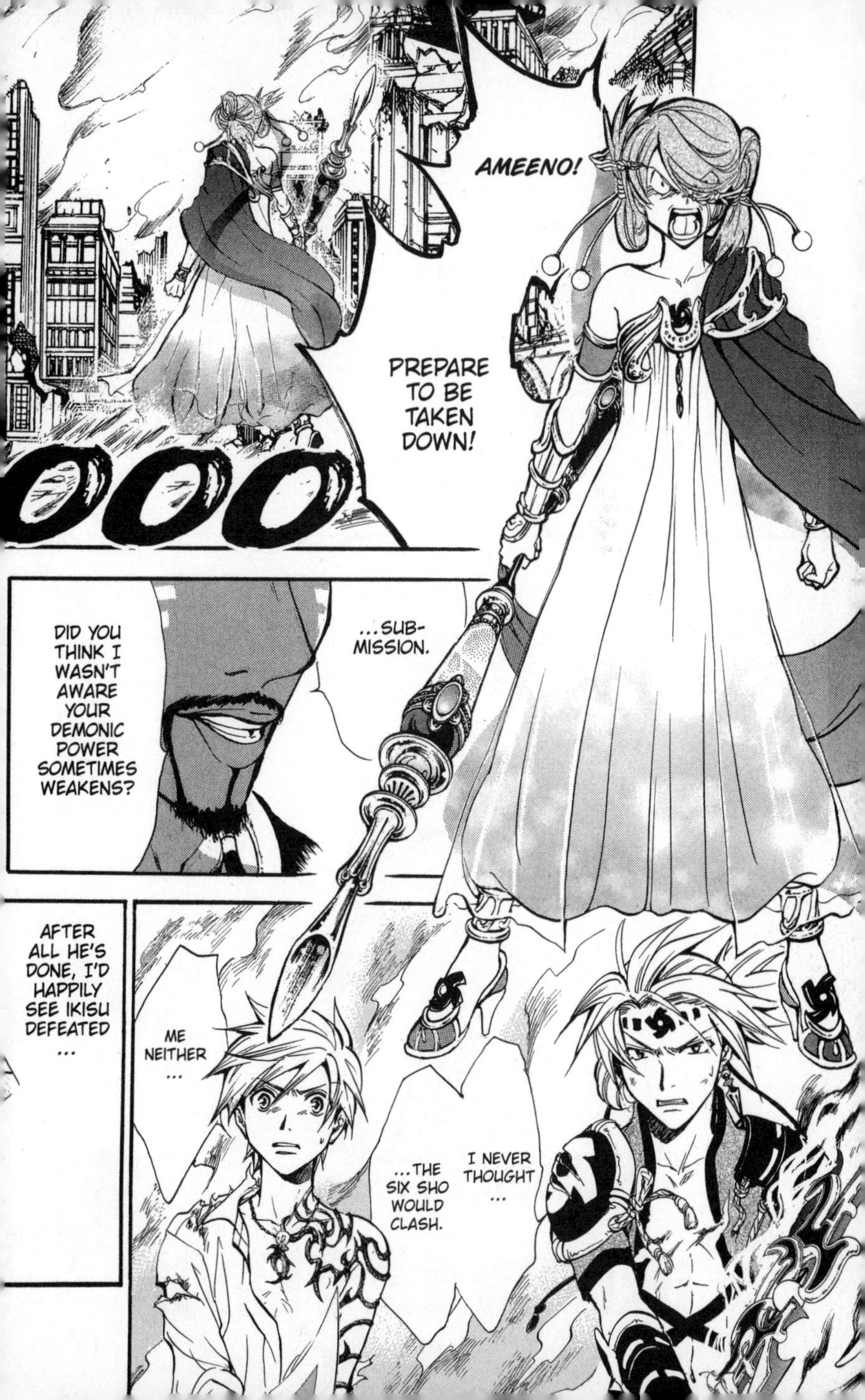

AMEENO!
PREPARE TO BE TAKEN DOWN!
OOO
...SUB-MISSION.
DID YOU THINK I WASN'T AWARE YOUR DEMONIC POWER SOMETIMES WEAKENS?
I NEVER THOUGHT ...
...THE SIX SHO WOULD CLASH.
ME NEITHER ...
AFTER ALL HE'S DONE, I'D HAPPILY SEE IKISU DEFEATED ...

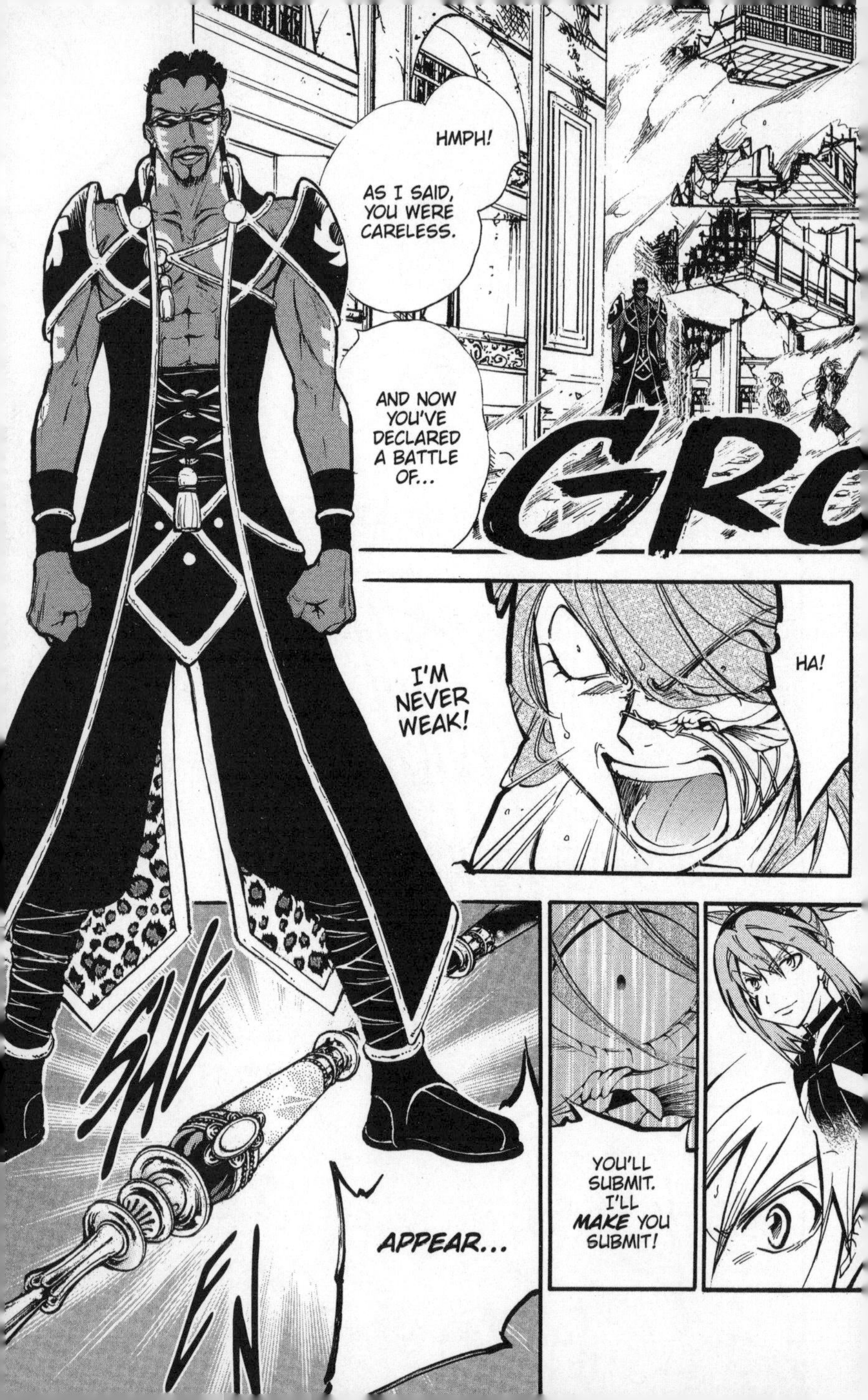
HMPH!
AS I SAID, YOU WERE CARELESS.
AND NOW YOU'VE DECLARED A BATTLE OF...
GRO
HA!
I'M NEVER WEAK!
YOU'LL SUBMIT. I'LL *MAKE* YOU SUBMIT!
APPEAR...

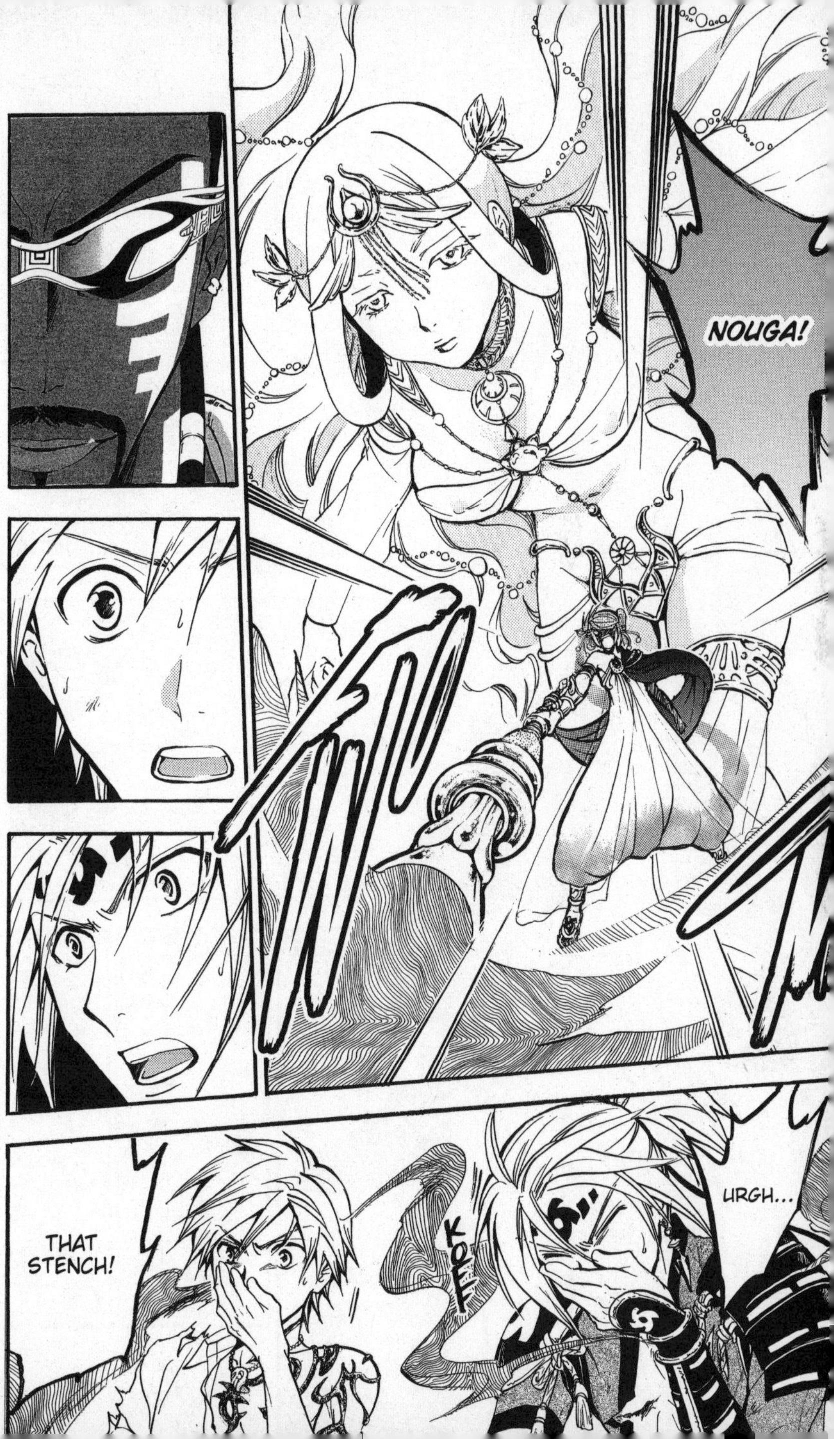
NOUGA!
URGH...
KOFF
THAT STENCH!

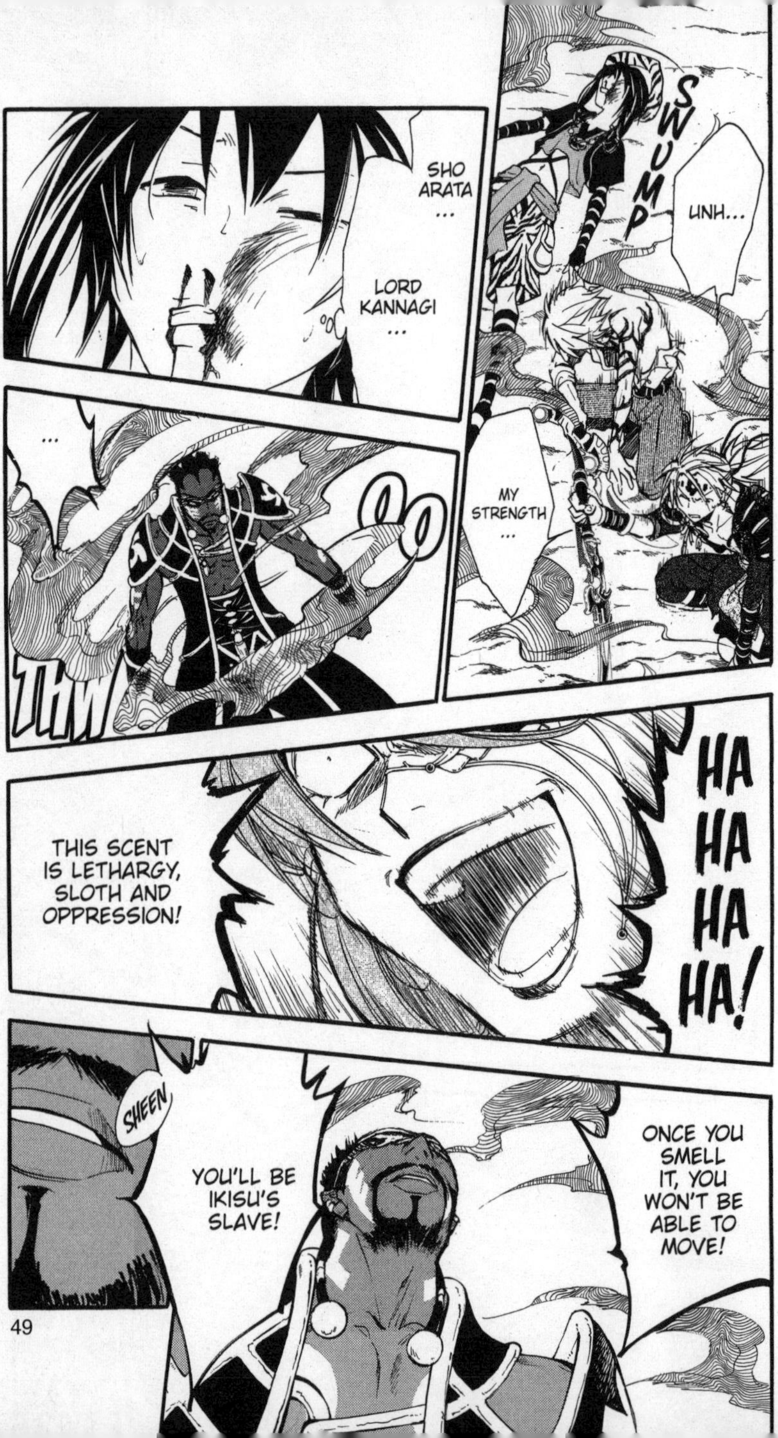
SWUMP
UNH...
MY STRENGTH ...
SHO ARATA ...
LORD KANNAGI ...
...
THW
HA HA HA HA HA!
THIS SCENT IS LETHARGY, SLOTH AND OPPRESSION!
ONCE YOU SMELL IT, YOU WON'T BE ABLE TO MOVE!
YOU'LL BE IKISU'S SLAVE!
SHEEN

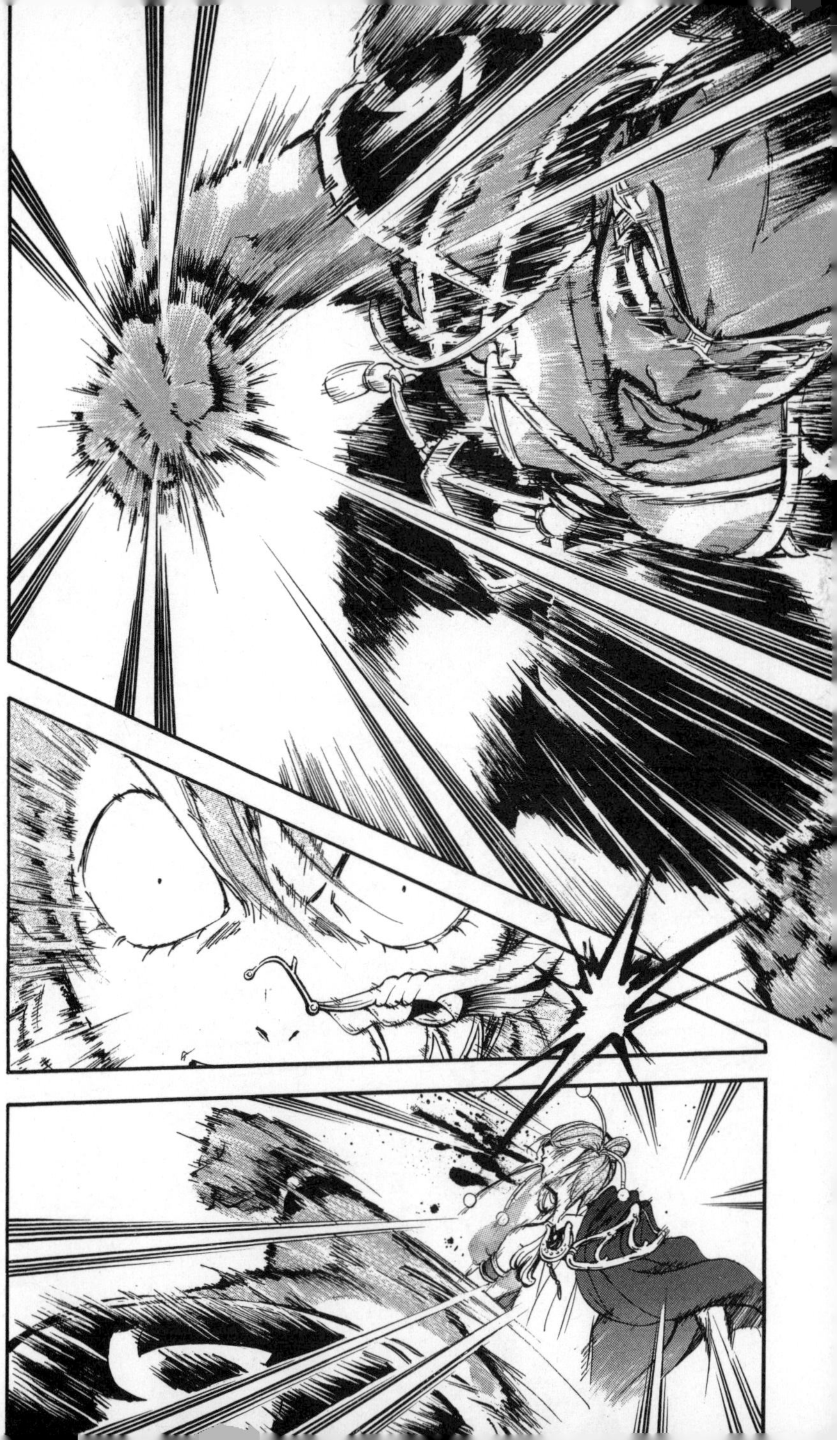

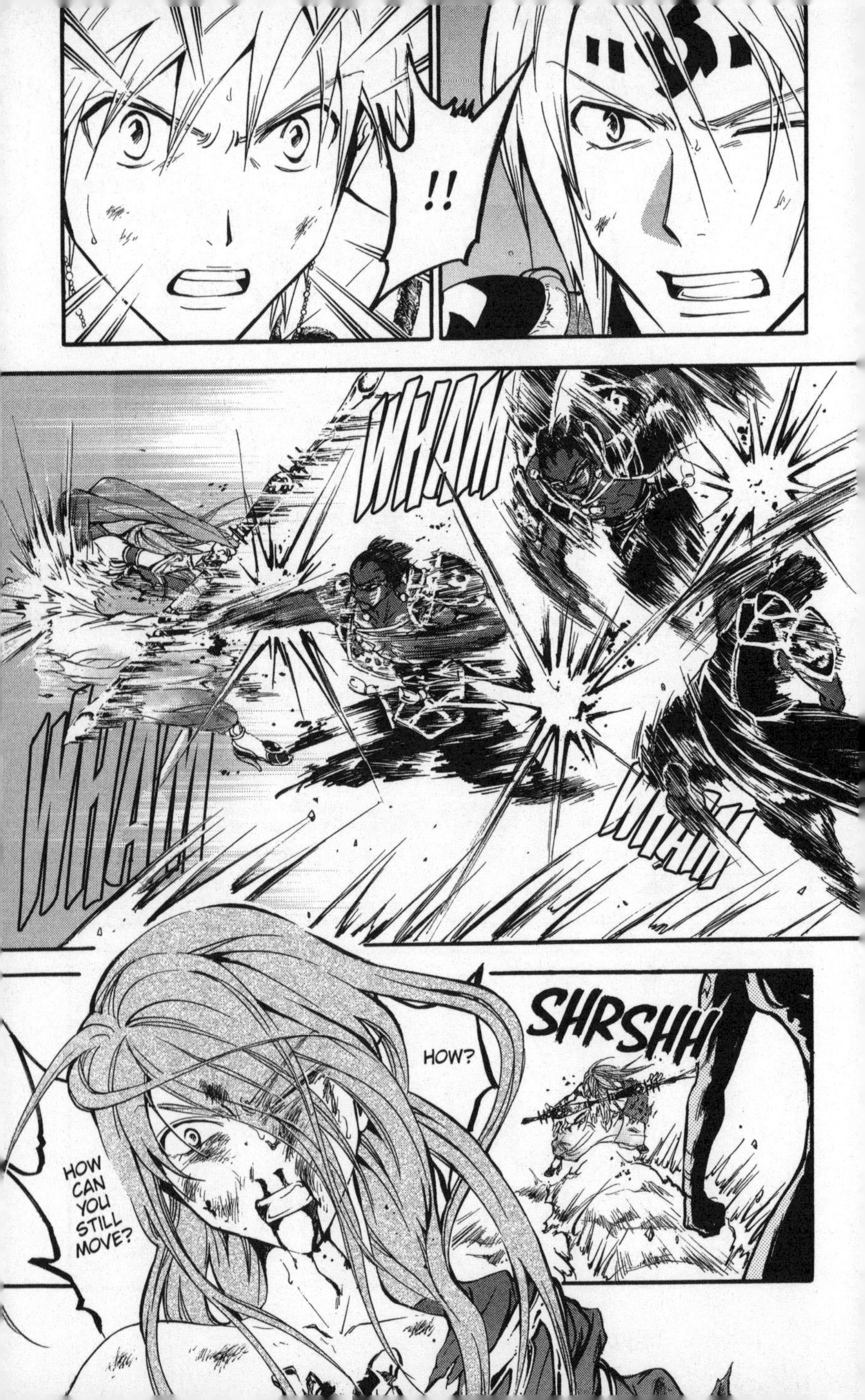
!!
WHAM
WHAM
WHAM
SHRSHH
HOW?
HOW CAN YOU STILL MOVE?

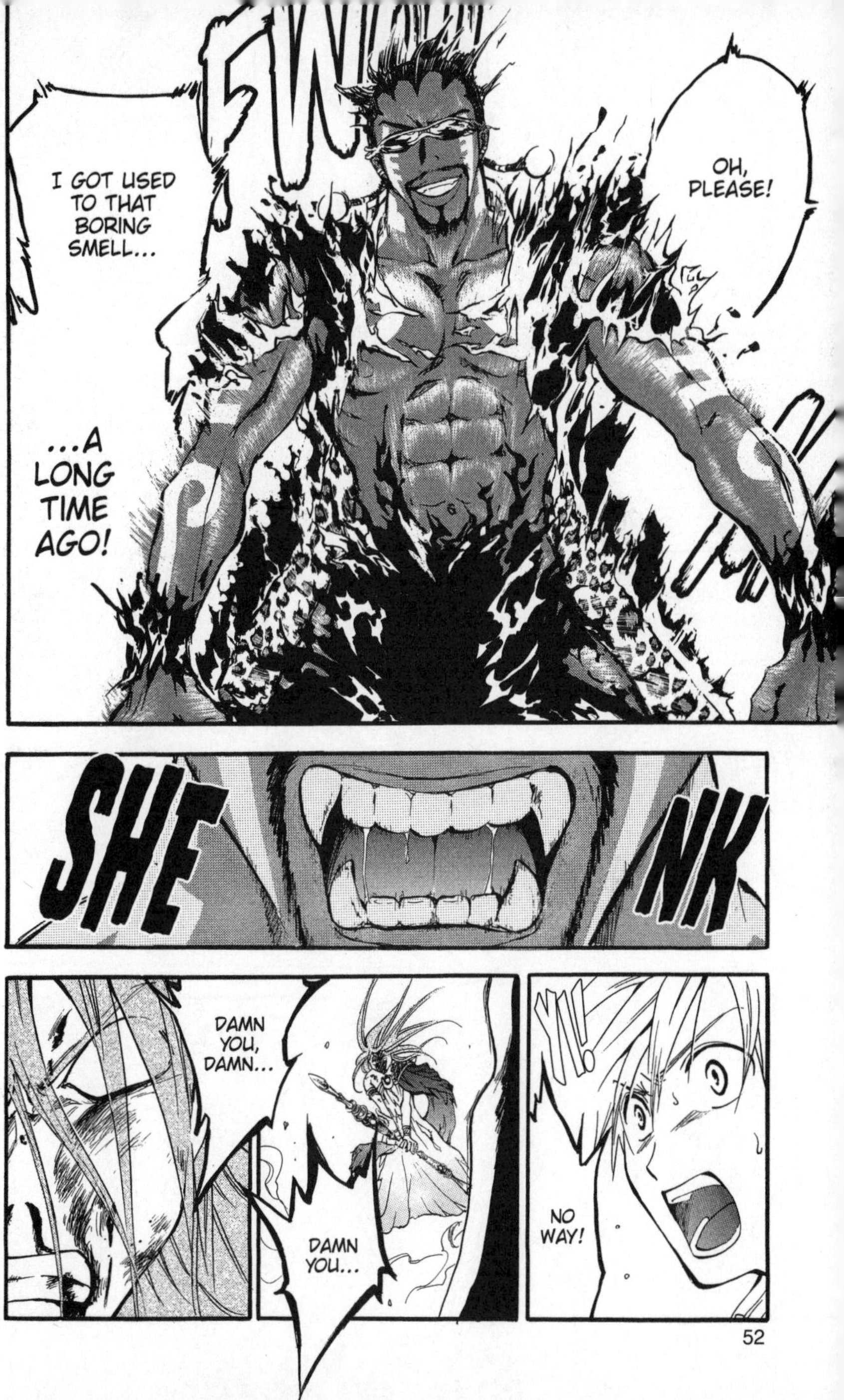

OH, PLEASE!
I GOT USED TO THAT BORING SMELL...
...A LONG TIME AGO!
SHE
NK
NO WAY!
DAMN YOU, DAMN...
DAMN YOU...

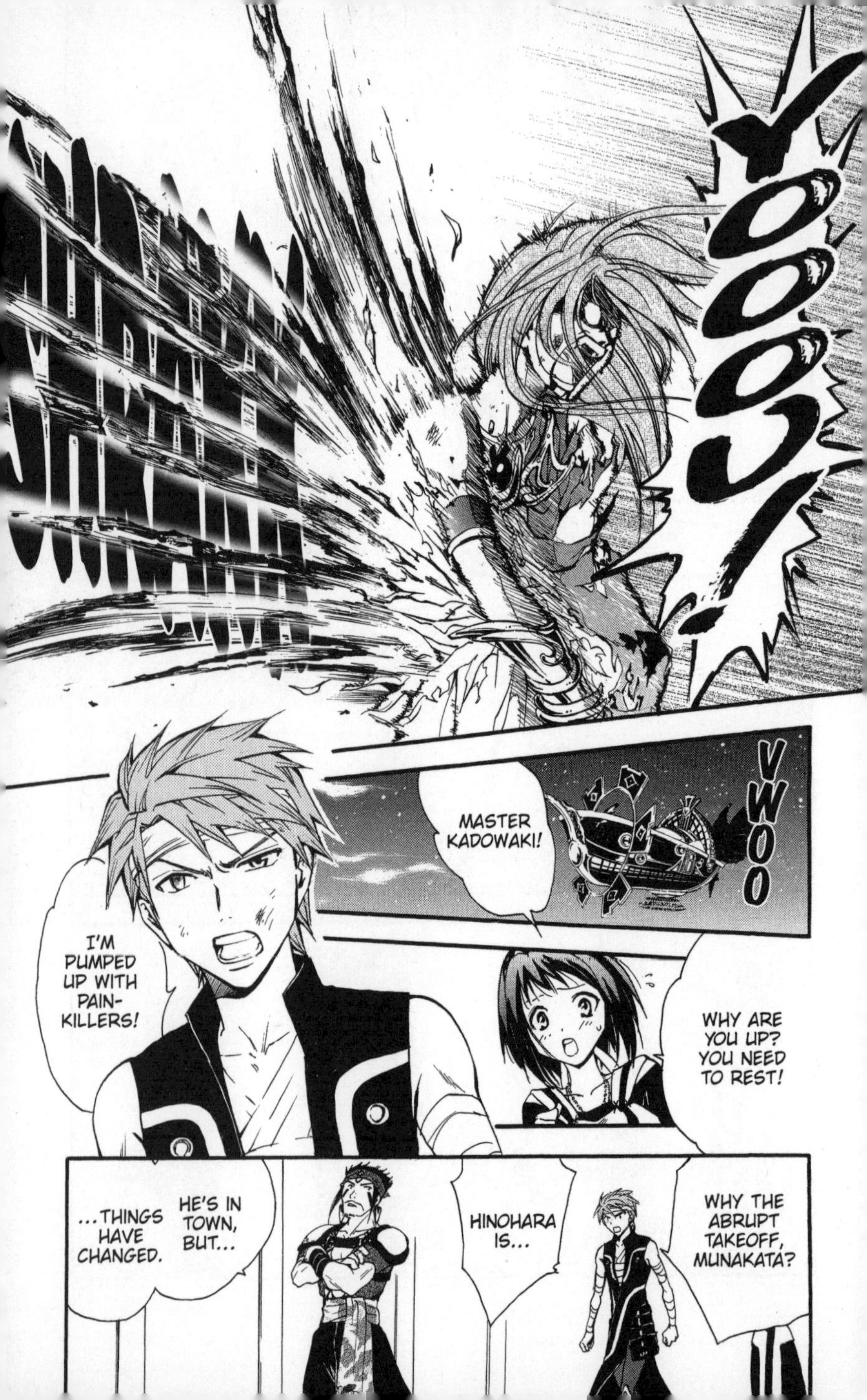
YOOOJ!
VWOO
MASTER KADOWAKI!
WHY ARE YOU UP? YOU NEED TO REST!
I'M PUMPED UP WITH PAIN-KILLERS!
WHY THE ABRUPT TAKEOFF, MUNAKATA?
HINOHARA IS...
HE'S IN TOWN, BUT...
...THINGS HAVE CHANGED.

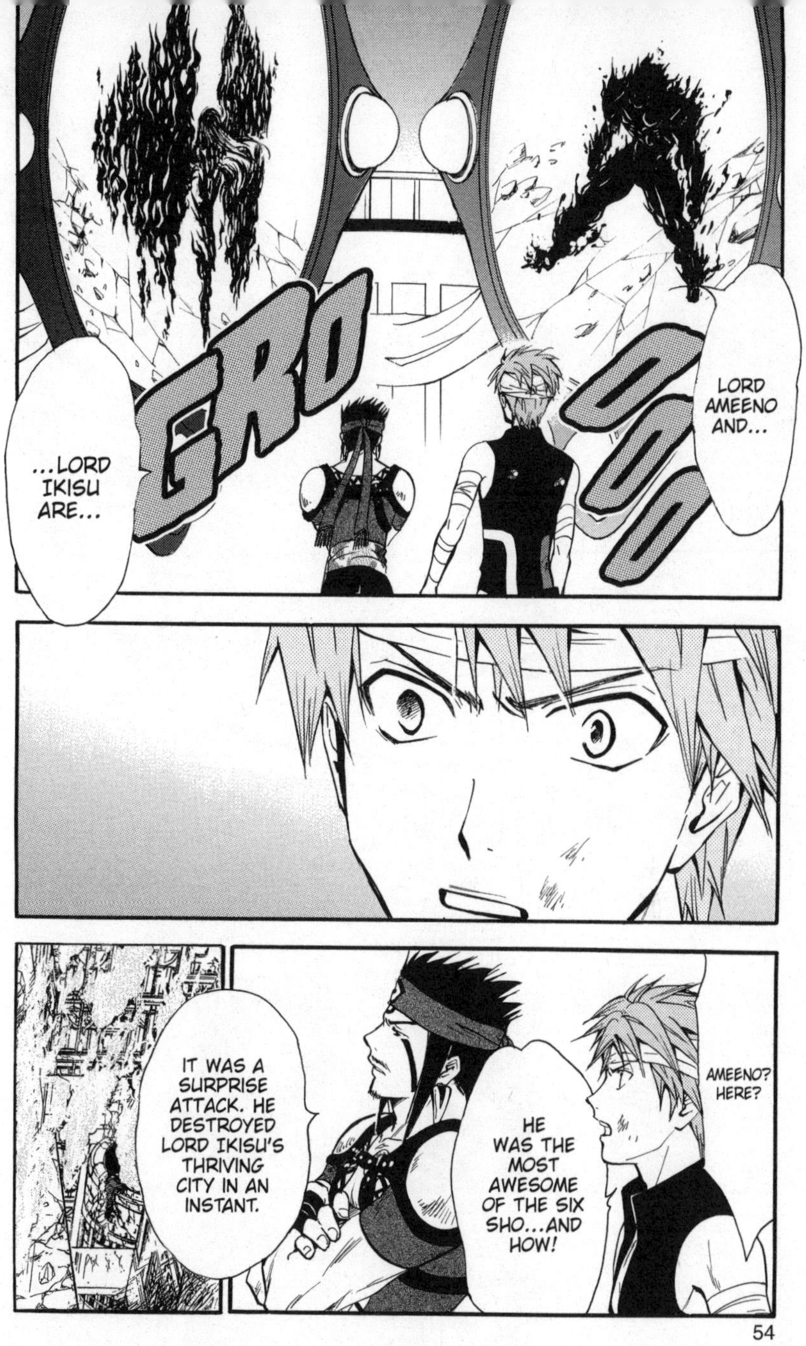
LORD AMEENO AND...
GROOO
...LORD IKISU ARE...
AMEENO? HERE?
HE WAS THE MOST AWESOME OF THE SIX SHO...AND HOW!
IT WAS A SURPRISE ATTACK. HE DESTROYED LORD IKISU'S THRIVING CITY IN AN INSTANT.

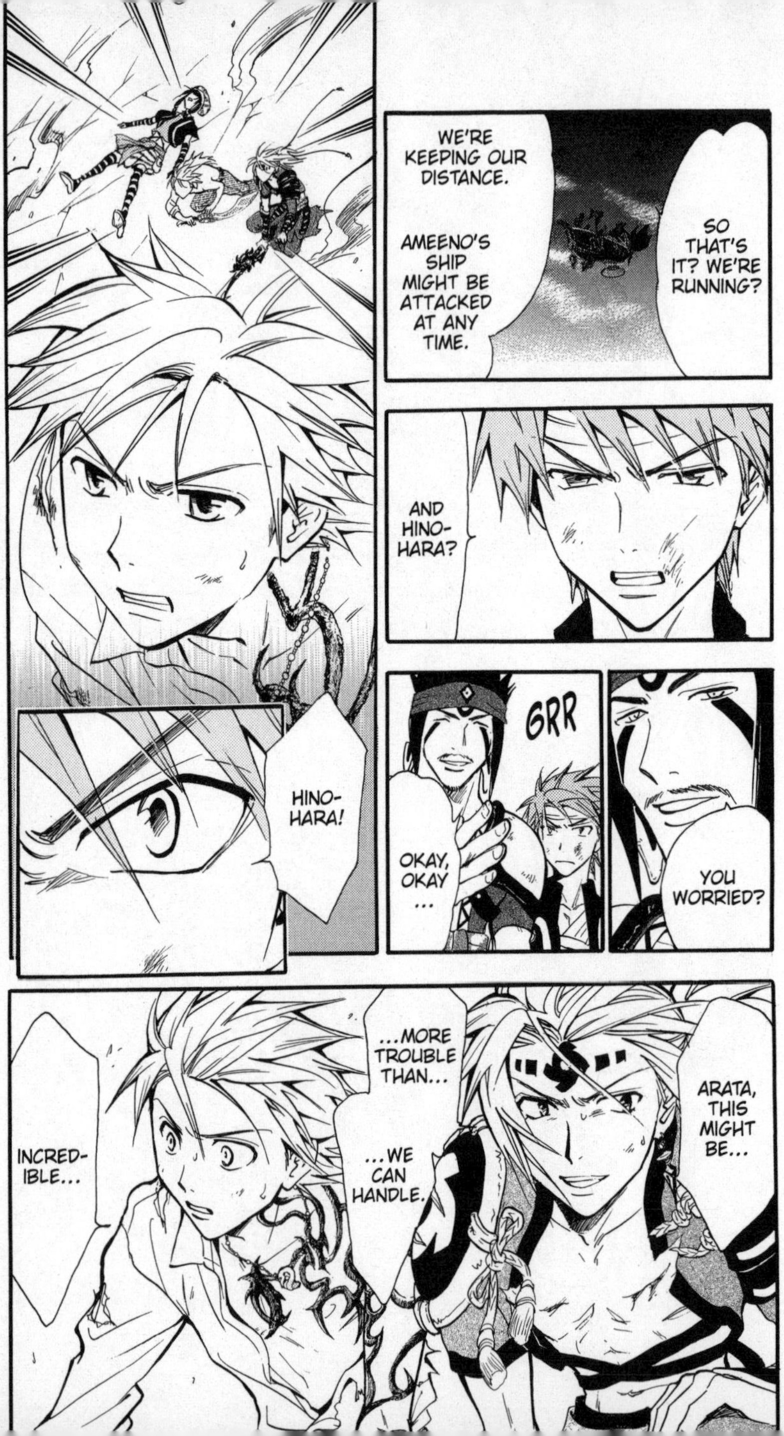
SO THAT'S IT? WE'RE RUNNING?
WE'RE KEEPING OUR DISTANCE.
AMEENO'S SHIP MIGHT BE ATTACKED AT ANY TIME.
AND HINO-HARA?
YOU WORRIED?
GRR
OKAY, OKAY ...
HINO-HARA!
ARATA, THIS MIGHT BE...
...MORE TROUBLE THAN...
...WE CAN HANDLE.
INCRED-IBLE...

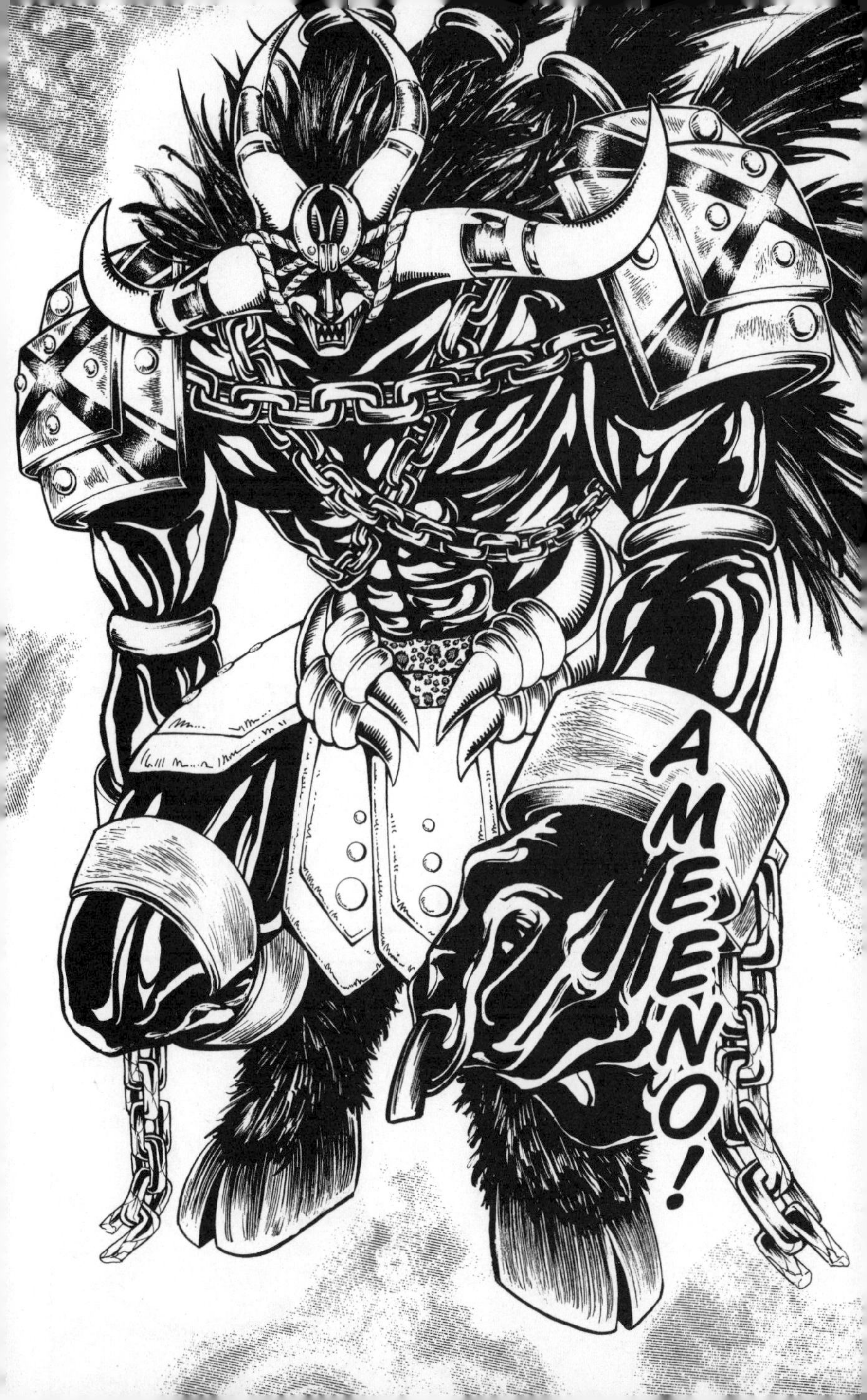
AMEENO!

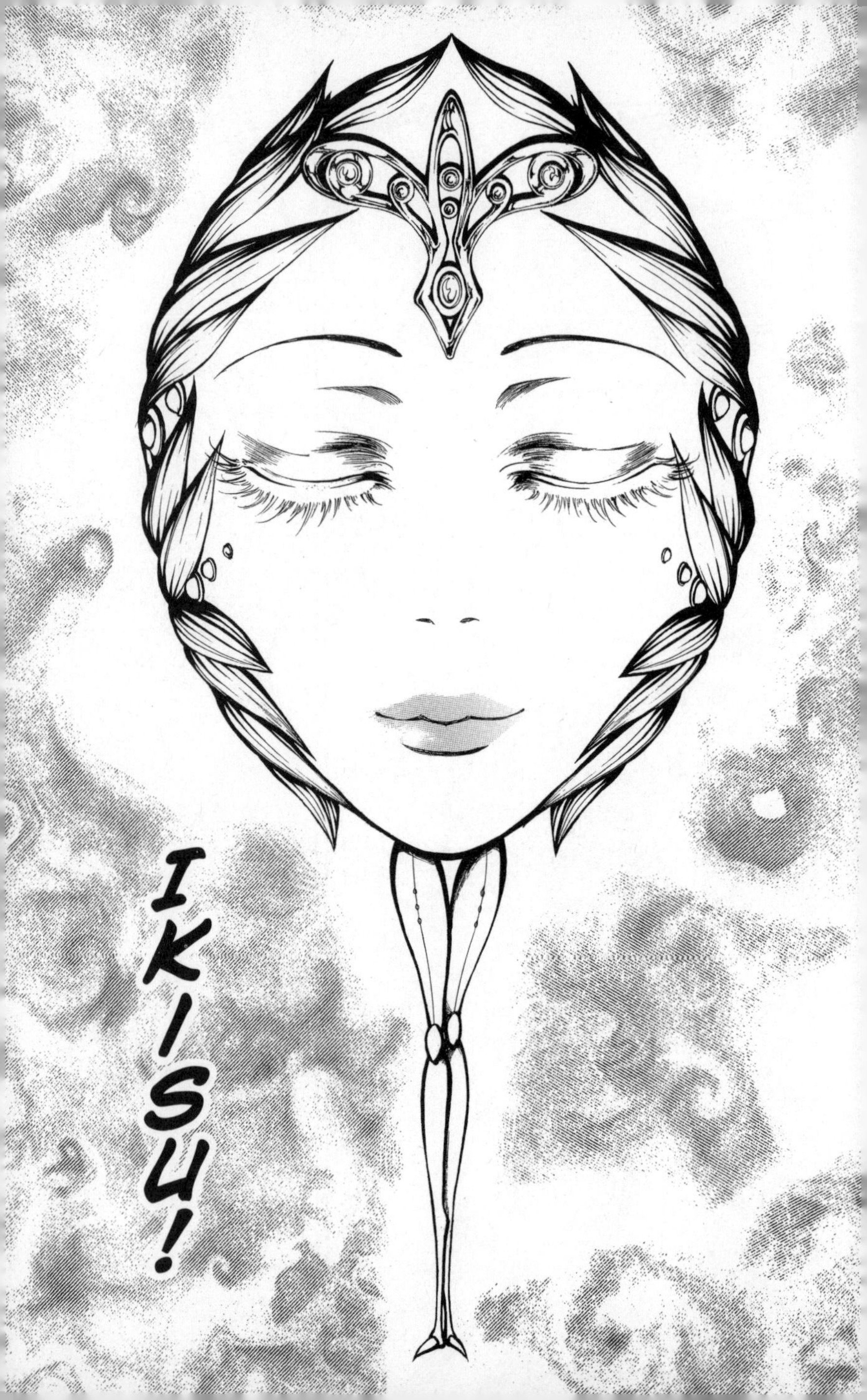
IKISU!

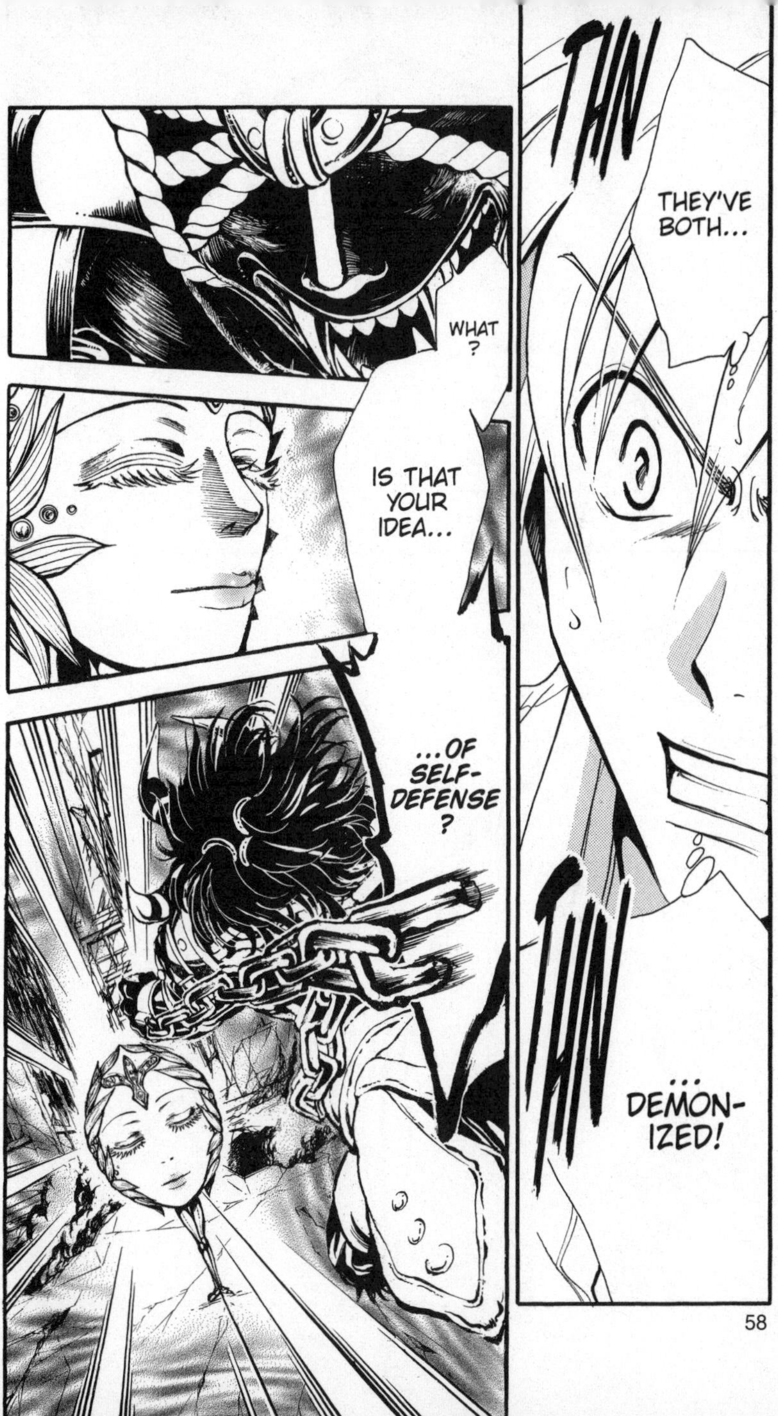
THAN
THEY'VE BOTH...
THAN
...DEMONIZED!
WHAT?
IS THAT YOUR IDEA...
...OF SELF-DEFENSE?

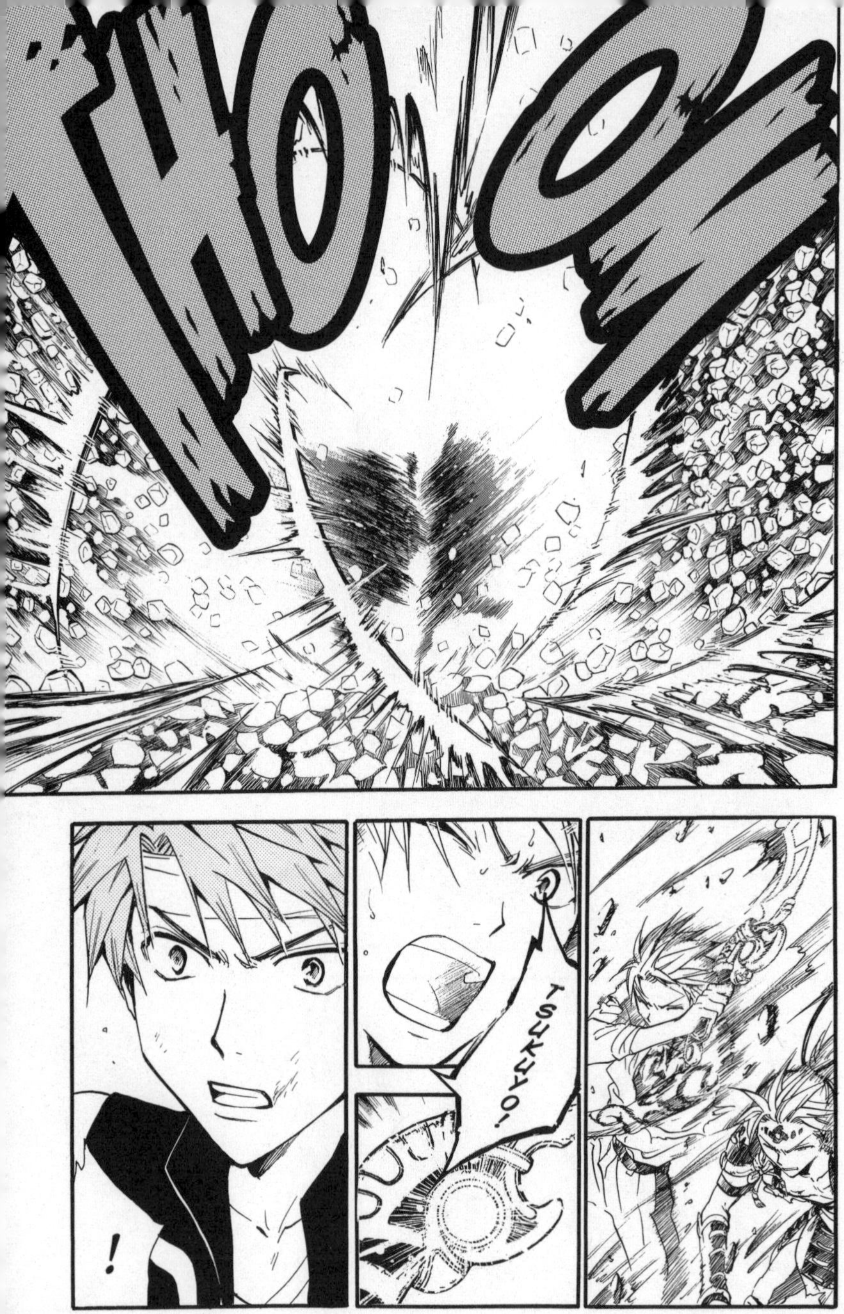
THOOM
TSUKUYO!
!

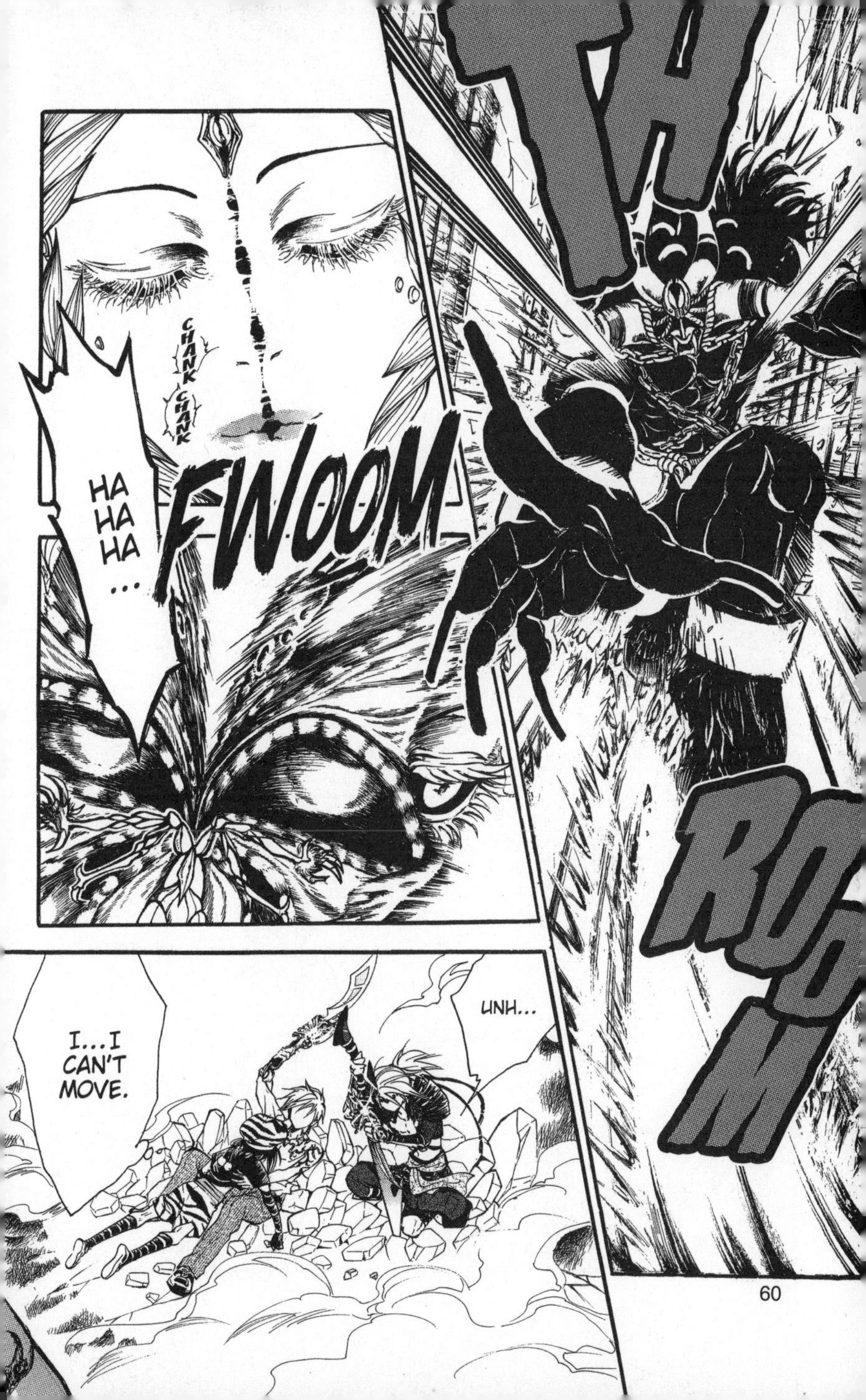
CHANK CHANK
HA HA HA ...
FWOOM
UNH...
I...I CAN'T MOVE.

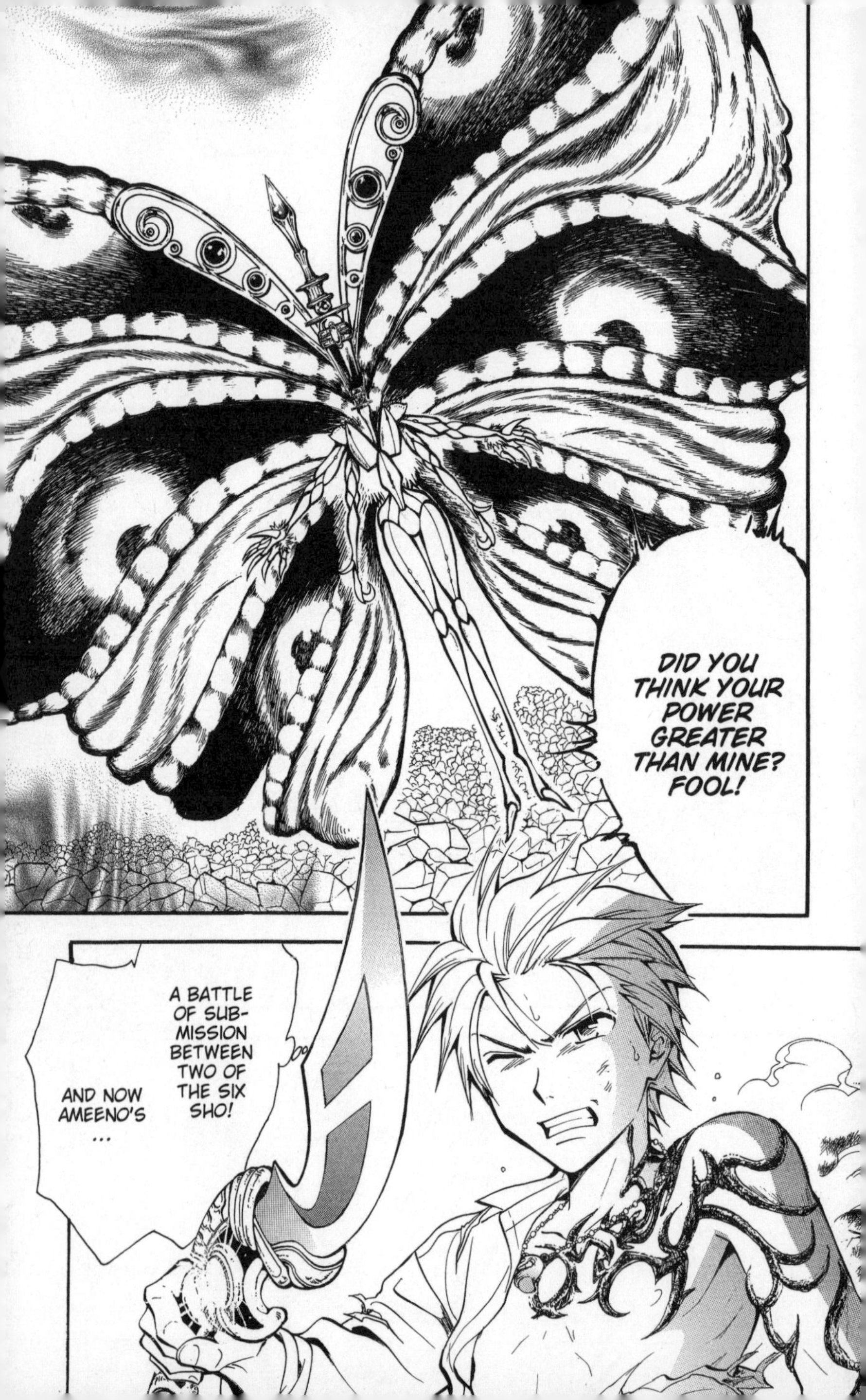
DID YOU THINK YOUR POWER GREATER THAN MINE? FOOL!
A BATTLE OF SUB-MISSION BETWEEN TWO OF THE SIX SHO!
AND NOW AMEENO'S ...

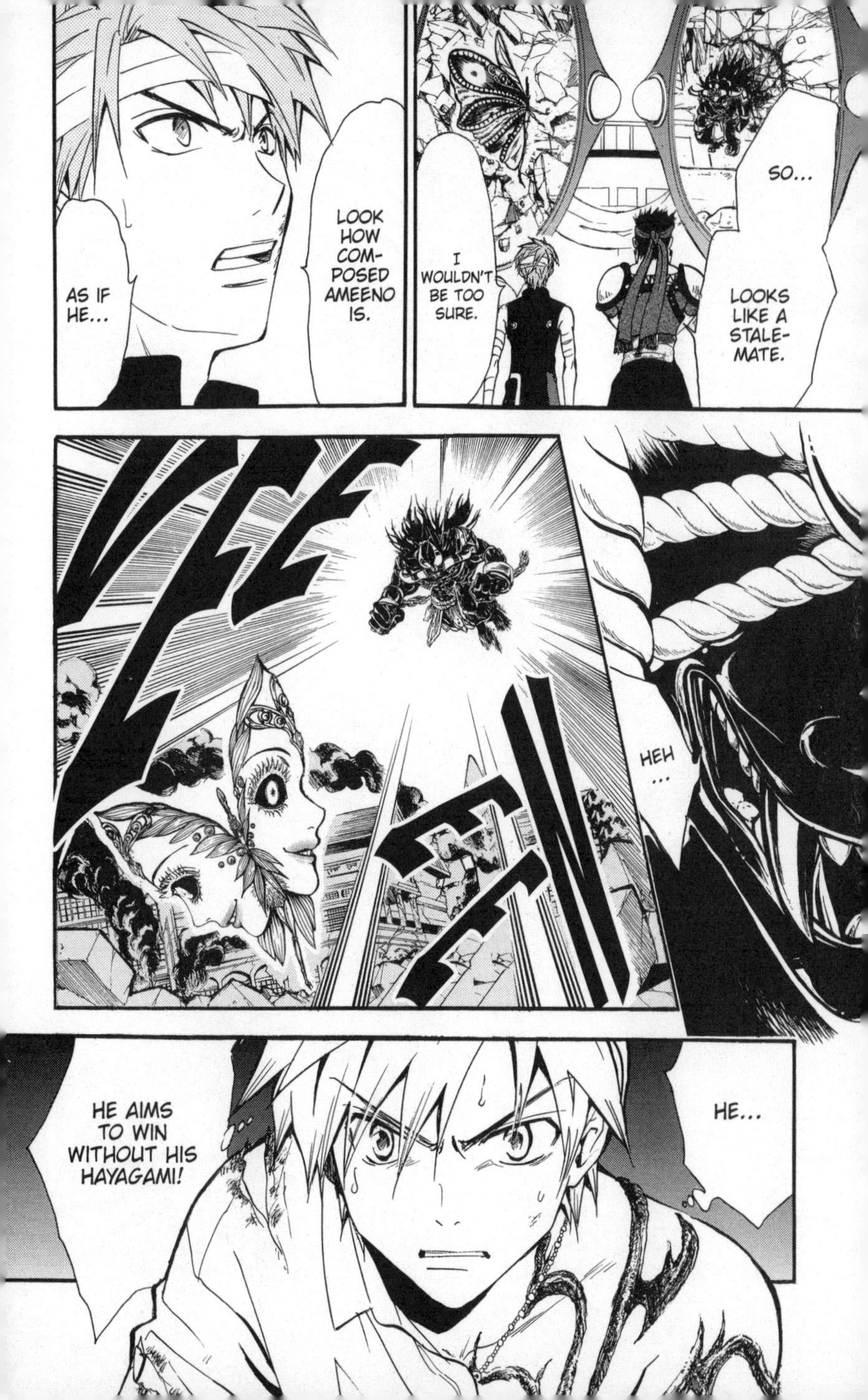
SO...
LOOKS LIKE A STALE-MATE.
I WOULDN'T BE TOO SURE.
LOOK HOW COM-POSED AMEENO IS.
AS IF HE...
HEH ...
HE...
HE AIMS TO WIN WITHOUT HIS HAYAGAMI!

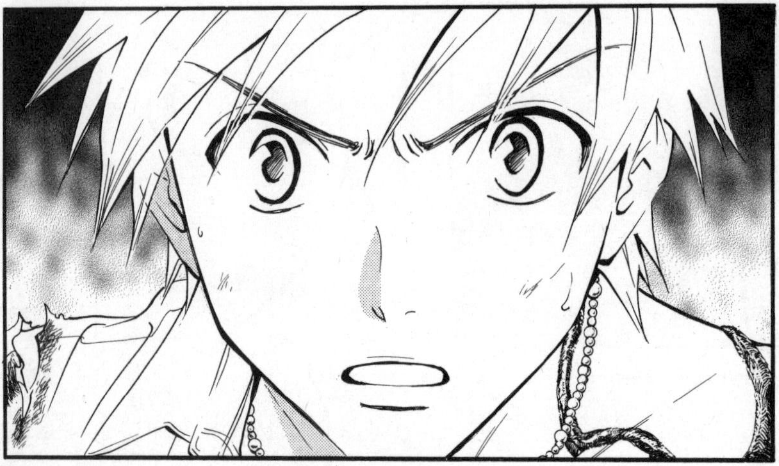

Chapter 211

ARMOR

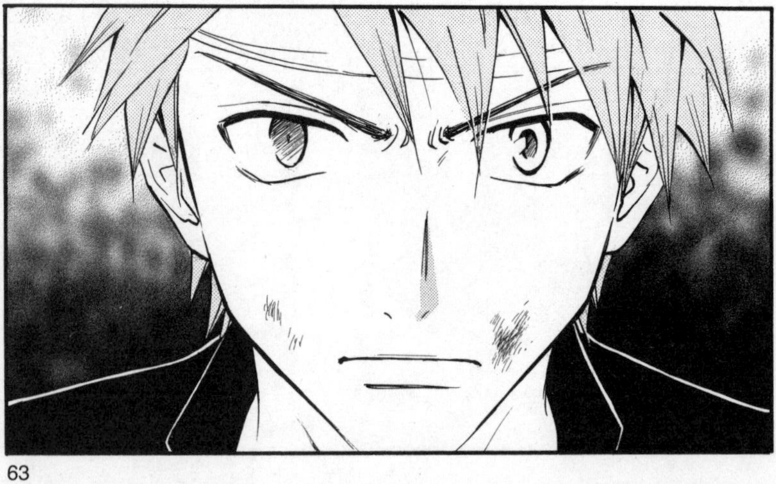

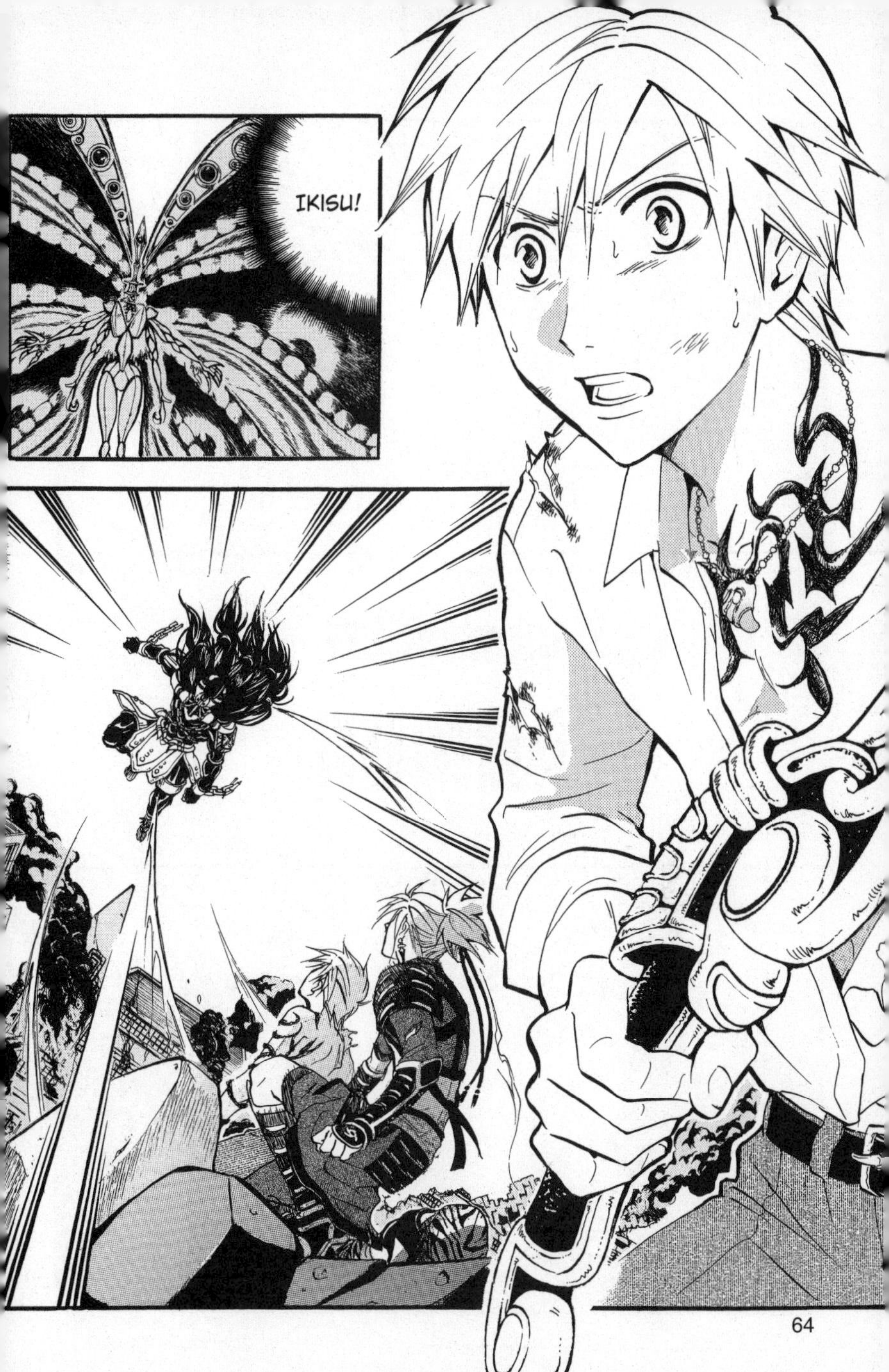
IKISU!

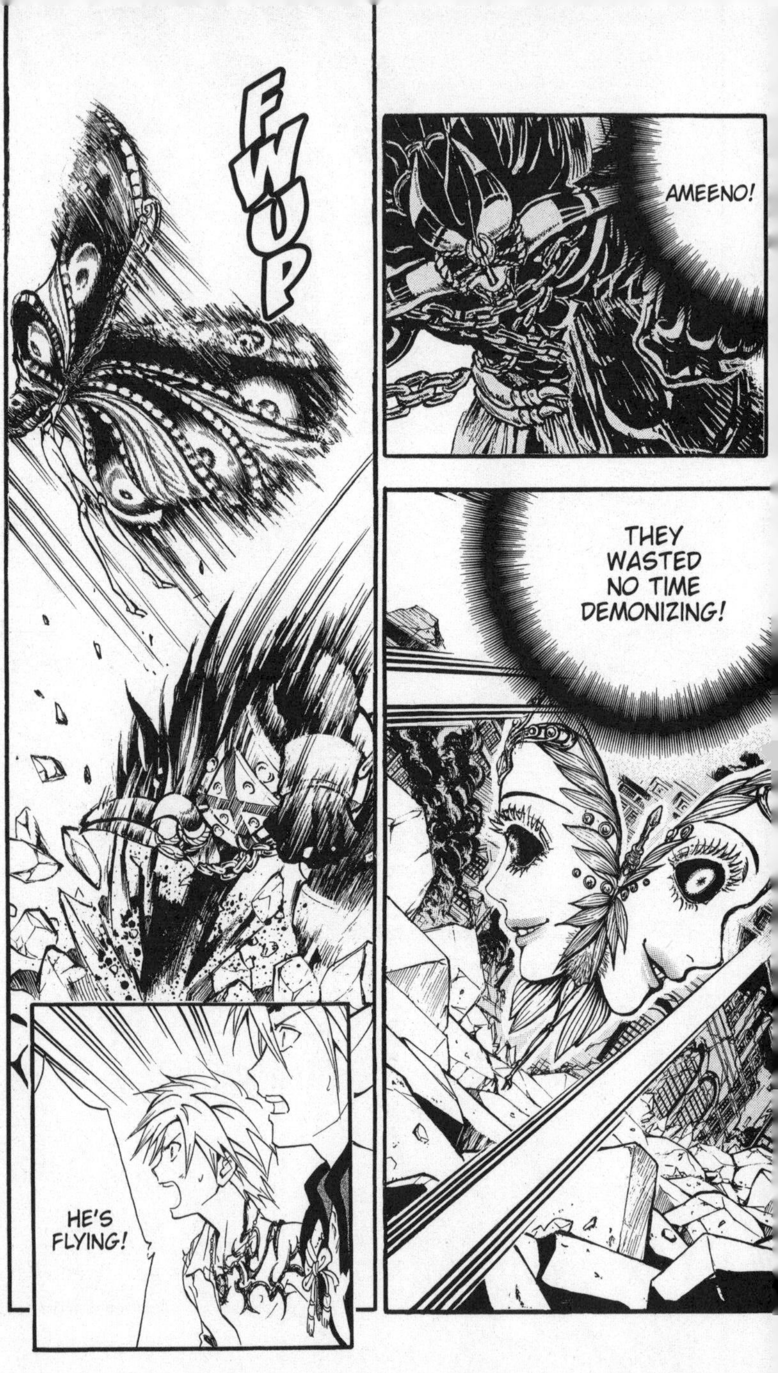
AMEENO!
THEY WASTED NO TIME DEMONIZING!
FWUP
HE'S FLYING!

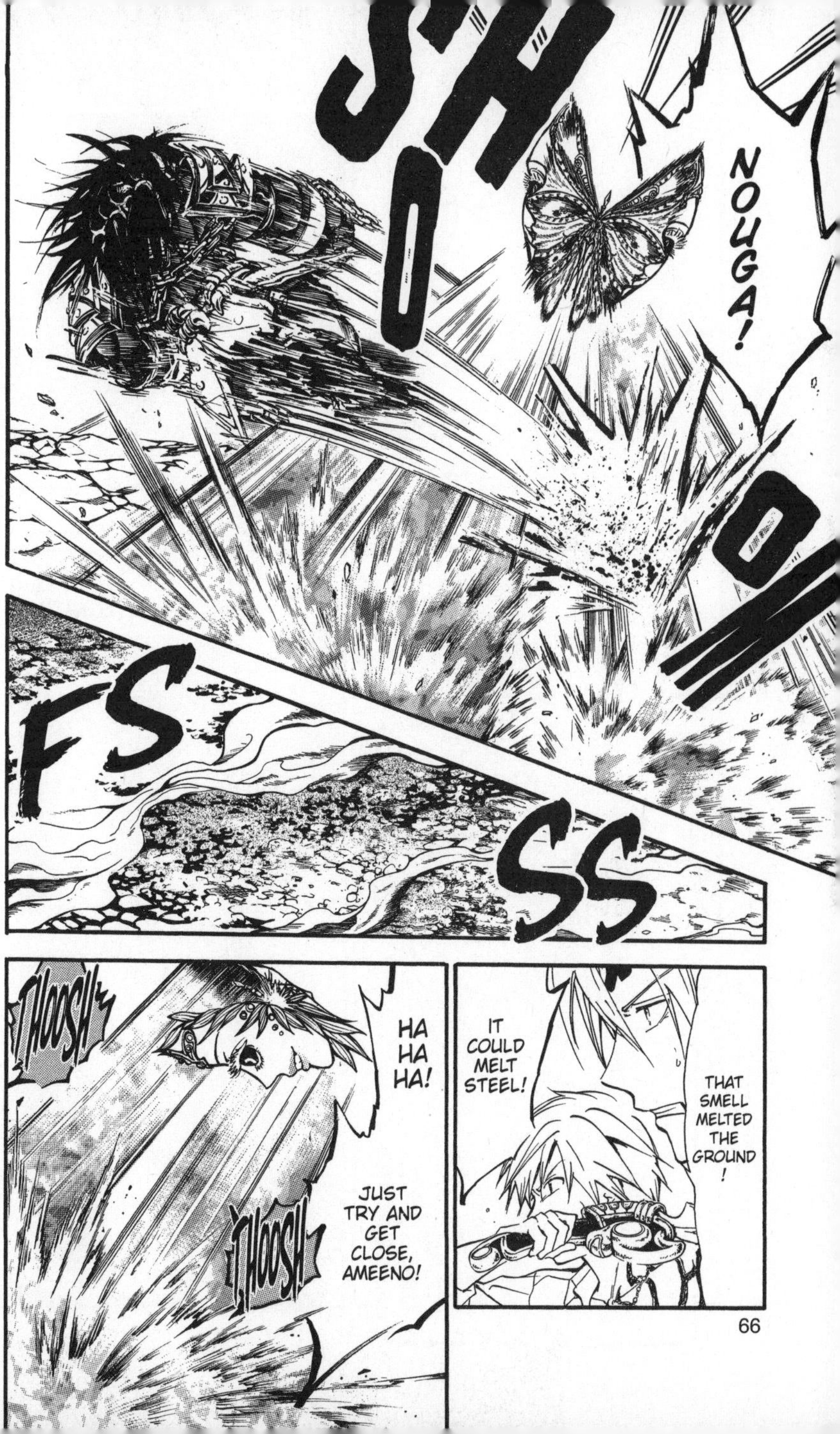
NOUGA!
FSSS
THAT SMELL MELTED THE GROUND!
IT COULD MELT STEEL!
HA HA HA!
THOOSH
JUST TRY AND GET CLOSE, AMEENO!
THOOSH

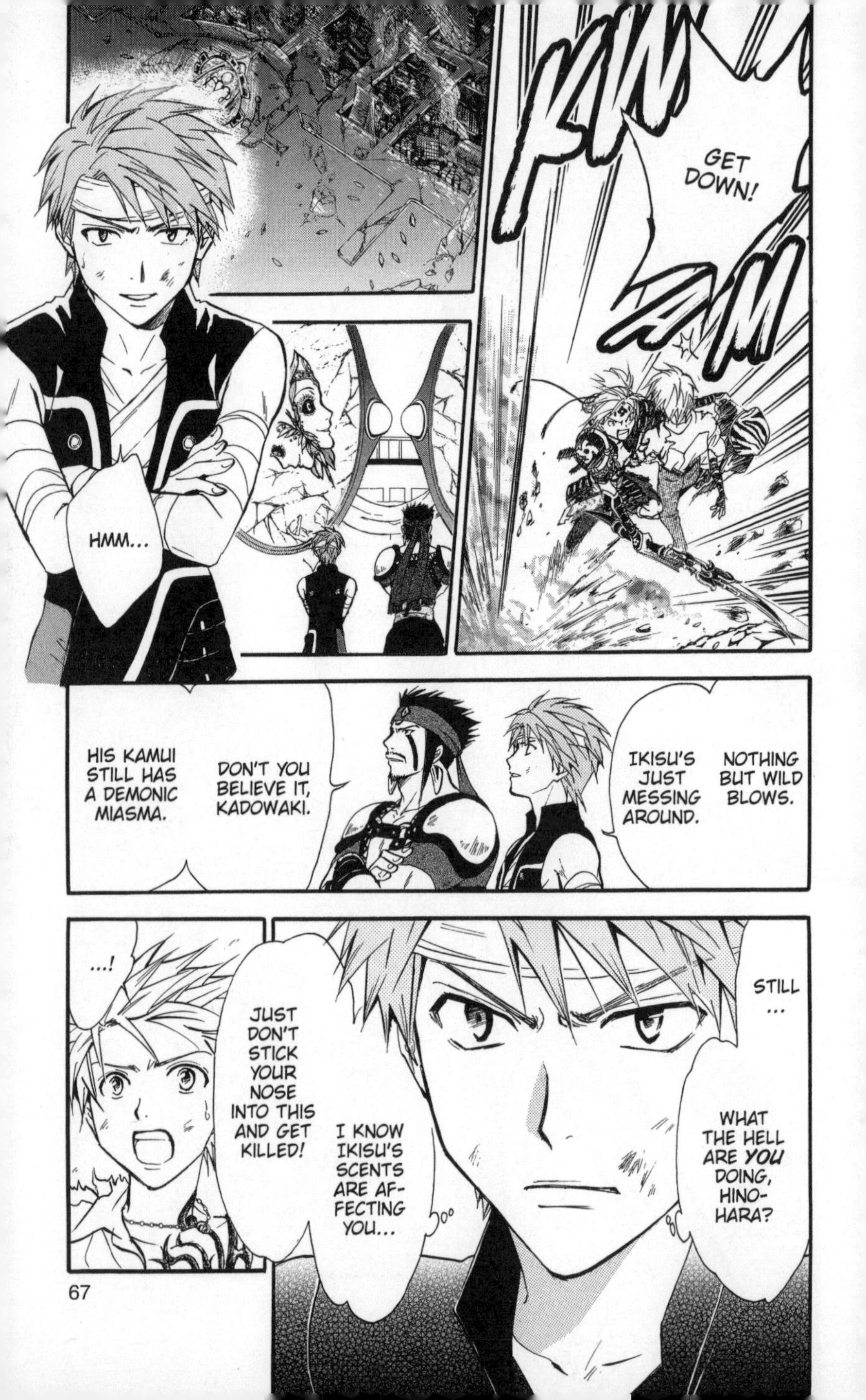
KAM
AM
GET DOWN!
HMM...
NOTHING BUT WILD BLOWS.
IKISU'S JUST MESSING AROUND.
DON'T YOU BELIEVE IT, KADOWAKI.
HIS KAMUI STILL HAS A DEMONIC MIASMA.
STILL...
WHAT THE HELL ARE YOU DOING, HINO-HARA?
I KNOW IKISU'S SCENTS ARE AF-FECTING YOU...
JUST DON'T STICK YOUR NOSE INTO THIS AND GET KILLED!
...!

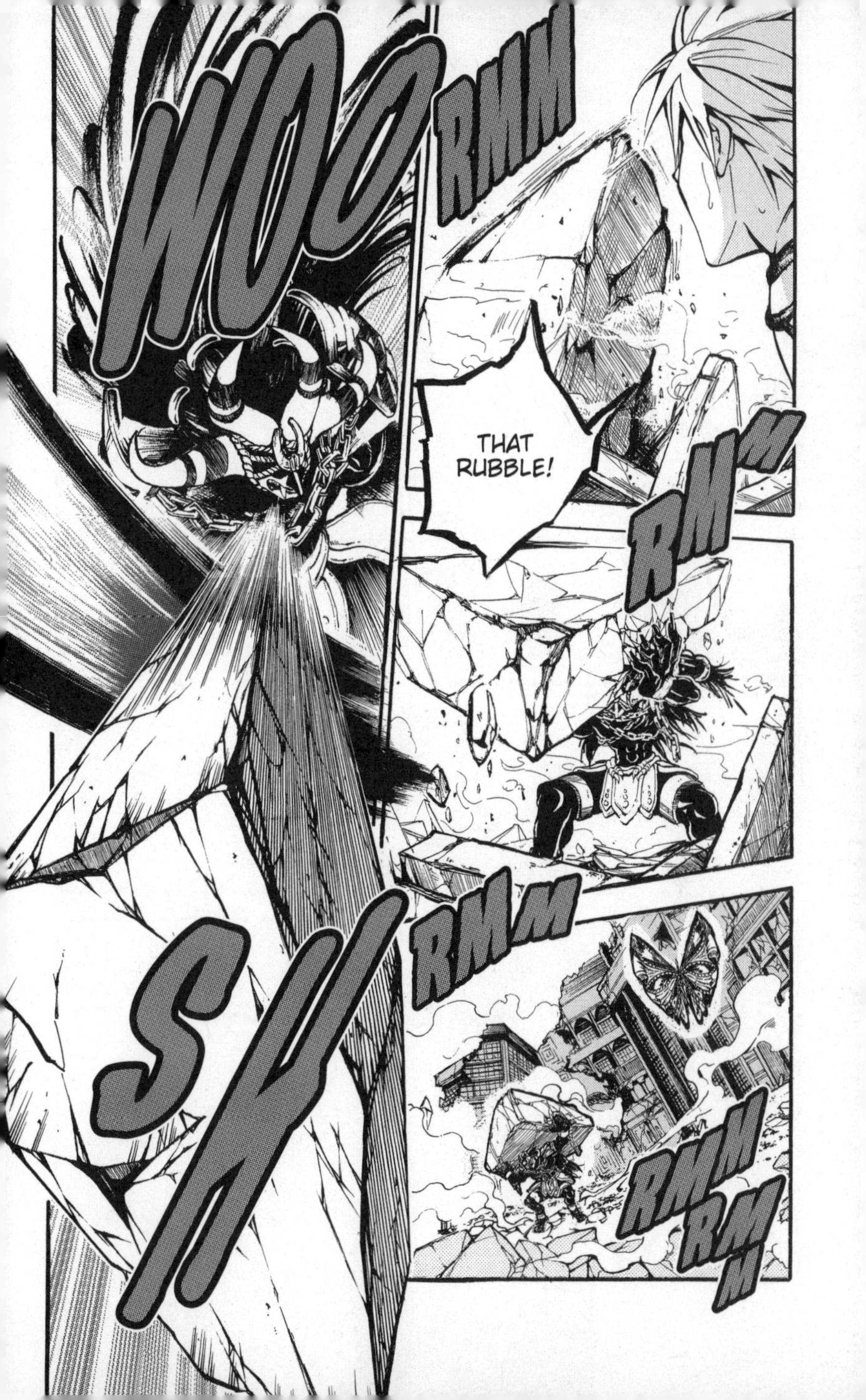
THAT RUBBLE!
RMM
RMMM
RMM
WHOORMMM
SHRMM

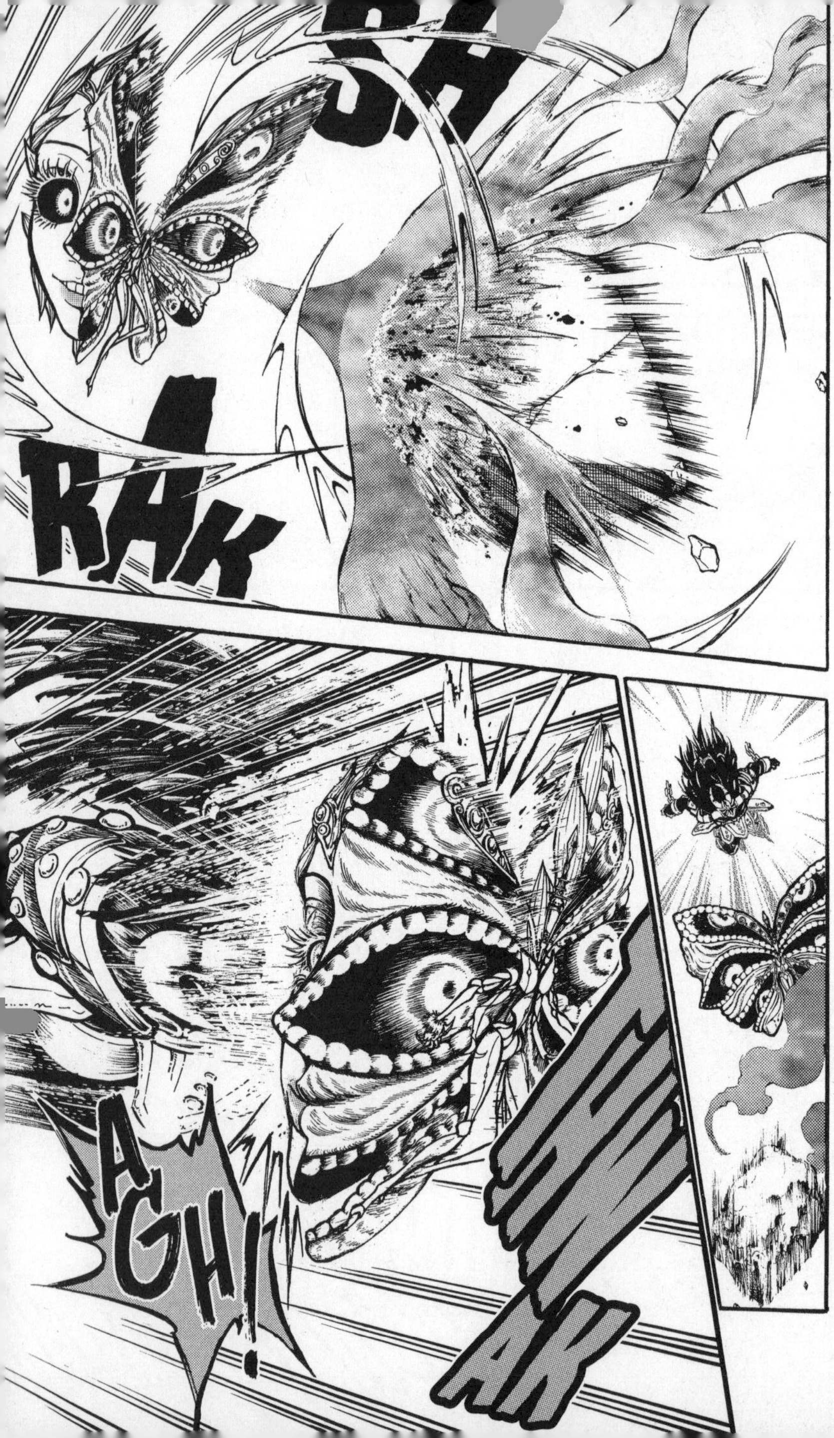
RAK
AGH!

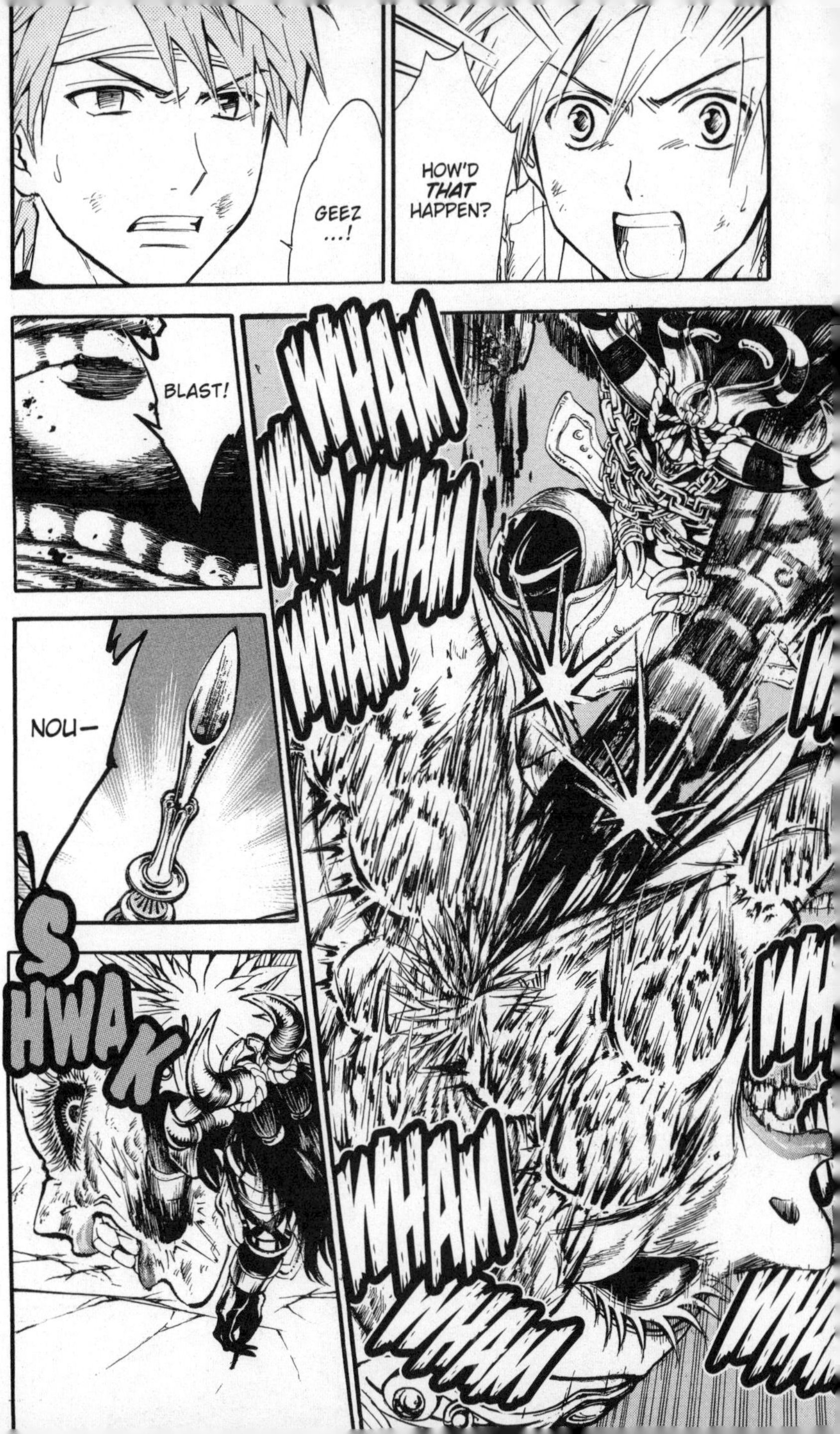
HOW'D *THAT* HAPPEN?
GEEZ ...!
WHAM
WHAM
WHAM
WHAM
WHAM
WHAM
BLAST!
NOU—
SHWAK

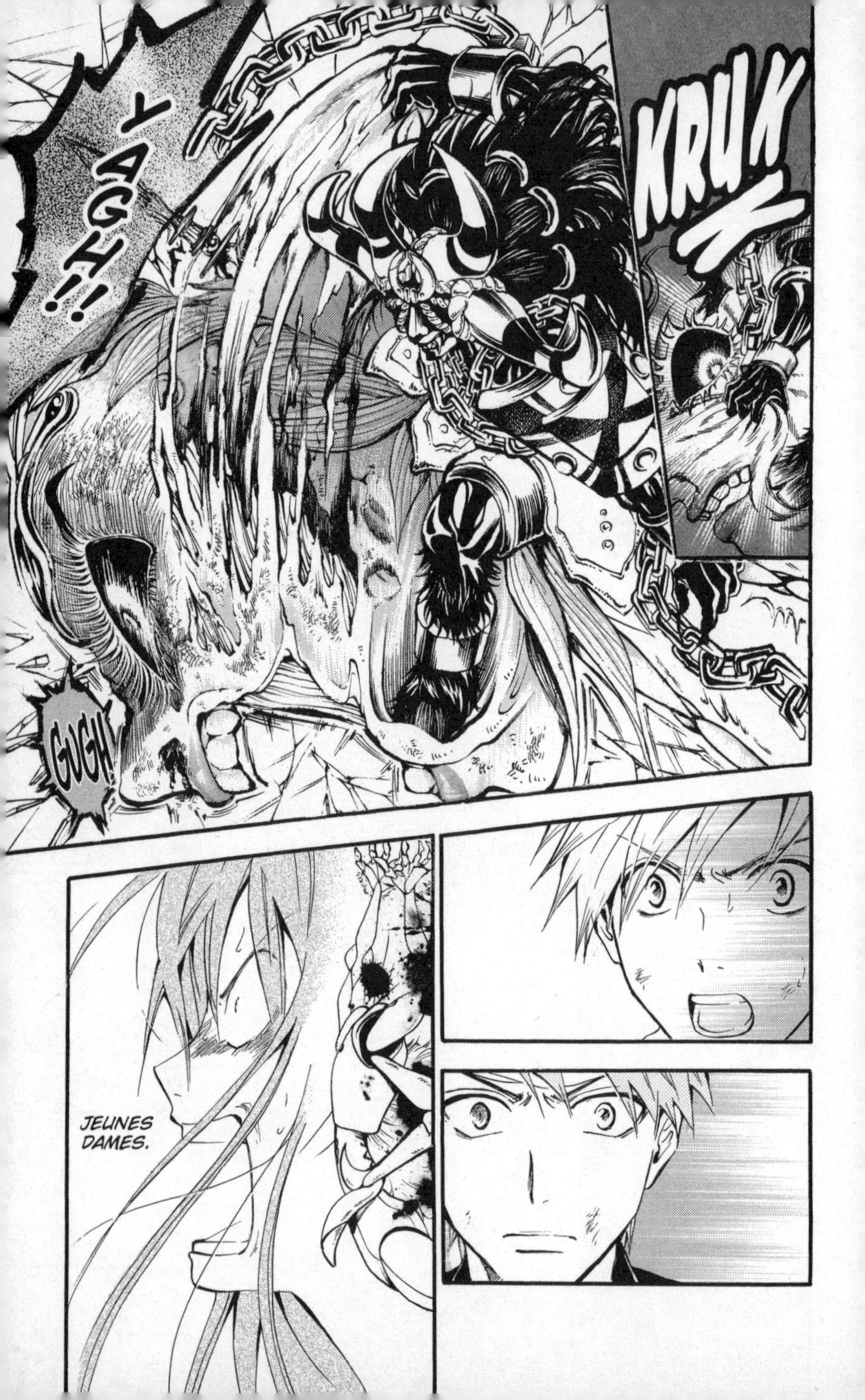
KRUNK
YAGH!!
GUGH
JEUNES DAMES.

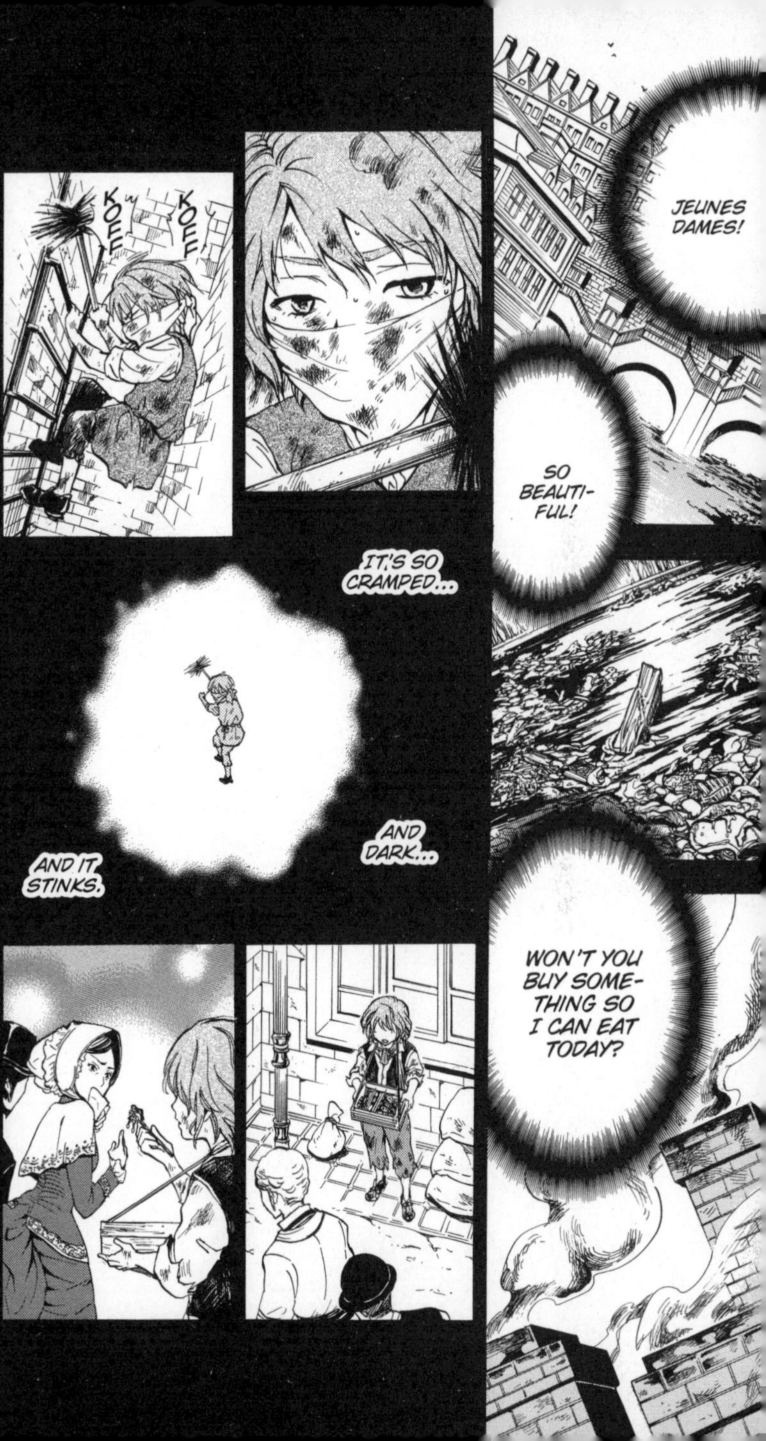
JEUNES DAMES!
SO BEAUTI-FUL!
WON'T YOU BUY SOME-THING SO I CAN EAT TODAY?
KOFF KOFF
IT'S SO CRAMPED...
AND DARK...
AND IT STINKS.

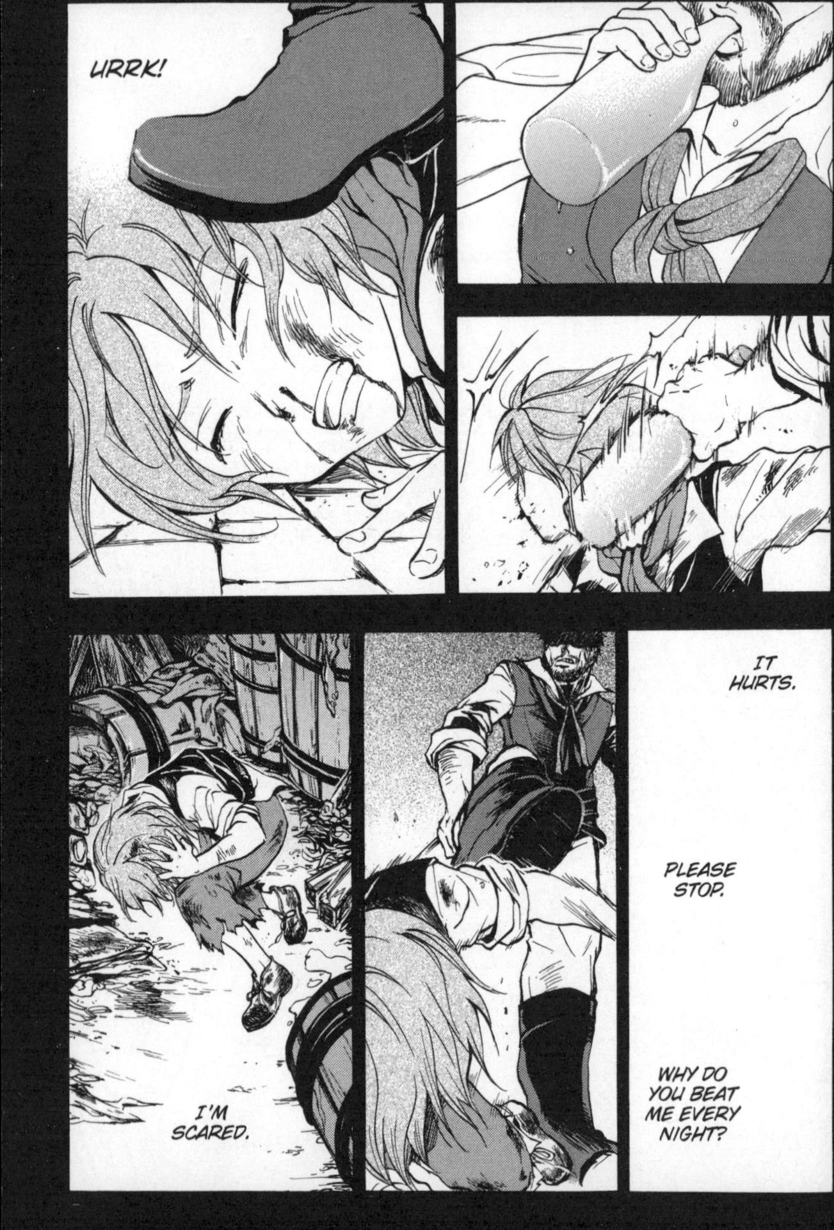
URRK!
IT HURTS.
PLEASE STOP.
WHY DO YOU BEAT ME EVERY NIGHT?
I'M SCARED.

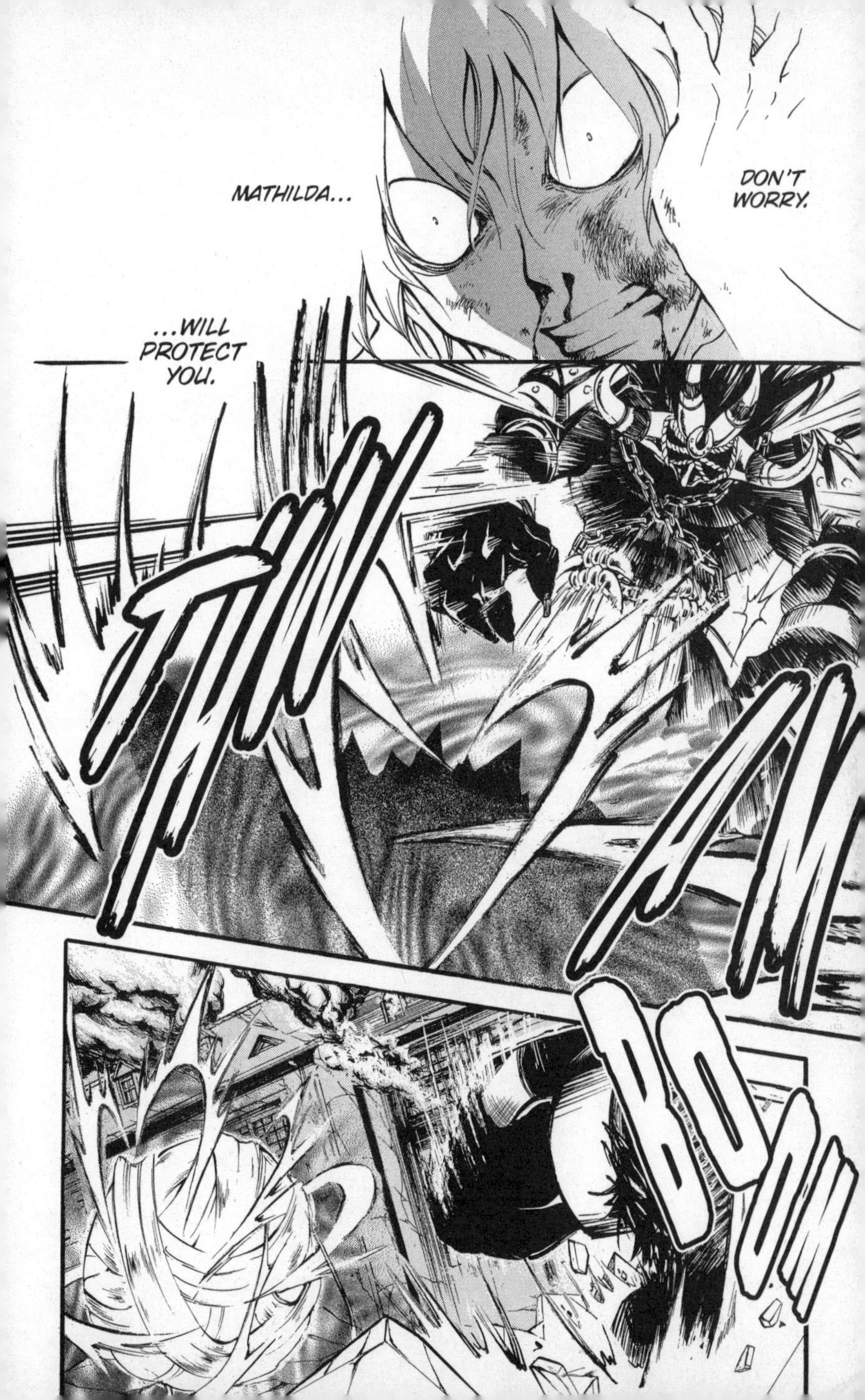
DON'T WORRY.
MATHILDA...
...WILL PROTECT YOU.

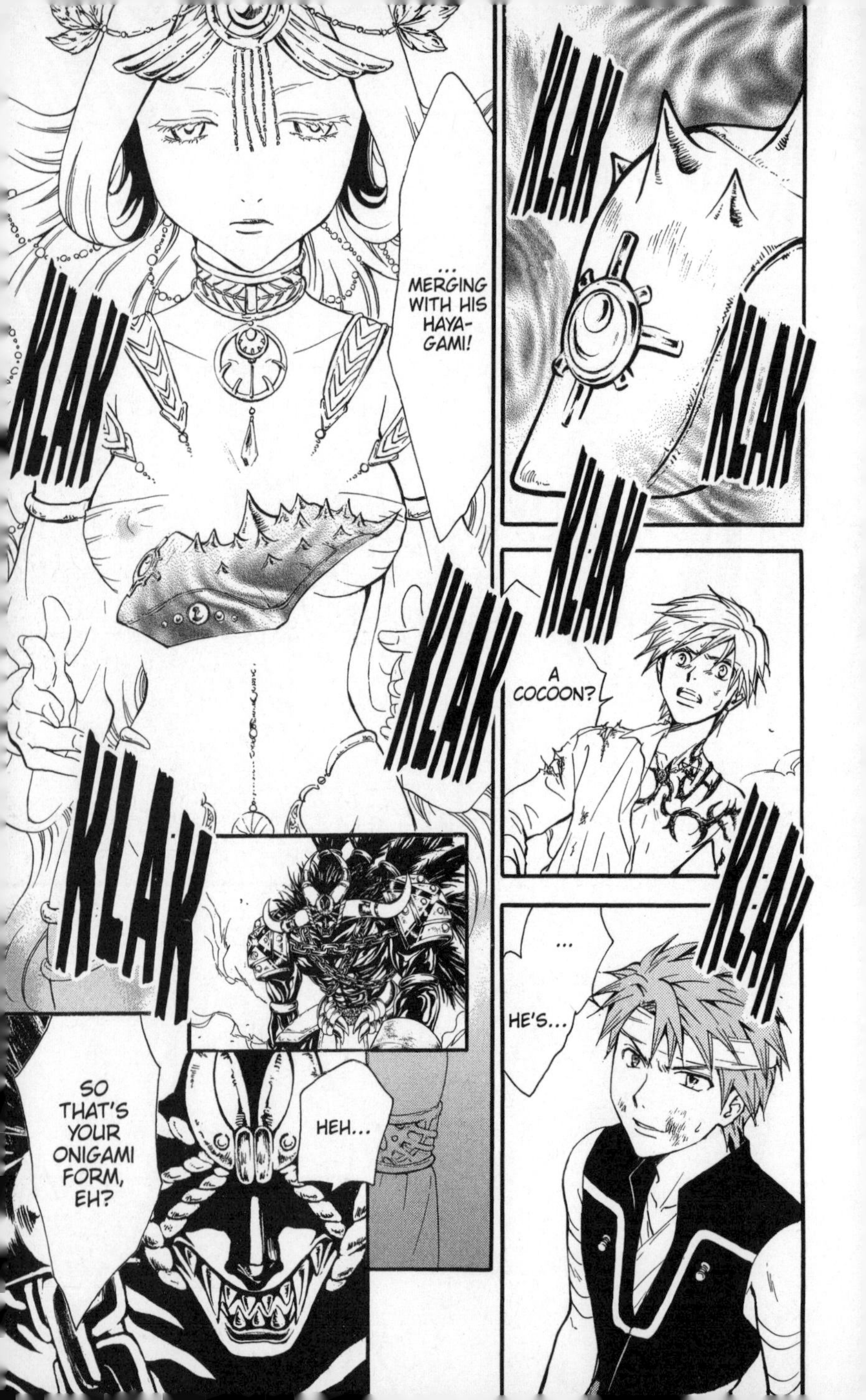
KLAK
KLAK
KLAK
A COCOON?
KLAK
...
HE'S...
...MERGING WITH HIS HAYA-GAMI!
KLAK
KLAK
KLAK
HEH...
SO THAT'S YOUR ONIGAMI FORM, EH?

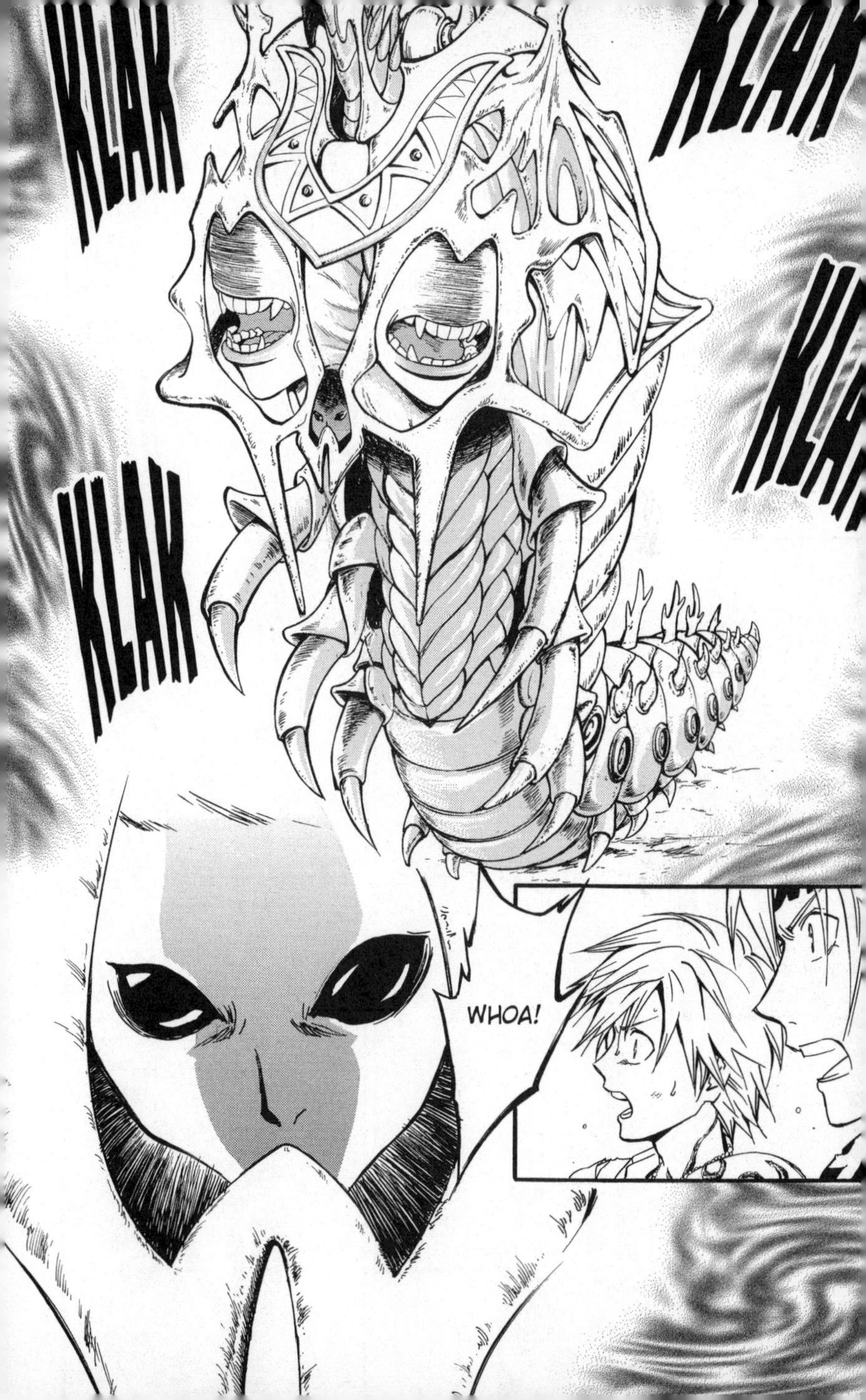
KLAK
KLAK
KLAK
KLAK
WHOA!

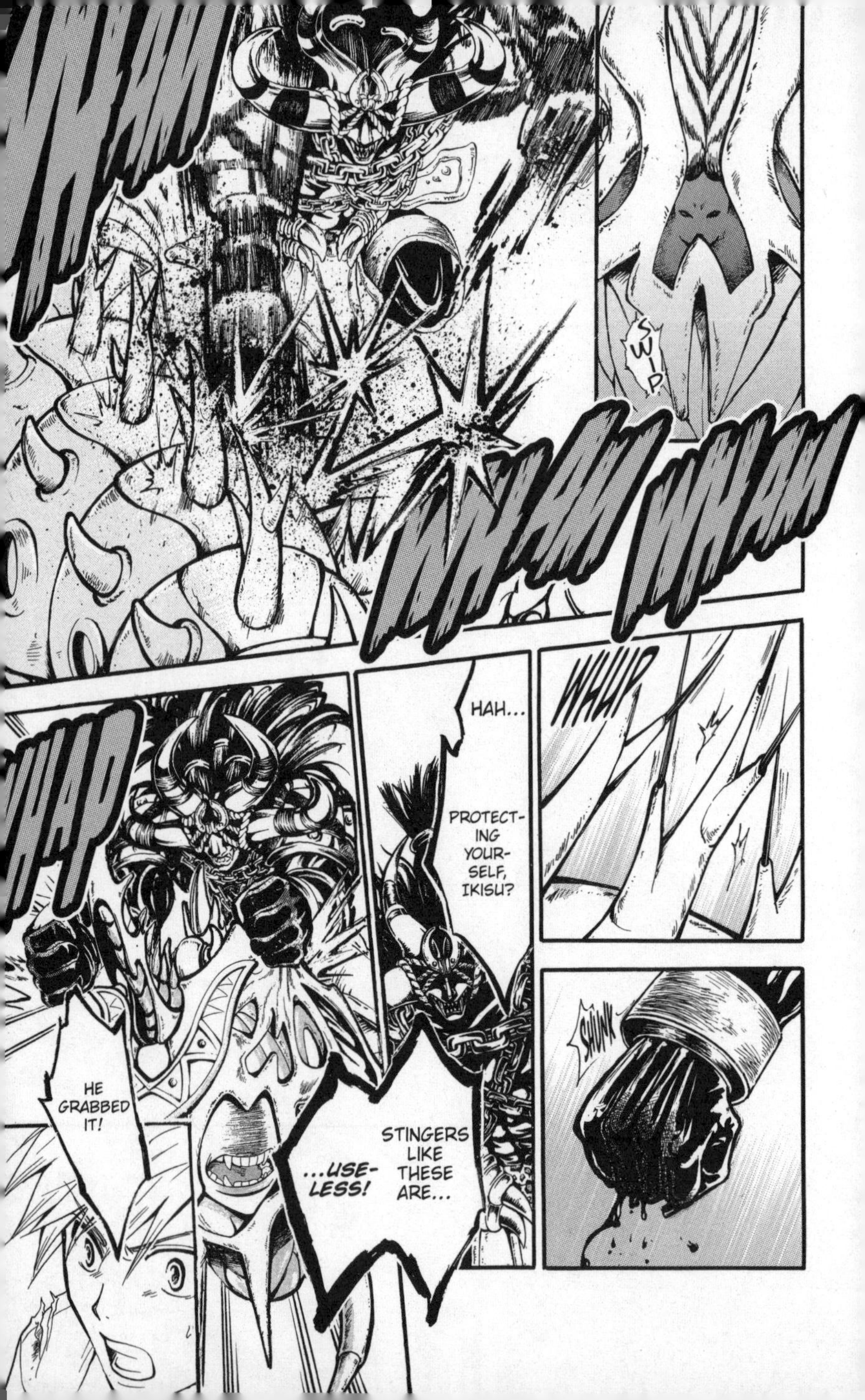
SWIP
WHAM WHAM WHAM
WHAP
WHUP
HAH...
PROTECT-ING YOUR-SELF, IKISU?
SHUNK
STINGERS LIKE THESE ARE...
...USE-LESS!
HE GRABBED IT!

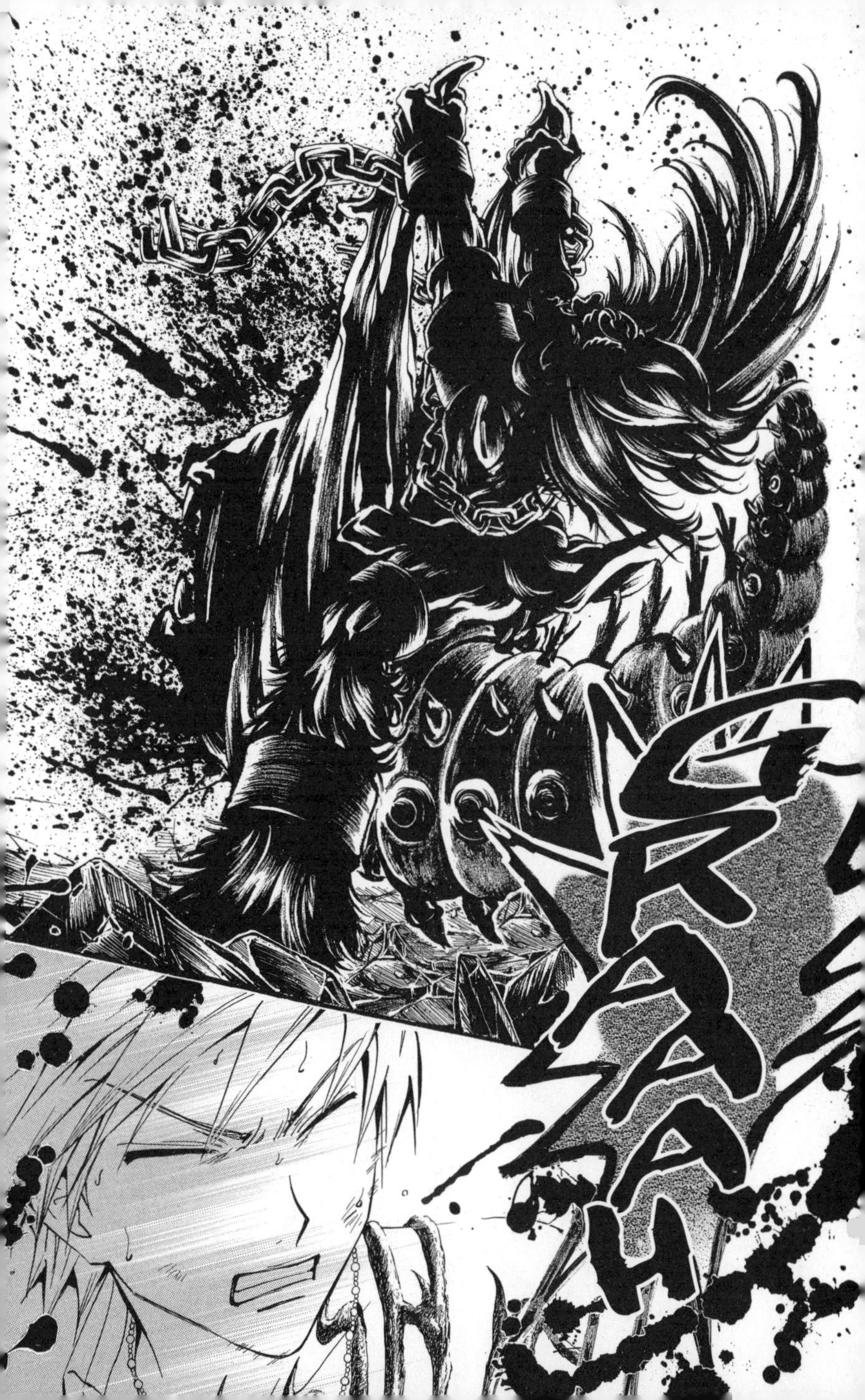

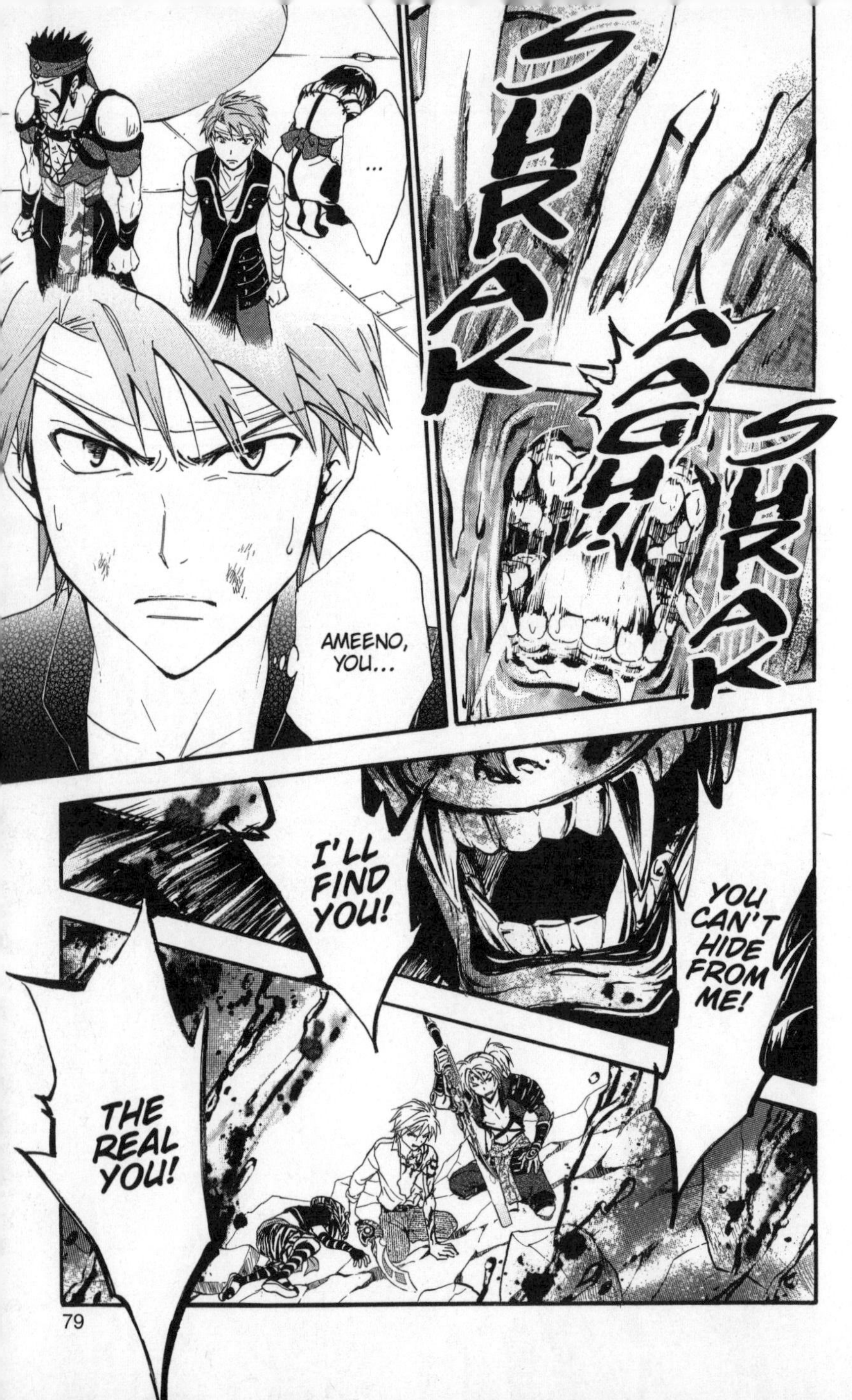
SHRAK
AAGH!
SHRAK
...
AMEENO, YOU...
YOU CAN'T HIDE FROM ME!
I'LL FIND YOU!
THE REAL YOU!

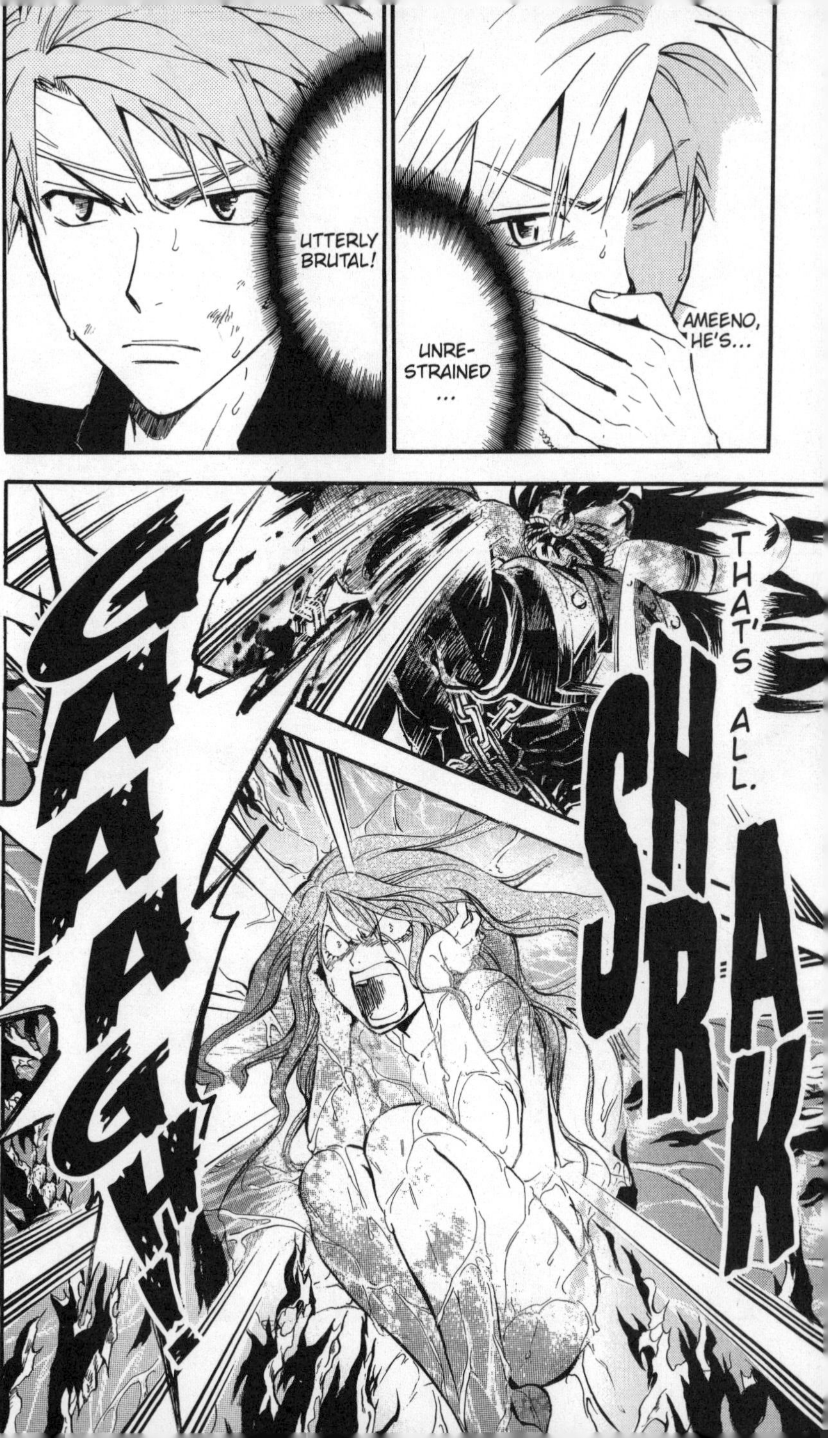
AMEENO, HE'S...
UNRE-STRAINED...
UTTERLY BRUTAL!
THAT'S ALL.
SHRAK
GAAAGH!

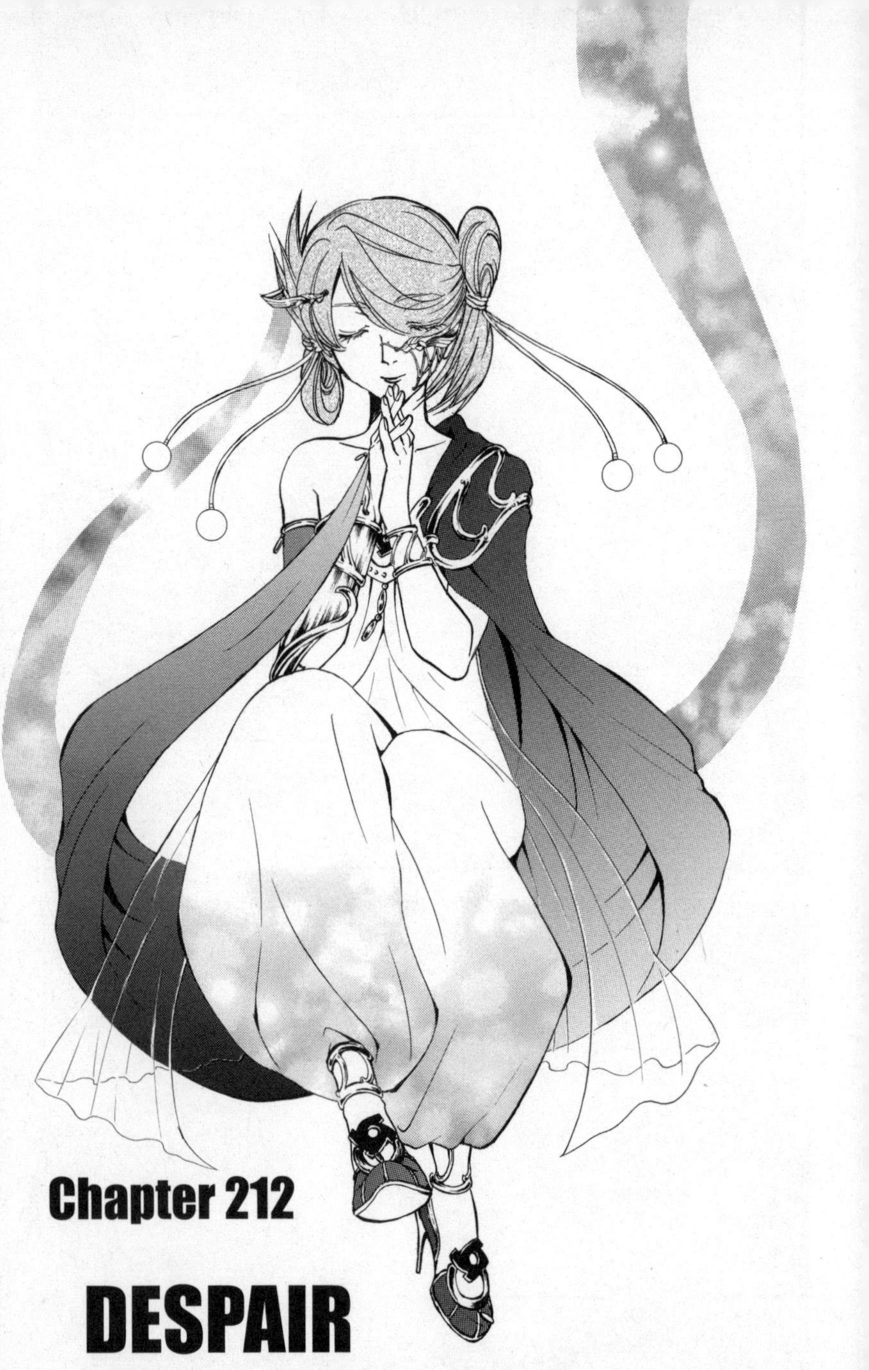

Chapter 212

DESPAIR

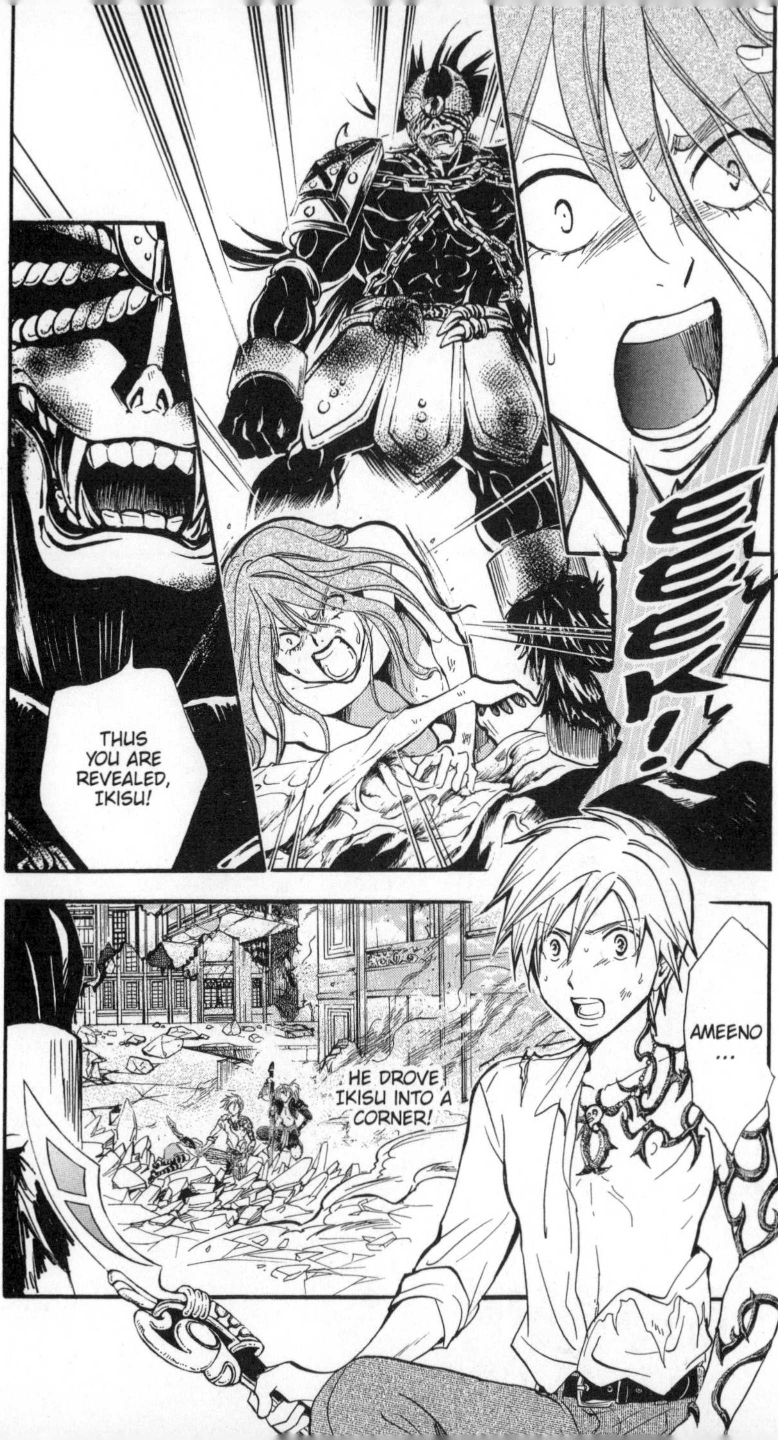
EEEK!!
THUS YOU ARE REVEALED, IKISU!
AMEENO ...
HE DROVE IKISU INTO A CORNER!

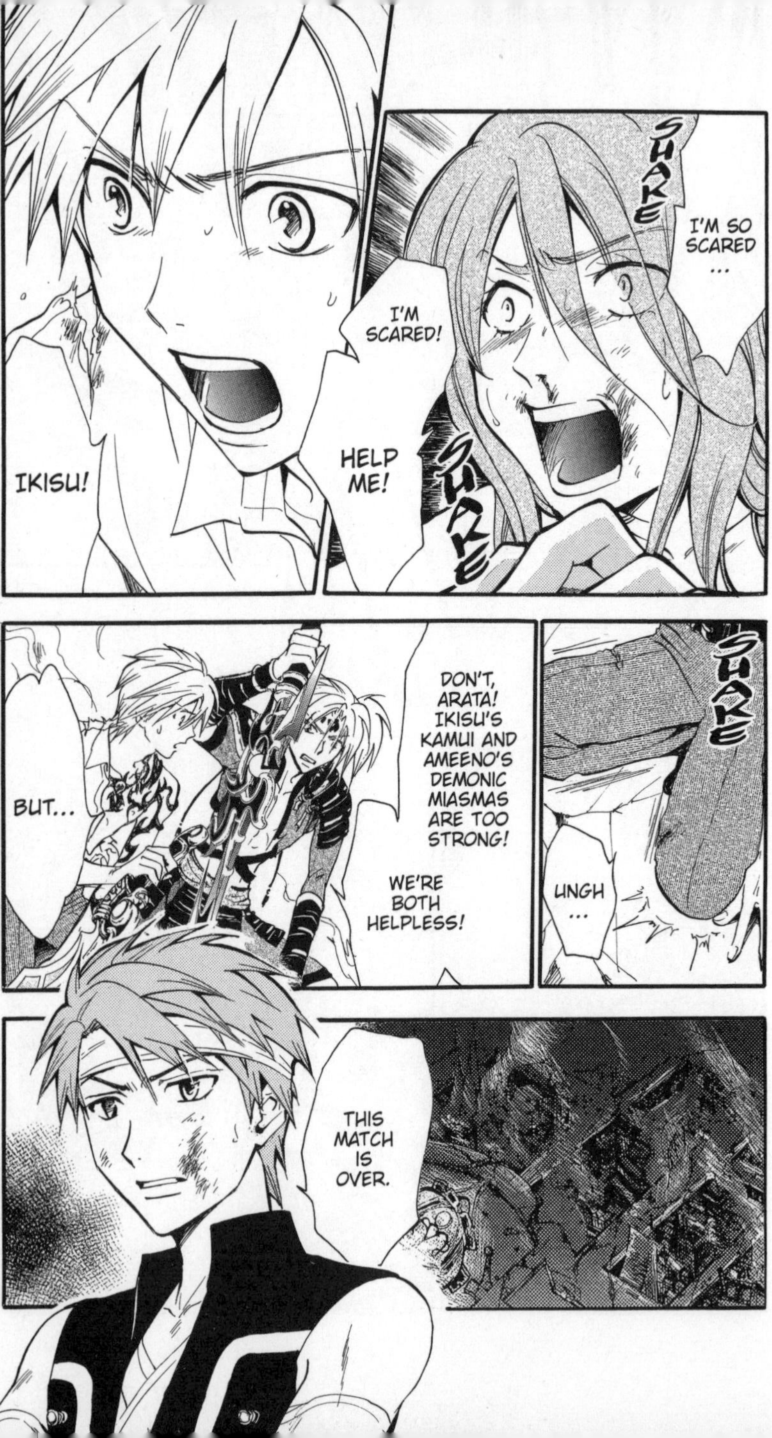
SHAKE
I'M SO SCARED ...
I'M SCARED!
HELP ME!
SHAKE
IKISU!
SHAKE
UNGH ...
DON'T, ARATA! IKISU'S KAMUI AND AMEENO'S DEMONIC MIASMAS ARE TOO STRONG!
WE'RE BOTH HELPLESS!
BUT...
THIS MATCH IS OVER.

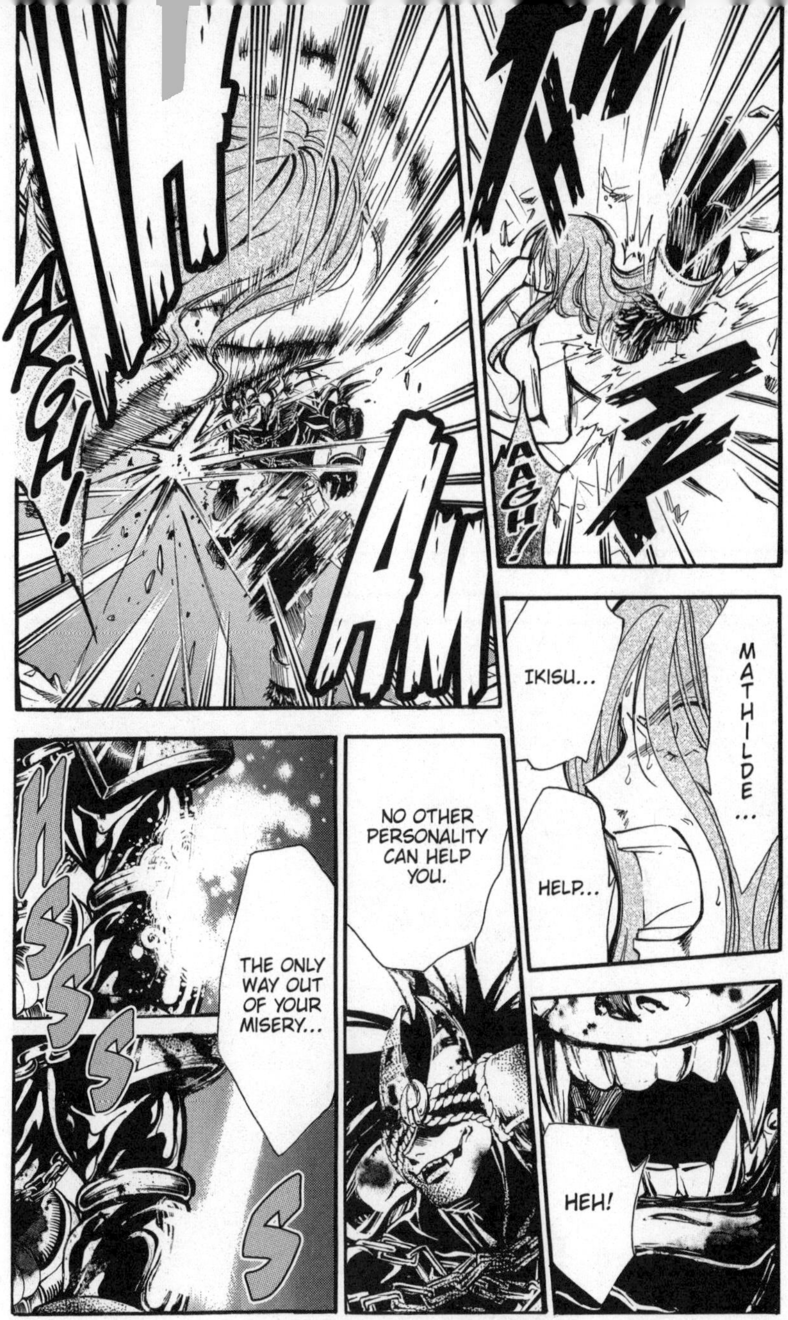
AAGH!
ARGH!
MATHILDE...
IKISU...
HELP...
HEH!
NO OTHER PERSONALITY CAN HELP YOU.
THE ONLY WAY OUT OF YOUR MISERY...

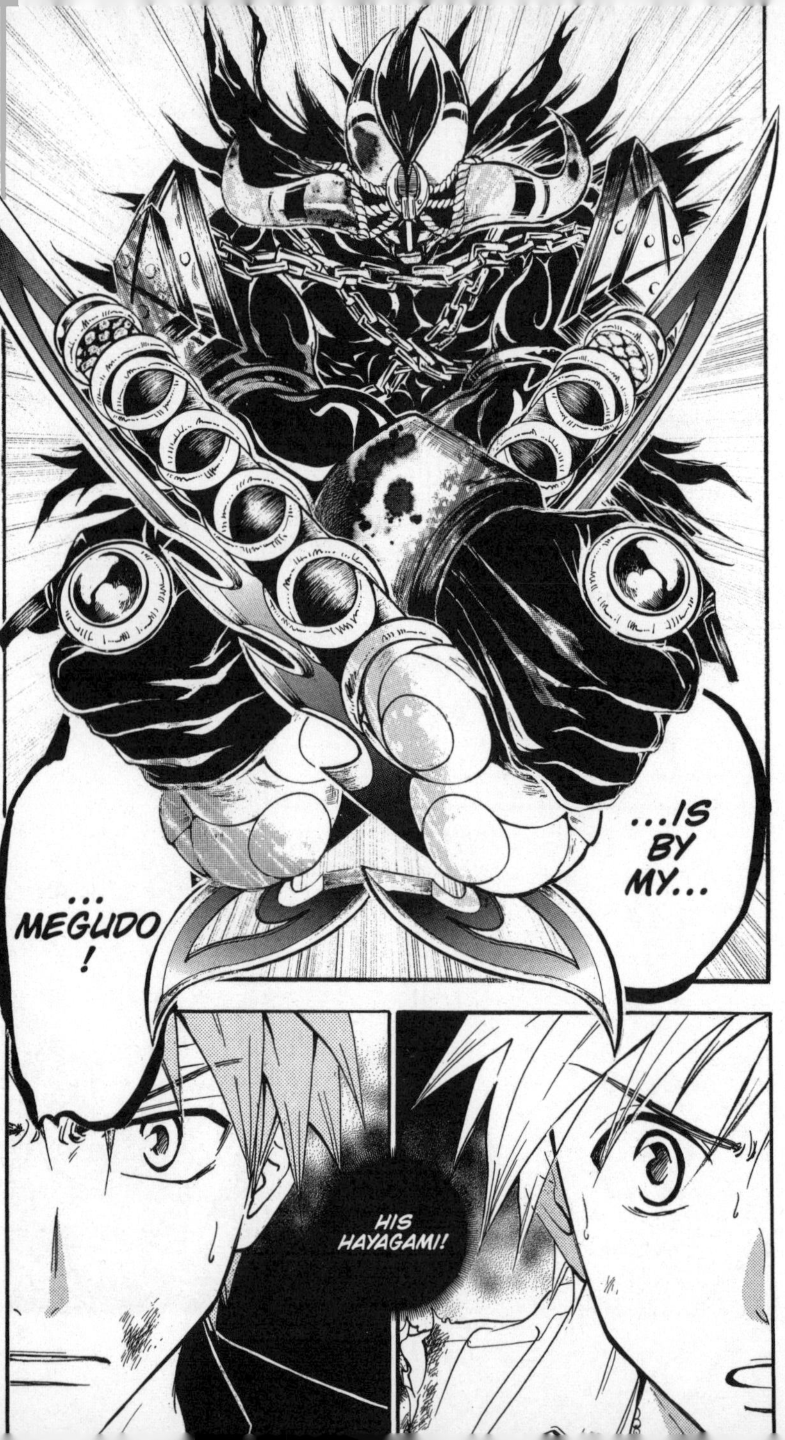
...IS BY MY...
...MEGUDO!
HIS HAYAGAMI!

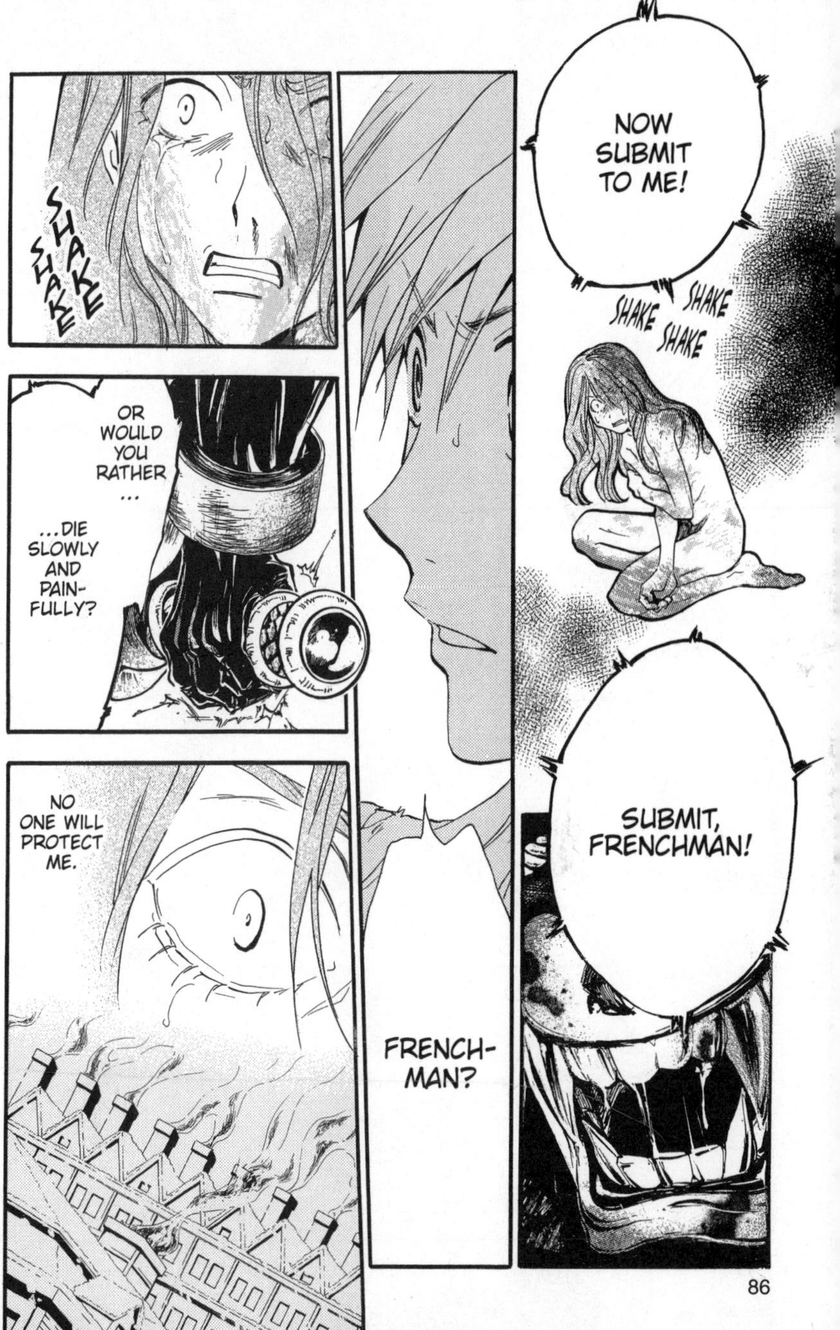
NOW SUBMIT TO ME!
SHAKE SHAKE SHAKE
SUBMIT, FRENCHMAN!
FRENCH-MAN?
SHAKE SHAKE
OR WOULD YOU RATHER ...
...DIE SLOWLY AND PAIN-FULLY?
NO ONE WILL PROTECT ME.

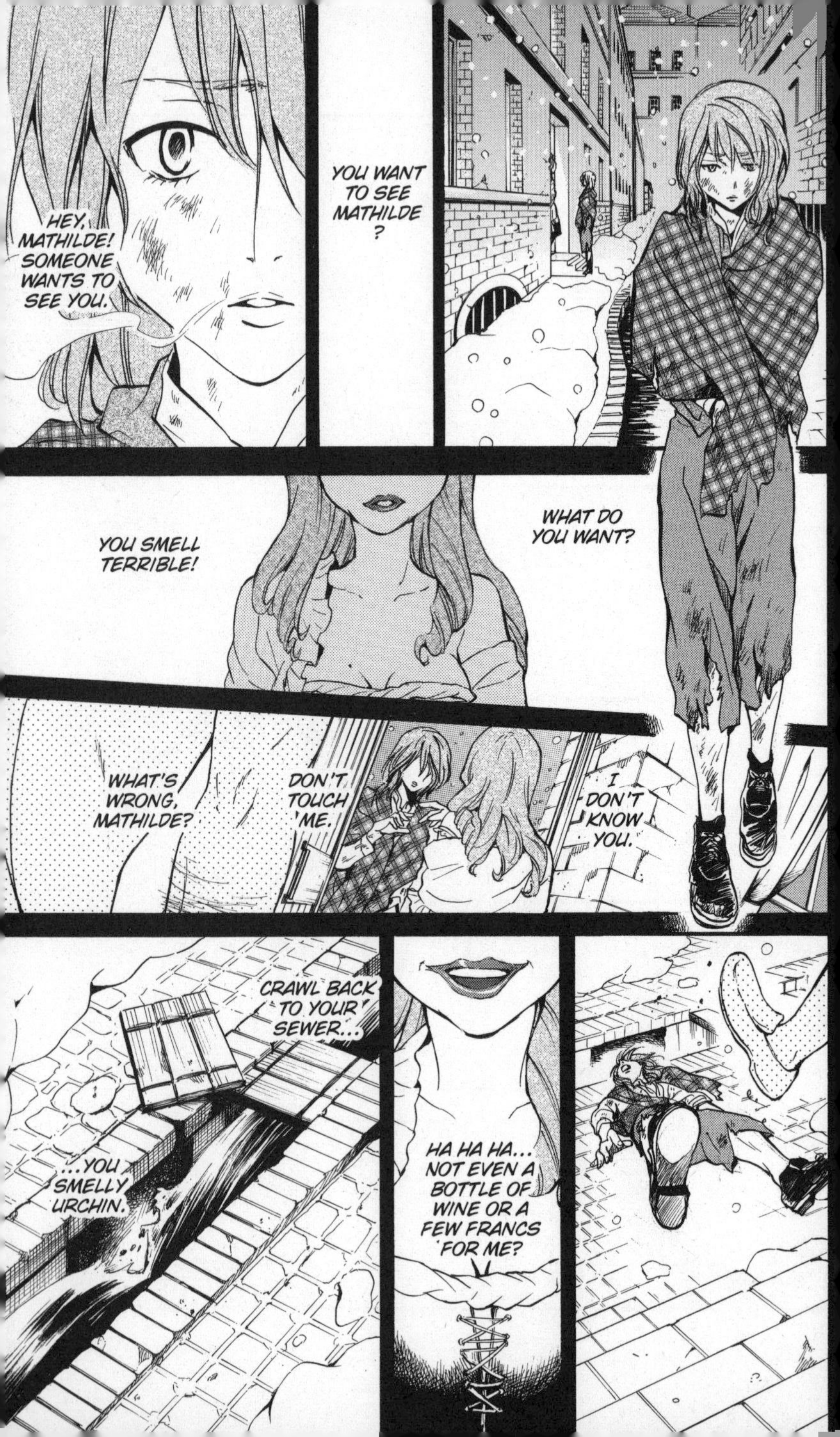
YOU WANT TO SEE MATHILDE?
HEY, MATHILDE! SOMEONE WANTS TO SEE YOU.
WHAT DO YOU WANT?
YOU SMELL TERRIBLE!
I DON'T KNOW YOU.
DON'T TOUCH ME.
WHAT'S WRONG, MATHILDE?
HA HA HA... NOT EVEN A BOTTLE OF WINE OR A FEW FRANCS FOR ME?
CRAWL BACK TO YOUR SEWER...
...YOU SMELLY URCHIN.

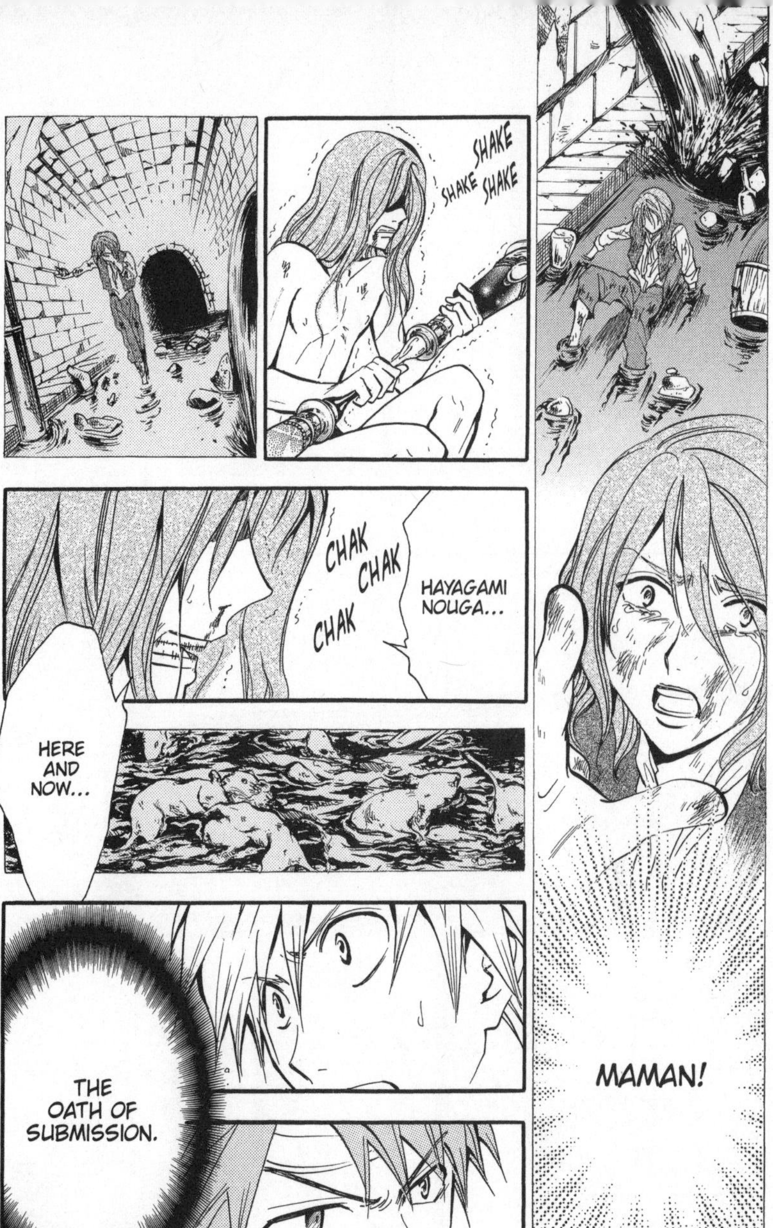
MAMAN!
SHAKE SHAKE SHAKE
HAYAGAMI NOUGA...
CHAK CHAK CHAK
HERE AND NOW...
THE OATH OF SUBMISSION.

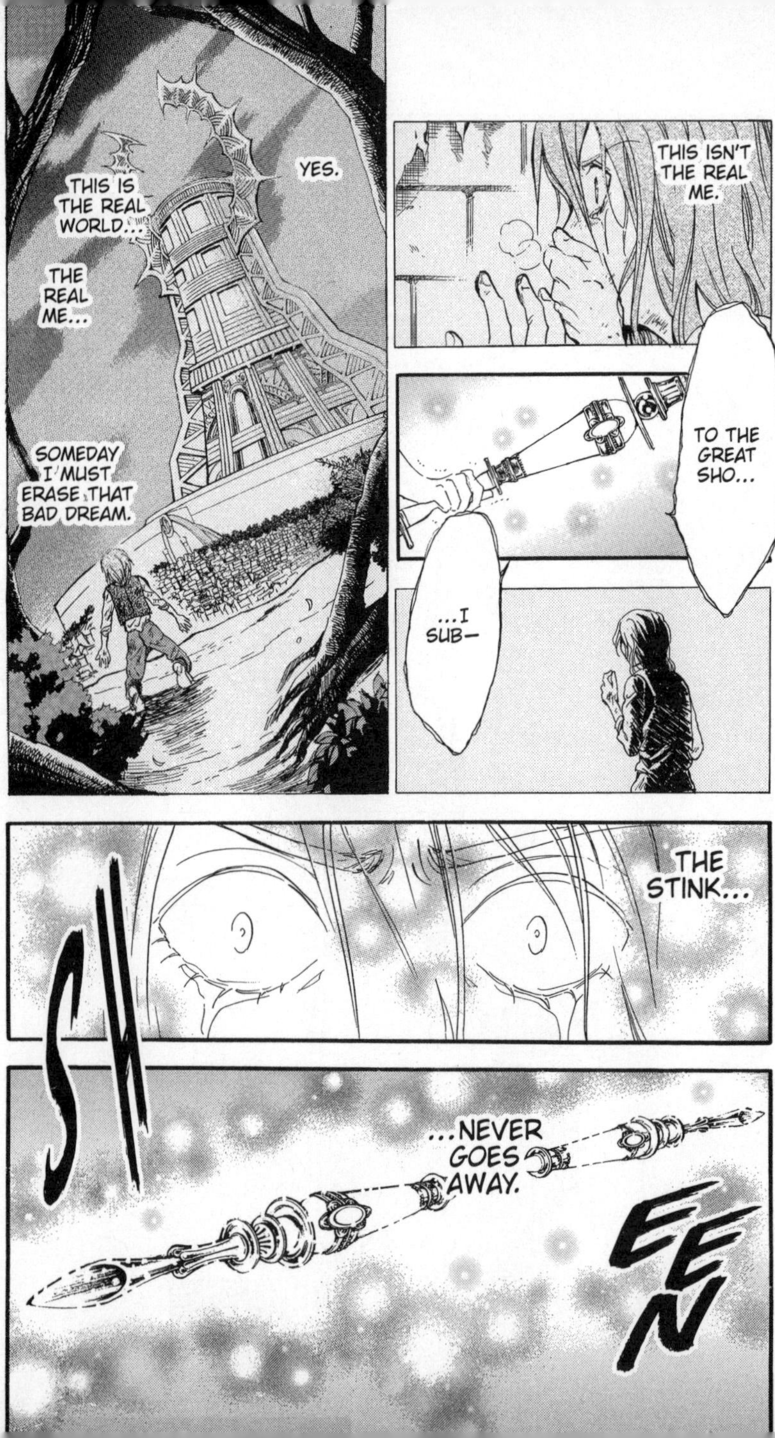
THIS ISN'T THE REAL ME.
TO THE GREAT SHO...
...I SUB—
YES.
THIS IS THE REAL WORLD...
THE REAL ME...
SOMEDAY I MUST ERASE THAT BAD DREAM.
THE STINK...
SH
...NEVER GOES AWAY.
EEN

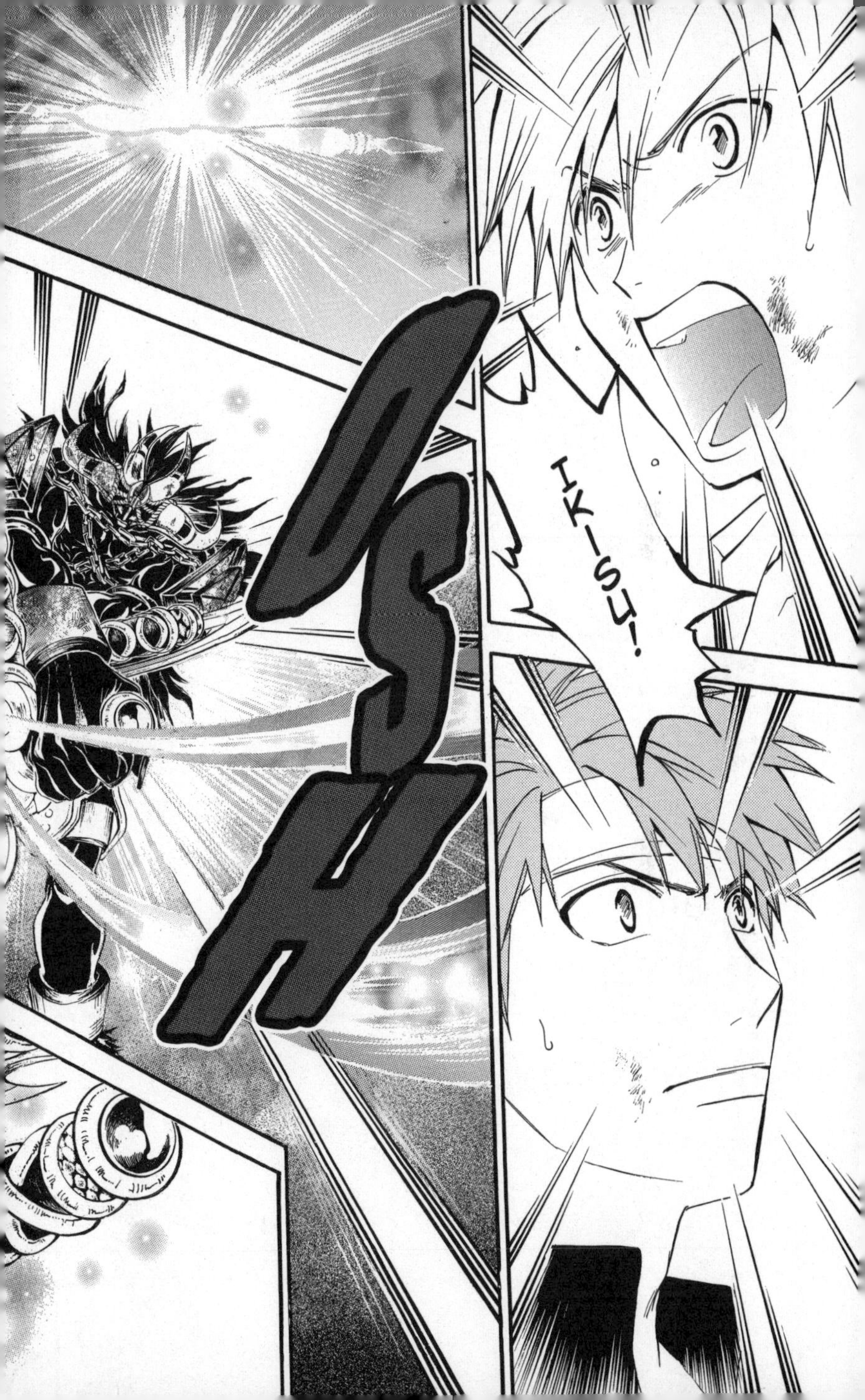
IKISU!

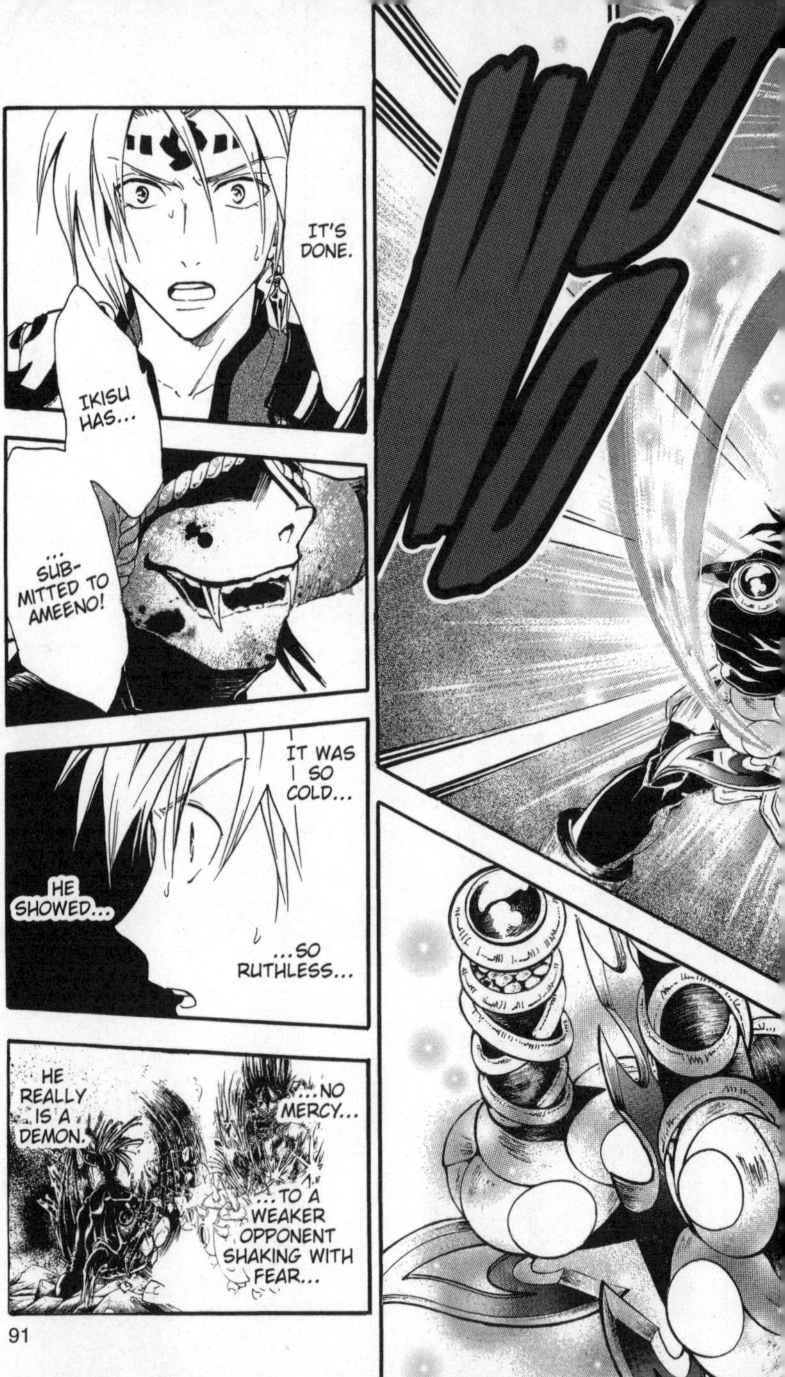
IT'S DONE.
IKISU HAS...
...SUB-MITTED TO AMEENO!
IT WAS SO COLD...
HE SHOWED...
...SO RUTHLESS...
...NO MERCY...
...TO A WEAKER OPPONENT SHAKING WITH FEAR...
HE REALLY IS A DEMON.

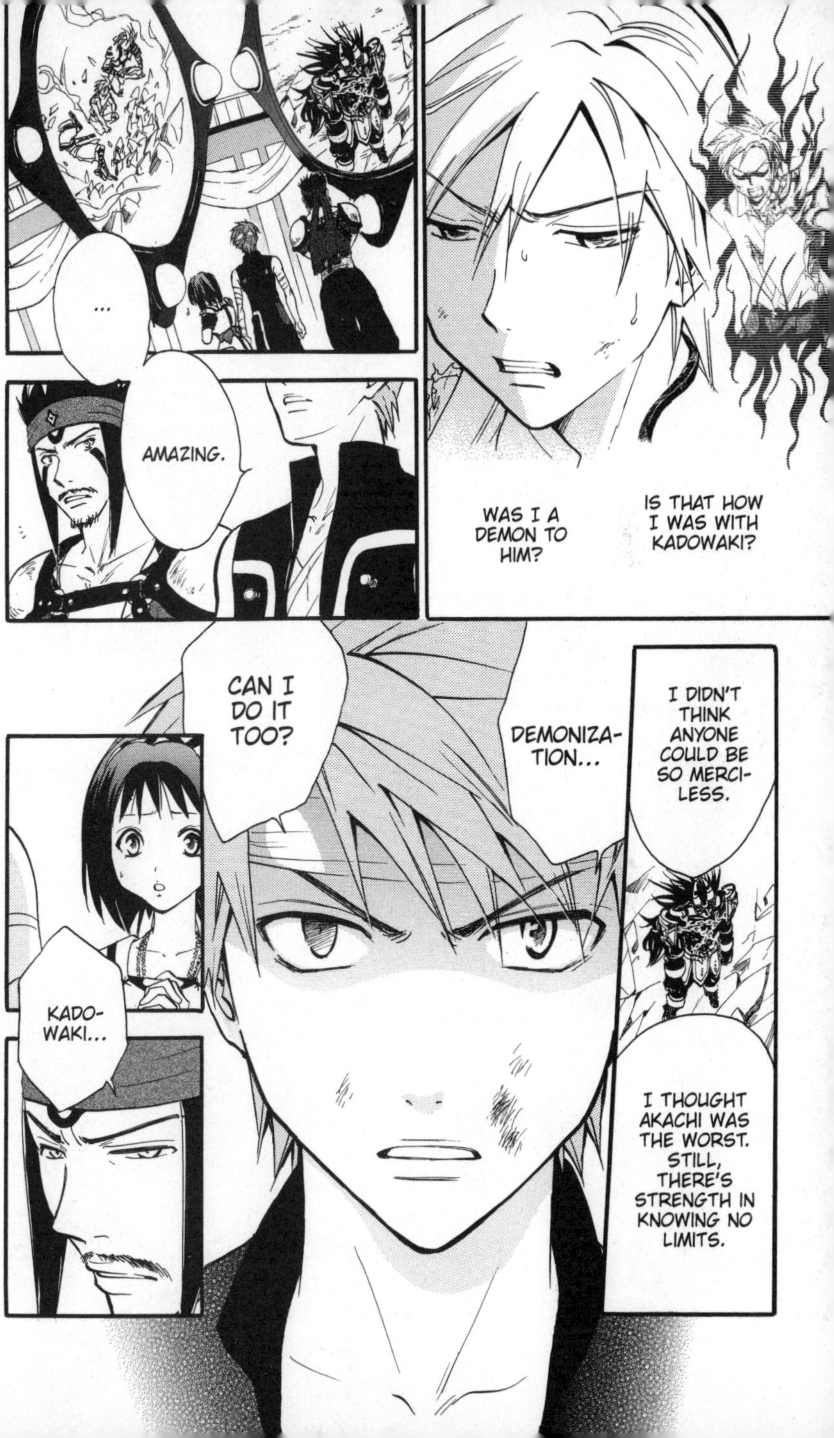

IS THAT HOW I WAS WITH KADOWAKI?
WAS I A DEMON TO HIM?
...
AMAZING.
I DIDN'T THINK ANYONE COULD BE SO MERCILESS.
DEMONIZATION...
CAN I DO IT TOO?
I THOUGHT AKACHI WAS THE WORST. STILL, THERE'S STRENGTH IN KNOWING NO LIMITS.
KADOWAKI...

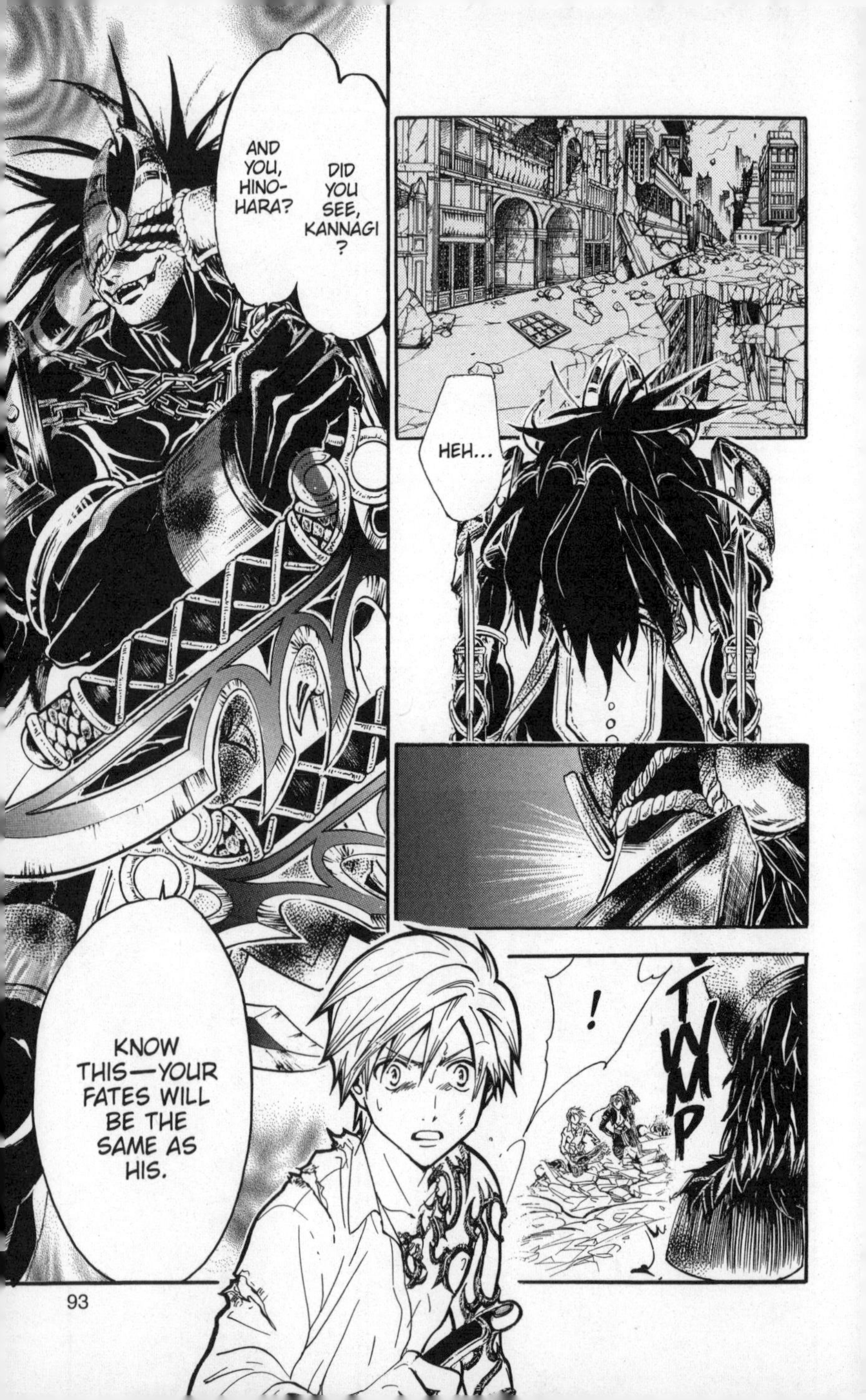
HEH...
!
THUMP
DID YOU SEE, KANNAGI?
AND YOU, HINO-HARA?
KNOW THIS—YOUR FATES WILL BE THE SAME AS HIS.

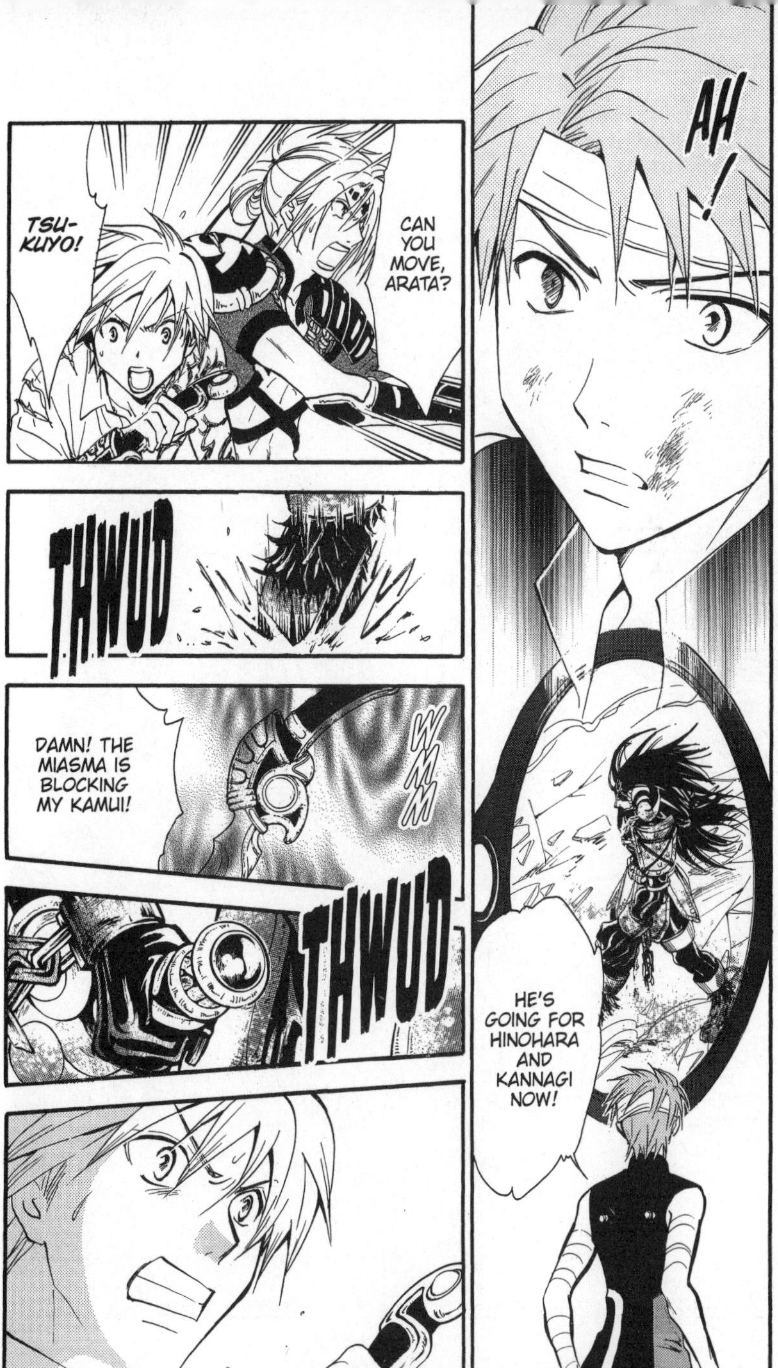
AH!
HE'S GOING FOR HINOHARA AND KANNAGI NOW!
CAN YOU MOVE, ARATA?
TSU-KUYO!
THWUD
WMM
DAMN! THE MIASMA IS BLOCKING MY KAMUI!
THWUD

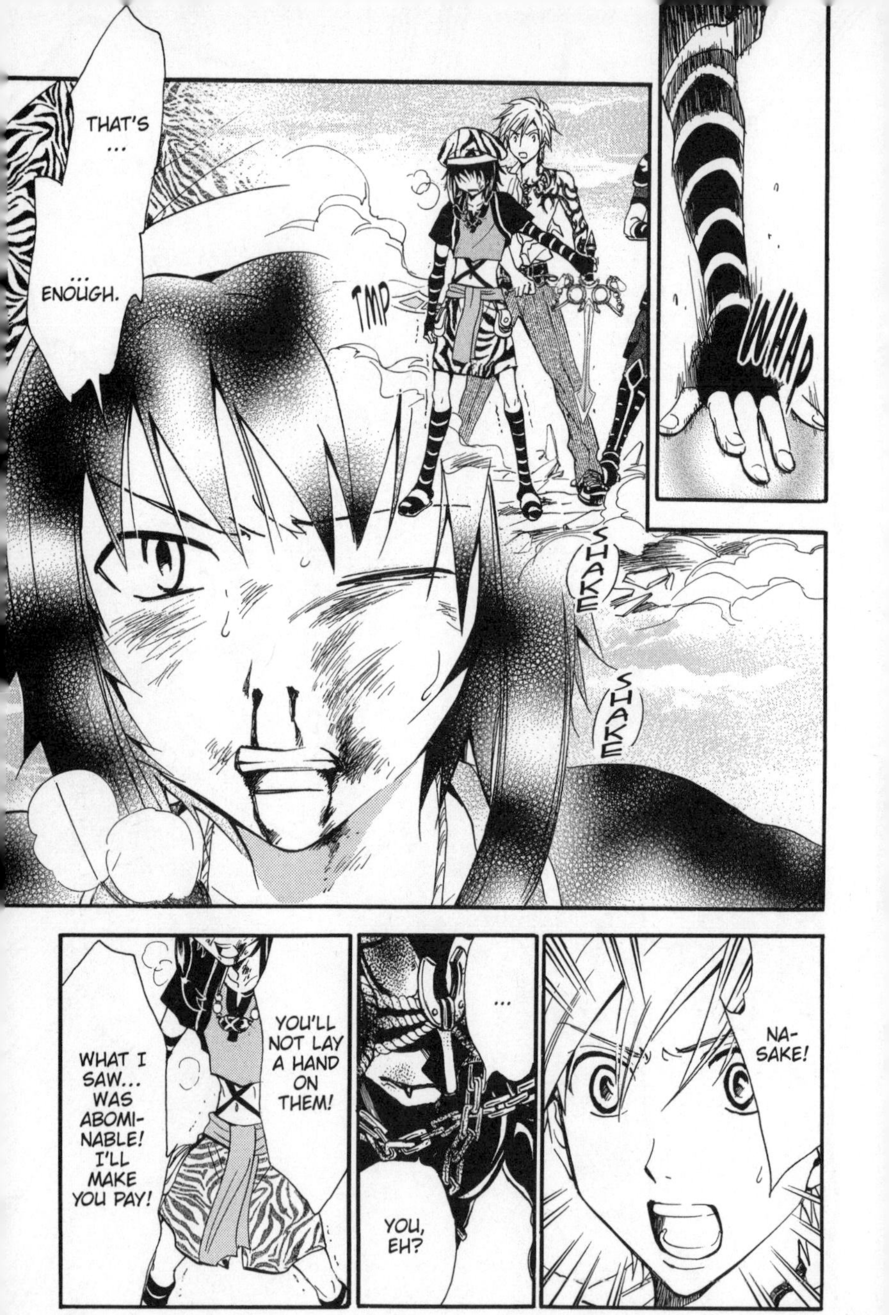
WHAP
TMP
SHAKE
SHAKE
THAT'S ...
... ENOUGH.
NA-SAKE!
...
YOU, EH?
YOU'LL NOT LAY A HAND ON THEM!
WHAT I SAW... WAS ABOMI-NABLE! I'LL MAKE YOU PAY!

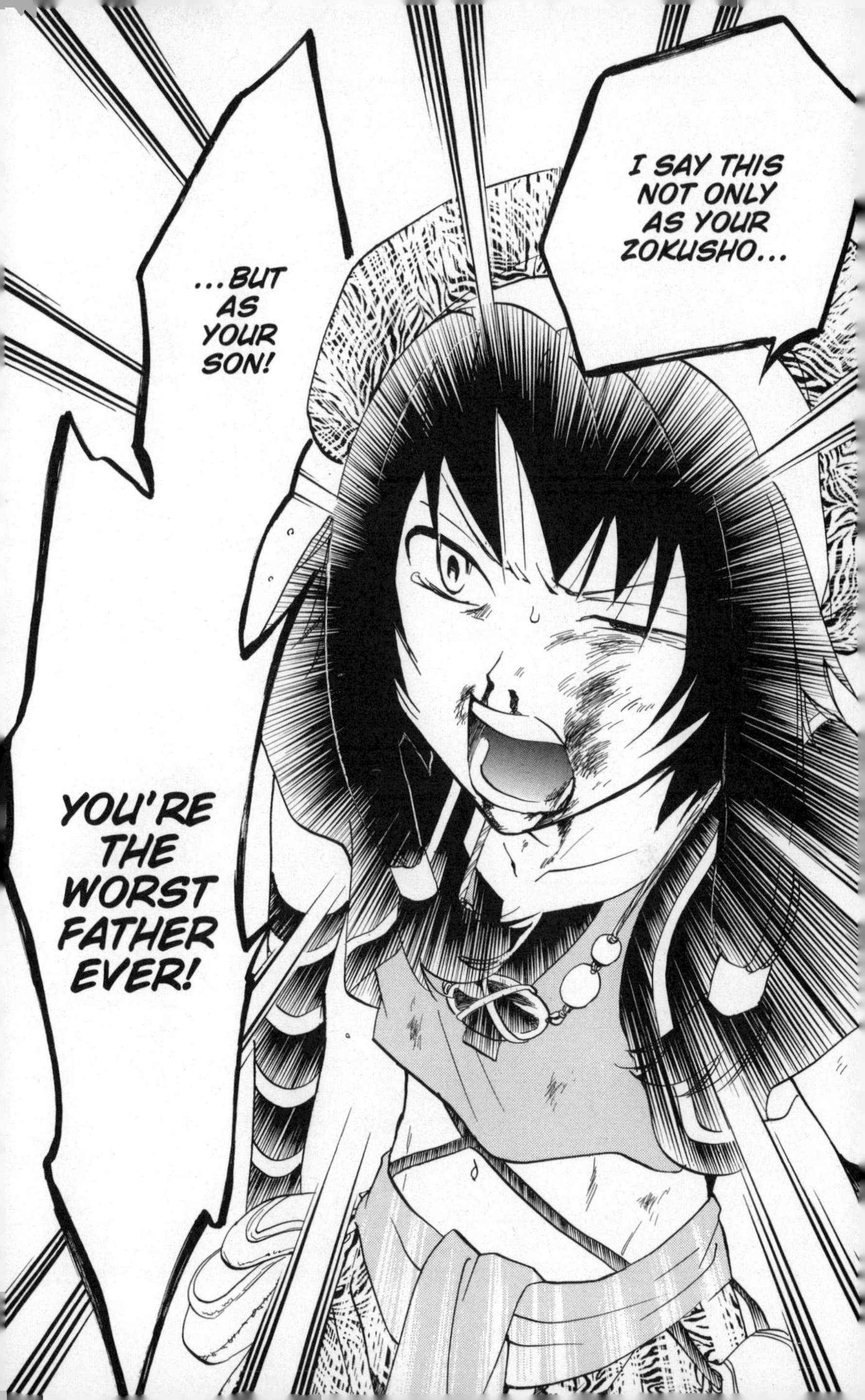
I SAY THIS NOT ONLY AS YOUR ZOKUSHO...
...BUT AS YOUR SON!
YOU'RE THE WORST FATHER EVER!

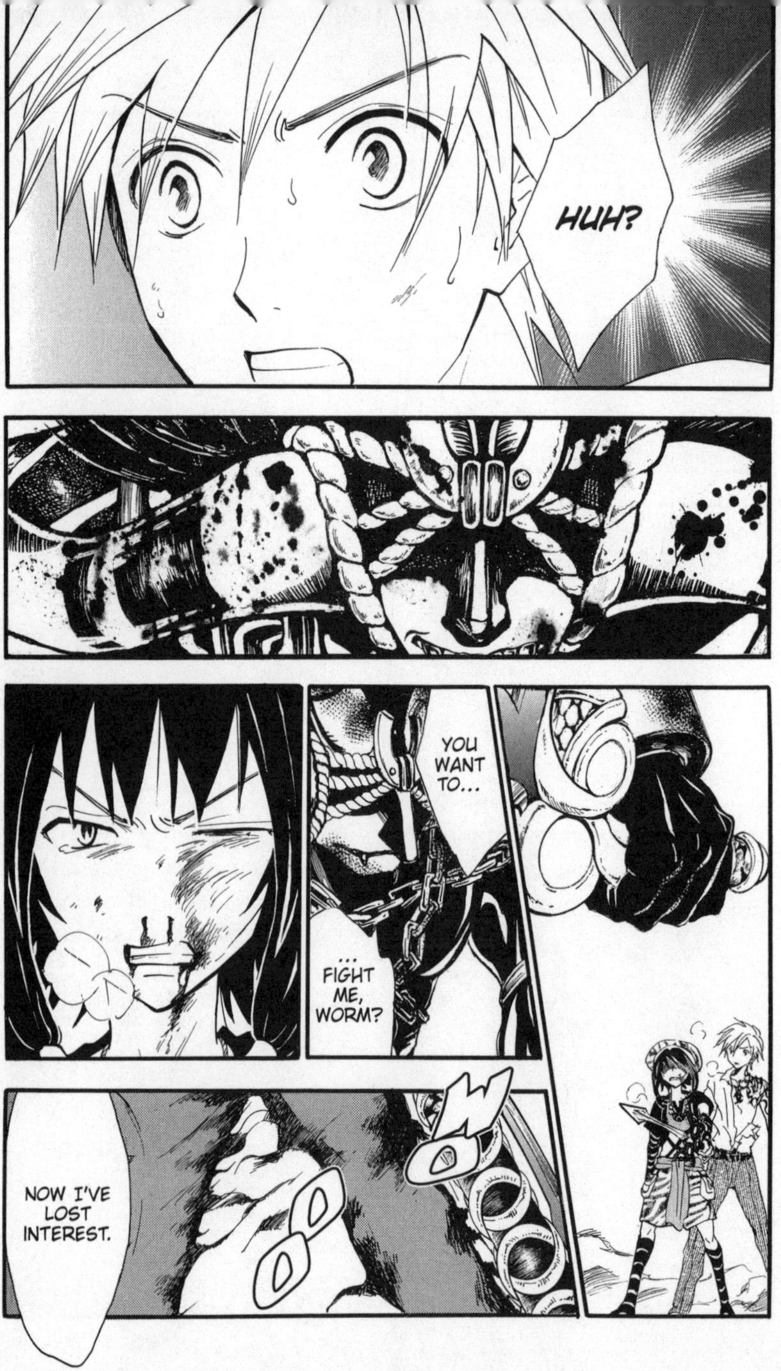
HUH?
YOU WANT TO...
...FIGHT ME, WORM?
NOW I'VE LOST INTEREST.

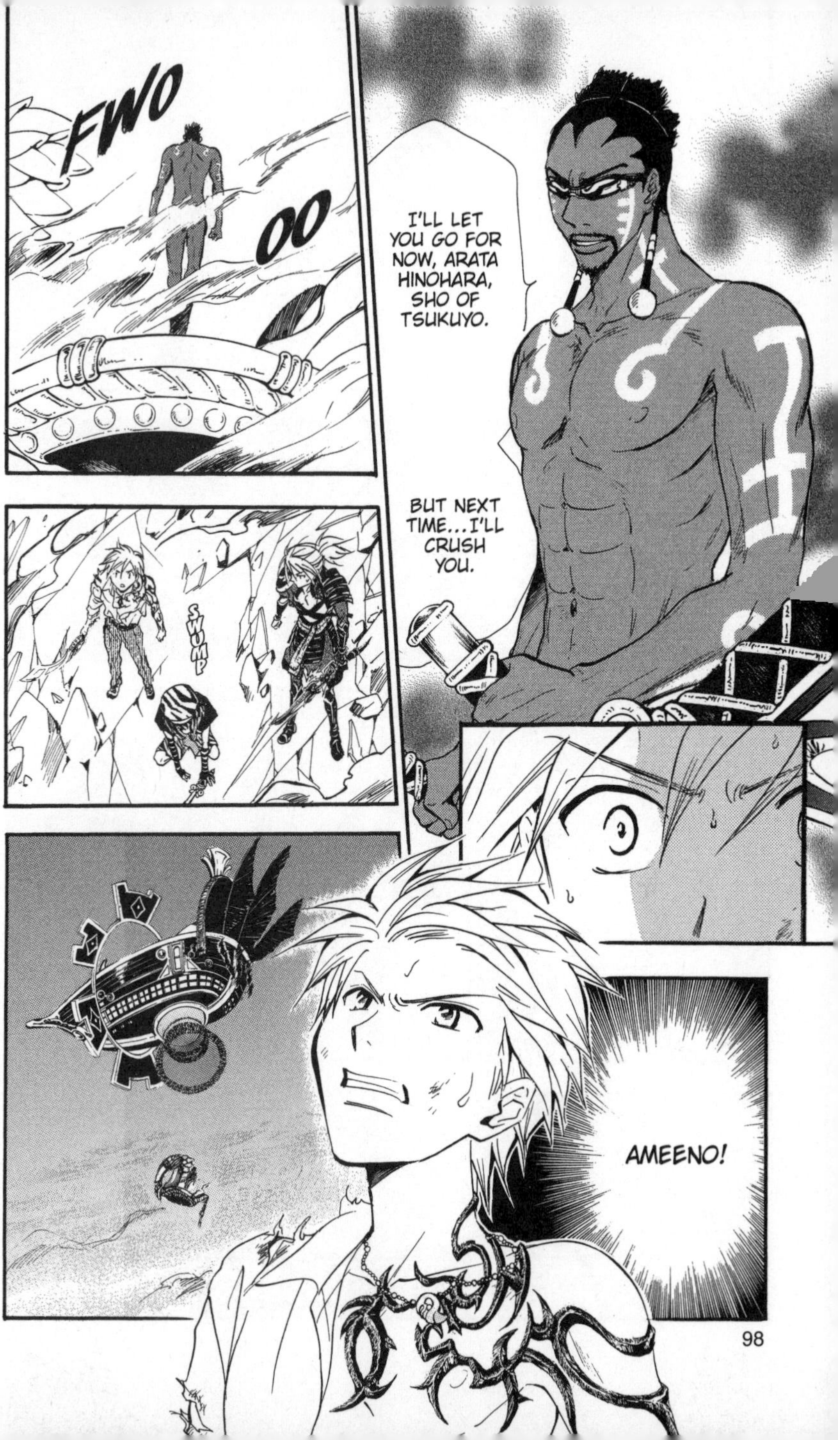
I'LL LET YOU GO FOR NOW, ARATA HINOHARA, SHO OF TSUKUYO.
BUT NEXT TIME...I'LL CRUSH YOU.
FWOOO
SWUMP
AMEENO!

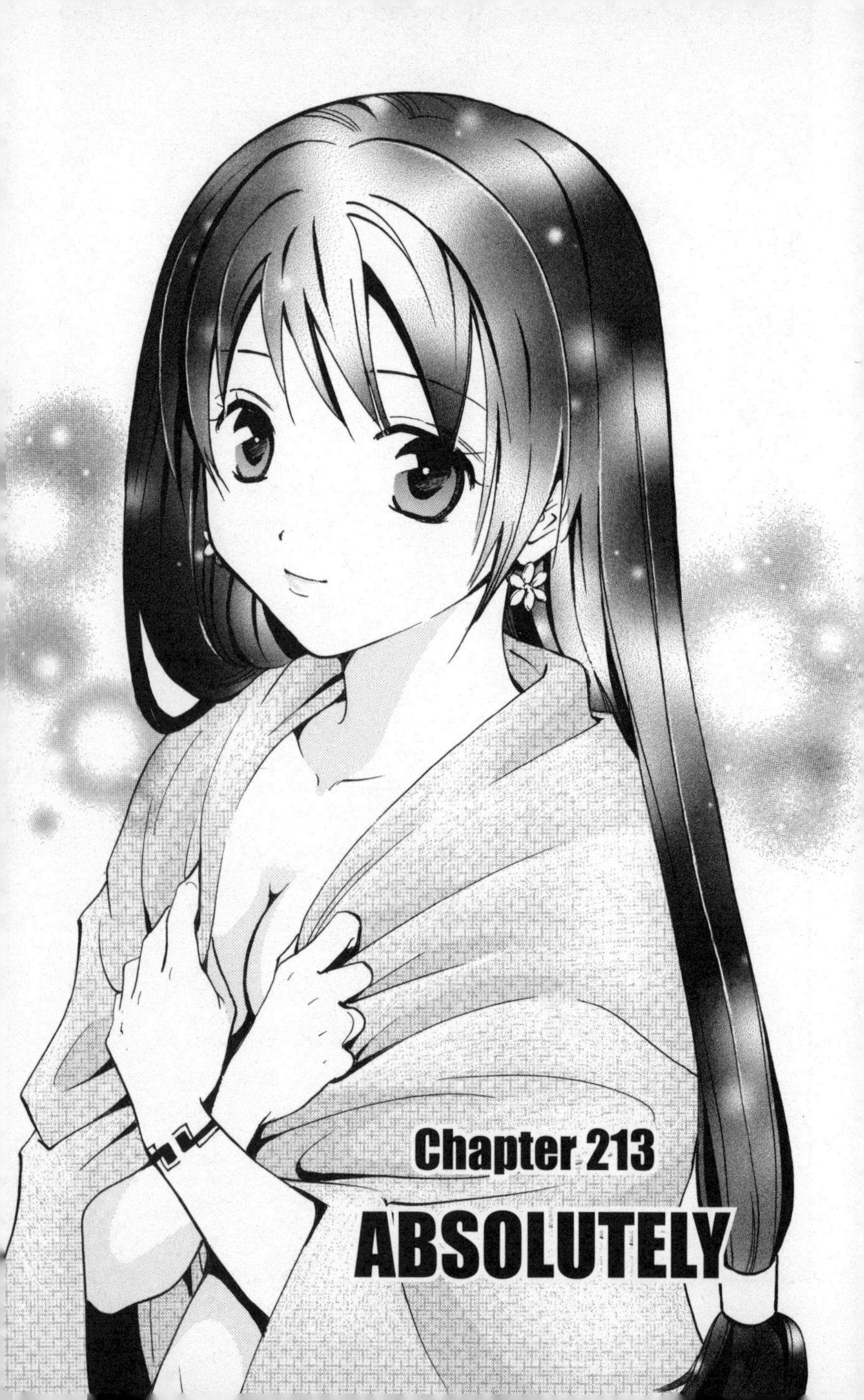
Chapter 213
ABSOLUTELY

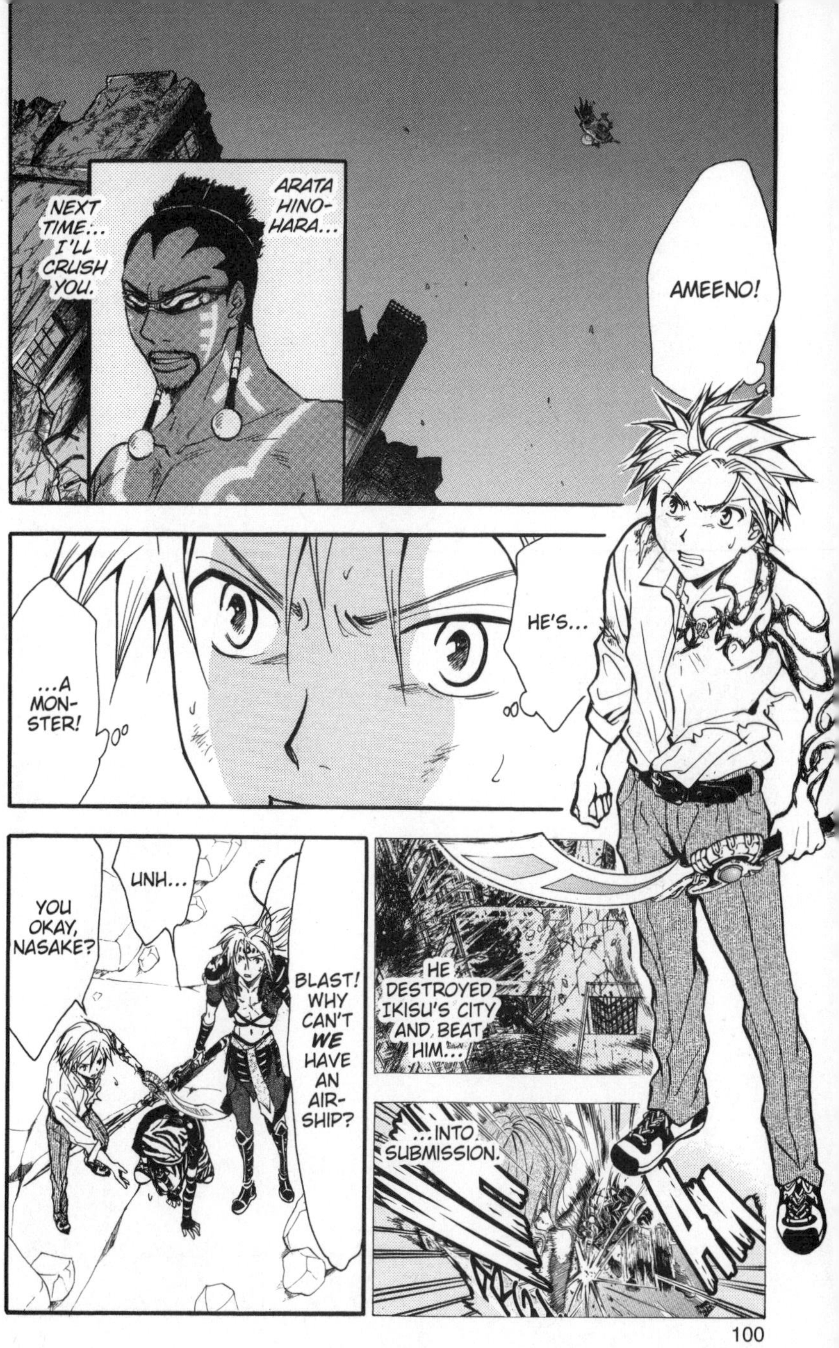
AMEENO!
ARATA HINO-HARA...
NEXT TIME... I'LL CRUSH YOU.
HE'S...
...A MON-STER!
HE DESTROYED IKISU'S CITY AND BEAT HIM...
...INTO SUBMISSION.
UNH...
YOU OKAY, NASAKE?
BLAST! WHY CAN'T *WE* HAVE AN AIR-SHIP?

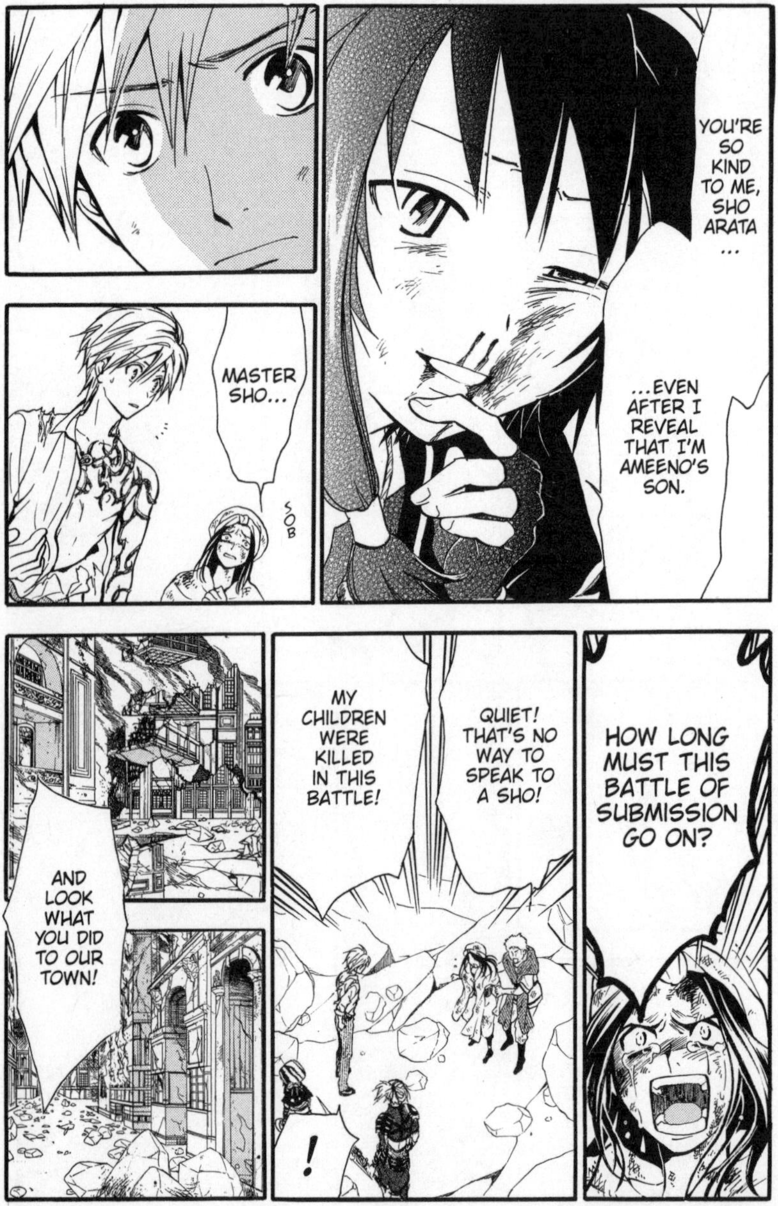
YOU'RE SO KIND TO ME, SHO ARATA...
...EVEN AFTER I REVEAL THAT I'M AMEENO'S SON.
MASTER SHO...
SOB
HOW LONG MUST THIS BATTLE OF SUBMISSION GO ON?
QUIET! THAT'S NO WAY TO SPEAK TO A SHO!
MY CHILDREN WERE KILLED IN THIS BATTLE!
!
AND LOOK WHAT YOU DID TO OUR TOWN!

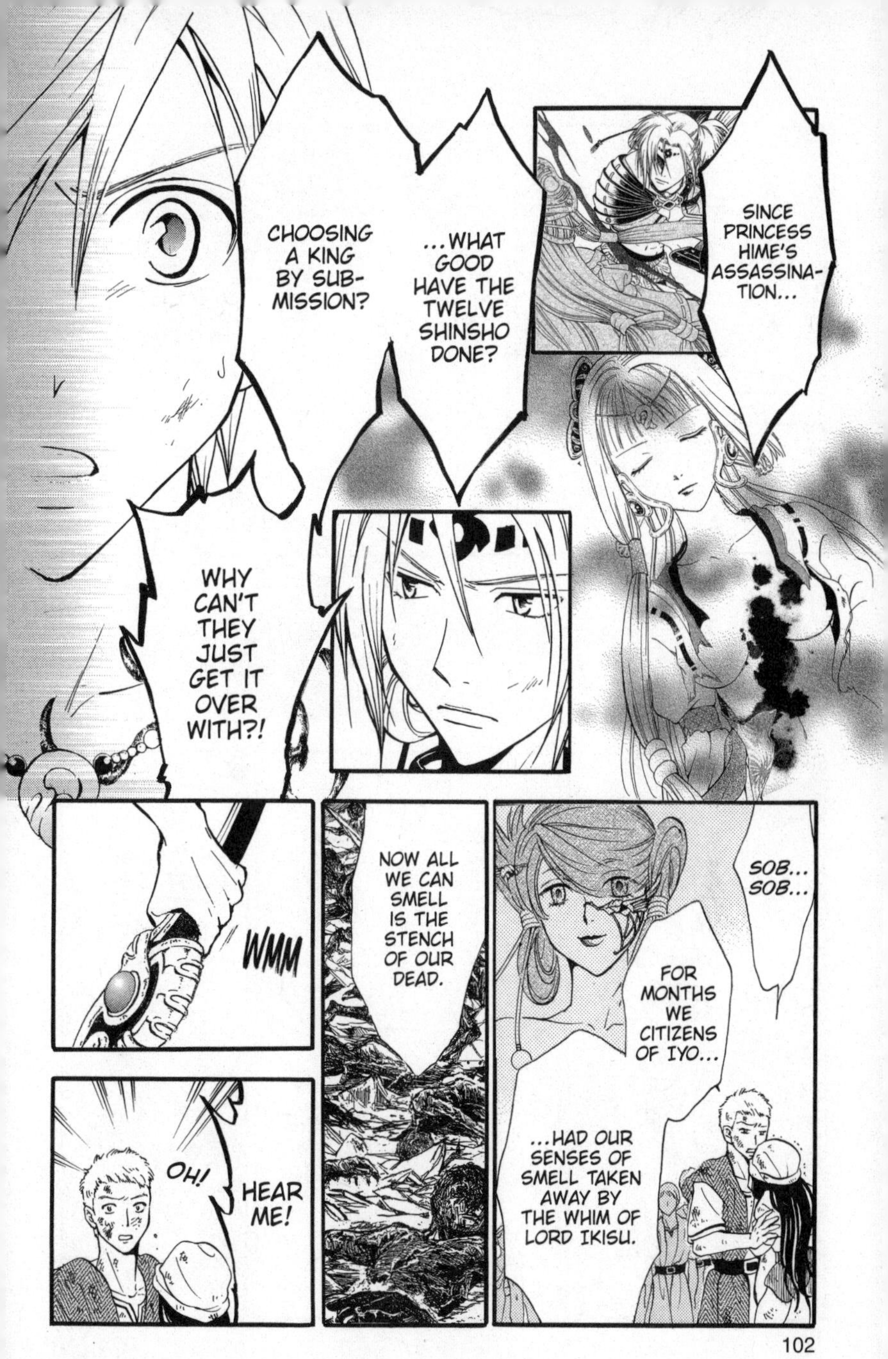
SINCE PRINCESS HIME'S ASSASSINATION...
...WHAT GOOD HAVE THE TWELVE SHINSHO DONE?
CHOOSING A KING BY SUBMISSION?
WHY CAN'T THEY JUST GET IT OVER WITH?!
SOB... SOB...
FOR MONTHS WE CITIZENS OF IYO...
...HAD OUR SENSES OF SMELL TAKEN AWAY BY THE WHIM OF LORD IKISU.
NOW ALL WE CAN SMELL IS THE STENCH OF OUR DEAD.
WMM
HEAR ME!
OH!

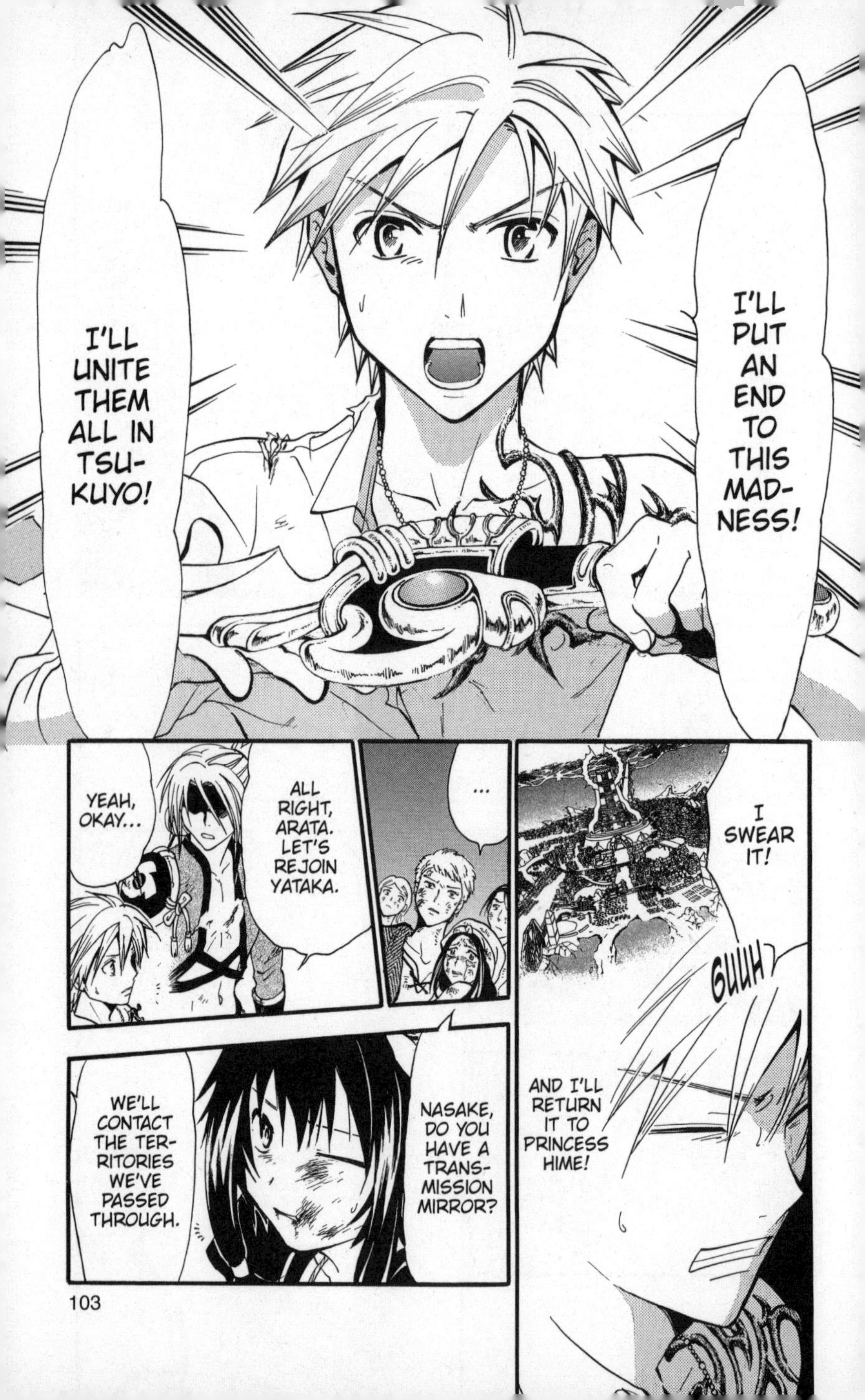
I'LL PUT AN END TO THIS MAD-NESS!
I'LL UNITE THEM ALL IN TSU-KUYO!
I SWEAR IT!
GUUH
AND I'LL RETURN IT TO PRINCESS HIME!
...
ALL RIGHT, ARATA. LET'S REJOIN YATAKA.
YEAH, OKAY...
NASAKE, DO YOU HAVE A TRANS-MISSION MIRROR?
WE'LL CONTACT THE TER-RITORIES WE'VE PASSED THROUGH.

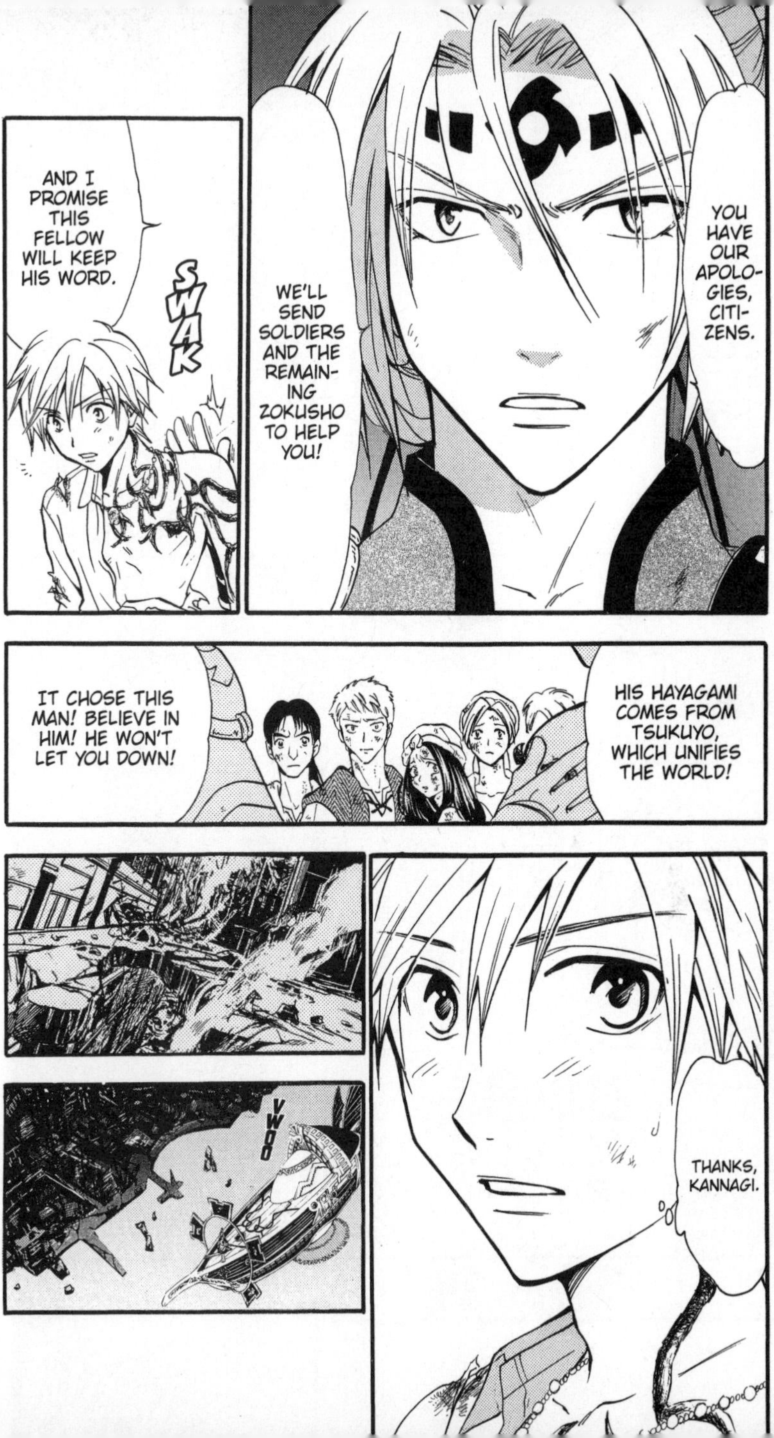
YOU HAVE OUR APOLOGIES, CITIZENS.
WE'LL SEND SOLDIERS AND THE REMAINING ZOKUSHO TO HELP YOU!
AND I PROMISE THIS FELLOW WILL KEEP HIS WORD.
SWAK
HIS HAYAGAMI COMES FROM TSUKUYO, WHICH UNIFIES THE WORLD!
IT CHOSE THIS MAN! BELIEVE IN HIM! HE WON'T LET YOU DOWN!
THANKS, KANNAGI.
VWOO

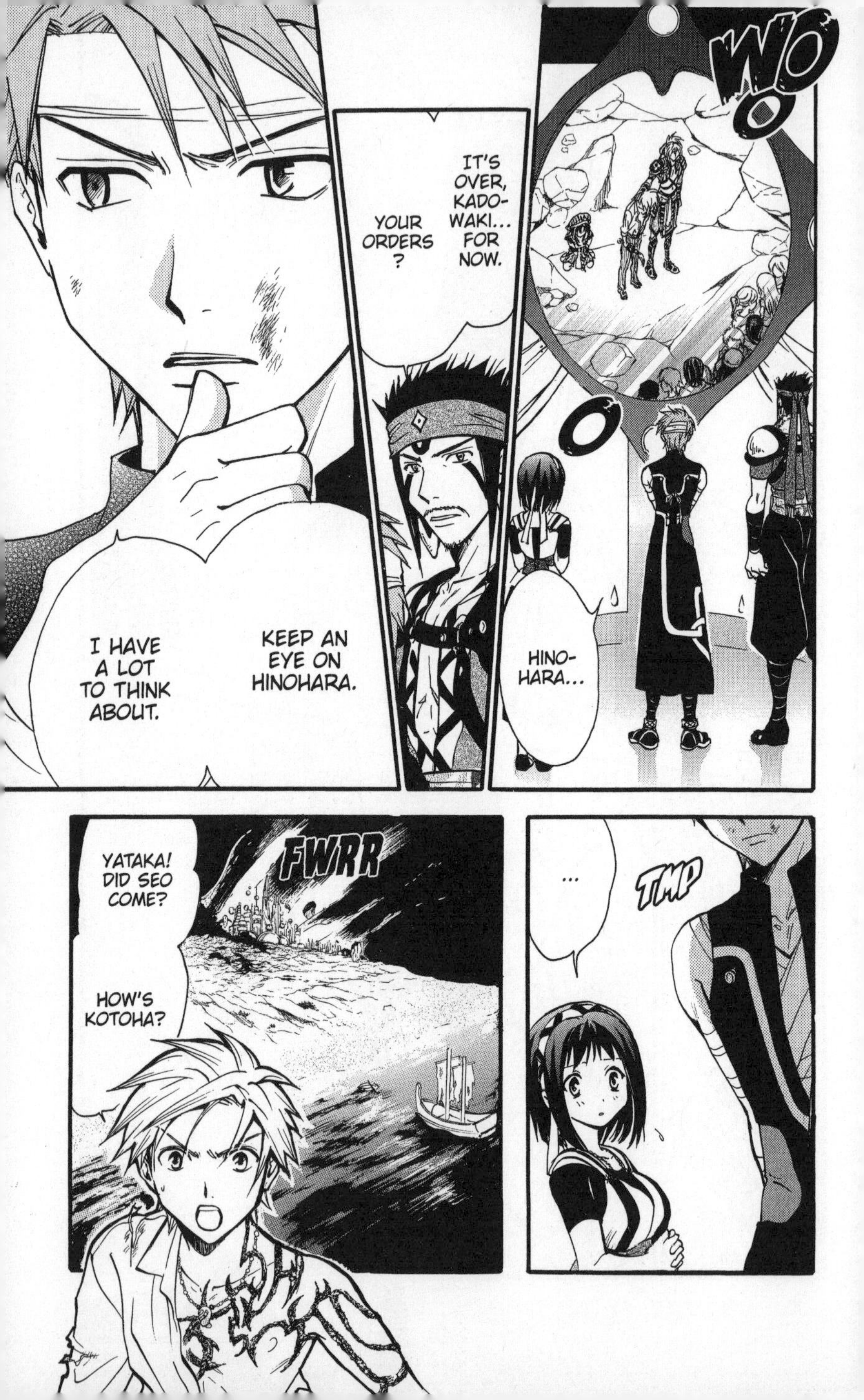
WOOO
HINO-HARA...
IT'S OVER, KADO-WAKI... FOR NOW.
YOUR ORDERS?
KEEP AN EYE ON HINOHARA.
I HAVE A LOT TO THINK ABOUT.
TMP
...
FWRR
YATAKA! DID SEO COME?
HOW'S KOTOHA?

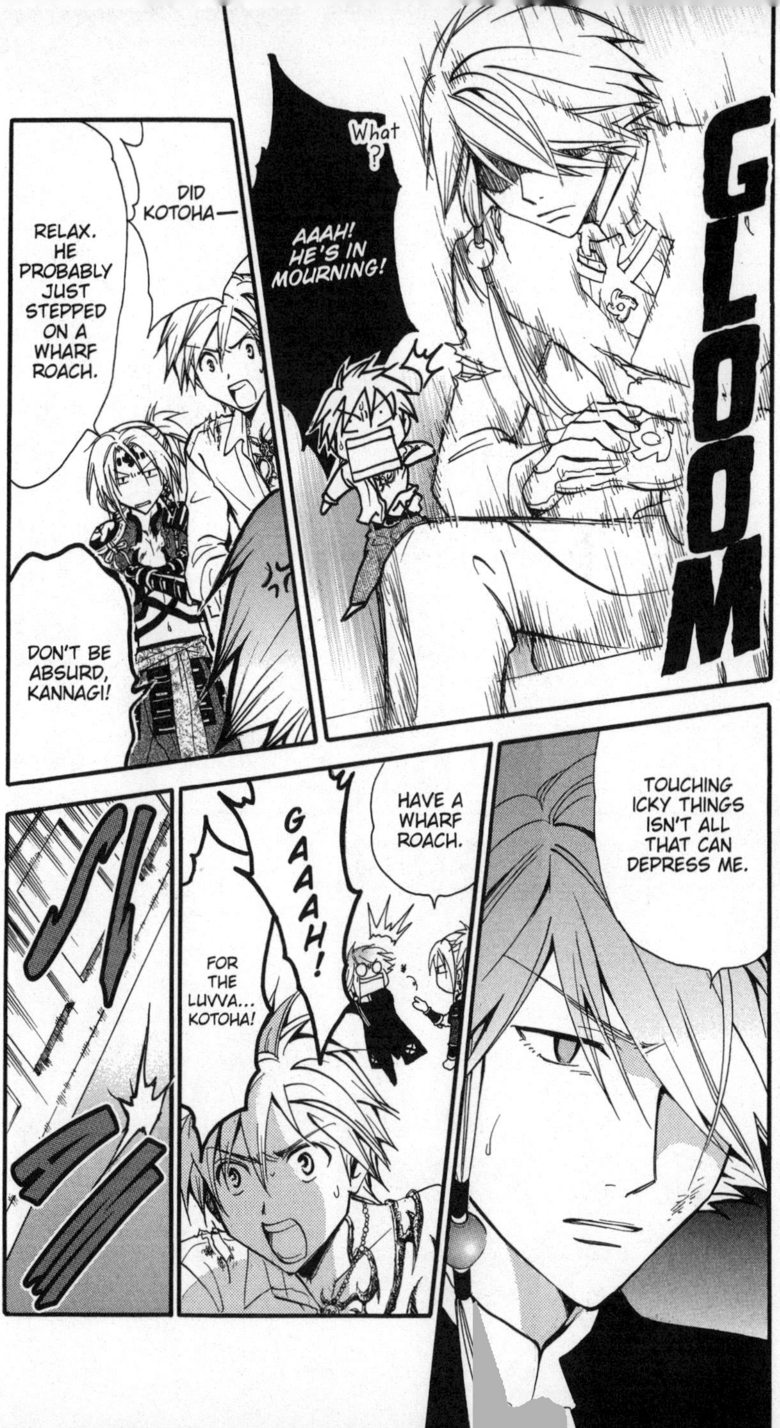
GLOOM
What?
AAAH! HE'S IN MOURNING!
DID KOTOHA—
RELAX. HE PROBABLY JUST STEPPED ON A WHARF ROACH.
DON'T BE ABSURD, KANNAGI!
TOUCHING ICKY THINGS ISN'T ALL THAT CAN DEPRESS ME.
HAVE A WHARF ROACH.
GAAAAH!
FOR THE LUVVA... KOTOHA!

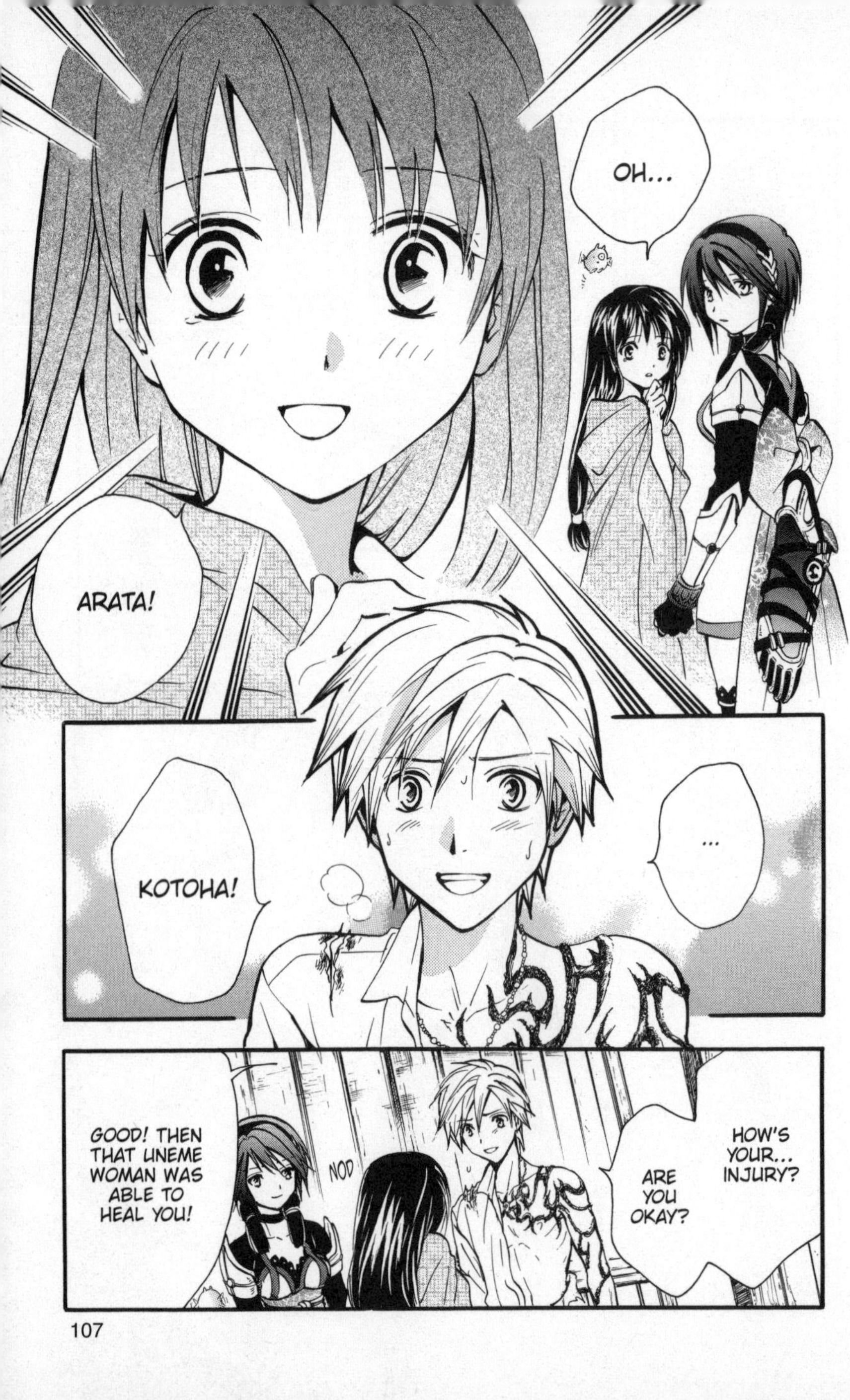
OH...
ARATA!
...
KOTOHA!
HOW'S YOUR... INJURY?
ARE YOU OKAY?
NOD
GOOD! THEN THAT UNEME WOMAN WAS ABLE TO HEAL YOU!

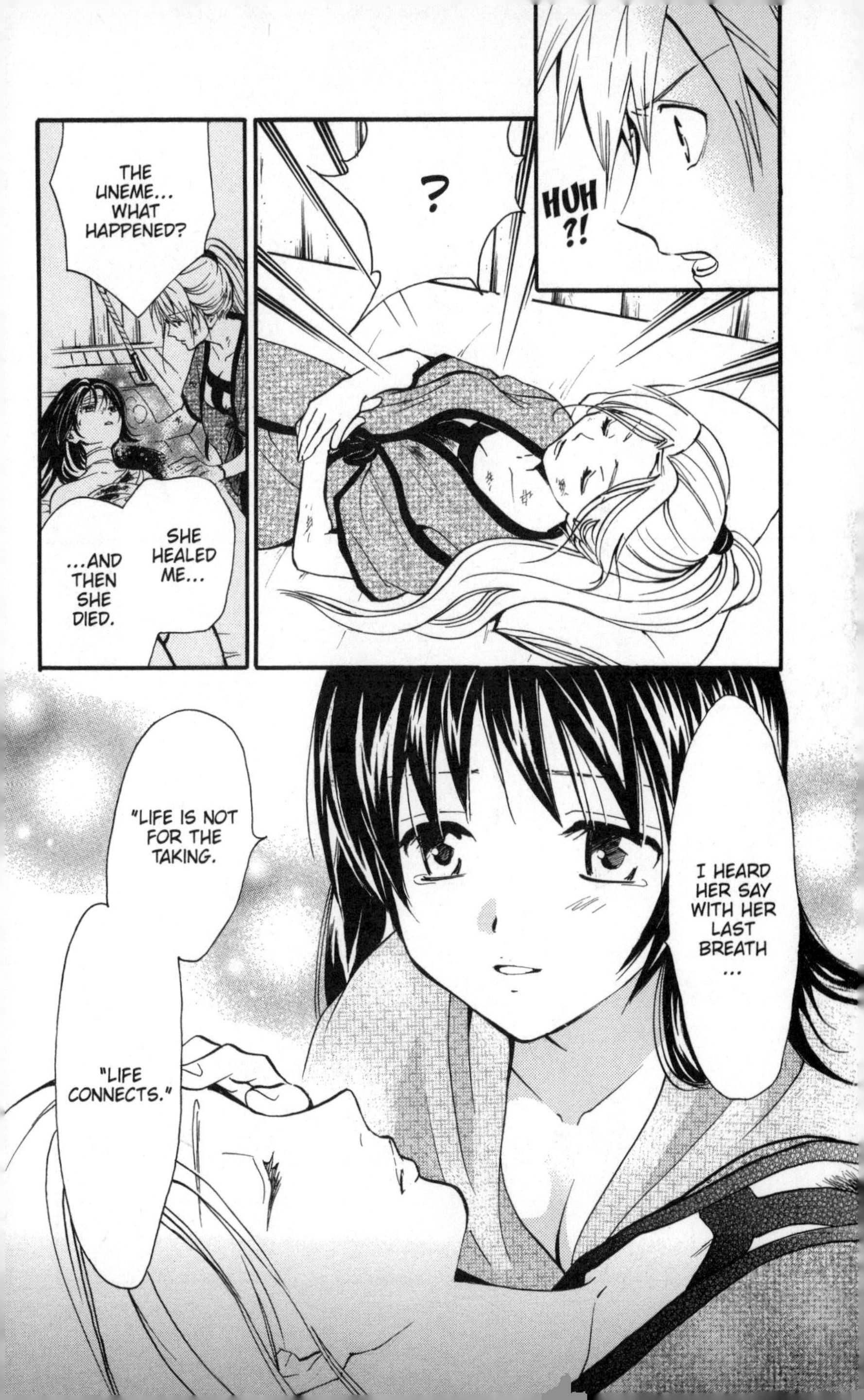
HUH?!
?
THE UNEME... WHAT HAPPENED?
SHE HEALED ME...
...AND THEN SHE DIED.
I HEARD HER SAY WITH HER LAST BREATH...
"LIFE IS NOT FOR THE TAKING.
"LIFE CONNECTS."

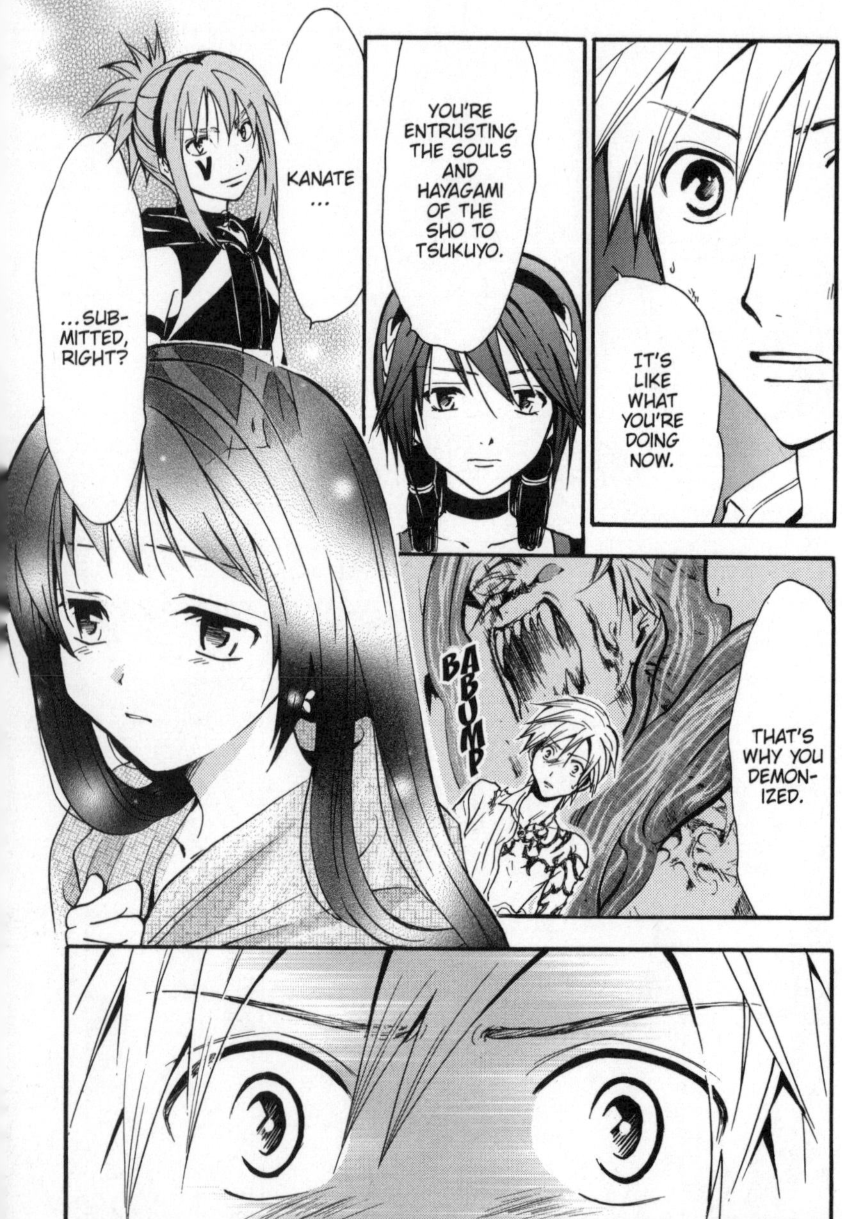
IT'S LIKE WHAT YOU'RE DOING NOW.
YOU'RE ENTRUSTING THE SOULS AND HAYAGAMI OF THE SHO TO TSUKUYO.
BABUMP
THAT'S WHY YOU DEMON-IZED.
KANATE ...
...SUB-MITTED, RIGHT?

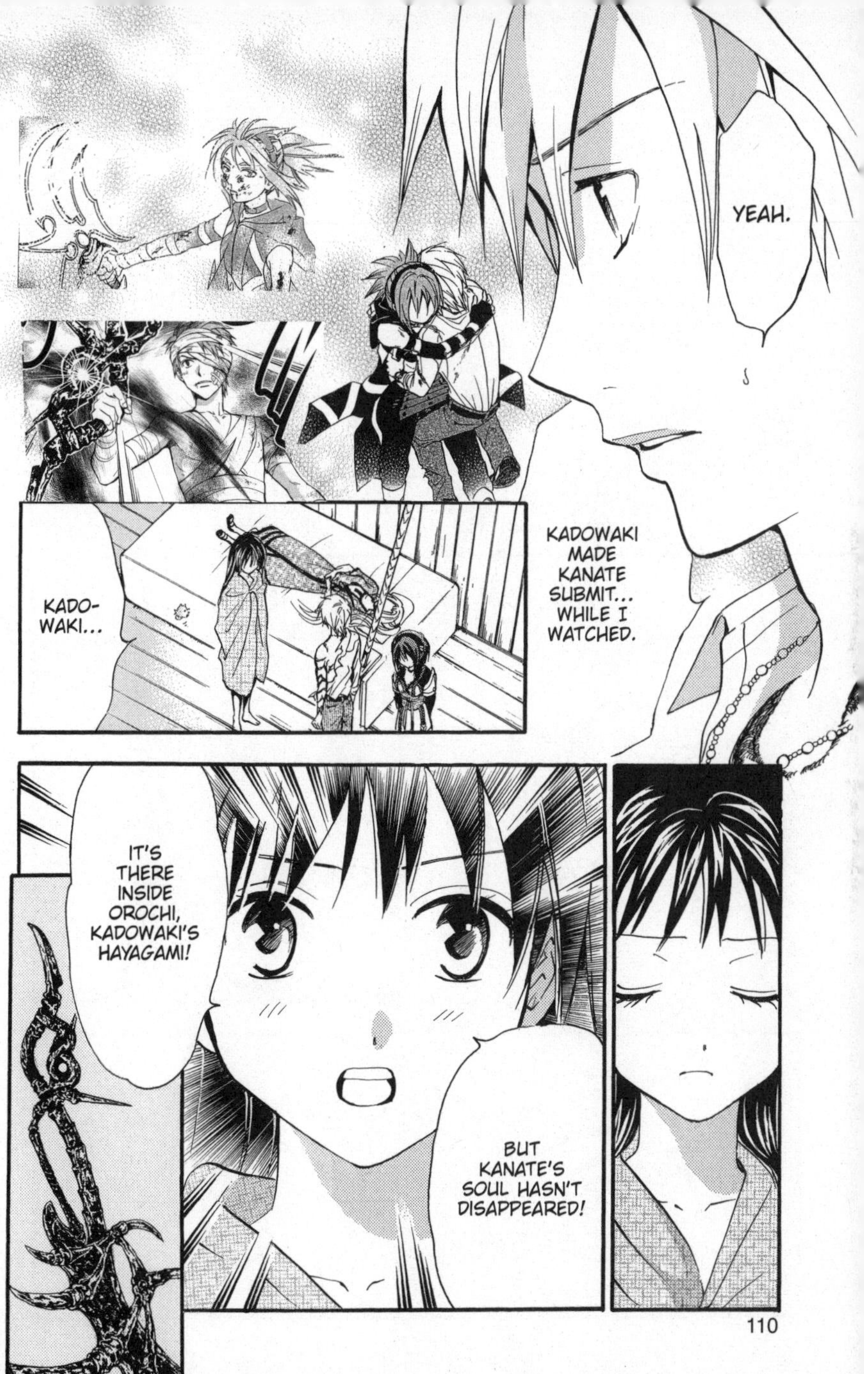
YEAH.
KADOWAKI MADE KANATE SUBMIT... WHILE I WATCHED.
KADO-WAKI...
BUT KANATE'S SOUL HASN'T DISAPPEARED!
IT'S THERE INSIDE OROCHI, KADOWAKI'S HAYAGAMI!

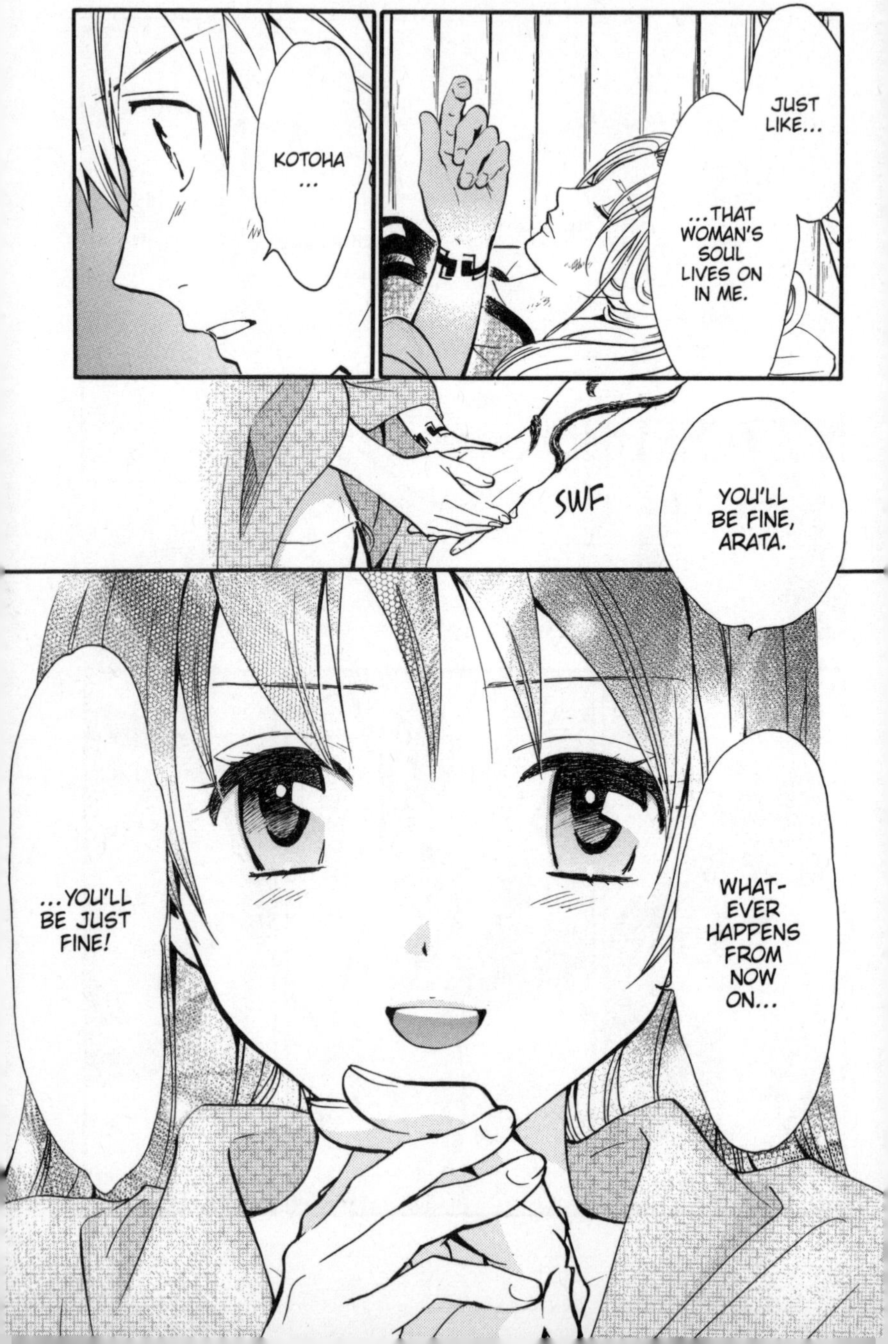
JUST LIKE... ...THAT WOMAN'S SOUL LIVES ON IN ME.
KOTOHA...
YOU'LL BE FINE, ARATA.
SWF
WHAT-EVER HAPPENS FROM NOW ON...
...YOU'LL BE JUST FINE!

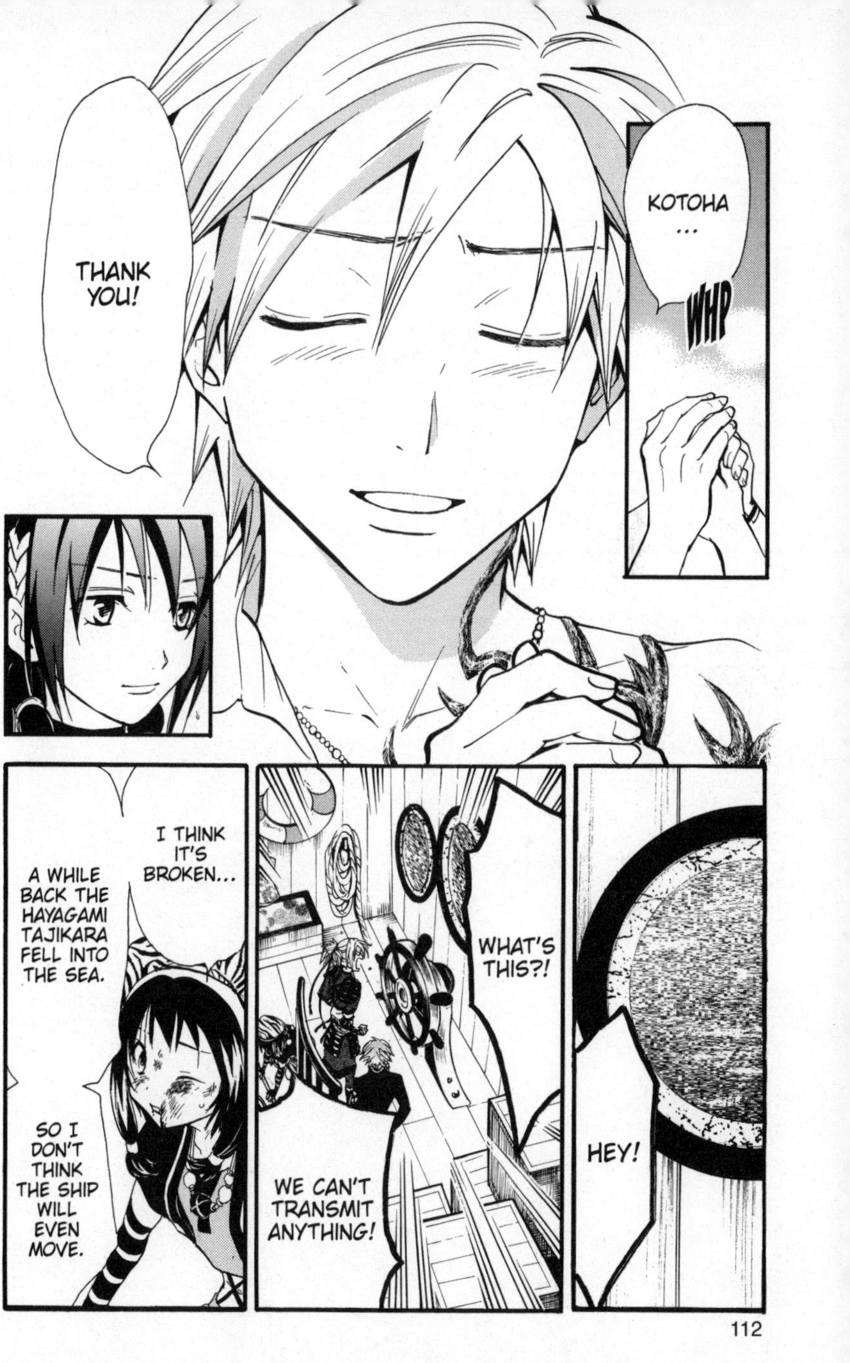
KOTOHA...
WHP
THANK YOU!
HEY!
WHAT'S THIS?!
WE CAN'T TRANSMIT ANYTHING!
I THINK IT'S BROKEN...
A WHILE BACK THE HAYAGAMI TAJIKARA FELL INTO THE SEA.
SO I DON'T THINK THE SHIP WILL EVEN MOVE.

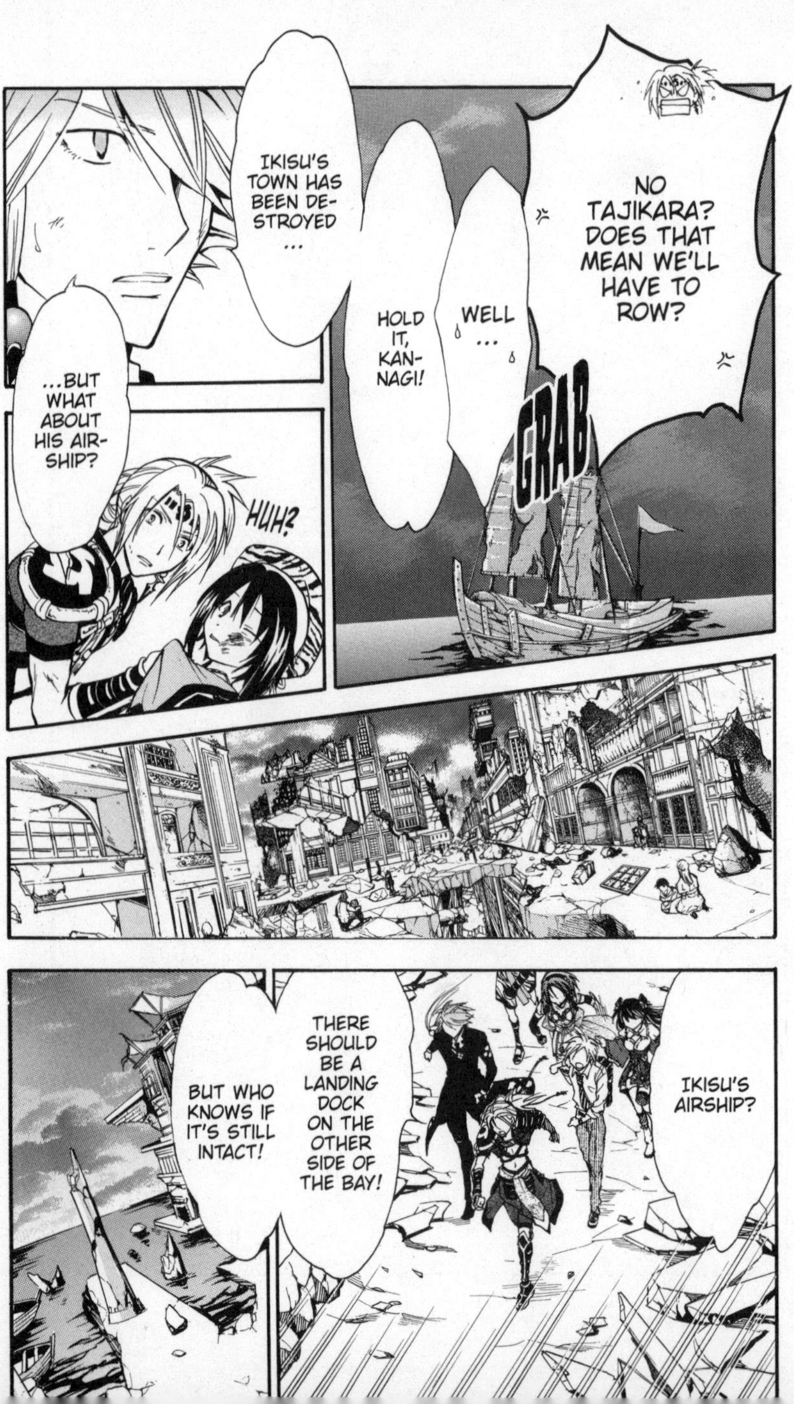
NO TAJIKARA? DOES THAT MEAN WE'LL HAVE TO ROW?
WELL ...
HOLD IT, KANNAGI!
GRAB
IKISU'S TOWN HAS BEEN DESTROYED ...
...BUT WHAT ABOUT HIS AIRSHIP?
HUH?
IKISU'S AIRSHIP?
THERE SHOULD BE A LANDING DOCK ON THE OTHER SIDE OF THE BAY!
BUT WHO KNOWS IF IT'S STILL INTACT!

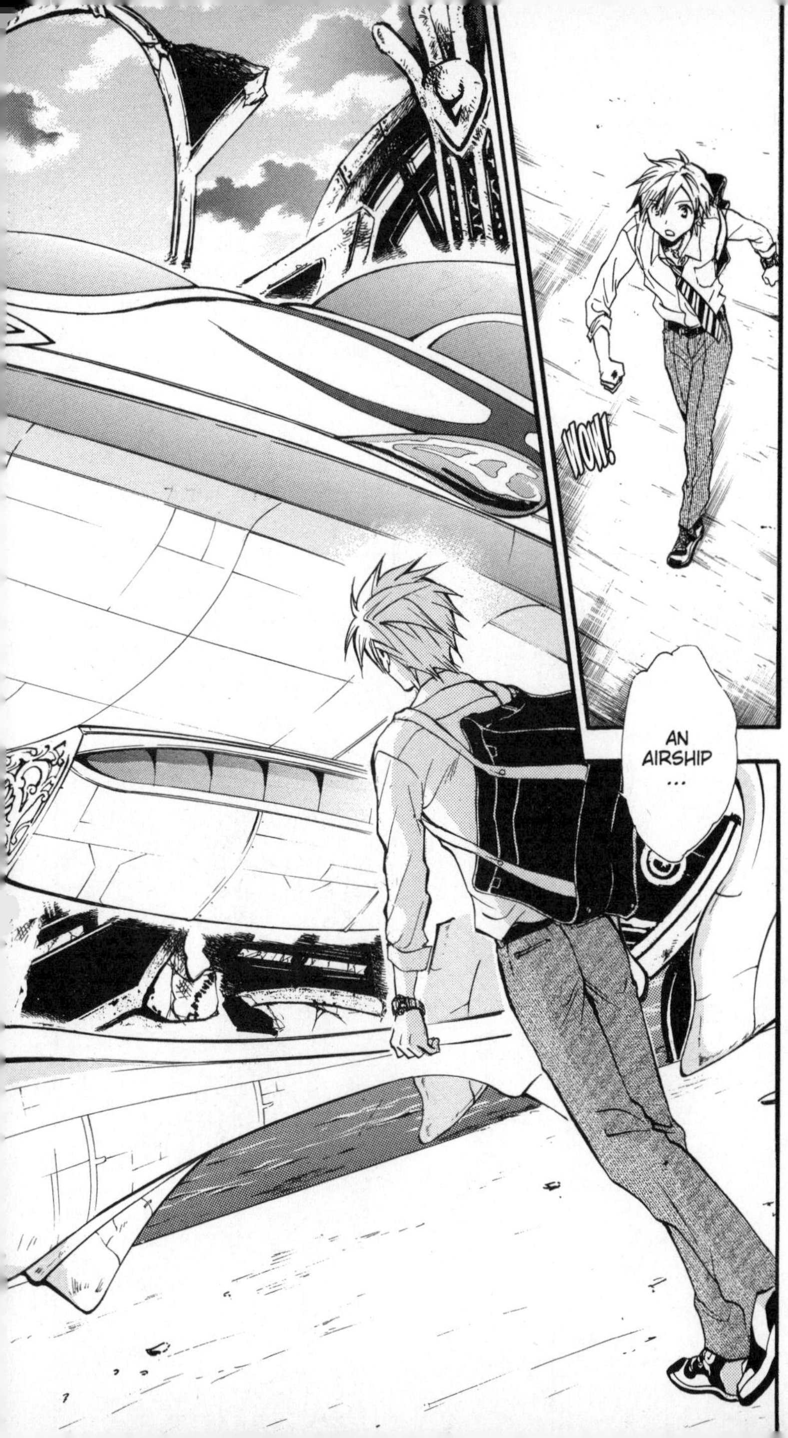
WOW!
AN AIRSHIP ...

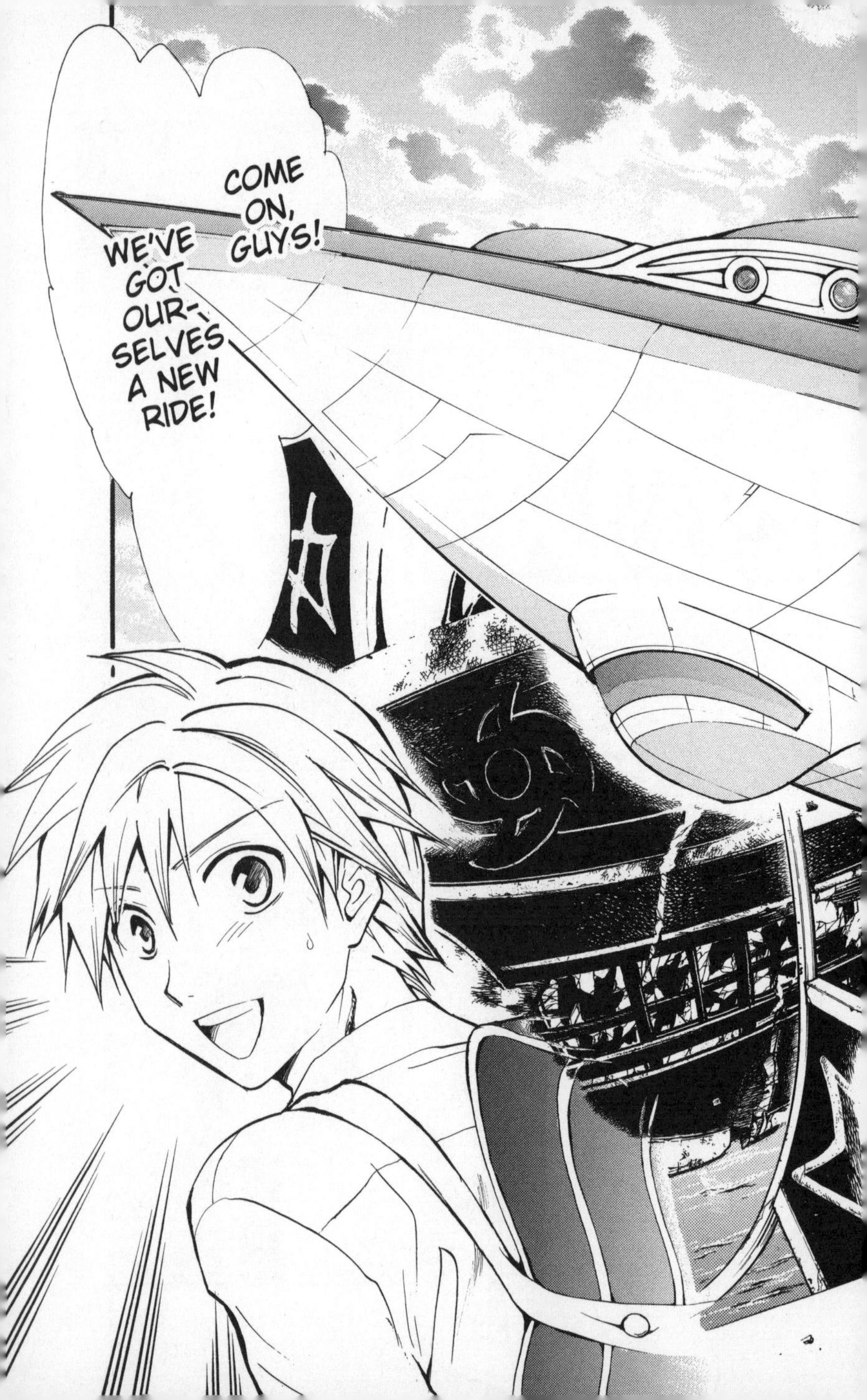
COME ON, GUYS!
WE'VE GOT OUR-SELVES A NEW RIDE!

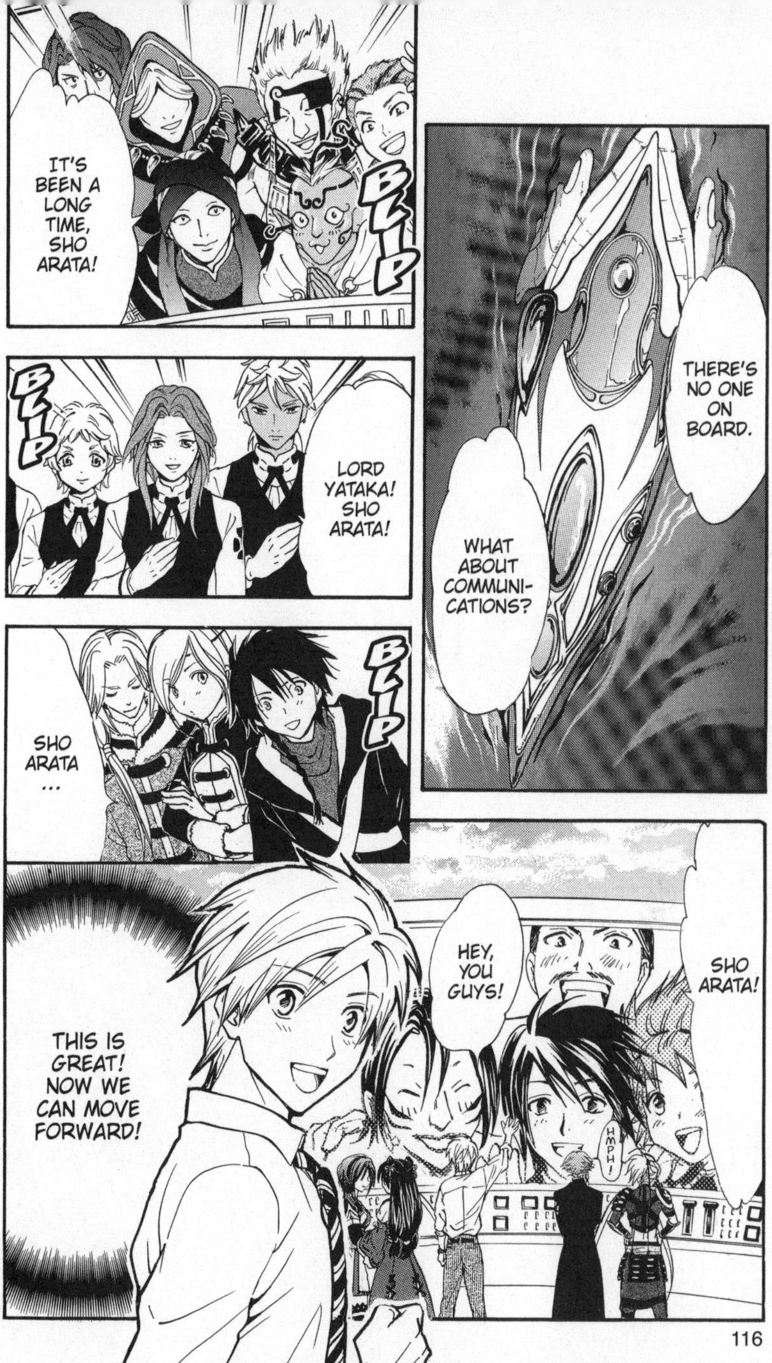
THERE'S NO ONE ON BOARD.
WHAT ABOUT COMMUNICATIONS?
BLIP
IT'S BEEN A LONG TIME, SHO ARATA!
LORD YATAKA! SHO ARATA!
BLIP
BLIP
SHO ARATA ...
SHO ARATA!
HEY, YOU GUYS!
HMPH!
THIS IS GREAT! NOW WE CAN MOVE FORWARD!

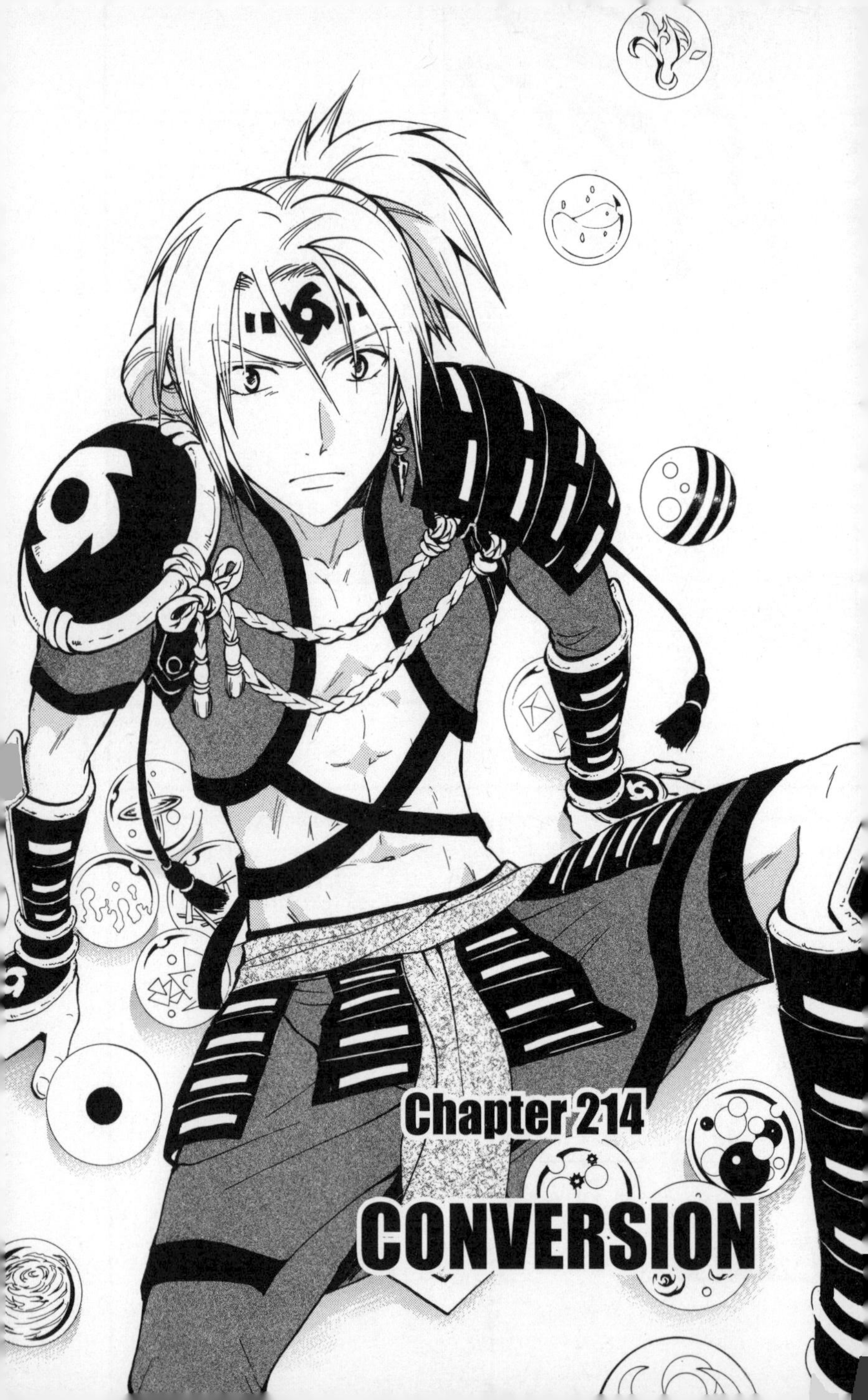
Chapter 214
CONVERSION

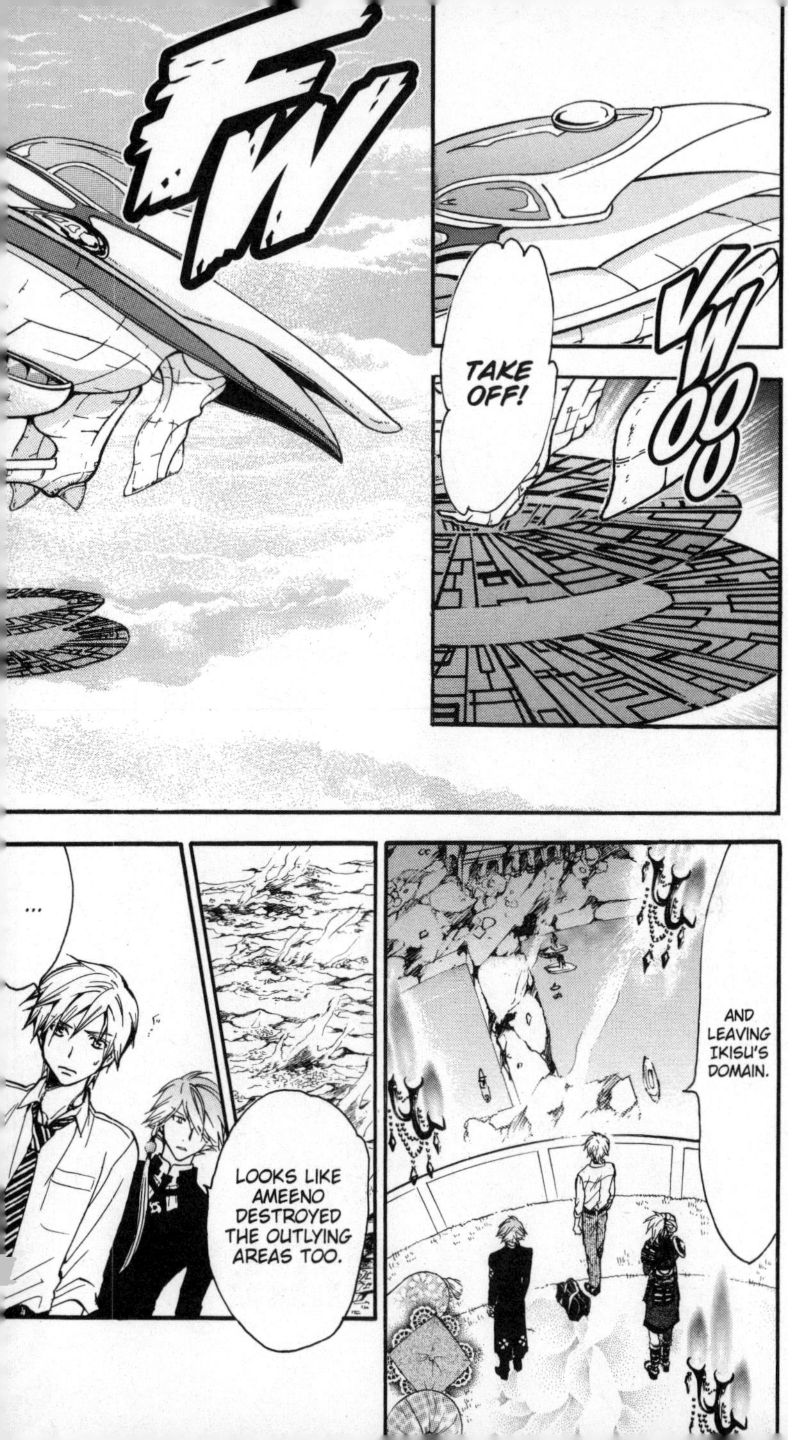
TAKE OFF!
VWOOO
FWN
AND LEAVING IKISU'S DOMAIN.
LOOKS LIKE AMEENO DESTROYED THE OUTLYING AREAS TOO.
...

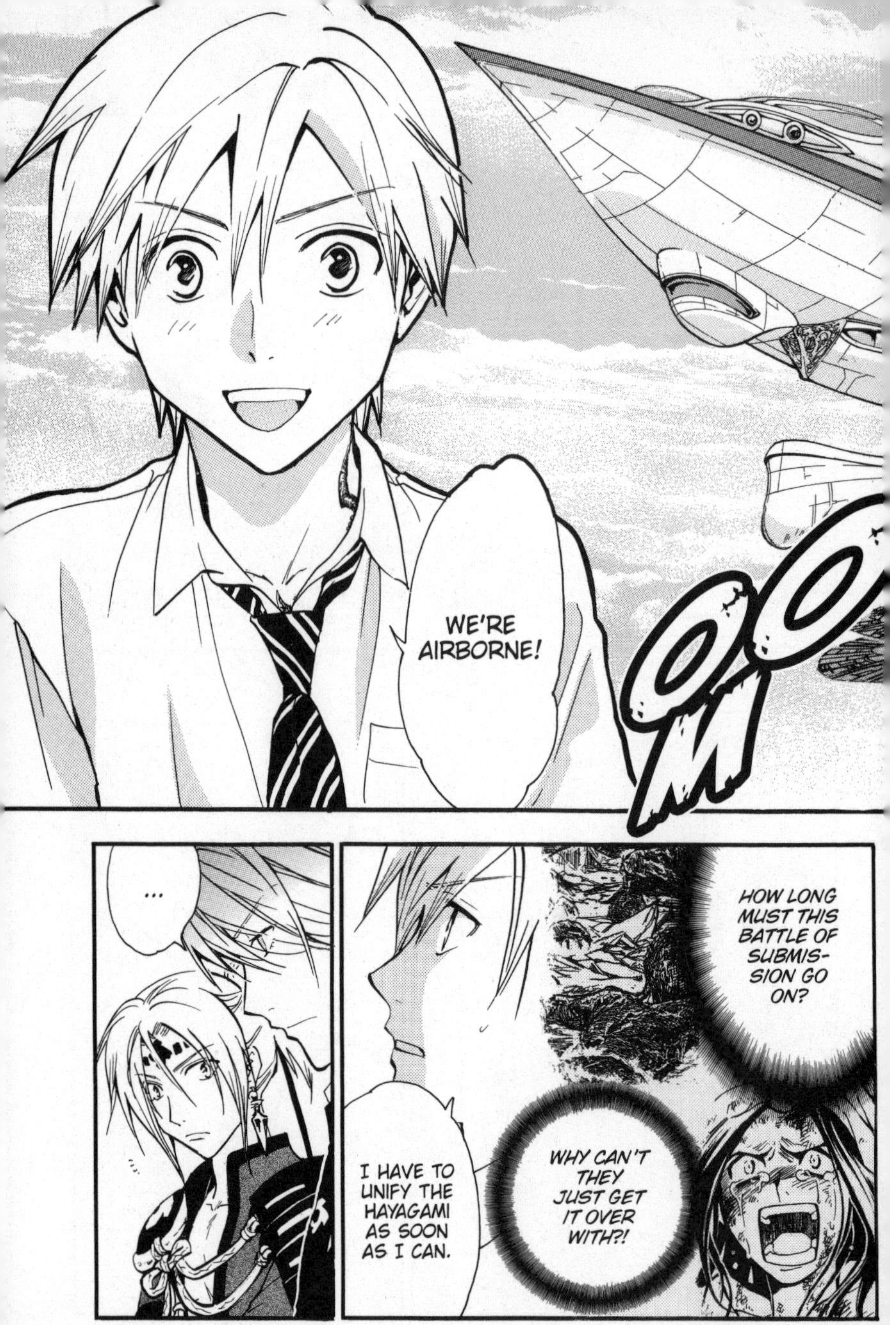
WE'RE AIRBORNE!
HOW LONG MUST THIS BATTLE OF SUBMISSION GO ON?
WHY CAN'T THEY JUST GET IT OVER WITH?!
I HAVE TO UNIFY THE HAYAGAMI AS SOON AS I CAN.
...

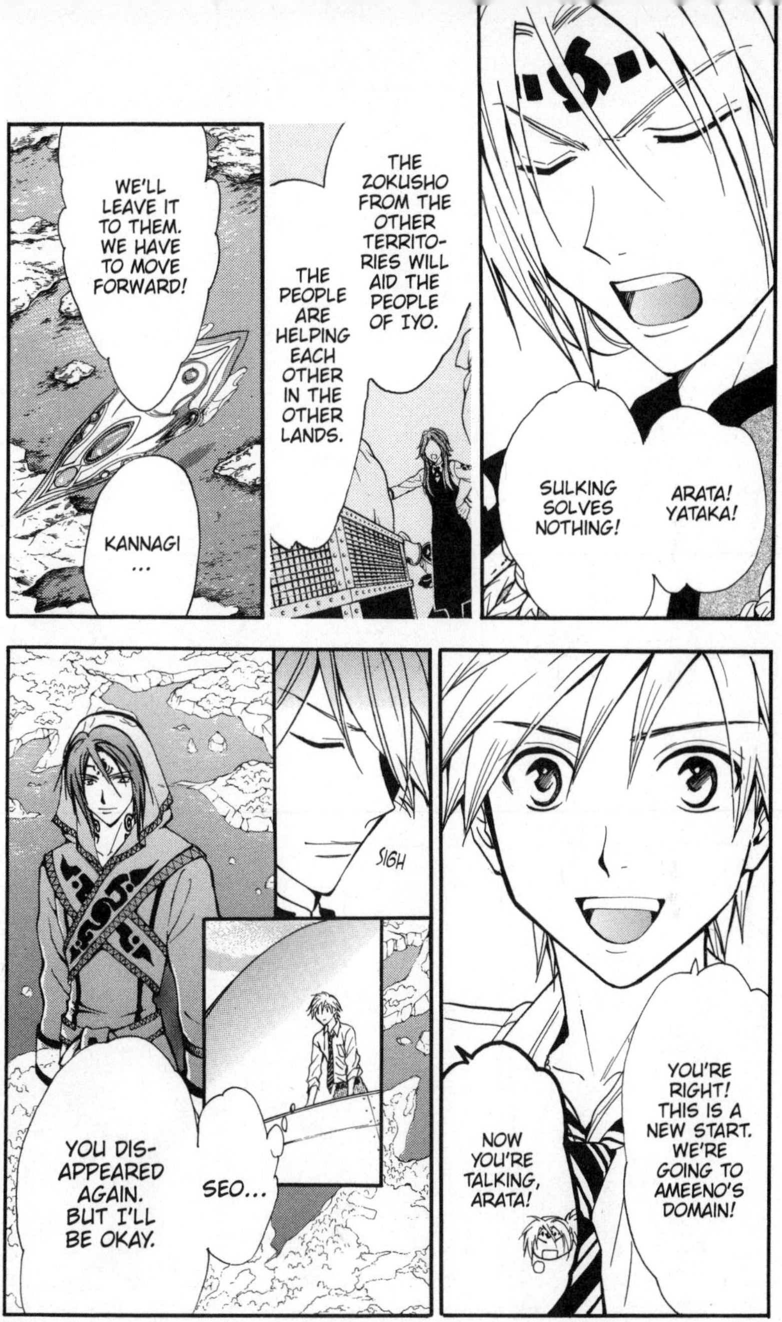
ARATA! YATAKA!
SULKING SOLVES NOTHING!
THE ZOKUSHO FROM THE OTHER TERRITO-RIES WILL AID THE PEOPLE OF IYO.
THE PEOPLE ARE HELPING EACH OTHER IN THE OTHER LANDS.
WE'LL LEAVE IT TO THEM. WE HAVE TO MOVE FORWARD!
KANNAGI ...
YOU'RE RIGHT! THIS IS A NEW START. WE'RE GOING TO AMEENO'S DOMAIN!
NOW YOU'RE TALKING, ARATA!
SIGH
SEO...
YOU DIS-APPEARED AGAIN. BUT I'LL BE OKAY.

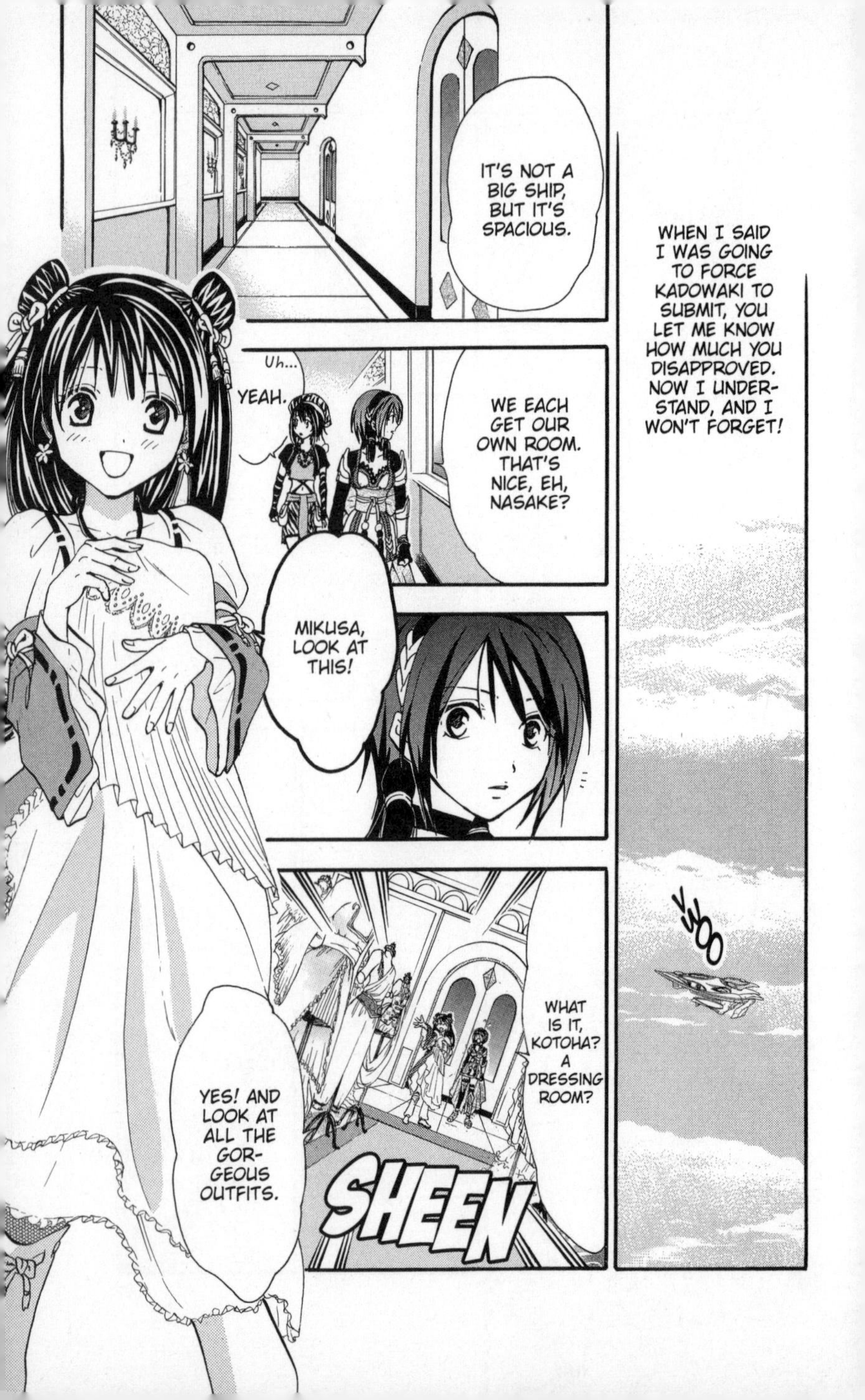
WHEN I SAID I WAS GOING TO FORCE KADOWAKI TO SUBMIT, YOU LET ME KNOW HOW MUCH YOU DISAPPROVED. NOW I UNDER-STAND, AND I WON'T FORGET!
IT'S NOT A BIG SHIP, BUT IT'S SPACIOUS.
WE EACH GET OUR OWN ROOM. THAT'S NICE, EH, NASAKE?
Uh...
YEAH.
MIKUSA, LOOK AT THIS!
WHAT IS IT, KOTOHA? A DRESSING ROOM?
SHEEN
YES! AND LOOK AT ALL THE GOR-GEOUS OUTFITS.

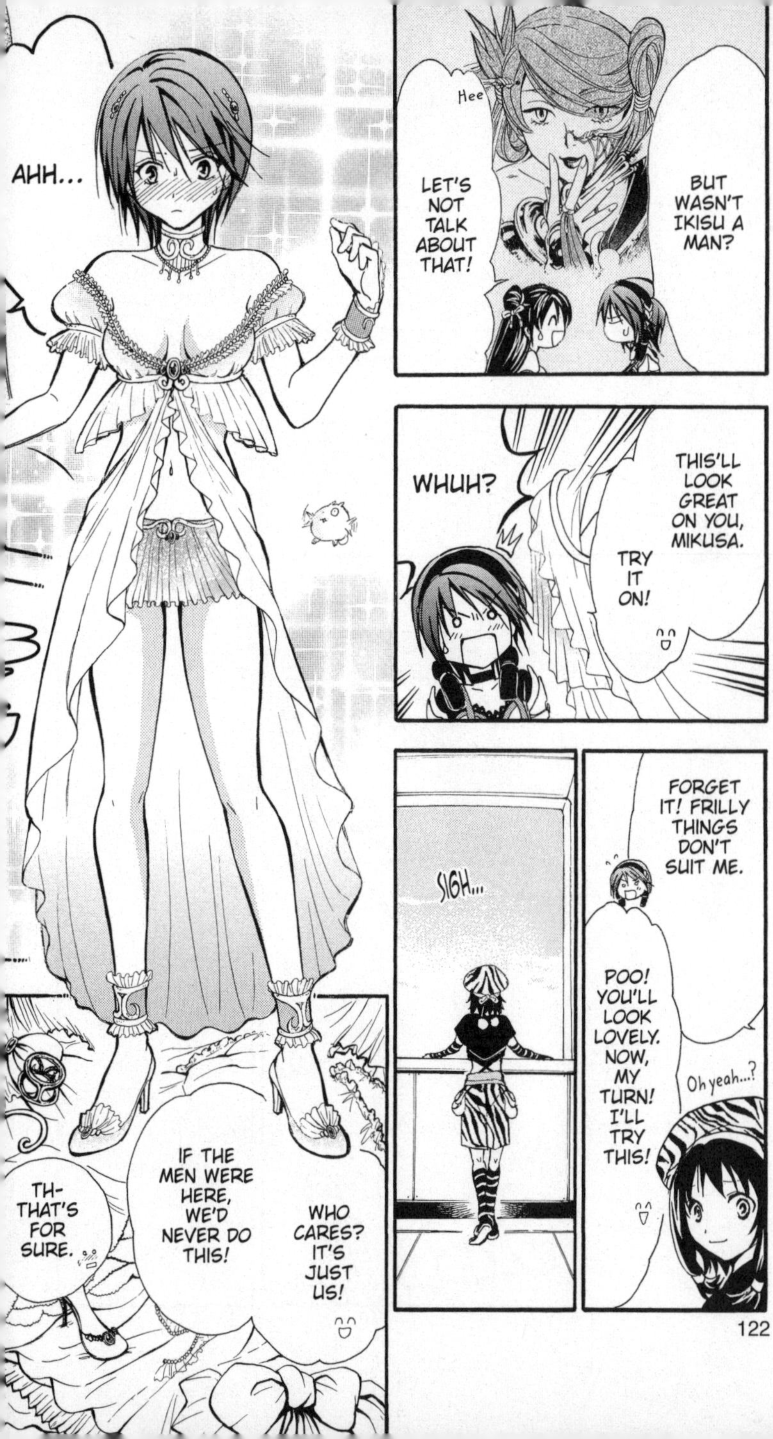
BUT WASN'T IKISU A MAN?
Hee
LET'S NOT TALK ABOUT THAT!
THIS'LL LOOK GREAT ON YOU, MIKUSA.
TRY IT ON!
WHUH?
FORGET IT! FRILLY THINGS DON'T SUIT ME.
POO! YOU'LL LOOK LOVELY. NOW, MY TURN! I'LL TRY THIS!
Oh yeah...?
SIGH...
AHH...
IF THE MEN WERE HERE, WE'D NEVER DO THIS!
WHO CARES? IT'S JUST US!
TH-THAT'S FOR SURE.

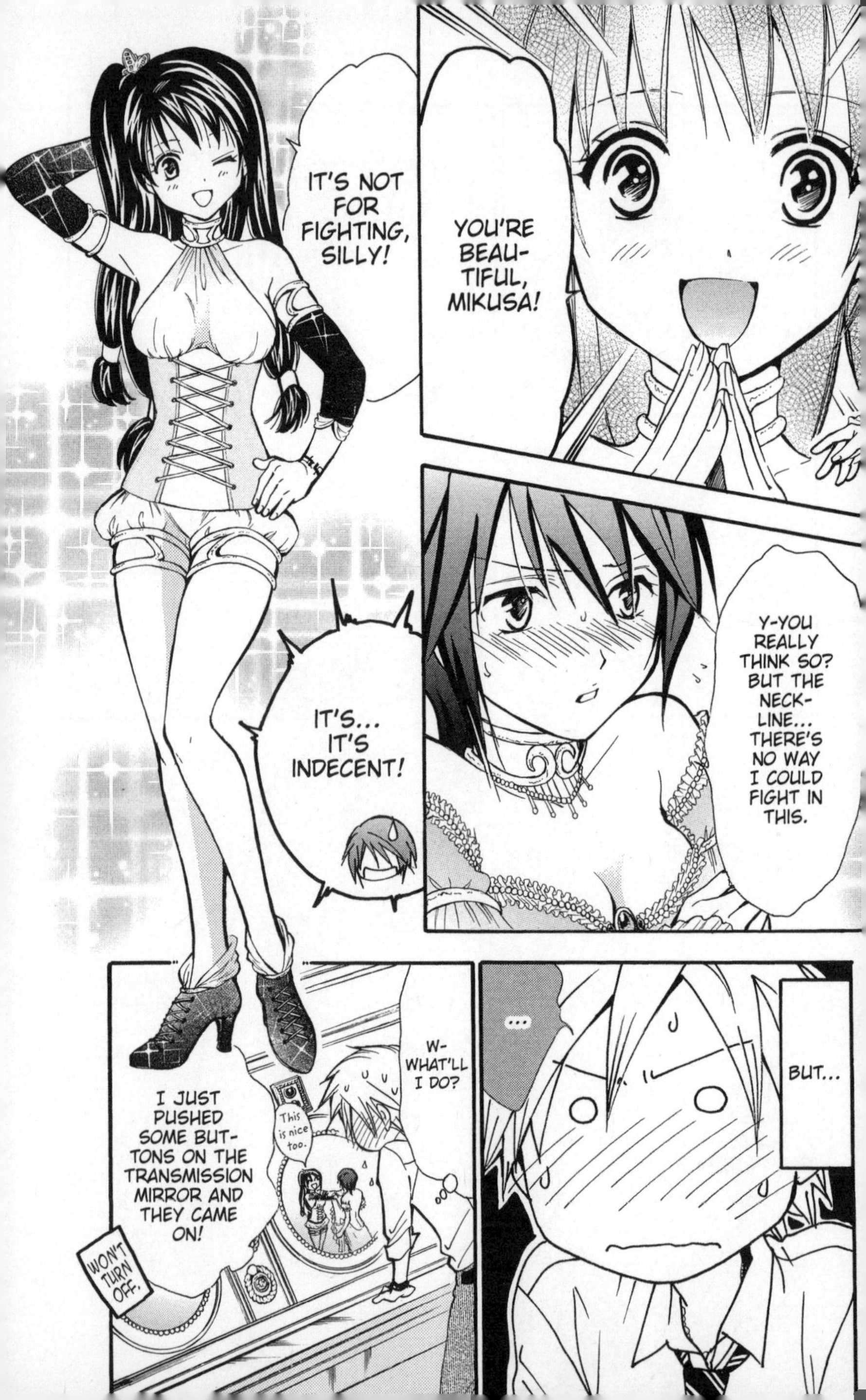
YOU'RE BEAUTIFUL, MIKUSA!
Y-YOU REALLY THINK SO? BUT THE NECKLINE... THERE'S NO WAY I COULD FIGHT IN THIS.
IT'S NOT FOR FIGHTING, SILLY!
IT'S... IT'S INDECENT!
...
BUT...
W-WHAT'LL I DO?
This is nice too.
I JUST PUSHED SOME BUTTONS ON THE TRANSMISSION MIRROR AND THEY CAME ON!
WON'T TURN OFF.

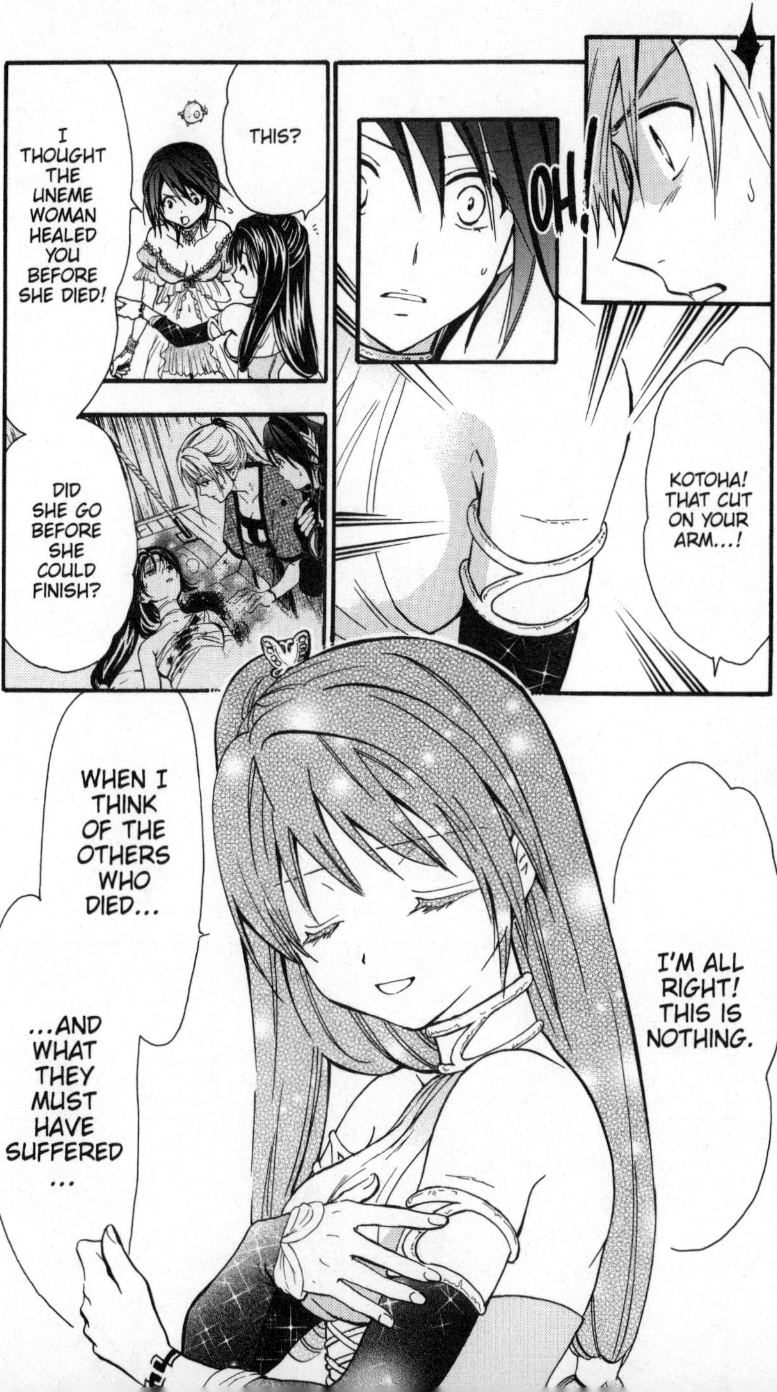
OH!
KOTOHA! THAT CUT ON YOUR ARM...!
THIS?
I THOUGHT THE UNEME WOMAN HEALED YOU BEFORE SHE DIED!
DID SHE GO BEFORE SHE COULD FINISH?
I'M ALL RIGHT! THIS IS NOTHING.
WHEN I THINK OF THE OTHERS WHO DIED...
...AND WHAT THEY MUST HAVE SUFFERED...

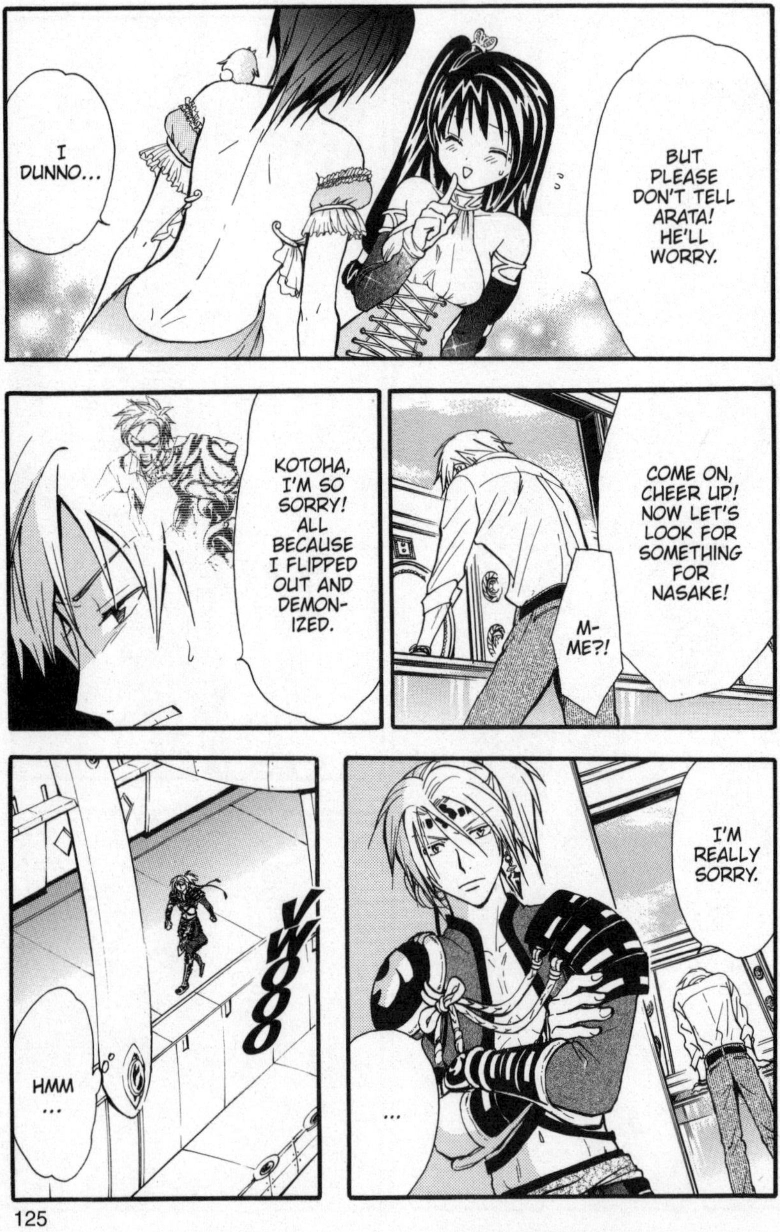
BUT PLEASE DON'T TELL ARATA! HE'LL WORRY.
I DUNNO...
COME ON, CHEER UP! NOW LET'S LOOK FOR SOMETHING FOR NASAKE!
M-ME?!
KOTOHA, I'M SO SORRY! ALL BECAUSE I FLIPPED OUT AND DEMON-IZED.
I'M REALLY SORRY.
...
VWOOO
HMM ...

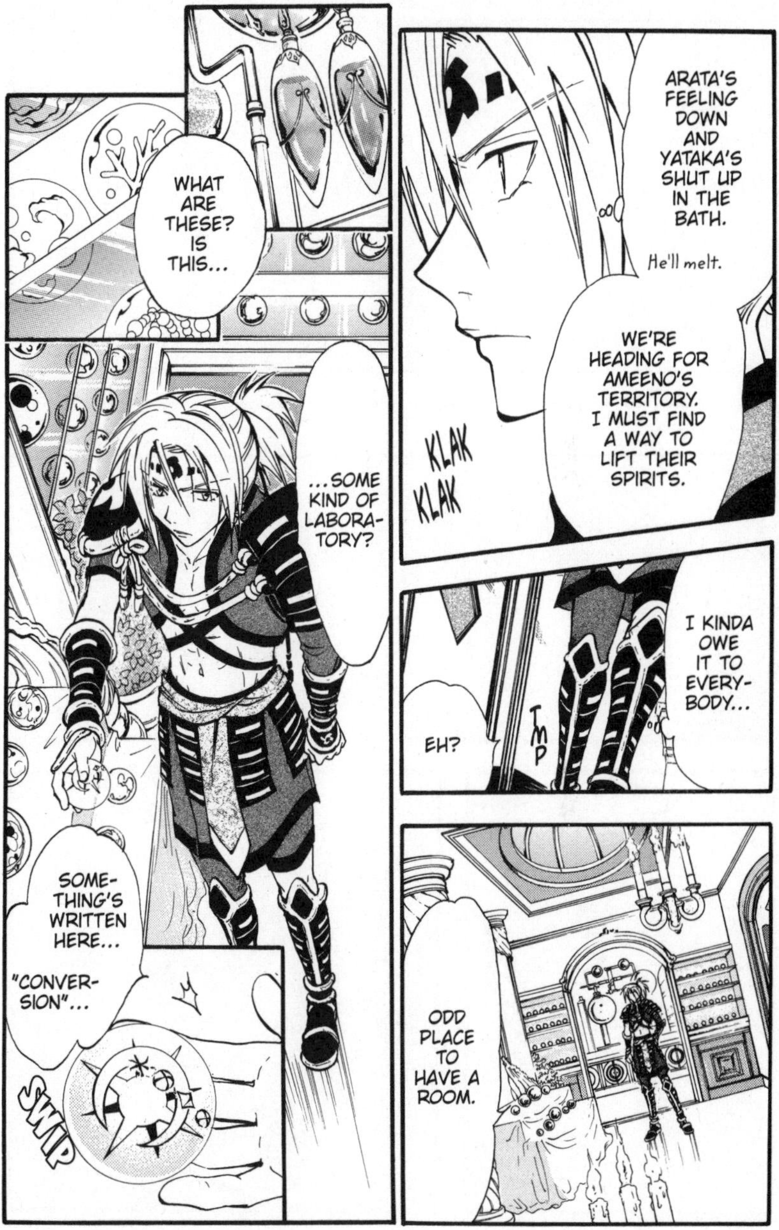
ARATA'S FEELING DOWN AND YATAKA'S SHUT UP IN THE BATH.
He'll melt.
WE'RE HEADING FOR AMEENO'S TERRITORY. I MUST FIND A WAY TO LIFT THEIR SPIRITS.
KLAK KLAK
I KINDA OWE IT TO EVERY-BODY...
EH?
TMP
ODD PLACE TO HAVE A ROOM.
WHAT ARE THESE? IS THIS...
...SOME KIND OF LABORA-TORY?
SOME-THING'S WRITTEN HERE...
"CONVER-SION"...
SWIP

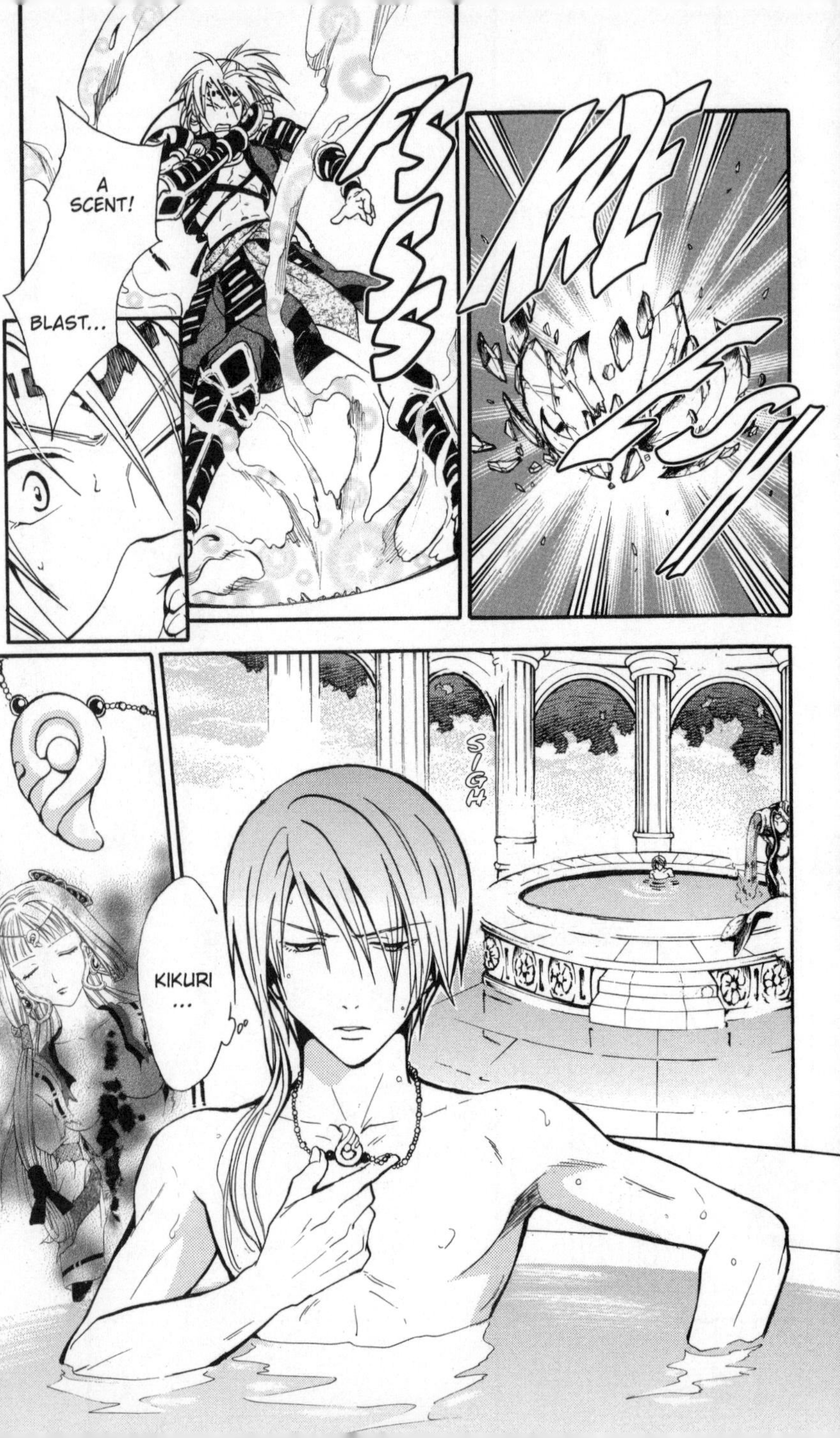
A SCENT!
BLAST...
SIGH
KIKURI ...

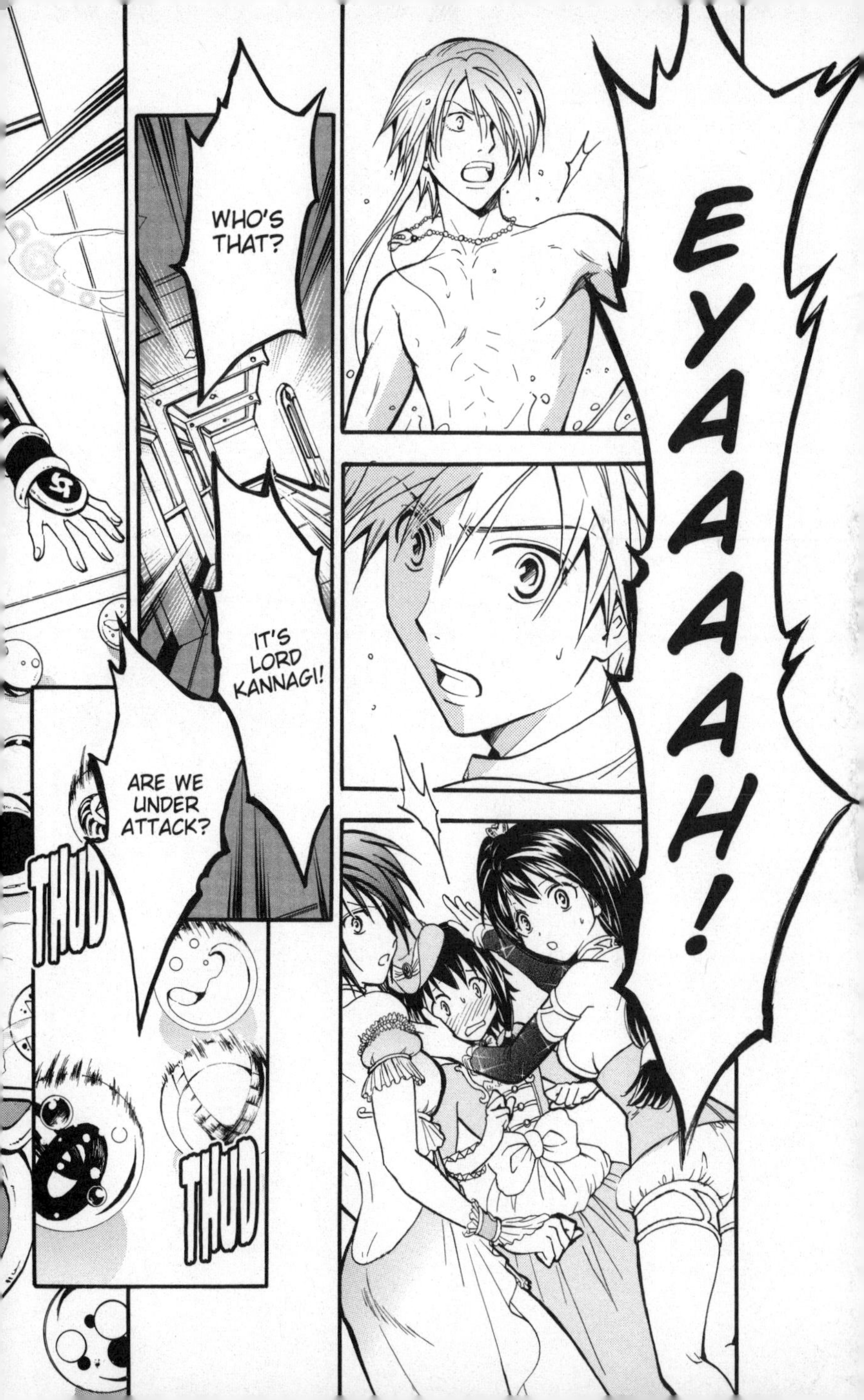
EYAAAAH!
WHO'S THAT?
IT'S LORD KANNAGI!
ARE WE UNDER ATTACK?
THUD
THUD

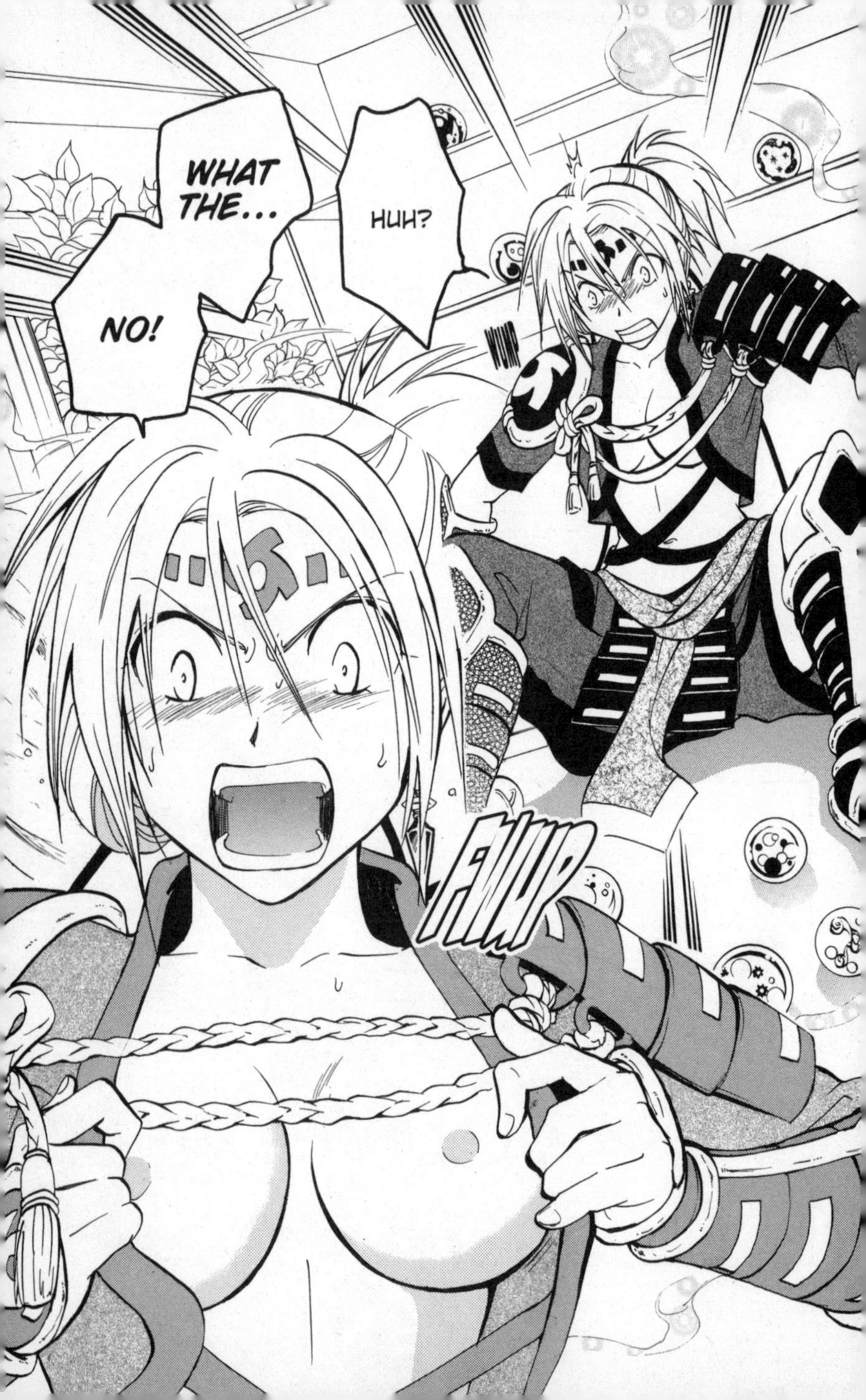
HUH?
WHUMP
WHAT THE...
NO!
FWUP

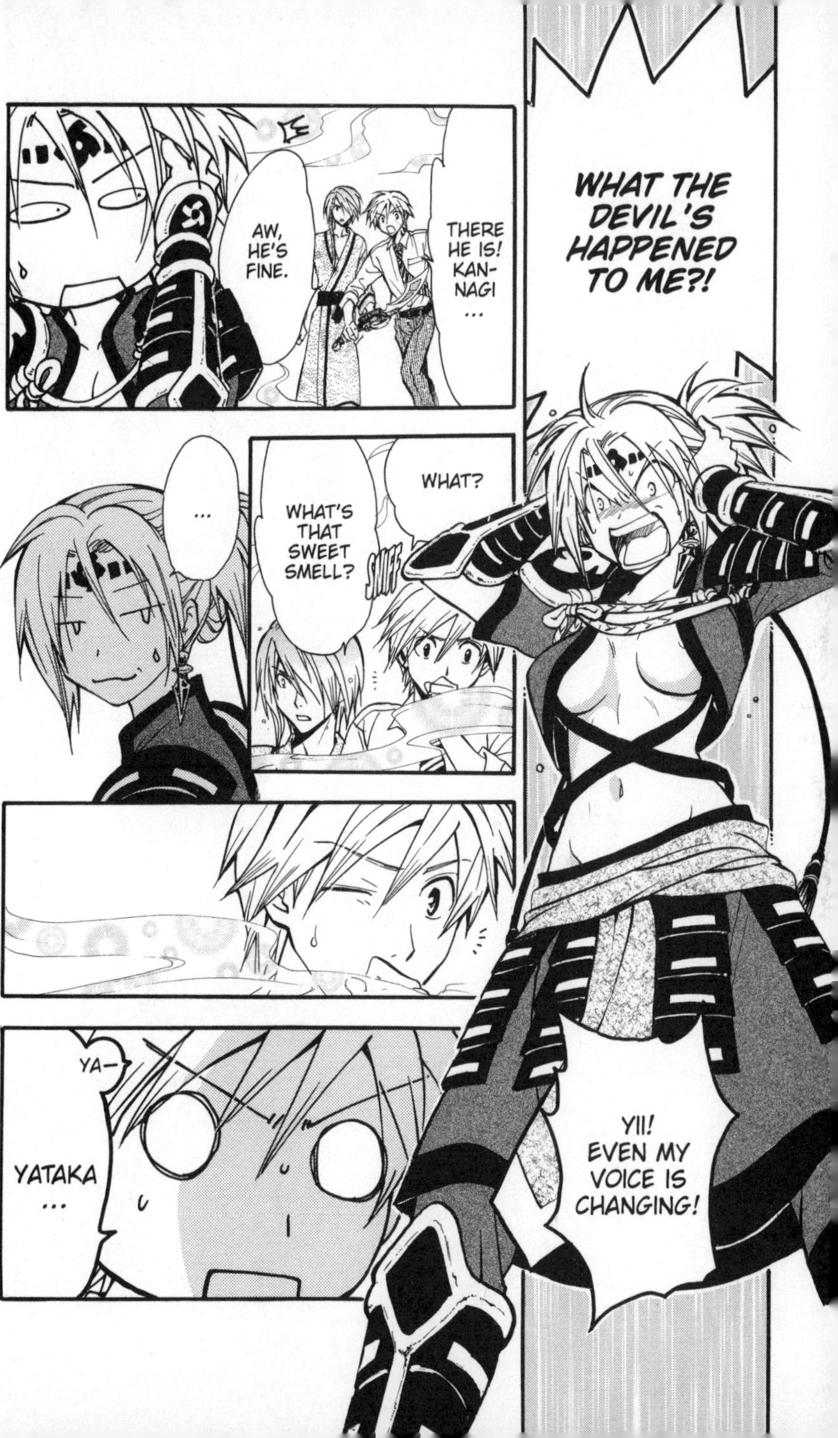
WHAT THE DEVIL'S HAPPENED TO ME?!
YII! EVEN MY VOICE IS CHANGING!
THERE HE IS! KAN-NAGI ...
AW, HE'S FINE.
WHAT?
WHAT'S THAT SWEET SMELL?
SNIFF
...
YA—
YATAKA ...

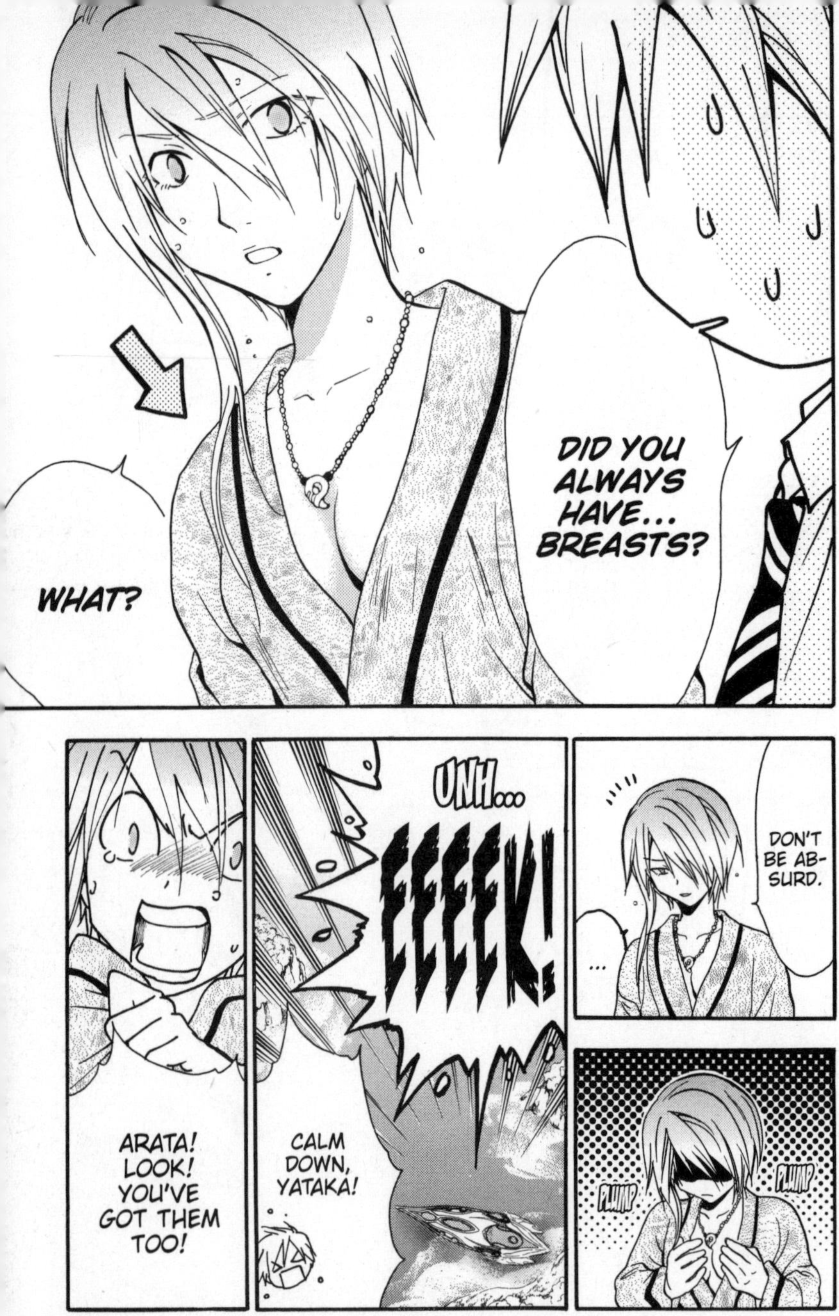
DID YOU ALWAYS HAVE... BREASTS?
WHAT?
DON'T BE AB-SURD.
...
PLUMP
PLUMP
UNH...
EEEK!
CALM DOWN, YATAKA!
ARATA! LOOK! YOU'VE GOT THEM TOO!

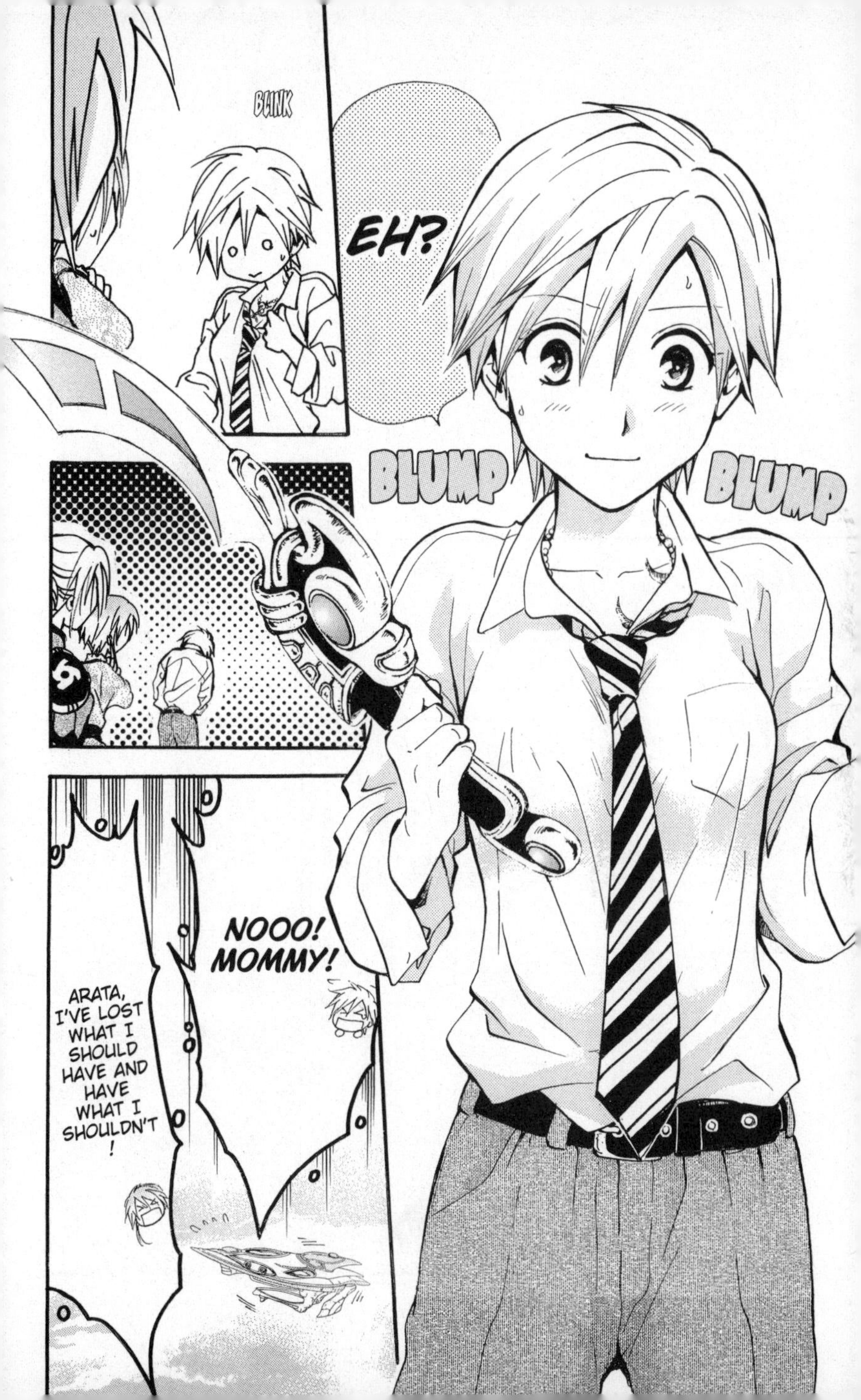
EH?
BLUMP
BLUMP
BLINK
NOOO! MOMMY!
ARATA, I'VE LOST WHAT I SHOULD HAVE AND HAVE WHAT I SHOULDN'T!

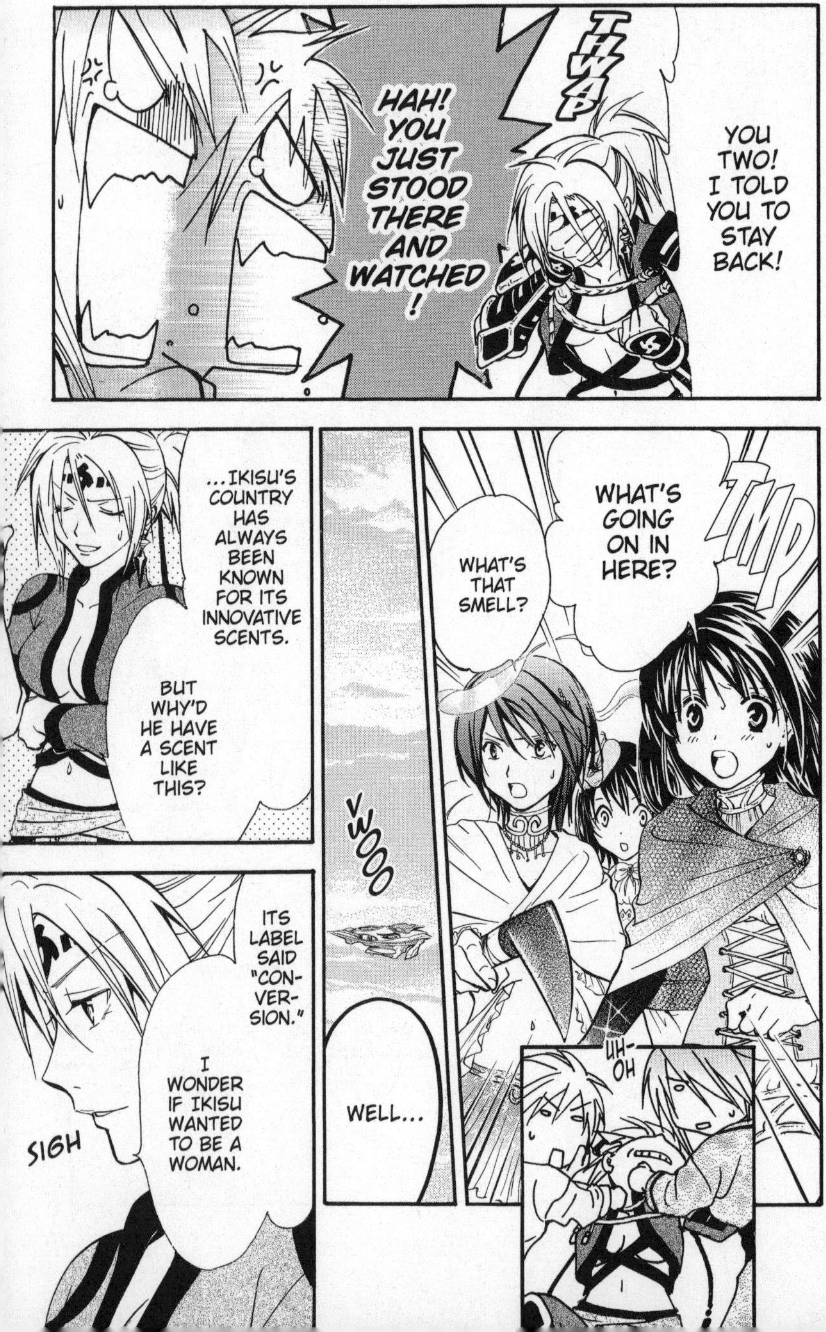
THWAP
YOU TWO! I TOLD YOU TO STAY BACK!
HAH! YOU JUST STOOD THERE AND WATCHED!
TMP
WHAT'S GOING ON IN HERE?
WHAT'S THAT SMELL?
UH-OH
VWOOO
WELL...
...IKISU'S COUNTRY HAS ALWAYS BEEN KNOWN FOR ITS INNOVATIVE SCENTS.
BUT WHY'D HE HAVE A SCENT LIKE THIS?
ITS LABEL SAID "CON-VER-SION."
I WONDER IF IKISU WANTED TO BE A WOMAN.
SIGH

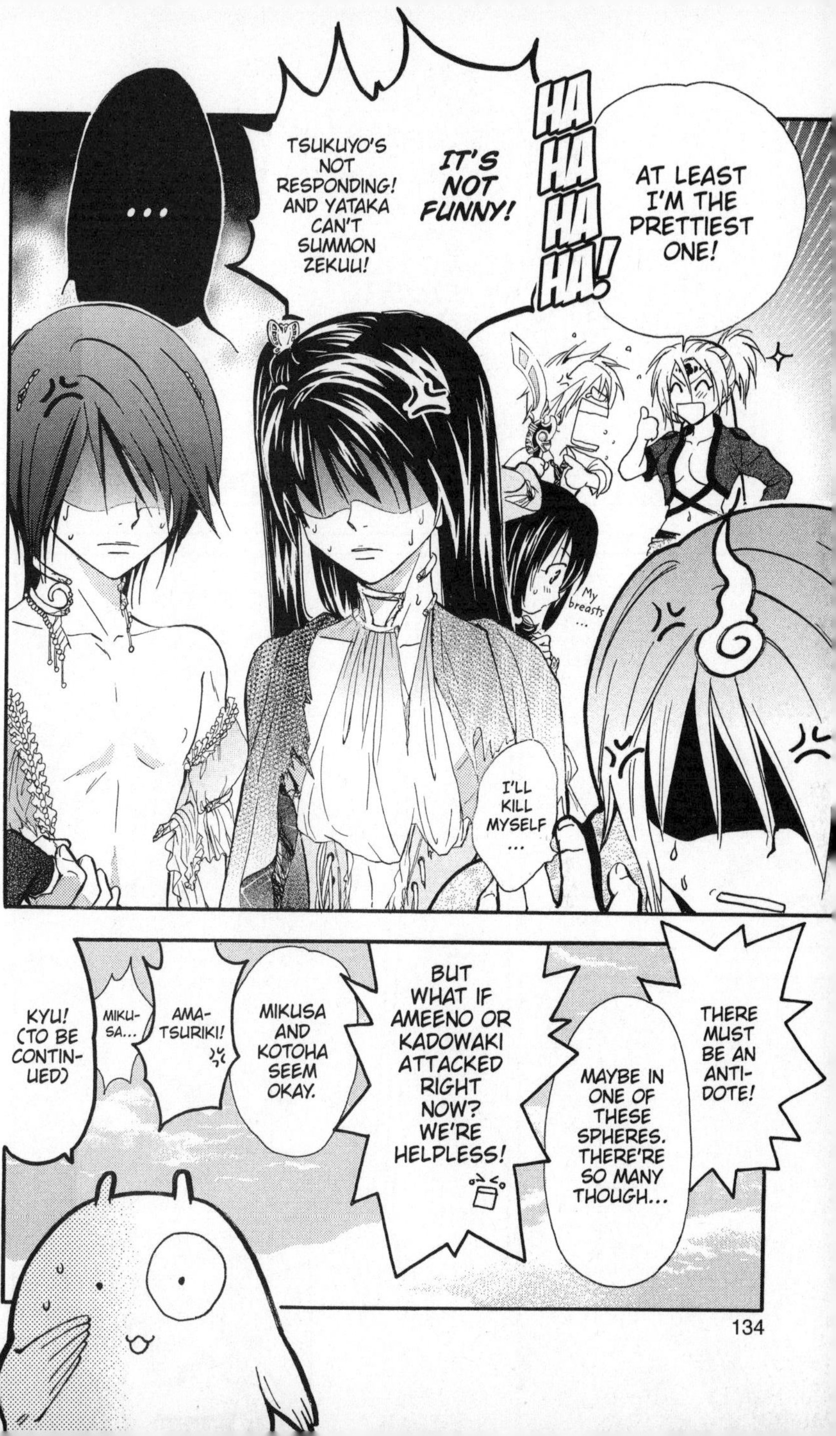
AT LEAST I'M THE PRETTIEST ONE!
HA HA HA HA!
IT'S NOT FUNNY!
TSUKUYO'S NOT RESPONDING! AND YATAKA CAN'T SUMMON ZEKUU!
...
My breasts ...
I'LL KILL MYSELF ...
THERE MUST BE AN ANTI-DOTE!
MAYBE IN ONE OF THESE SPHERES. THERE'RE SO MANY THOUGH...
BUT WHAT IF AMEENO OR KADOWAKI ATTACKED RIGHT NOW? WE'RE HELPLESS!
MIKUSA AND KOTOHA SEEM OKAY.
AMA-TSURIKI!
MIKU-SA...
KYU! (TO BE CONTIN-UED)

Chapter 215
SECOND DISASTER

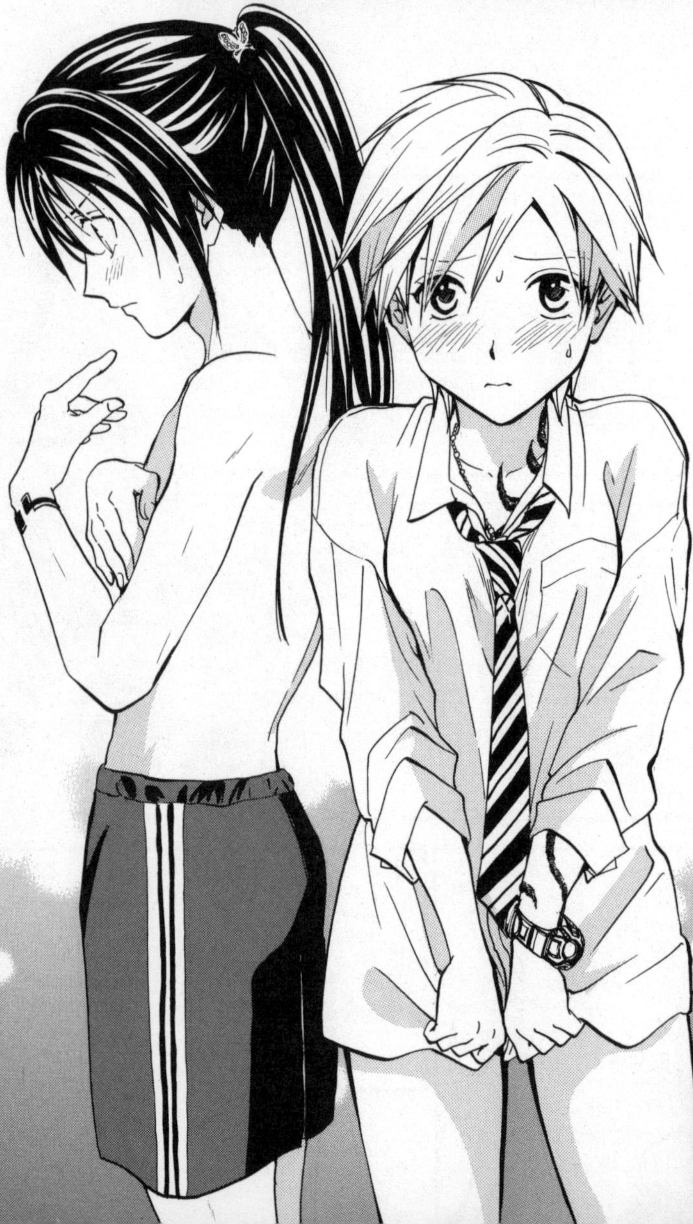

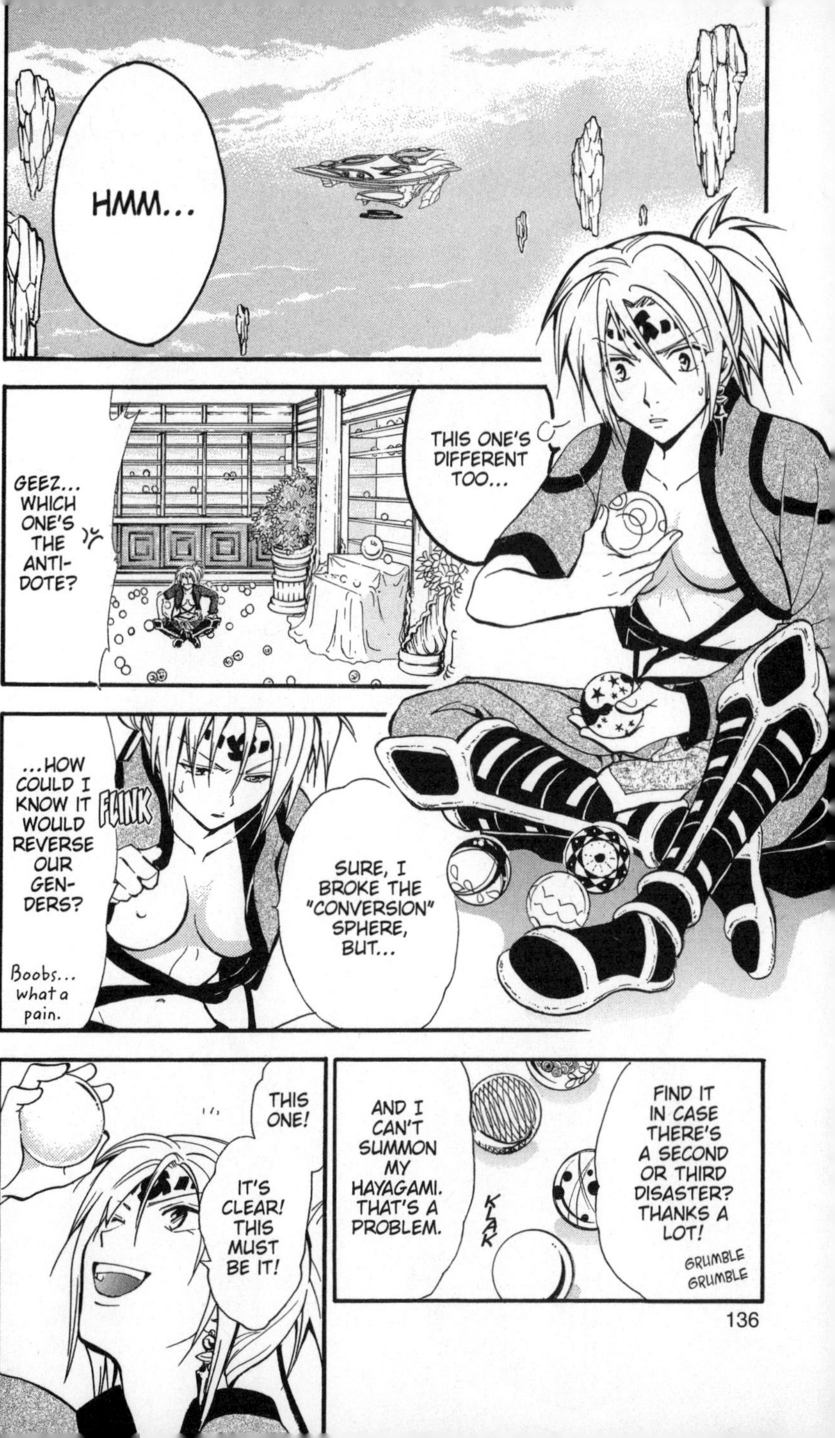
HMM...
THIS ONE'S DIFFERENT TOO...
GEEZ... WHICH ONE'S THE ANTI-DOTE?
SURE, I BROKE THE "CONVERSION" SPHERE, BUT...
FLINK
...HOW COULD I KNOW IT WOULD REVERSE OUR GEN-DERS?
Boobs... what a pain.
FIND IT IN CASE THERE'S A SECOND OR THIRD DISASTER? THANKS A LOT!
GRUMBLE GRUMBLE
AND I CAN'T SUMMON MY HAYAGAMI. THAT'S A PROBLEM.
KLAK
THIS ONE!
IT'S CLEAR! THIS MUST BE IT!

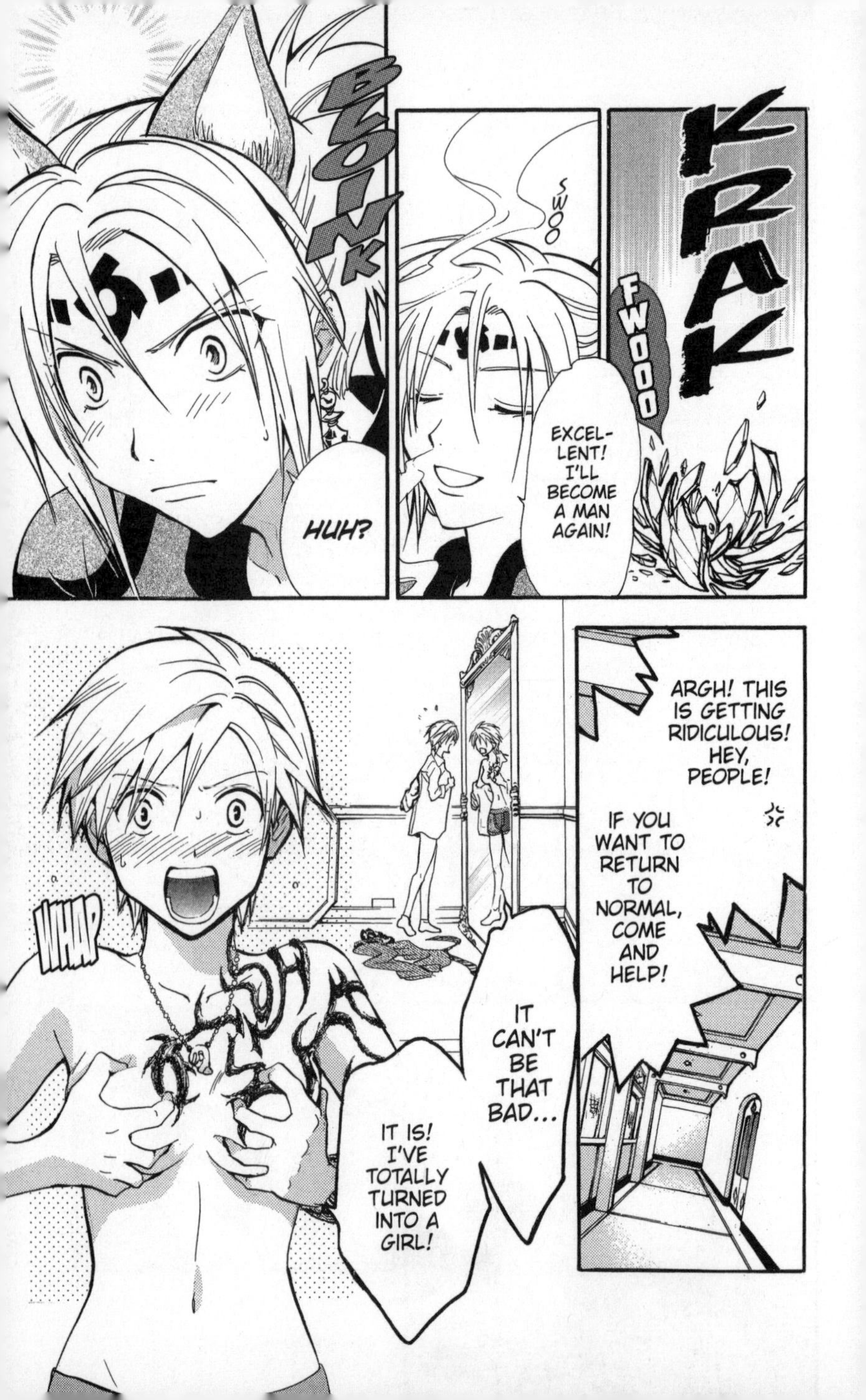
KRAK
FWOOO
SWOO
EXCEL-LENT! I'LL BECOME A MAN AGAIN!
BLOINK
HUH?
ARGH! THIS IS GETTING RIDICULOUS! HEY, PEOPLE!
IF YOU WANT TO RETURN TO NORMAL, COME AND HELP!
IT CAN'T BE THAT BAD...
WHAP
IT IS! I'VE TOTALLY TURNED INTO A GIRL!

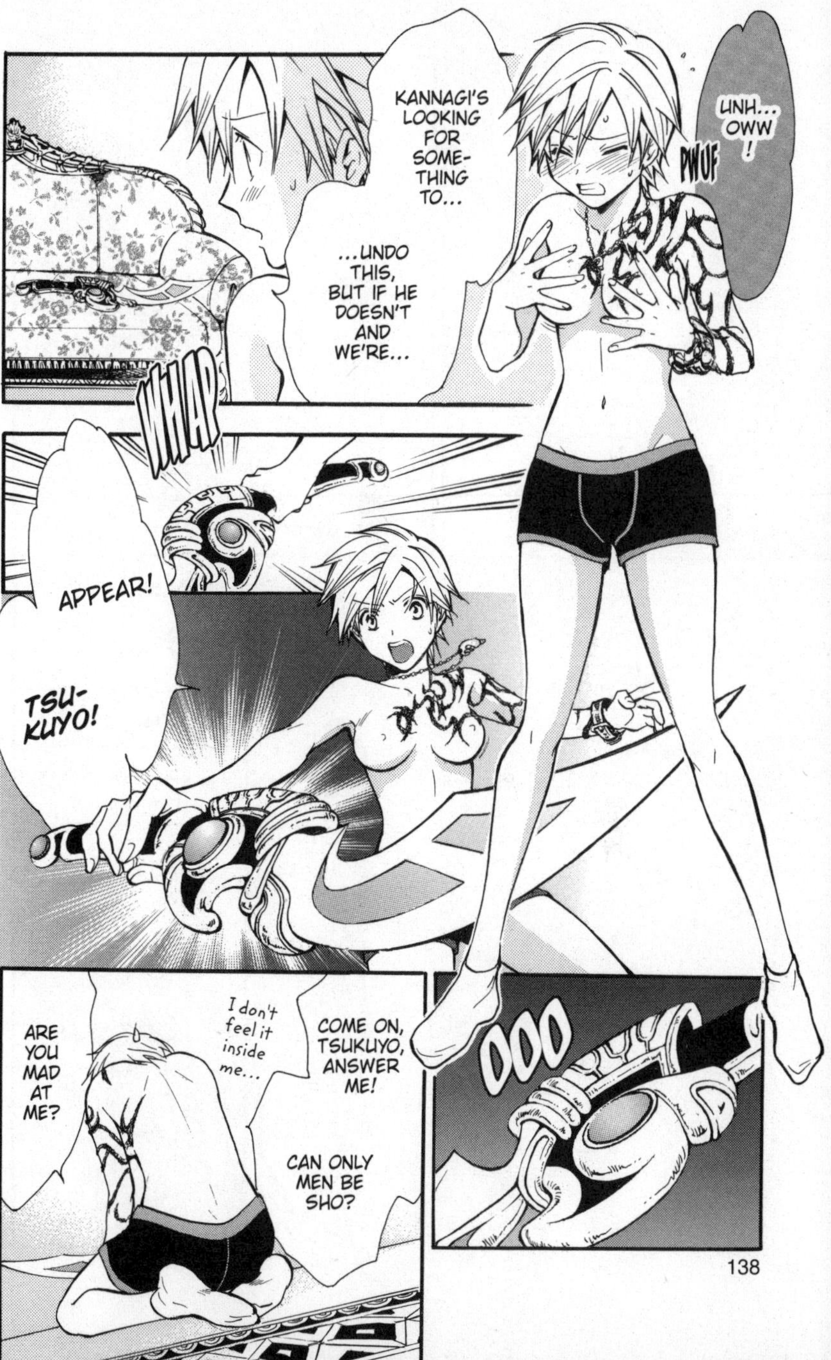
UNH... OWW!
PWUF
KANNAGI'S LOOKING FOR SOME-THING TO...
...UNDO THIS, BUT IF HE DOESN'T AND WE'RE...
WHAP
APPEAR!
TSU-KUYO!
OOO
COME ON, TSUKUYO, ANSWER ME!
I don't feel it inside me...
ARE YOU MAD AT ME?
CAN ONLY MEN BE SHO?

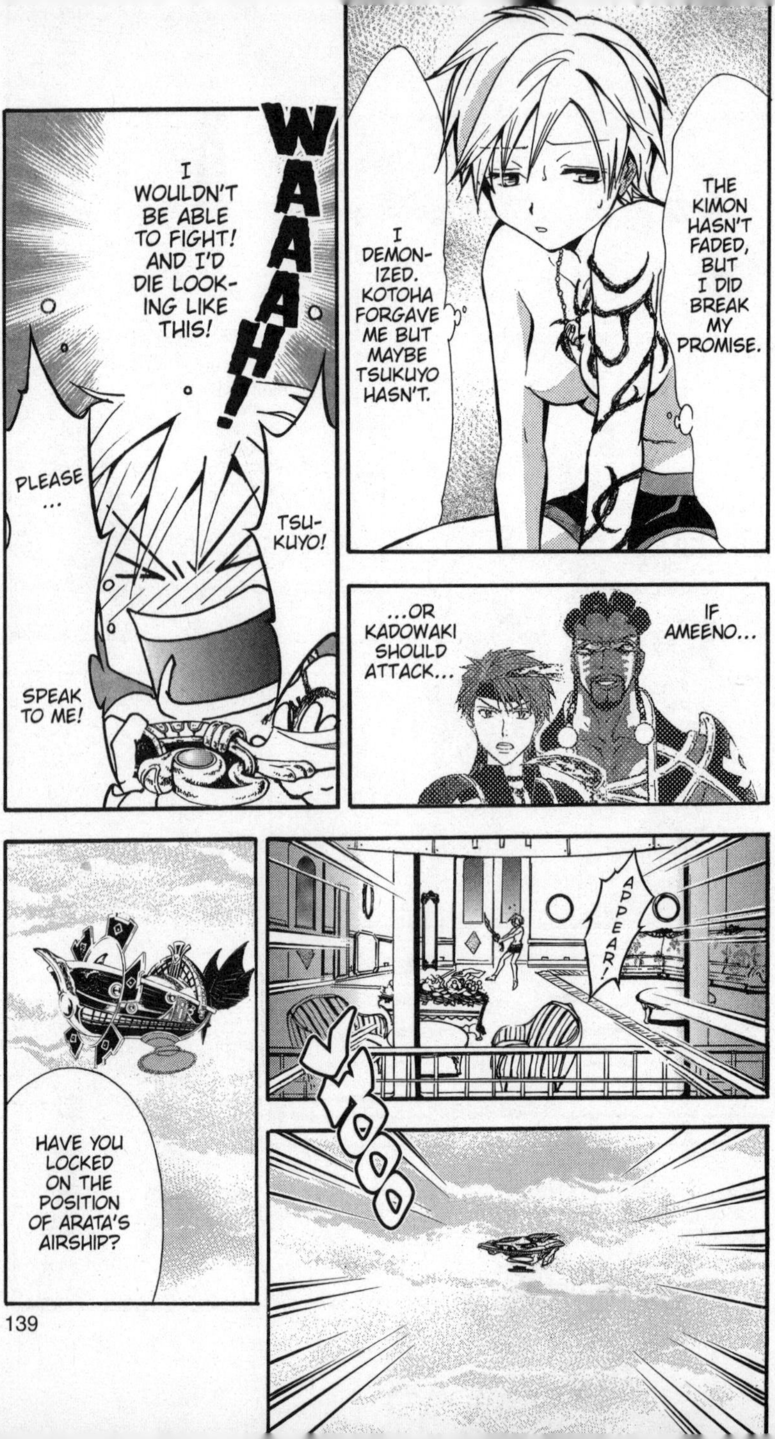
THE KIMON HASN'T FADED, BUT I DID BREAK MY PROMISE.
I DEMON-IZED. KOTOHA FORGAVE ME BUT MAYBE TSUKUYO HASN'T.
IF AMEENO...
...OR KADOWAKI SHOULD ATTACK...
WAAAAH!
I WOULDN'T BE ABLE TO FIGHT! AND I'D DIE LOOK-ING LIKE THIS!
TSU-KUYO!
PLEASE...
SPEAK TO ME!
APPEAR!
VOOOO
HAVE YOU LOCKED ON THE POSITION OF ARATA'S AIRSHIP?

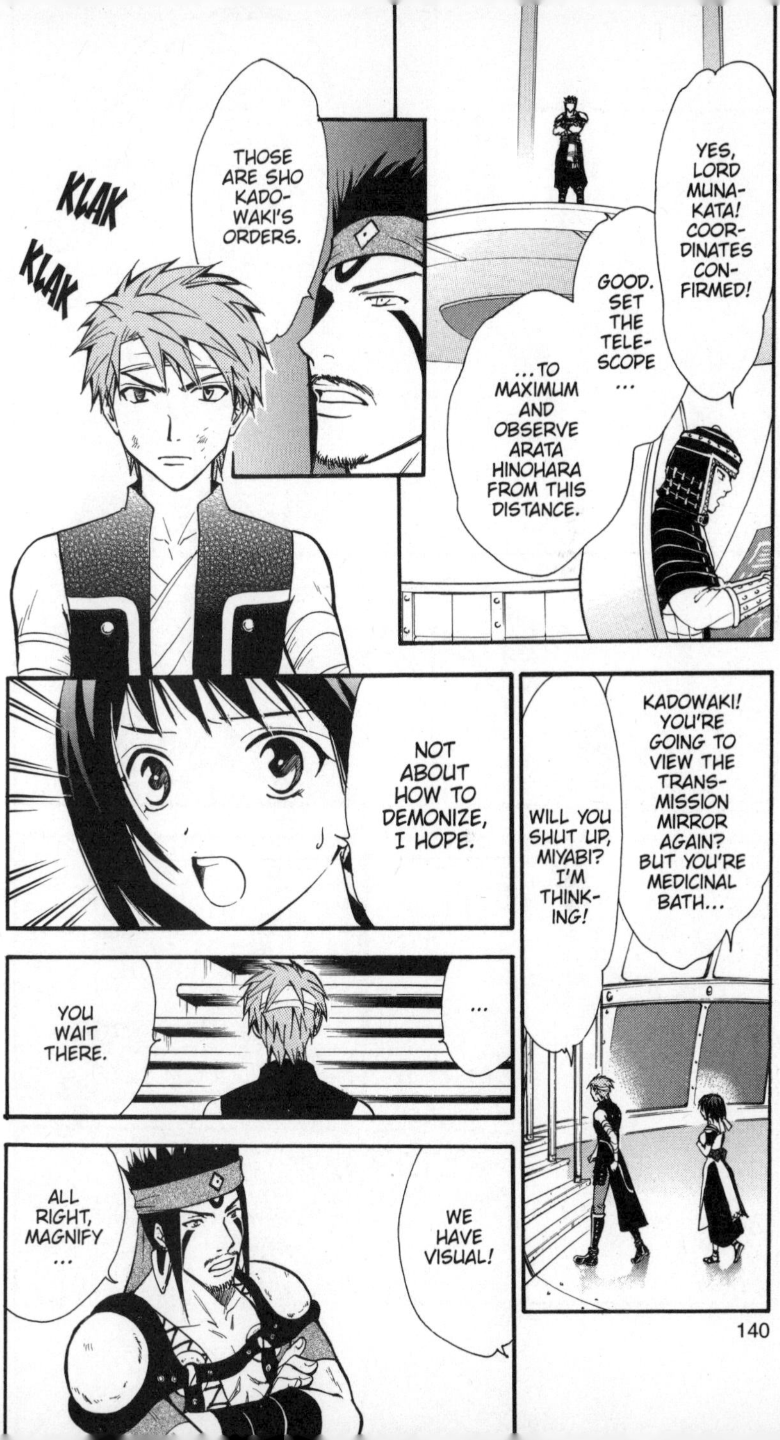
YES, LORD MUNAKATA! COORDINATES CONFIRMED!
GOOD. SET THE TELESCOPE...
...TO MAXIMUM AND OBSERVE ARATA HINOHARA FROM THIS DISTANCE.
THOSE ARE SHO KADOWAKI'S ORDERS.
KLAK
KLAK
KADOWAKI! YOU'RE GOING TO VIEW THE TRANSMISSION MIRROR AGAIN? BUT YOU'RE MEDICINAL BATH...
WILL YOU SHUT UP, MIYABI? I'M THINKING!
NOT ABOUT HOW TO DEMONIZE, I HOPE.
...
YOU WAIT THERE.
WE HAVE VISUAL!
ALL RIGHT, MAGNIFY...

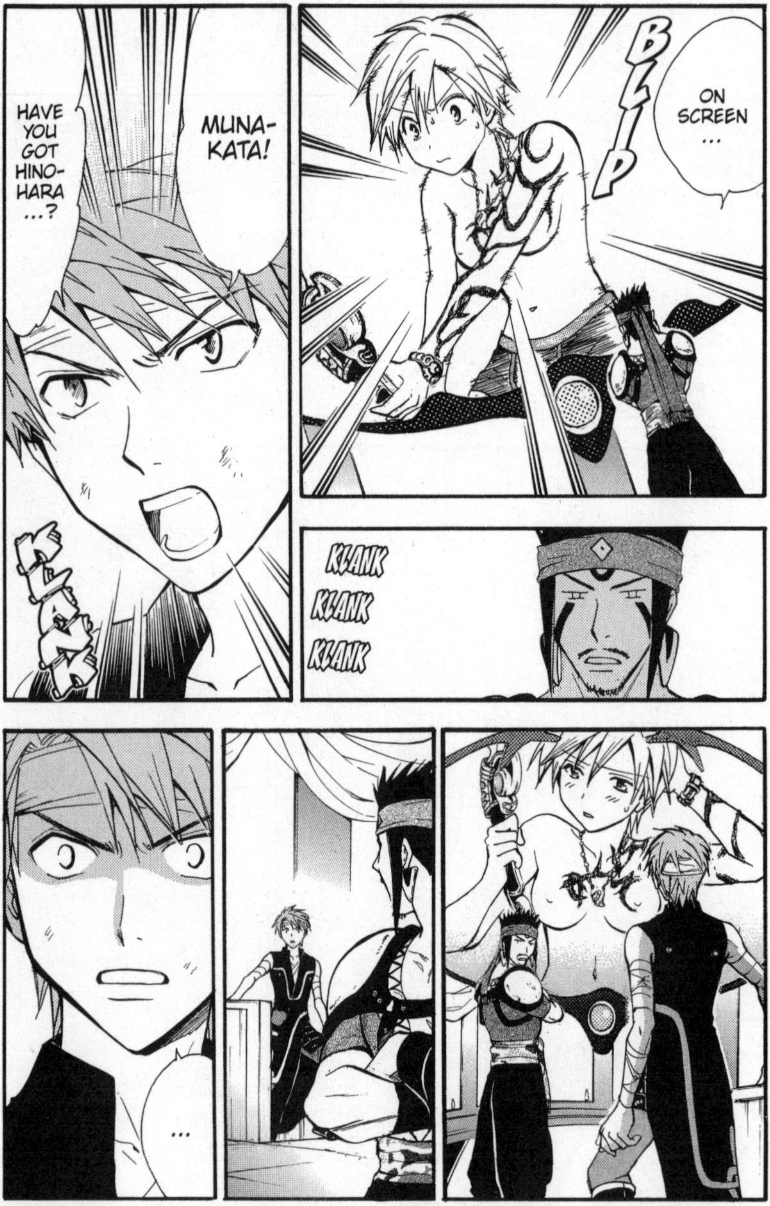
ON SCREEN ...
BLIP
KLANK
KLANK
KLANK
MUNA-KATA!
HAVE YOU GOT HINO-HARA ...?
...

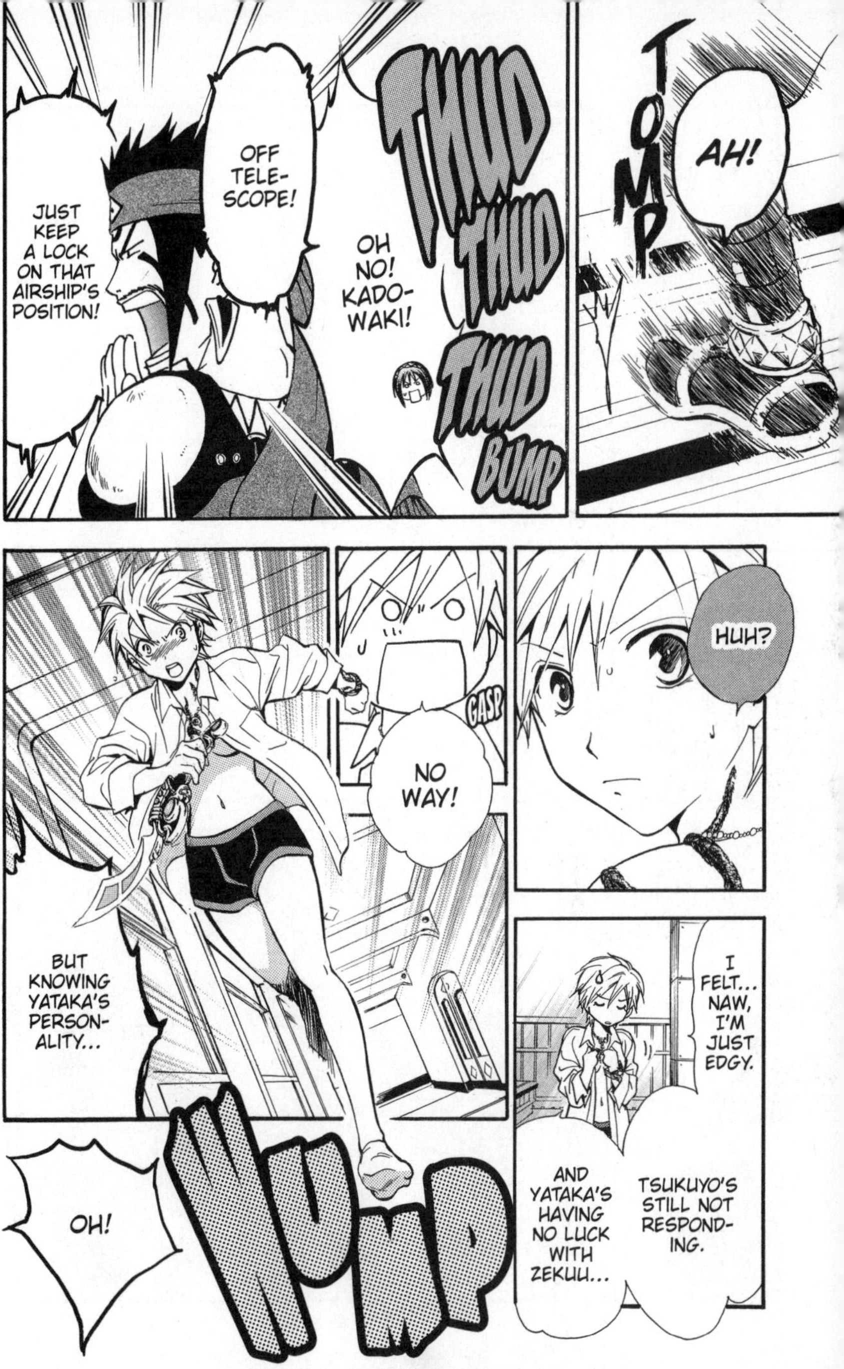
TOMP
AH!
THUD THUD
OH NO! KADOWAKI!
OFF TELESCOPE!
JUST KEEP A LOCK ON THAT AIRSHIP'S POSITION!
THUD BUMP
HUH?
I FELT... NAW, I'M JUST EDGY.
TSUKUYO'S STILL NOT RESPONDING.
AND YATAKA'S HAVING NO LUCK WITH ZEKUU...
GASP
NO WAY!
BUT KNOWING YATAKA'S PERSONALITY...
WUMP
OH!

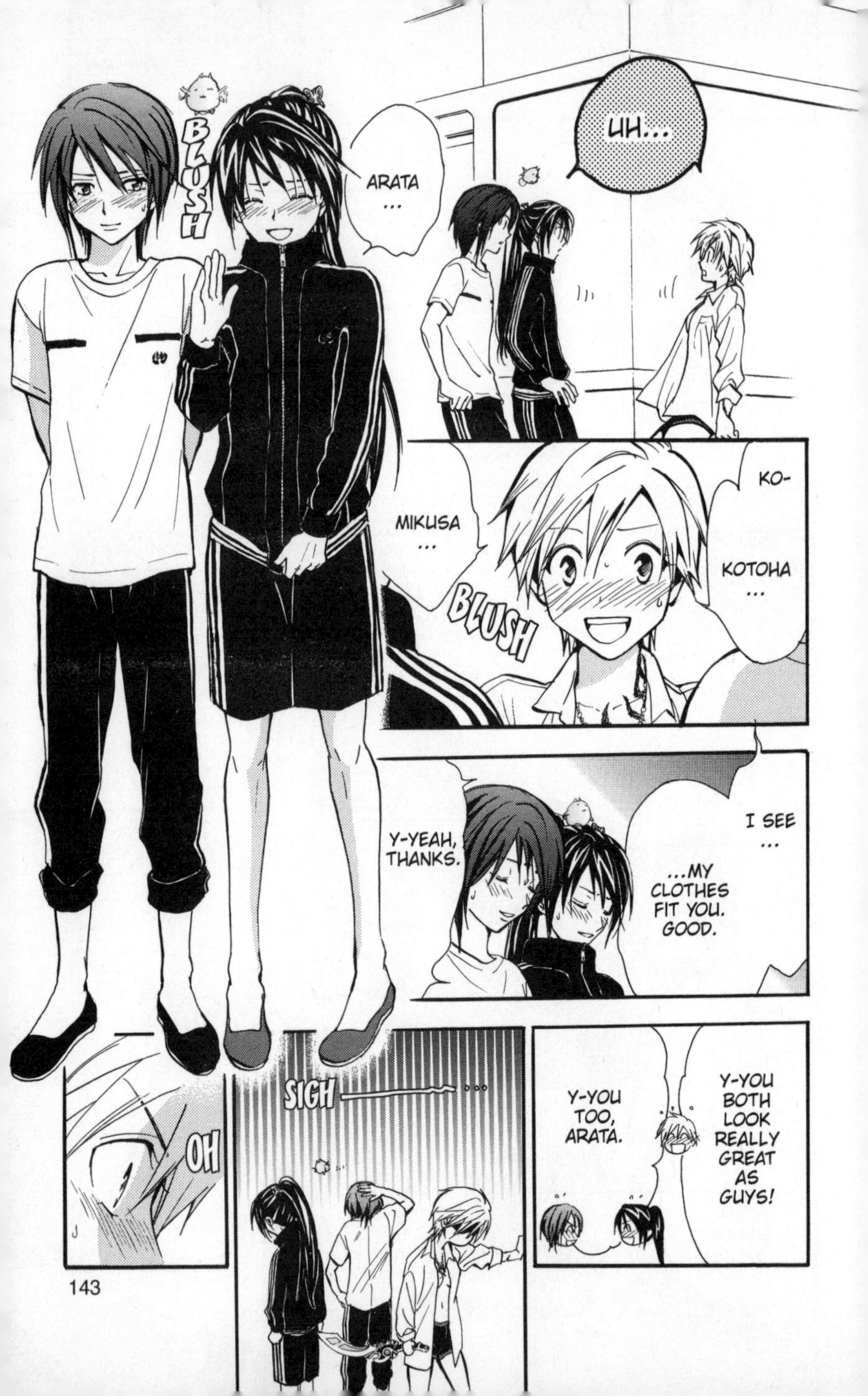
UH...
KO-
KOTOHA ...
MIKUSA ...
BLUSH
I SEE ...
...MY CLOTHES FIT YOU. GOOD.
Y-YEAH, THANKS.
BLUSH
ARATA ...
Y-YOU BOTH LOOK REALLY GREAT AS GUYS!
Y-YOU TOO, ARATA.
SIGH
OH

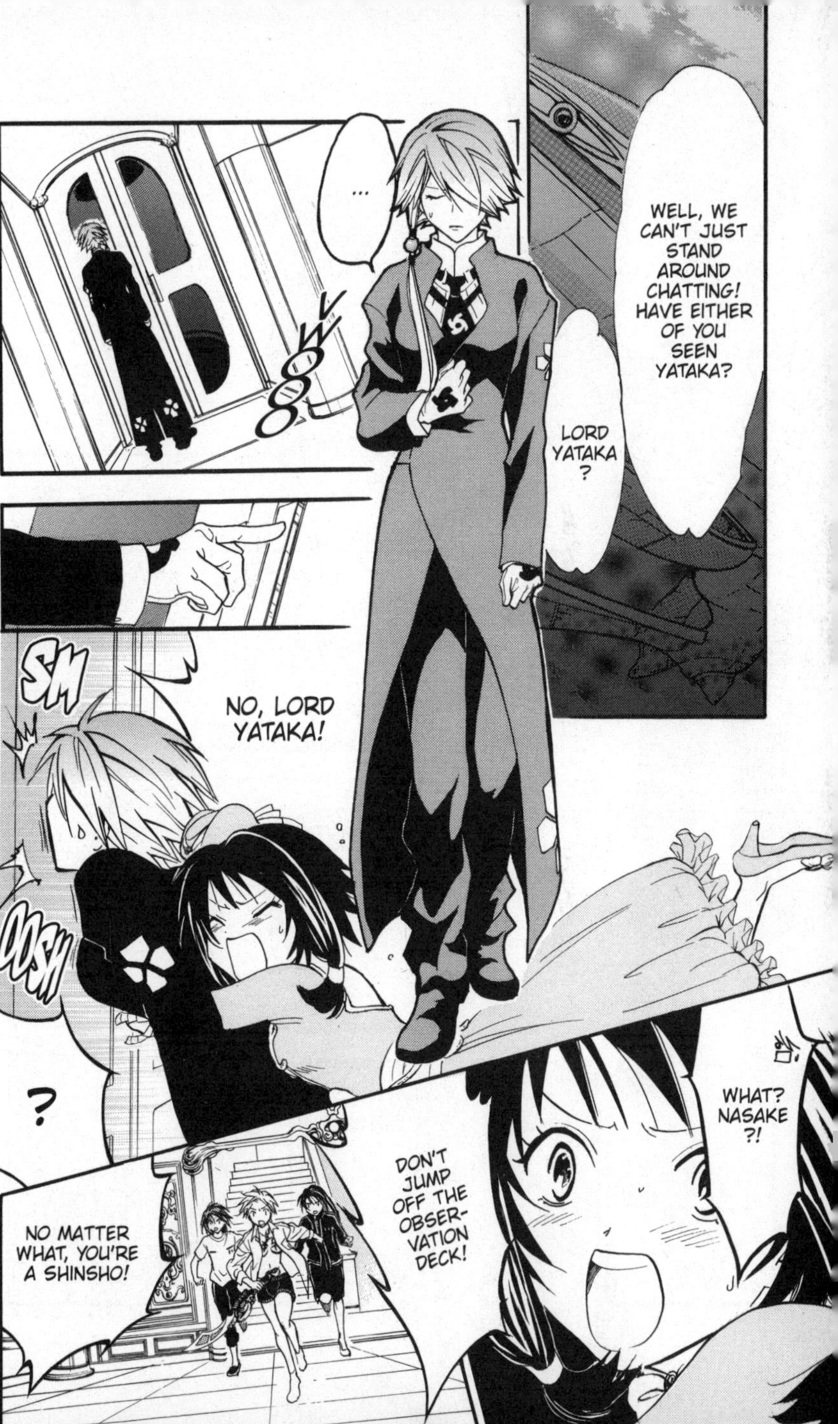
WELL, WE CAN'T JUST STAND AROUND CHATTING! HAVE EITHER OF YOU SEEN YATAKA?
LORD YATAKA?
...
VWOOO
SW
OOSH
NO, LORD YATAKA!
WHAT? NASAKE?!
DON'T JUMP OFF THE OBSER-VATION DECK!
NO MATTER WHAT, YOU'RE A SHINSHO!
?

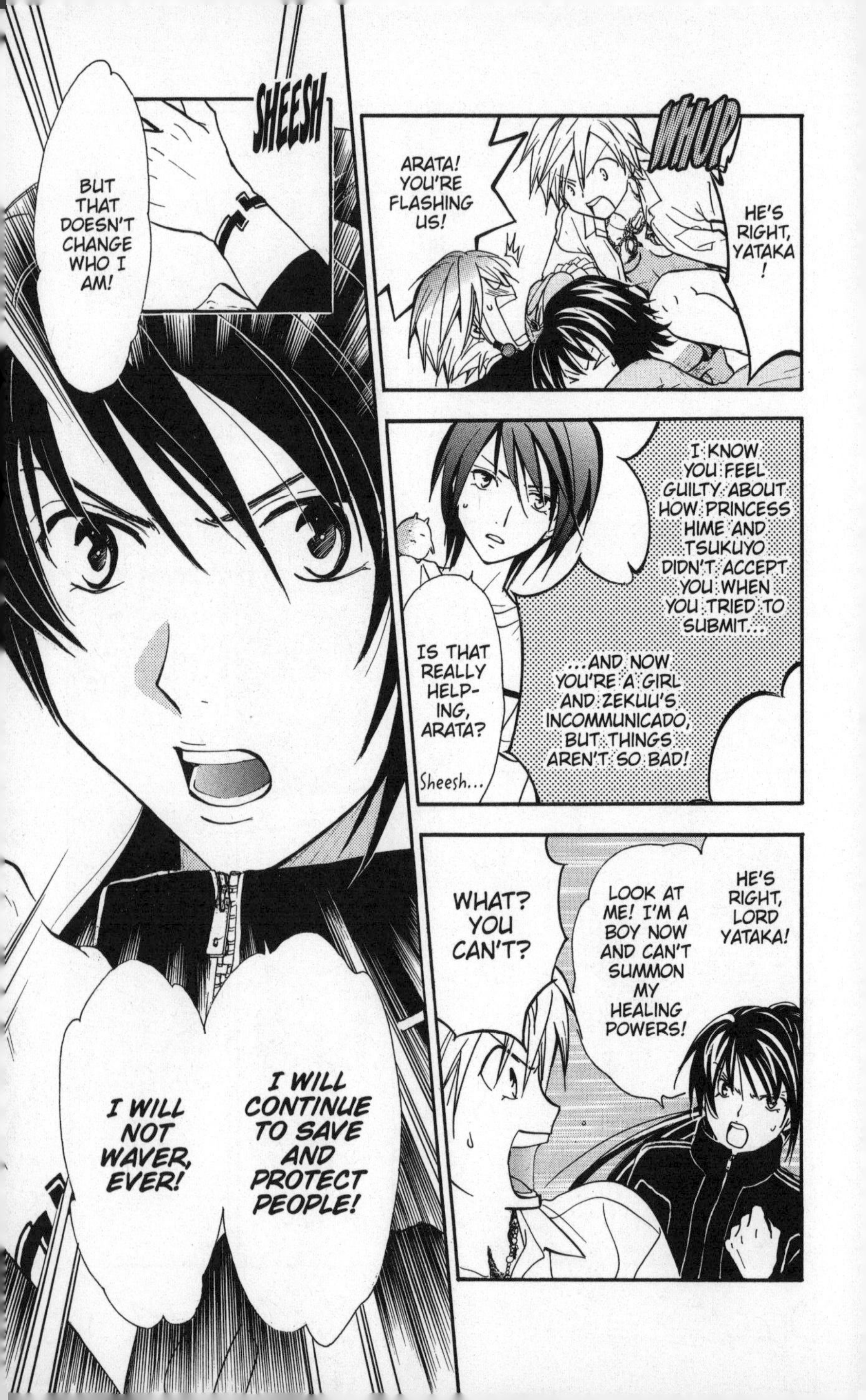
WHUP!
HE'S RIGHT, YATAKA!
ARATA! YOU'RE FLASHING US!
I KNOW YOU FEEL GUILTY ABOUT HOW PRINCESS HIME AND TSUKUYO DIDN'T ACCEPT YOU WHEN YOU TRIED TO SUBMIT...
...AND NOW YOU'RE A GIRL AND ZEKUU'S INCOMMUNICADO, BUT THINGS AREN'T SO BAD!
IS THAT REALLY HELPING, ARATA?
Sheesh...
HE'S RIGHT, LORD YATAKA!
LOOK AT ME! I'M A BOY NOW AND CAN'T SUMMON MY HEALING POWERS!
WHAT? YOU CAN'T?
SHEESH
BUT THAT DOESN'T CHANGE WHO I AM!
I WILL CONTINUE TO SAVE AND PROTECT PEOPLE!
I WILL NOT WAVER, EVER!

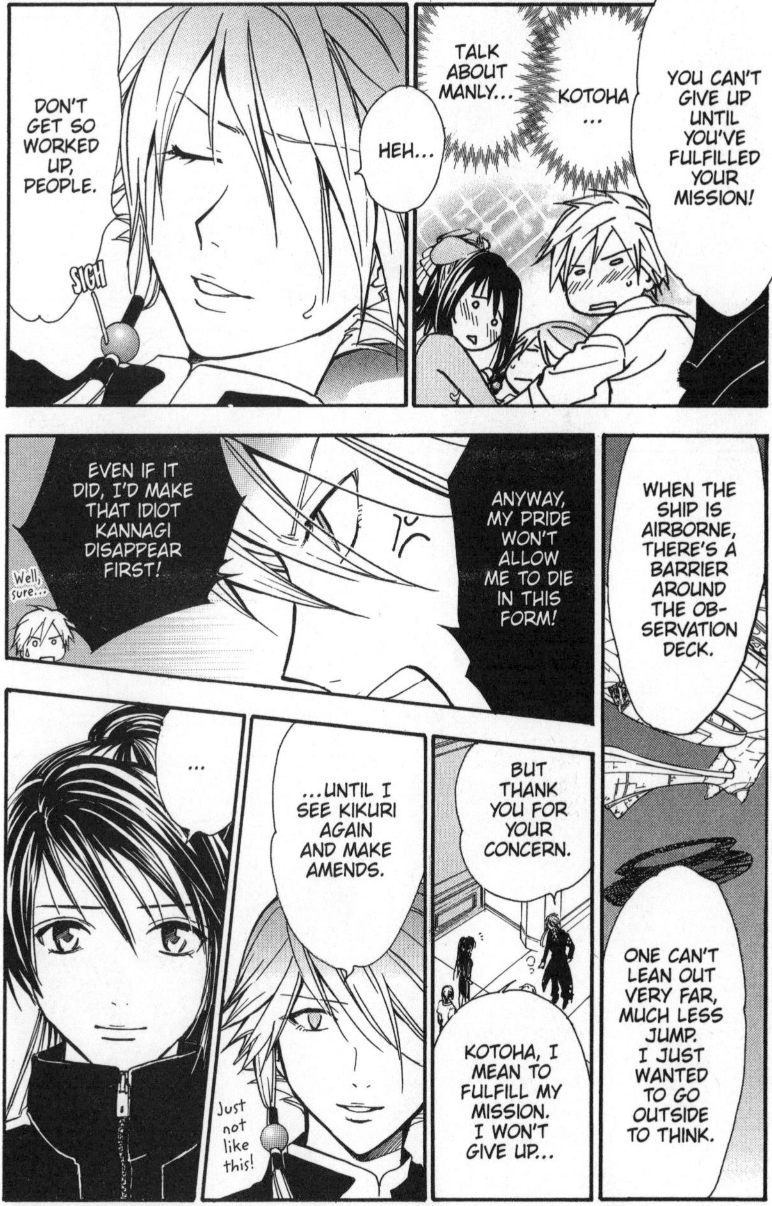
YOU CAN'T GIVE UP UNTIL YOU'VE FULFILLED YOUR MISSION!
KOTOHA ...
TALK ABOUT MANLY...
HEH...
DON'T GET SO WORKED UP, PEOPLE.
SIGH
WHEN THE SHIP IS AIRBORNE, THERE'S A BARRIER AROUND THE OB-SERVATION DECK.
ONE CAN'T LEAN OUT VERY FAR, MUCH LESS JUMP. I JUST WANTED TO GO OUTSIDE TO THINK.
ANYWAY, MY PRIDE WON'T ALLOW ME TO DIE IN THIS FORM!
EVEN IF IT DID, I'D MAKE THAT IDIOT KANNAGI DISAPPEAR FIRST!
Well, sure...
BUT THANK YOU FOR YOUR CONCERN.
KOTOHA, I MEAN TO FULFILL MY MISSION. I WON'T GIVE UP...
...UNTIL I SEE KIKURI AGAIN AND MAKE AMENDS.
Just not like this!
...

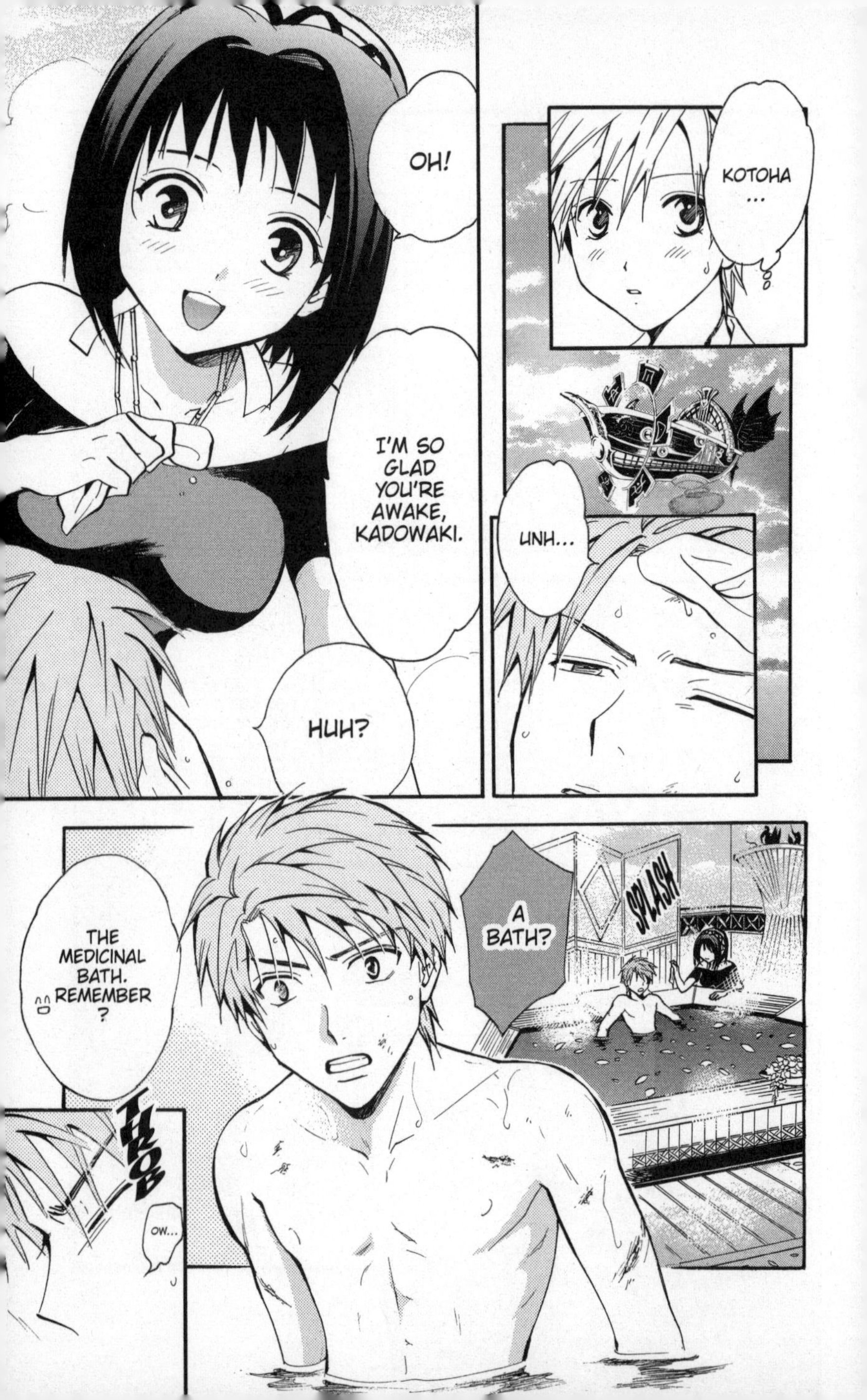
KOTOHA ...
UNH...
OH!
I'M SO GLAD YOU'RE AWAKE, KADOWAKI.
HUH?
A BATH?
SPLASH
THE MEDICINAL BATH. REMEMBER?
THROB
OW...

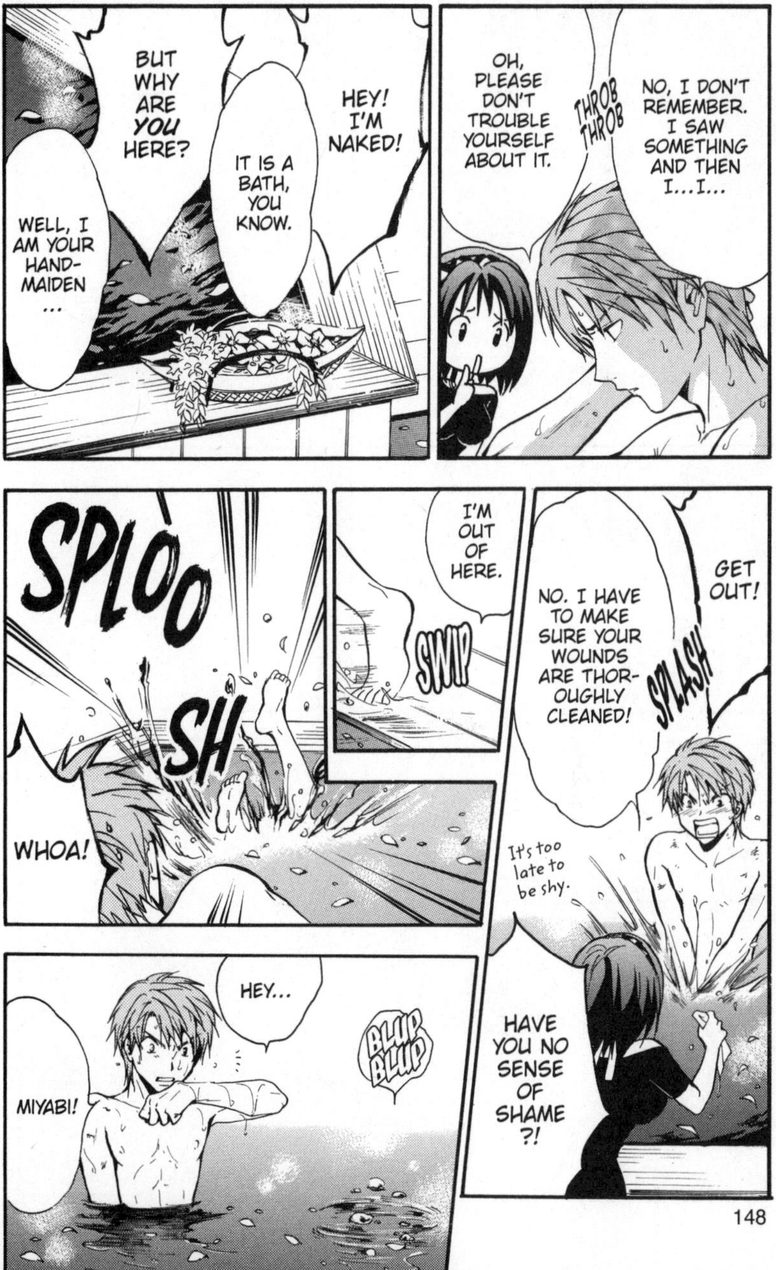
NO, I DON'T REMEMBER. I SAW SOMETHING AND THEN I...I...
THROB THROB
OH, PLEASE DON'T TROUBLE YOURSELF ABOUT IT.
HEY! I'M NAKED!
IT IS A BATH, YOU KNOW.
BUT WHY ARE *YOU* HERE?
WELL, I AM YOUR HAND-MAIDEN...
GET OUT!
SPLASH
NO. I HAVE TO MAKE SURE YOUR WOUNDS ARE THOR-OUGHLY CLEANED!
It's too late to be shy.
HAVE YOU NO SENSE OF SHAME?!
I'M OUT OF HERE.
SWIP
SPLOO
SH
WHOA!
BLUP BLUP
HEY...
MIYABI!

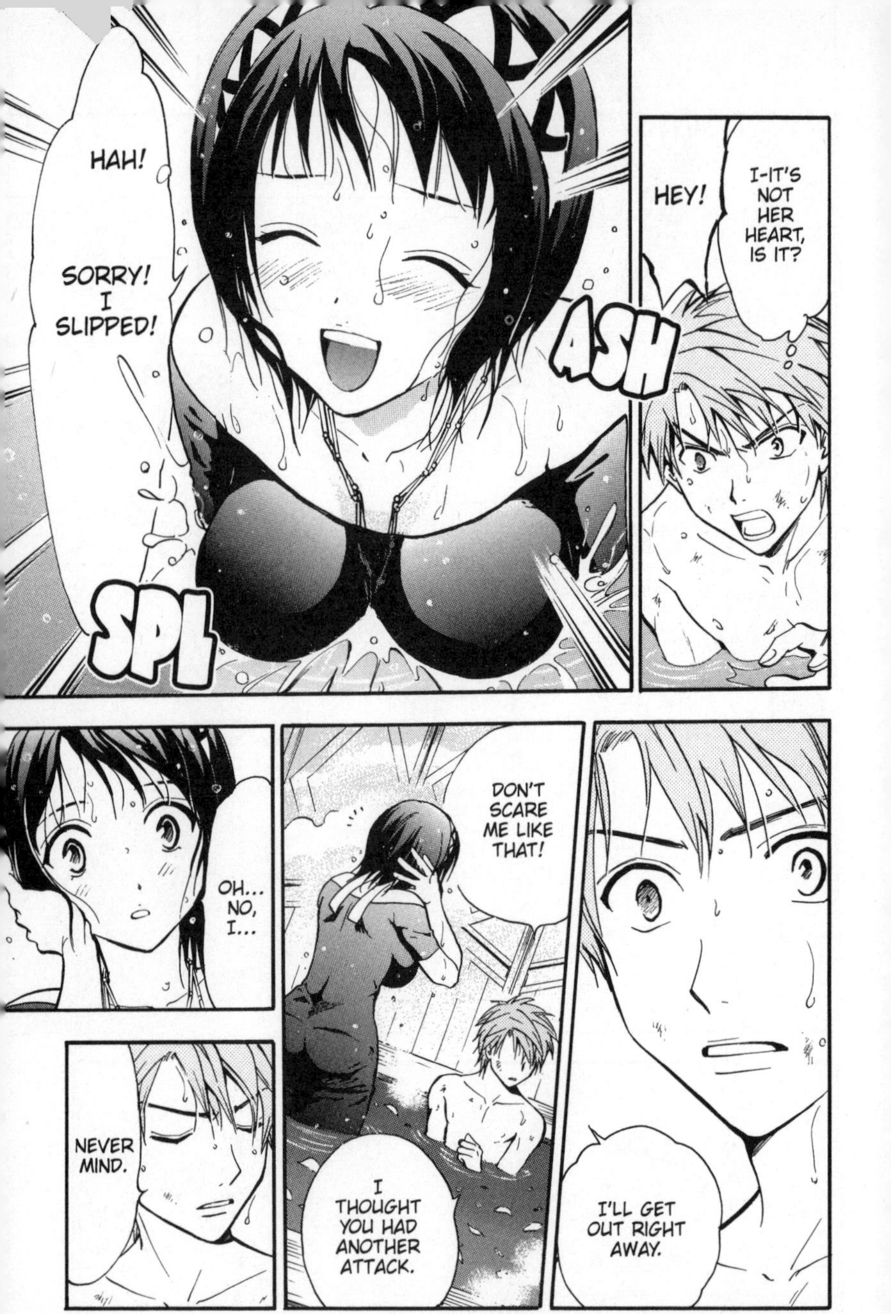
I-IT'S NOT HER HEART, IS IT?
HEY!
SPL
ASH
HAH!
SORRY! I SLIPPED!
I'LL GET OUT RIGHT AWAY.
DON'T SCARE ME LIKE THAT!
I THOUGHT YOU HAD ANOTHER ATTACK.
OH... NO, I...
NEVER MIND.

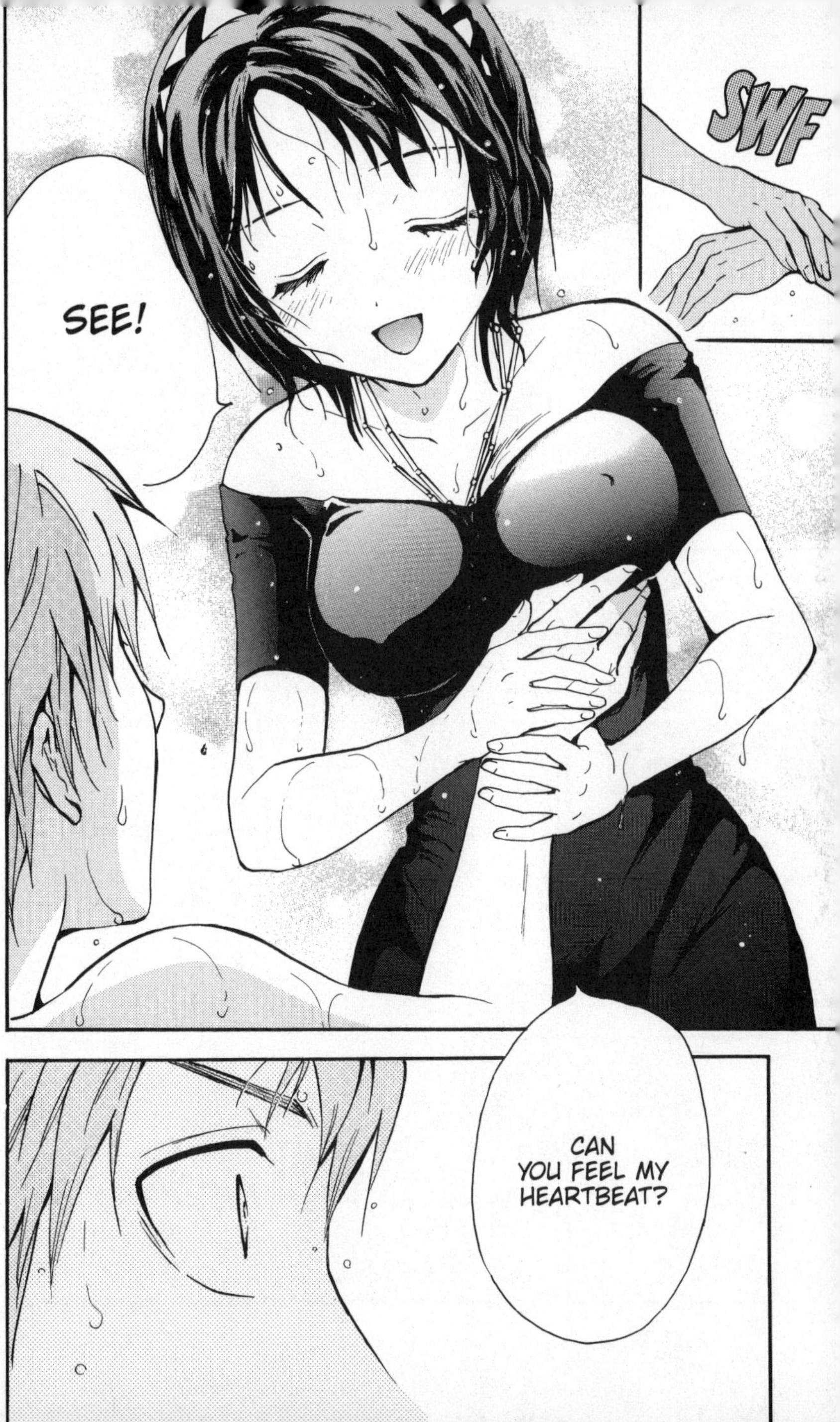
SWF
SEE!
CAN YOU FEEL MY HEARTBEAT?

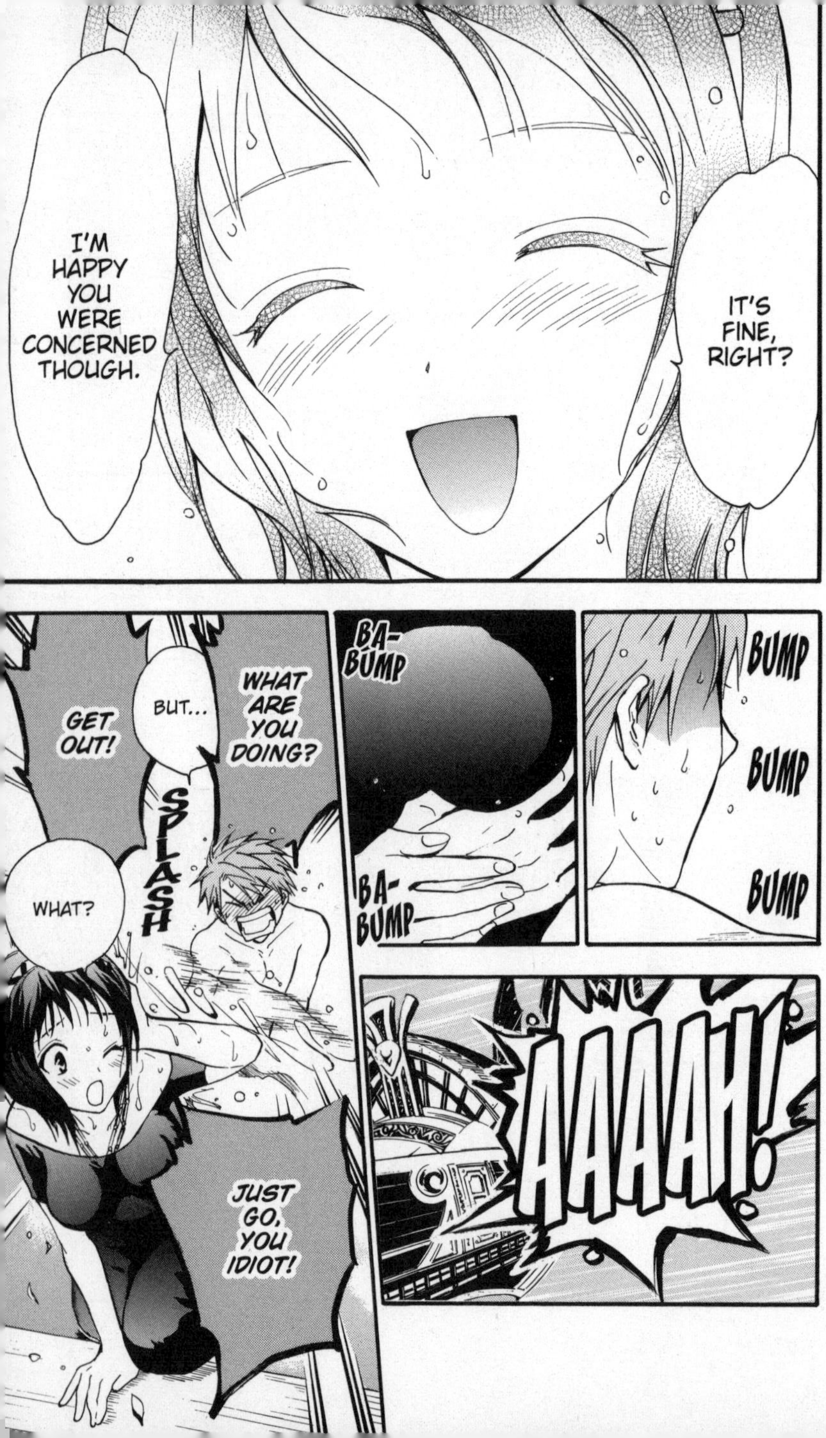

IT'S FINE, RIGHT?
I'M HAPPY YOU WERE CONCERNED THOUGH.
BUMP
BUMP
BUMP
BA-BUMP
BA-BUMP
AAAAH!
WHAT ARE YOU DOING?
BUT...
GET OUT!
SPLASH
WHAT?
JUST GO, YOU IDIOT!

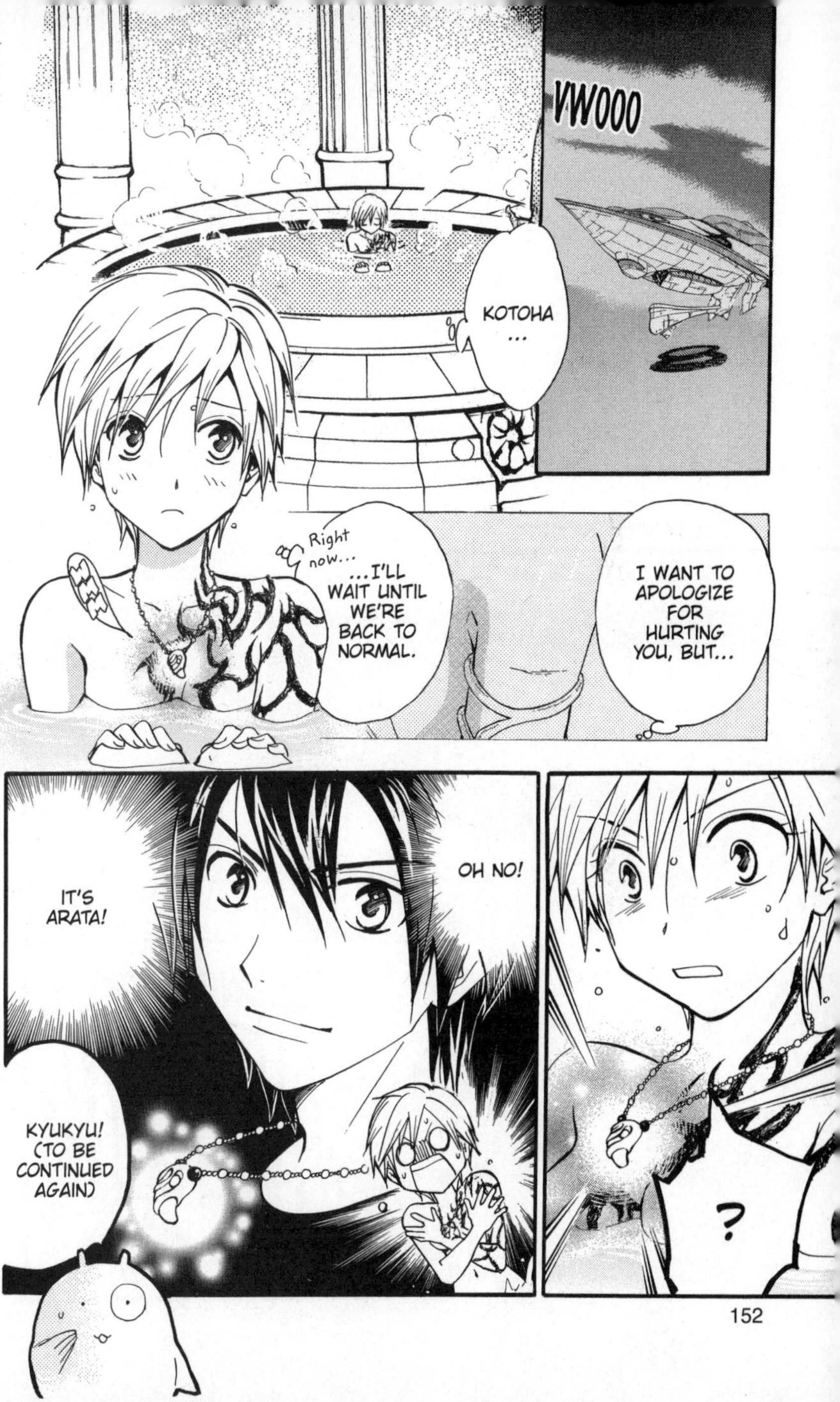
VWOOO
KOTOHA ...
I WANT TO APOLOGIZE FOR HURTING YOU, BUT...
...I'LL WAIT UNTIL WE'RE BACK TO NORMAL.
Right now...
?
OH NO!
IT'S ARATA!
KYUKYU! (TO BE CONTINUED AGAIN)

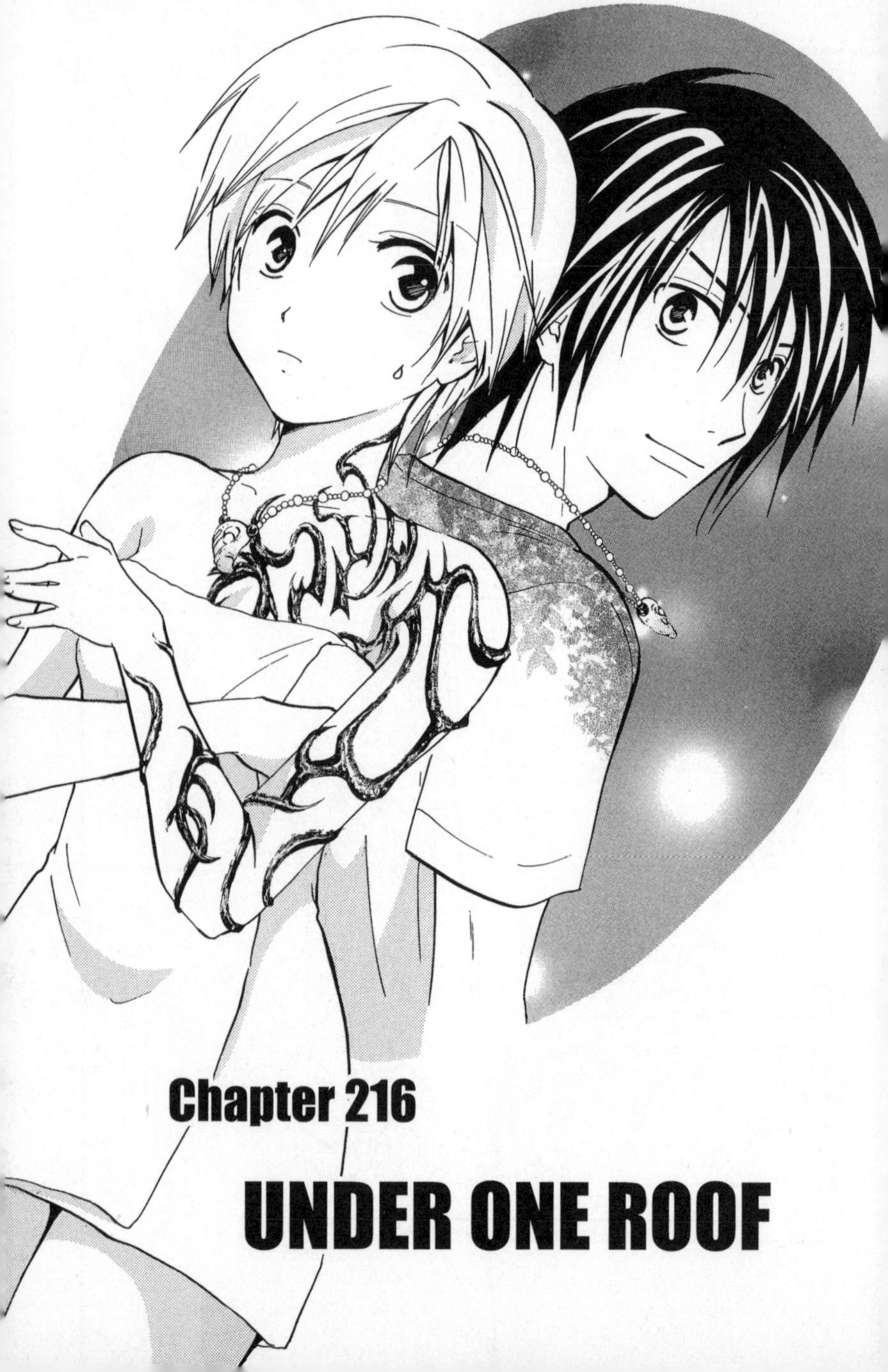

Chapter 216

UNDER ONE ROOF

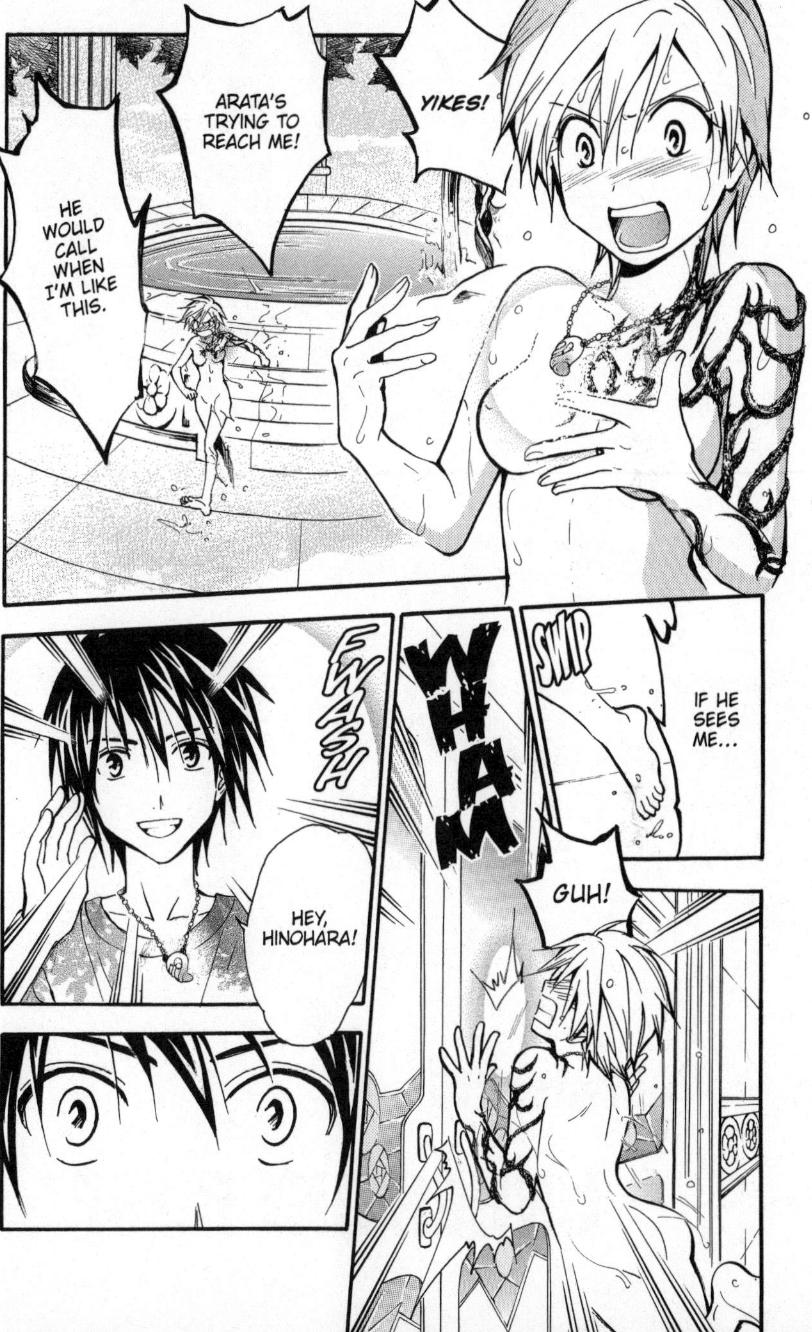
YIKES!
ARATA'S TRYING TO REACH ME!
HE WOULD CALL WHEN I'M LIKE THIS.
SWIP
IF HE SEES ME...
GUH!
WHAM
FWASH
HEY, HINOHARA!

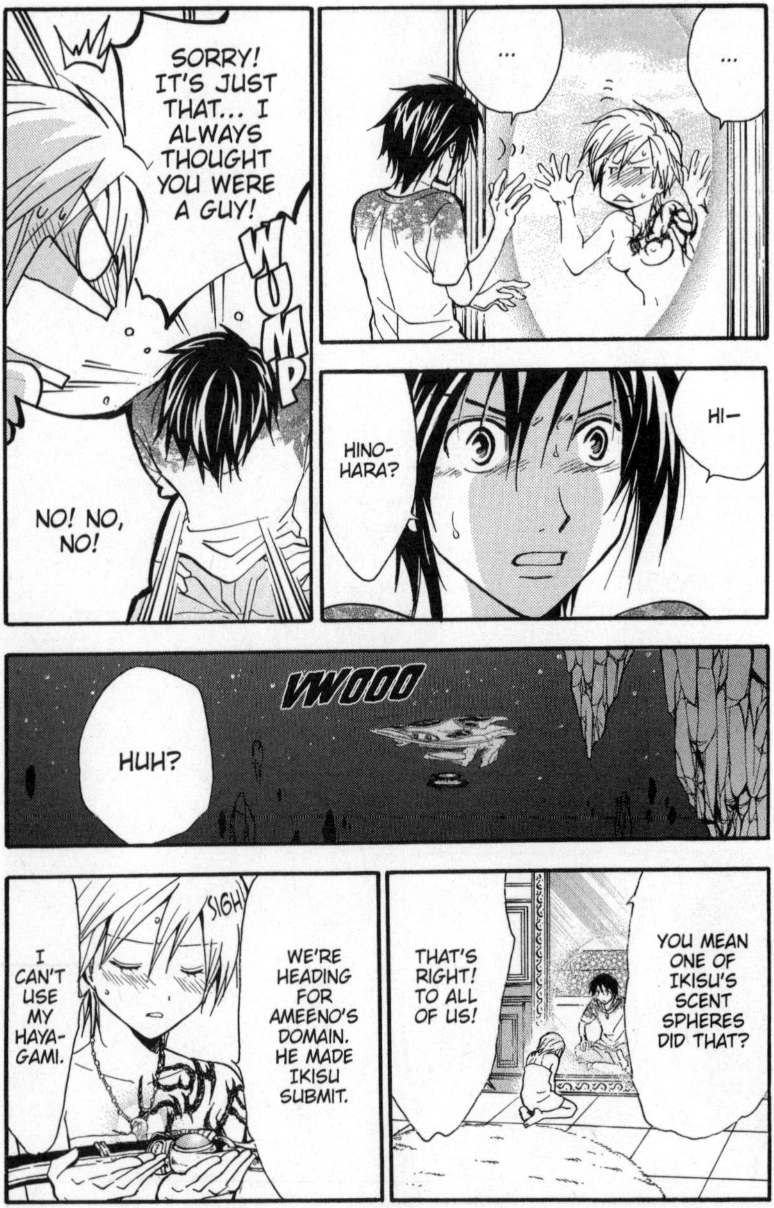
...
...
HI—
HINO-HARA?
SORRY! IT'S JUST THAT... I ALWAYS THOUGHT YOU WERE A GUY!
WUMP
NO! NO, NO!
VWOOO
HUH?
YOU MEAN ONE OF IKISU'S SCENT SPHERES DID THAT?
THAT'S RIGHT! TO ALL OF US!
WE'RE HEADING FOR AMEENO'S DOMAIN. HE MADE IKISU SUBMIT.
SIGH
I CAN'T USE MY HAYA-GAMI.

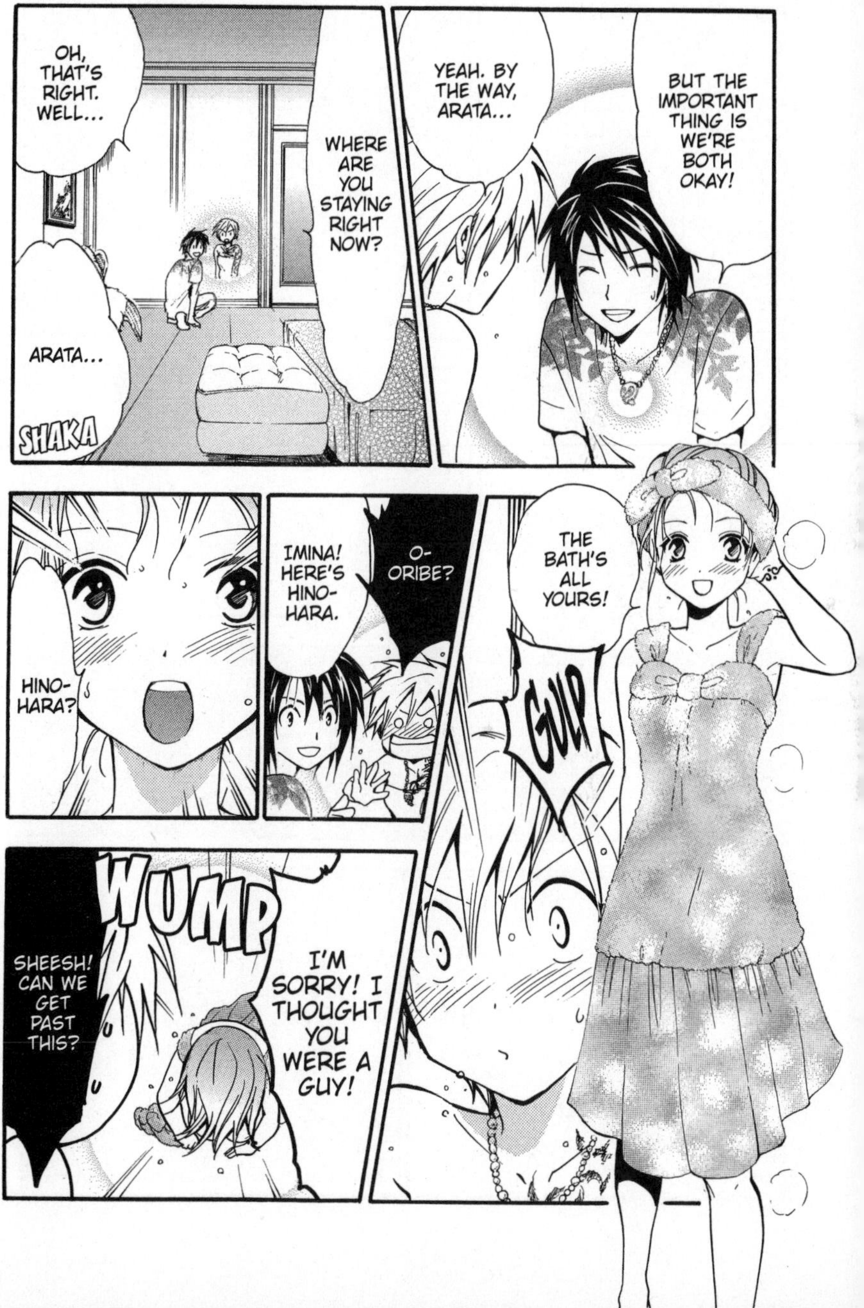
BUT THE IMPORTANT THING IS WE'RE BOTH OKAY!
YEAH. BY THE WAY, ARATA...
WHERE ARE YOU STAYING RIGHT NOW?
OH, THAT'S RIGHT. WELL...
ARATA...
SHAKA
THE BATH'S ALL YOURS!
GULP
O-ORIBE?
IMINA! HERE'S HINO-HARA.
HINO-HARA?
I'M SORRY! I THOUGHT YOU WERE A GUY!
WUMP
SHEESH! CAN WE GET PAST THIS?

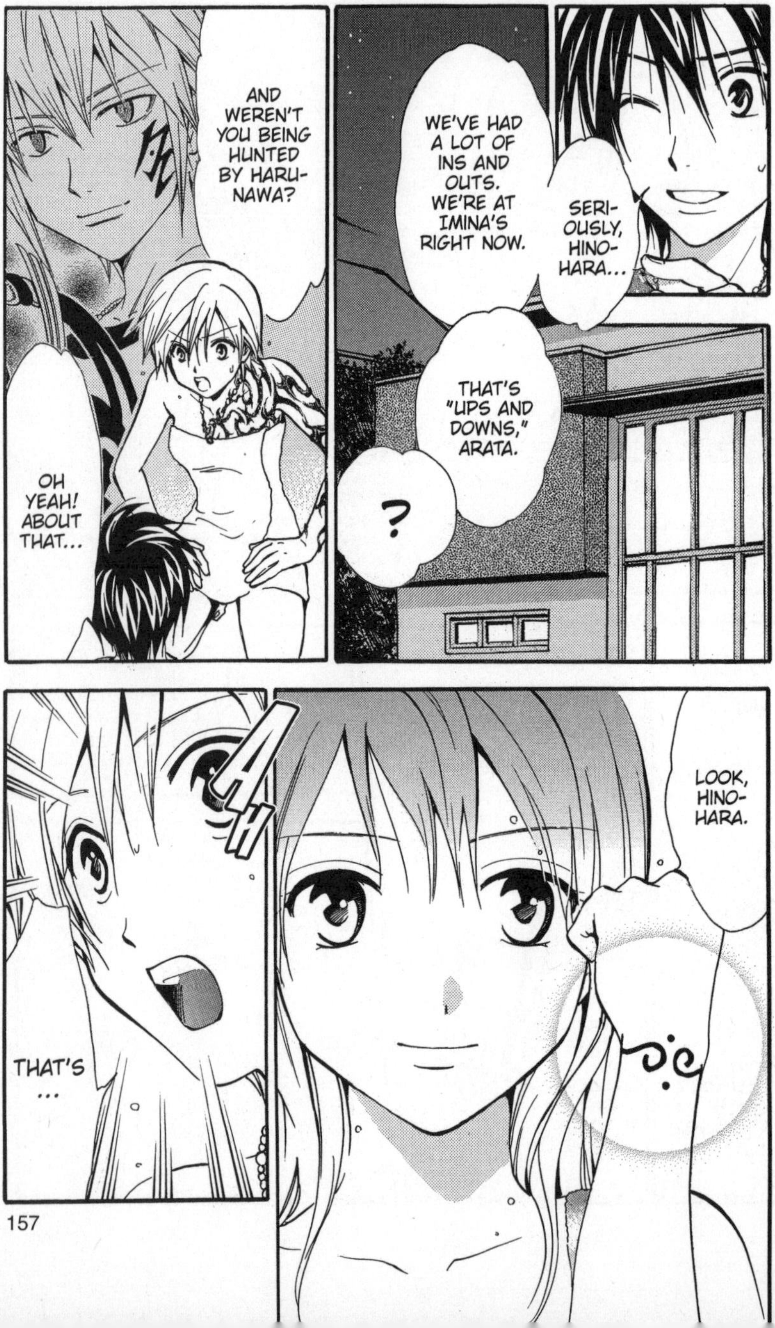

SERI-
OUSLY,
HINO-
HARA...
WE'VE HAD
A LOT OF
INS AND
OUTS.
WE'RE AT
IMINA'S
RIGHT NOW.
THAT'S
"UPS AND
DOWNS,"
ARATA.
?
AND
WEREN'T
YOU BEING
HUNTED
BY HARU-
NAWA?
OH
YEAH!
ABOUT
THAT...
LOOK,
HINO-
HARA.
AH
THAT'S
...

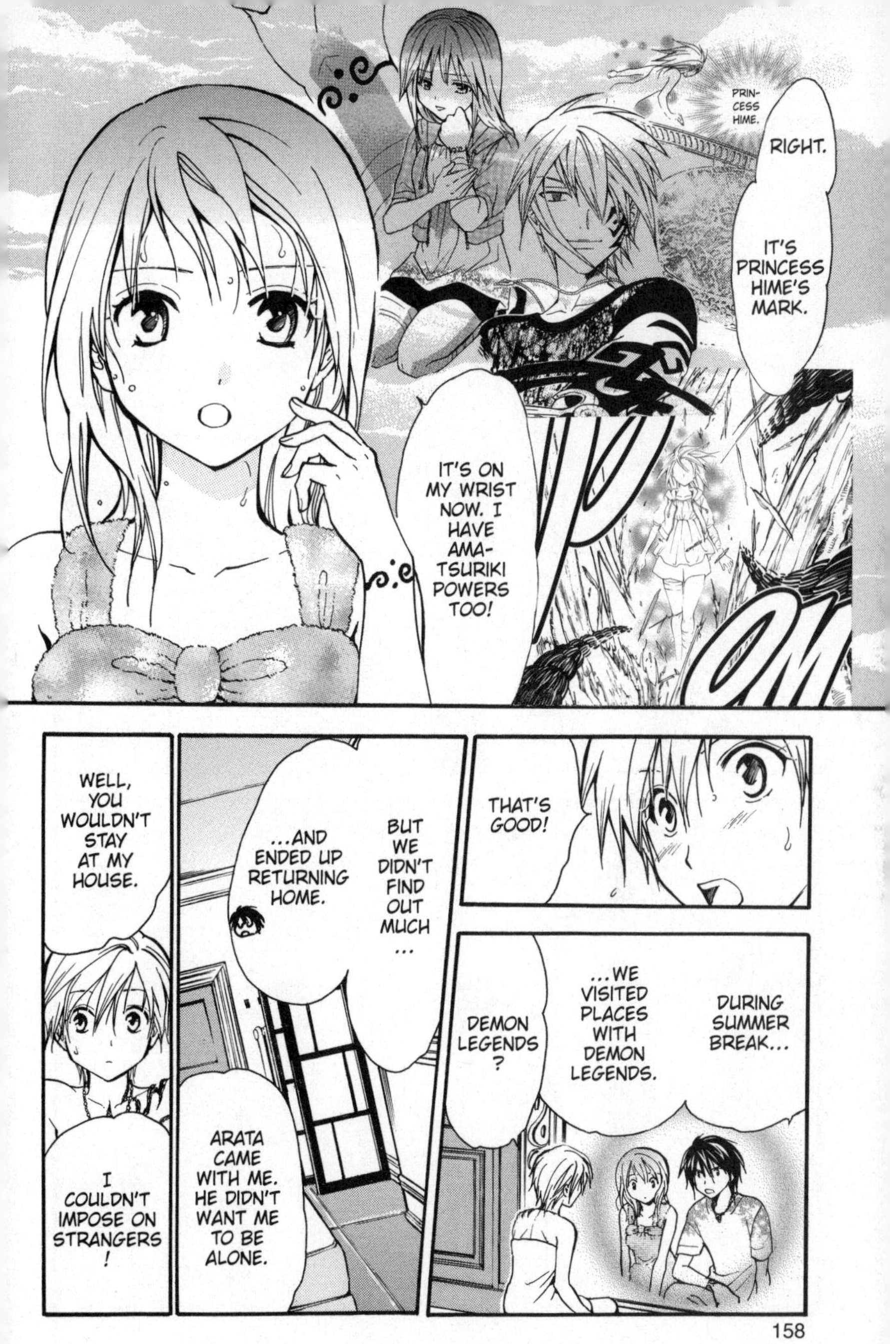
PRINCESS HIME.
RIGHT.
IT'S PRINCESS HIME'S MARK.
IT'S ON MY WRIST NOW. I HAVE AMATSURIKI POWERS TOO!
THAT'S GOOD!
DURING SUMMER BREAK...
...WE VISITED PLACES WITH DEMON LEGENDS.
DEMON LEGENDS?
BUT WE DIDN'T FIND OUT MUCH...
...AND ENDED UP RETURNING HOME.
ARATA CAME WITH ME. HE DIDN'T WANT ME TO BE ALONE.
WELL, YOU WOULDN'T STAY AT MY HOUSE.
I COULDN'T IMPOSE ON STRANGERS!

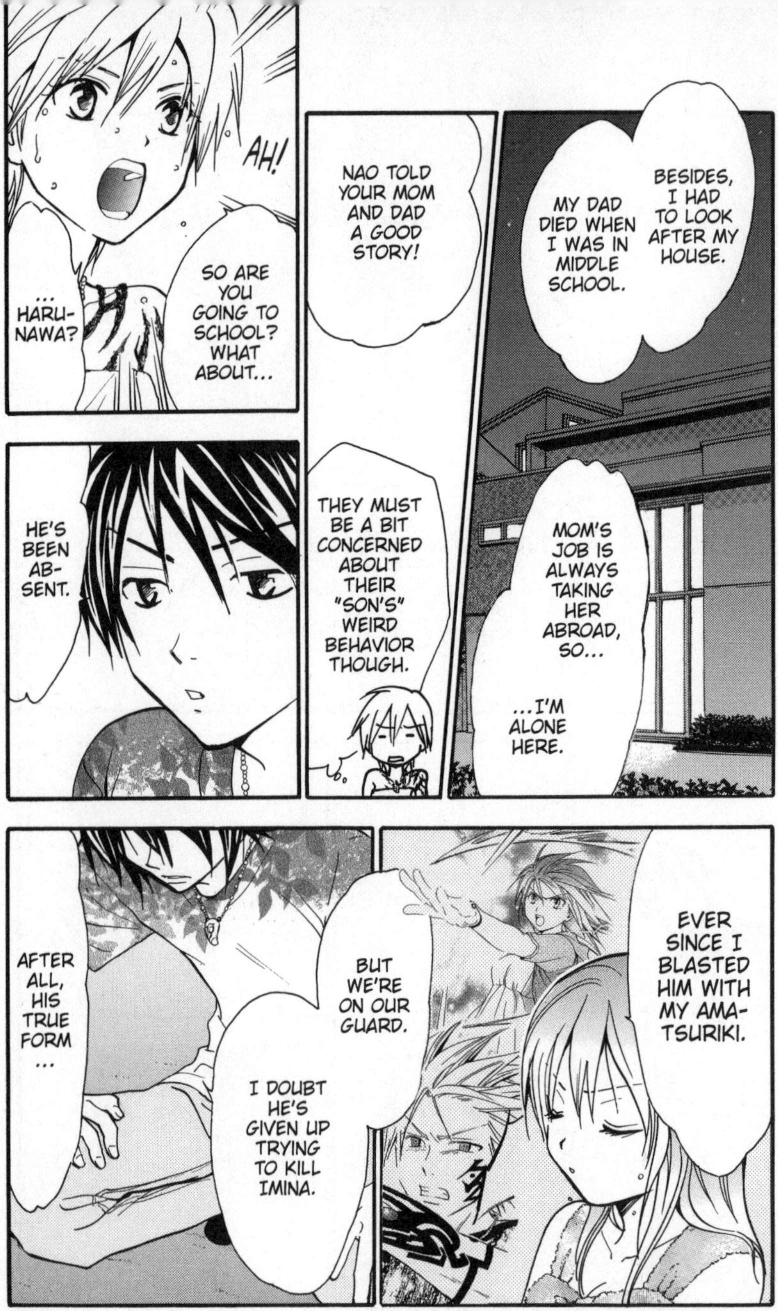
BESIDES, I HAD TO LOOK AFTER MY HOUSE.
MY DAD DIED WHEN I WAS IN MIDDLE SCHOOL.
MOM'S JOB IS ALWAYS TAKING HER ABROAD, SO...
...I'M ALONE HERE.
NAO TOLD YOUR MOM AND DAD A GOOD STORY!
THEY MUST BE A BIT CONCERNED ABOUT THEIR "SON'S" WEIRD BEHAVIOR THOUGH.
AH!
SO ARE YOU GOING TO SCHOOL? WHAT ABOUT...
... HARU-NAWA?
HE'S BEEN AB-SENT.
EVER SINCE I BLASTED HIM WITH MY AMA-TSURIKI.
BUT WE'RE ON OUR GUARD.
I DOUBT HE'S GIVEN UP TRYING TO KILL IMINA.
AFTER ALL, HIS TRUE FORM ...

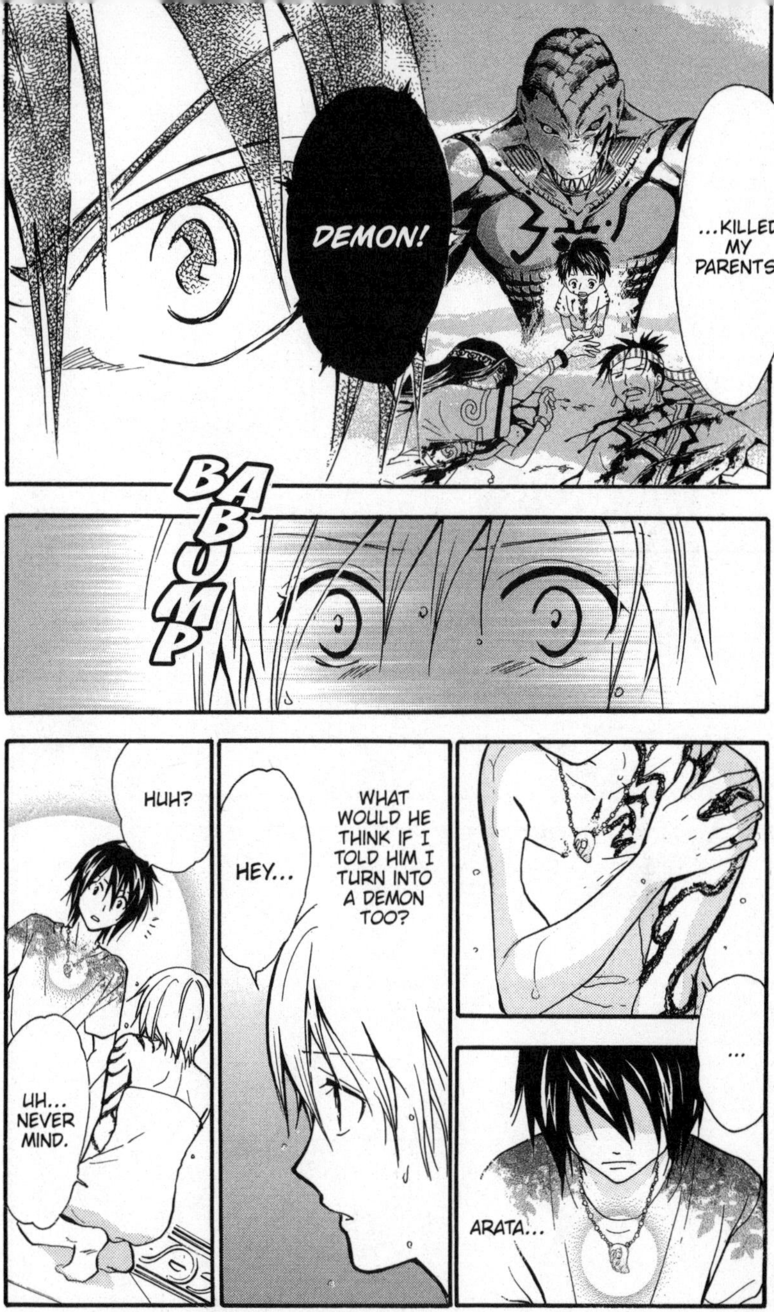
...KILLED MY PARENTS.
DEMON!
BA-BUMP
...
ARATA...
WHAT WOULD HE THINK IF I TOLD HIM I TURN INTO A DEMON TOO?
HEY...
HUH?
UH... NEVER MIND.

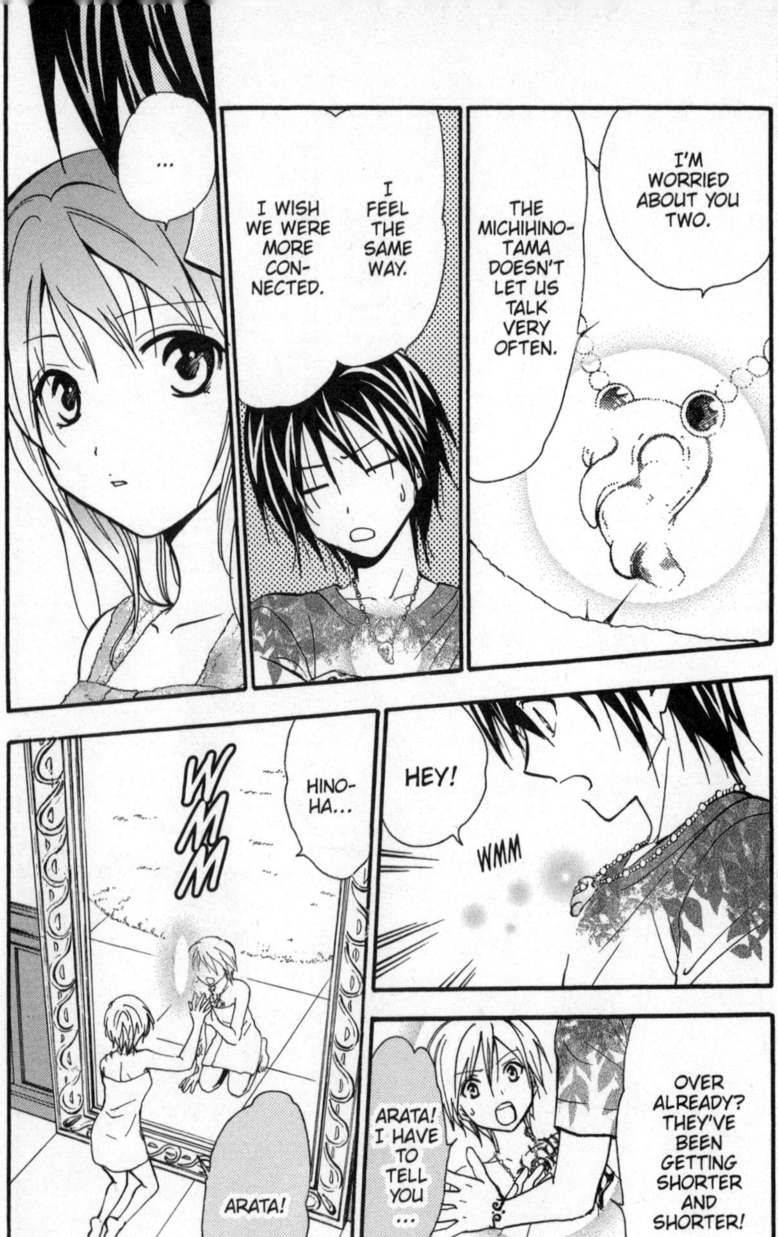
I'M WORRIED ABOUT YOU TWO.
THE MICHIHINO-TAMA DOESN'T LET US TALK VERY OFTEN.
I FEEL THE SAME WAY.
I WISH WE WERE MORE CON-NECTED.
...
HEY!
WMM
OVER ALREADY? THEY'VE BEEN GETTING SHORTER AND SHORTER!
ARATA! I HAVE TO TELL YOU ...
HINO-HA...
WMMM
ARATA!

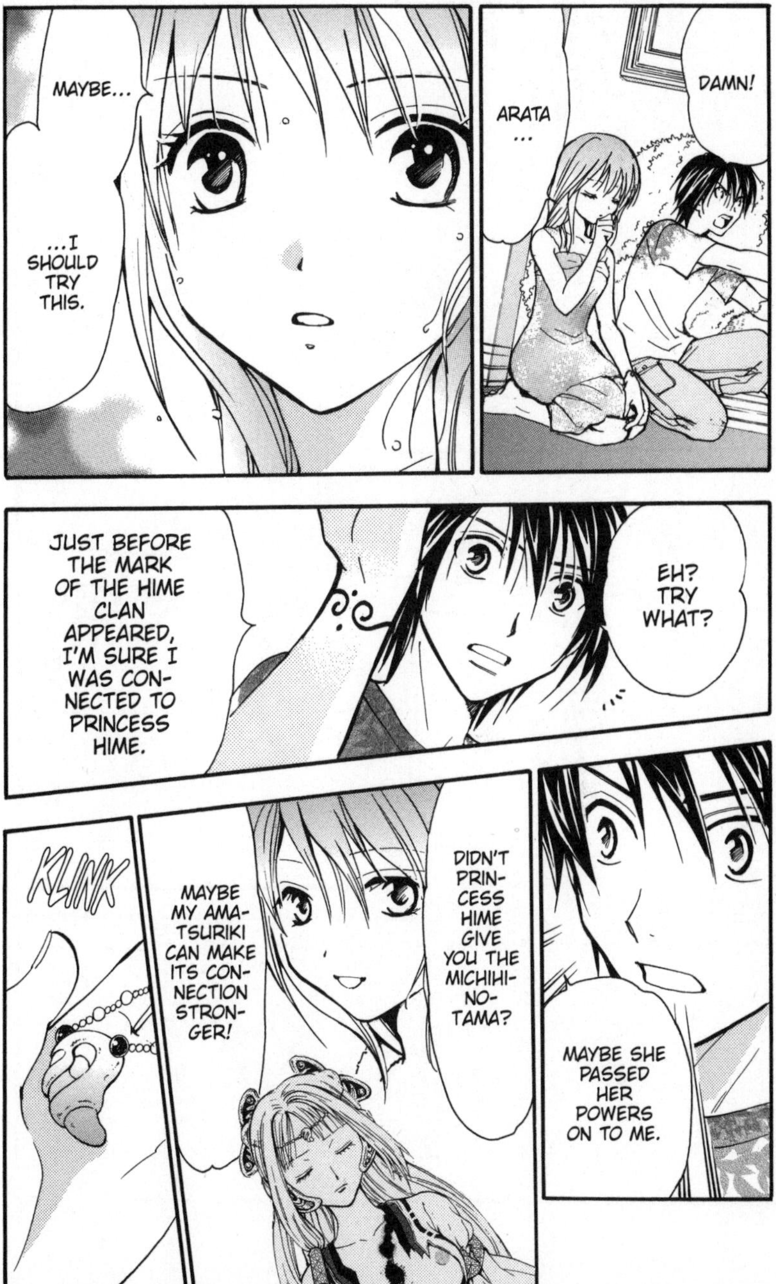
DAMN!
ARATA ...
MAYBE...
...I SHOULD TRY THIS.
EH? TRY WHAT?
JUST BEFORE THE MARK OF THE HIME CLAN APPEARED, I'M SURE I WAS CON-NECTED TO PRINCESS HIME.
MAYBE SHE PASSED HER POWERS ON TO ME.
DIDN'T PRIN-CESS HIME GIVE YOU THE MICHIHI-NO-TAMA?
MAYBE MY AMA-TSURIKI CAN MAKE ITS CON-NECTION STRON-GER!
KLINK

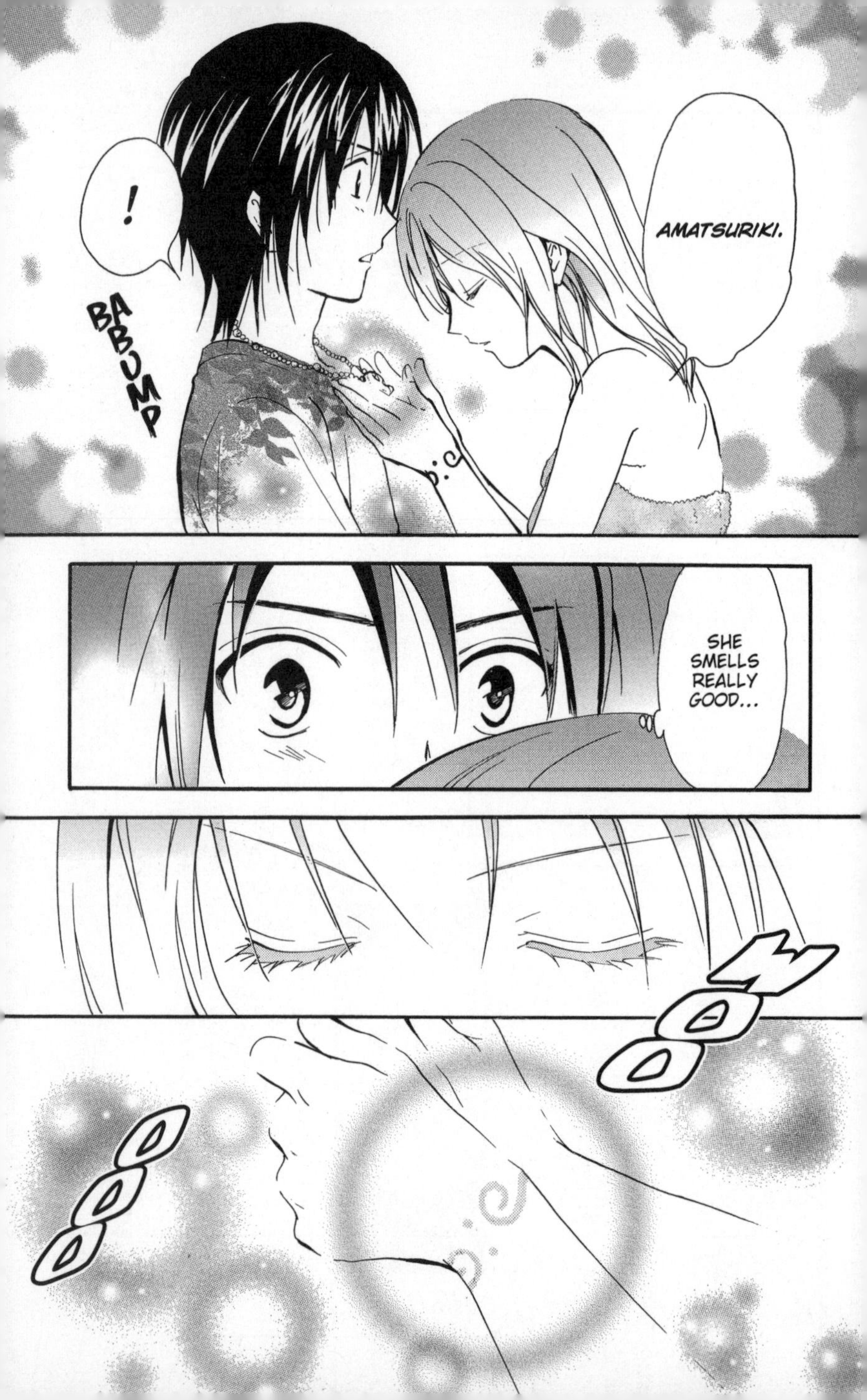
AMATSURIKI.
!
BABUMP
SHE SMELLS REALLY GOOD...
WOOO
OOOO

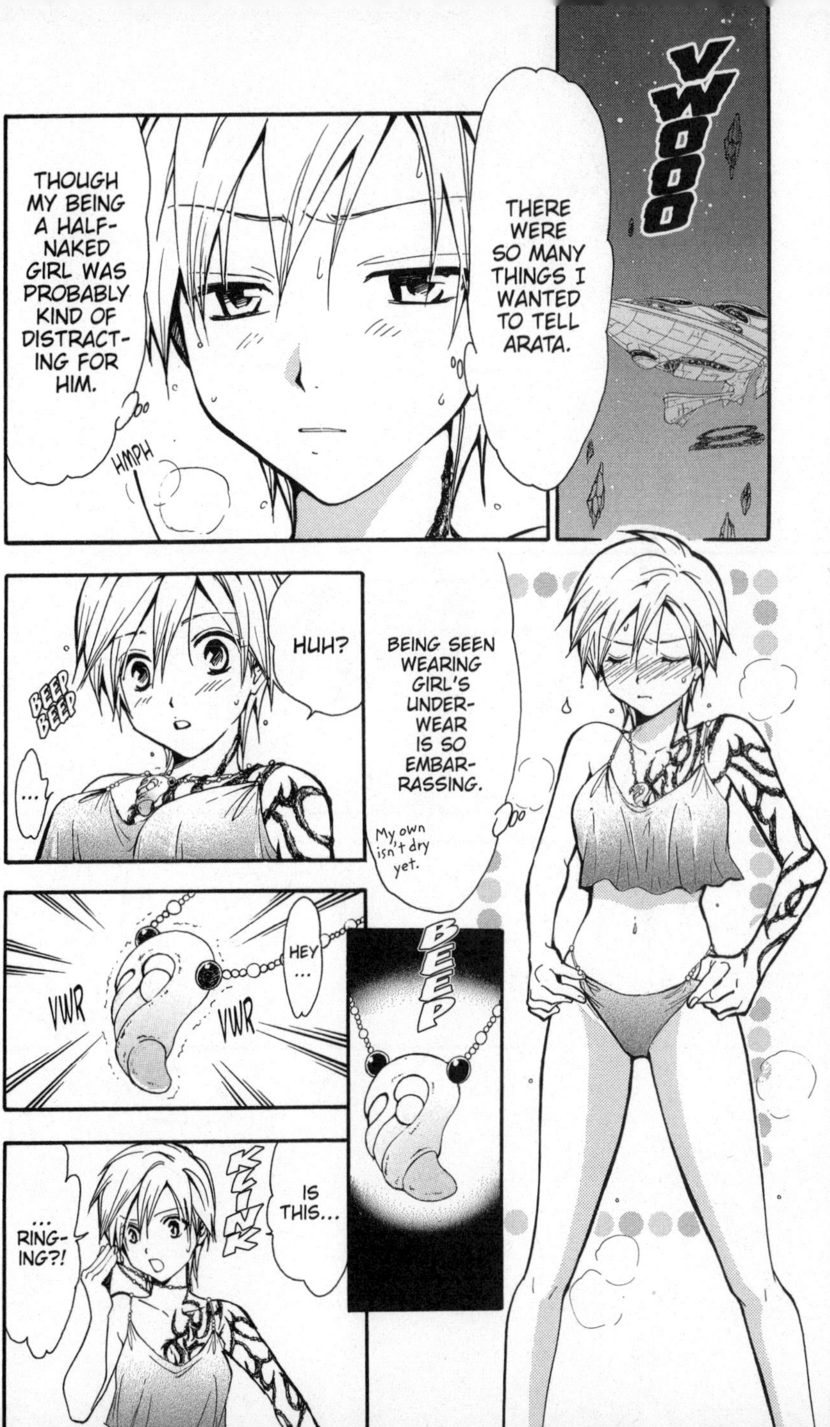
VWOOO
THERE WERE SO MANY THINGS I WANTED TO TELL ARATA.
THOUGH MY BEING A HALF-NAKED GIRL WAS PROBABLY KIND OF DISTRACTING FOR HIM.
HMPH
BEING SEEN WEARING GIRL'S UNDERWEAR IS SO EMBARRASSING.
My own isn't dry yet.
HUH?
BEEP BEEP
...
BEEP
HEY...
VWR
VWR
IS THIS...
KLINK
...RINGING?!

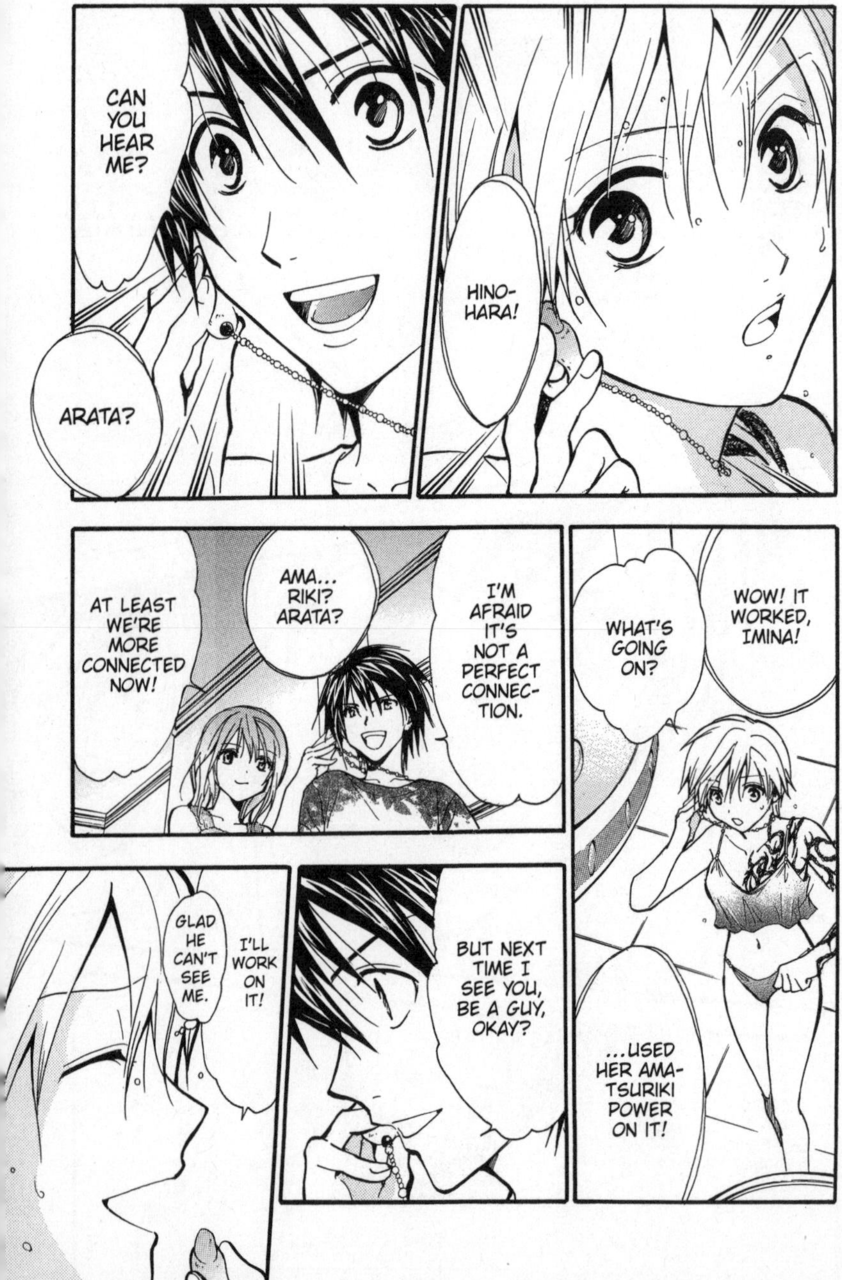
HINO-HARA!
CAN YOU HEAR ME?
ARATA?
WOW! IT WORKED, IMINA!
WHAT'S GOING ON?
...USED HER AMA-TSURIKI POWER ON IT!
I'M AFRAID IT'S NOT A PERFECT CONNEC-TION.
AMA... RIKI? ARATA?
AT LEAST WE'RE MORE CONNECTED NOW!
BUT NEXT TIME I SEE YOU, BE A GUY, OKAY?
I'LL WORK ON IT!
GLAD HE CAN'T SEE ME.

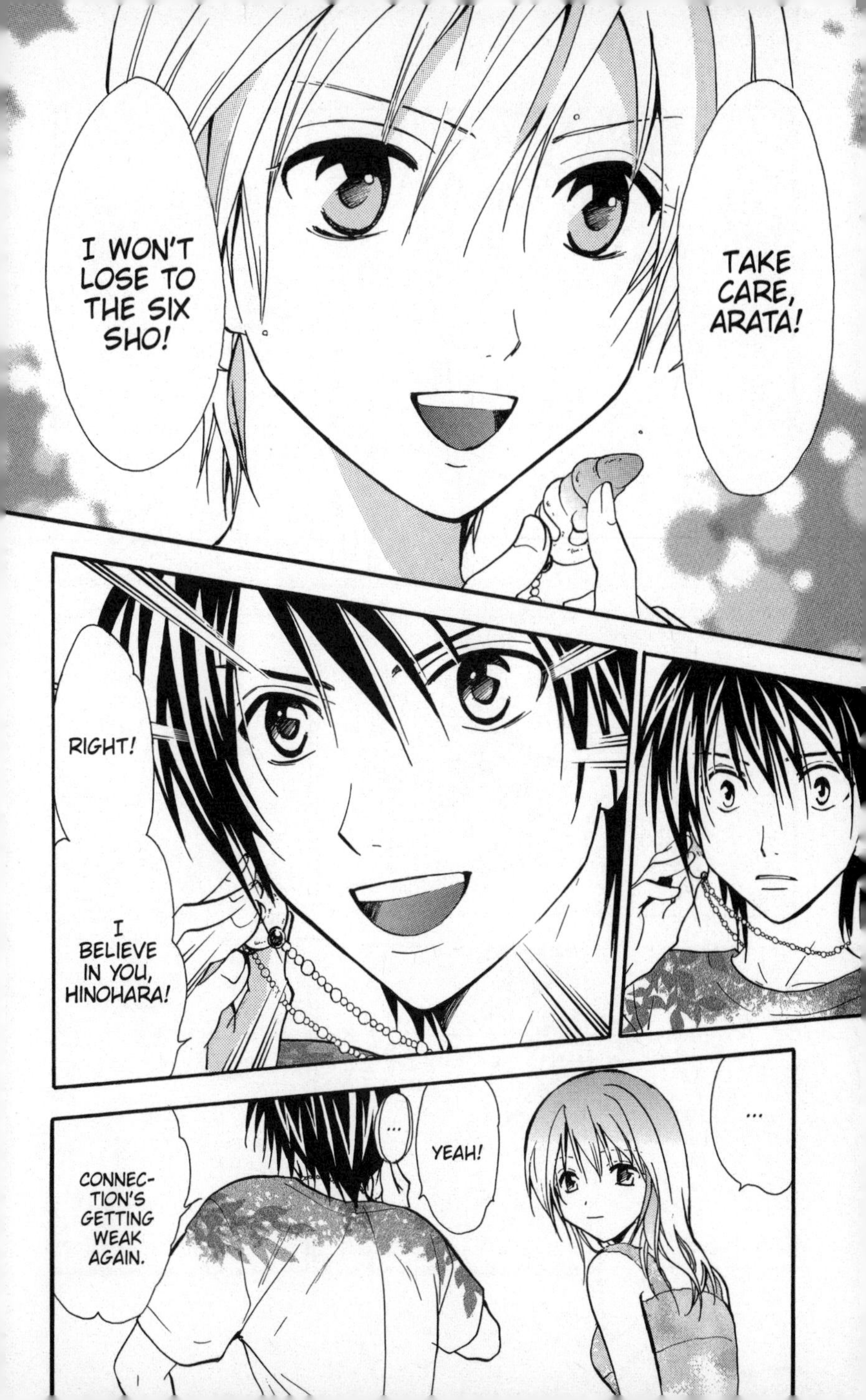
TAKE CARE, ARATA!
I WON'T LOSE TO THE SIX SHO!
RIGHT!
I BELIEVE IN YOU, HINOHARA!
...
... YEAH!
CONNEC-TION'S GETTING WEAK AGAIN.

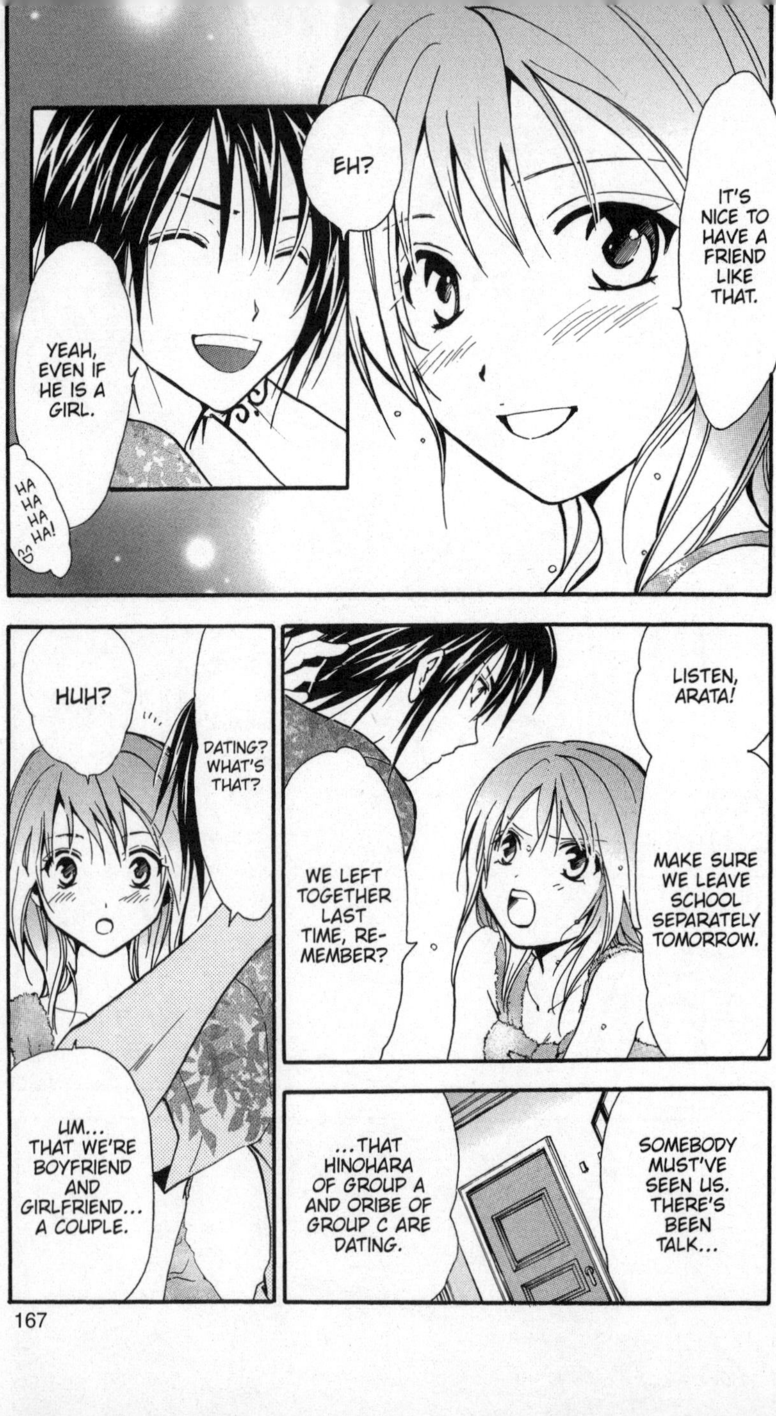
IT'S NICE TO HAVE A FRIEND LIKE THAT.
EH?
YEAH, EVEN IF HE IS A GIRL.
HA HA HA HA!
LISTEN, ARATA!
MAKE SURE WE LEAVE SCHOOL SEPARATELY TOMORROW.
WE LEFT TOGETHER LAST TIME, REMEMBER?
SOMEBODY MUST'VE SEEN US. THERE'S BEEN TALK...
...THAT HINOHARA OF GROUP A AND ORIBE OF GROUP C ARE DATING.
DATING? WHAT'S THAT?
HUH?
UM... THAT WE'RE BOYFRIEND AND GIRLFRIEND... A COUPLE.

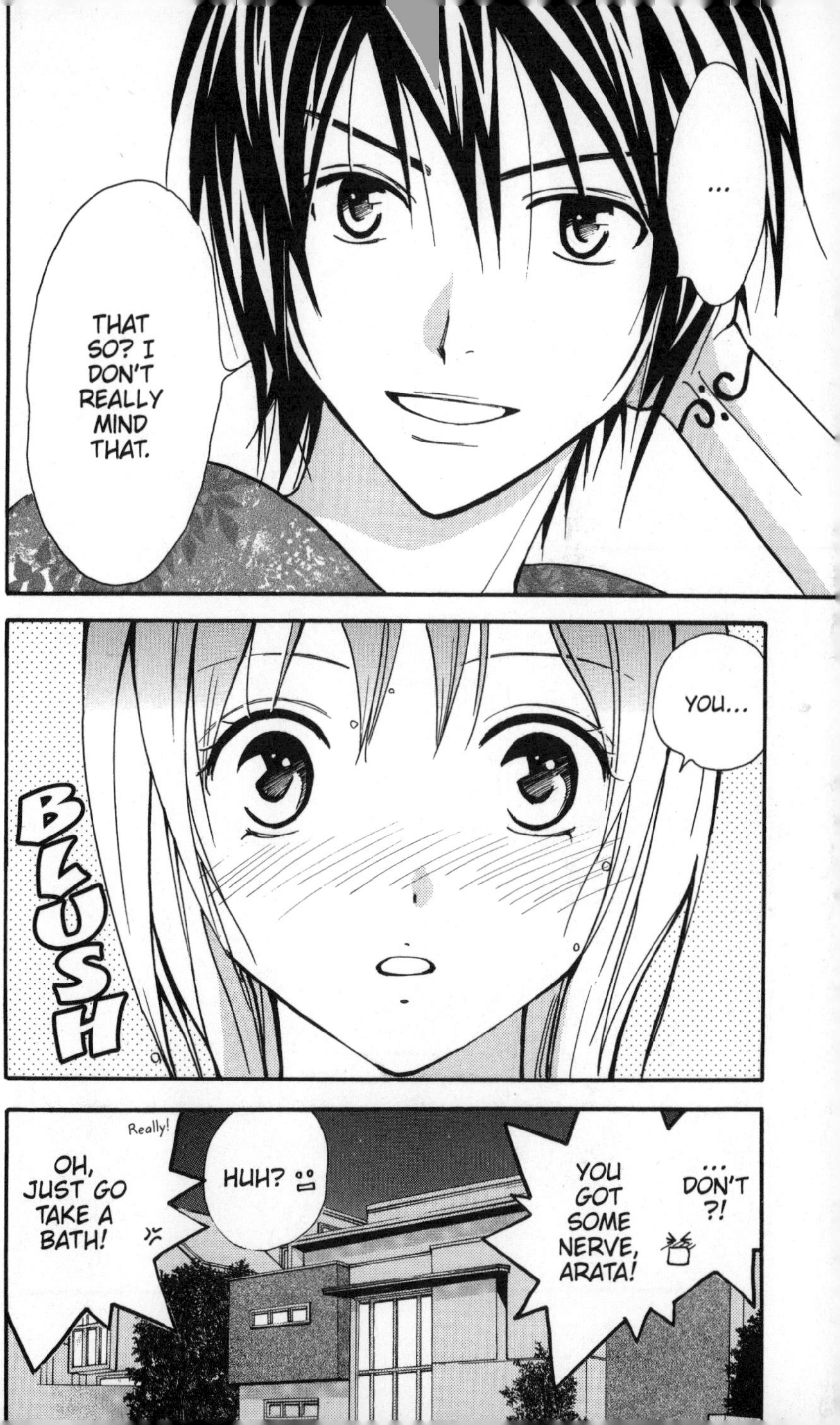
...
THAT SO? I DON'T REALLY MIND THAT.
YOU...
BLUSH
... DON'T ?!
YOU GOT SOME NERVE, ARATA!
HUH?
Really!
OH, JUST GO TAKE A BATH!

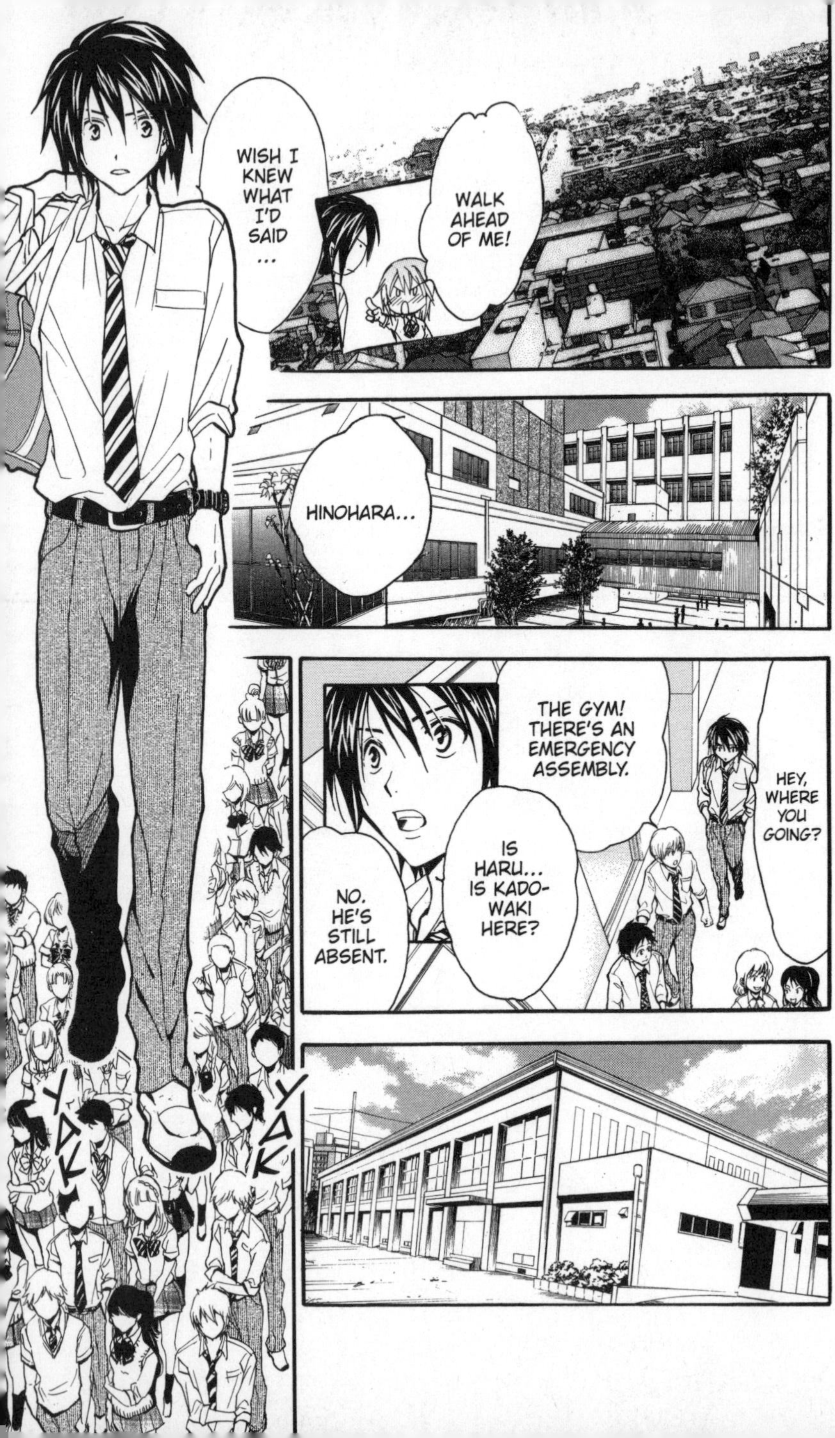

WALK AHEAD OF ME!
WISH I KNEW WHAT I'D SAID ...
HINOHARA...
HEY, WHERE YOU GOING?
THE GYM! THERE'S AN EMERGENCY ASSEMBLY.
IS HARU... IS KADO-WAKI HERE?
NO. HE'S STILL ABSENT.
YAK
YAK

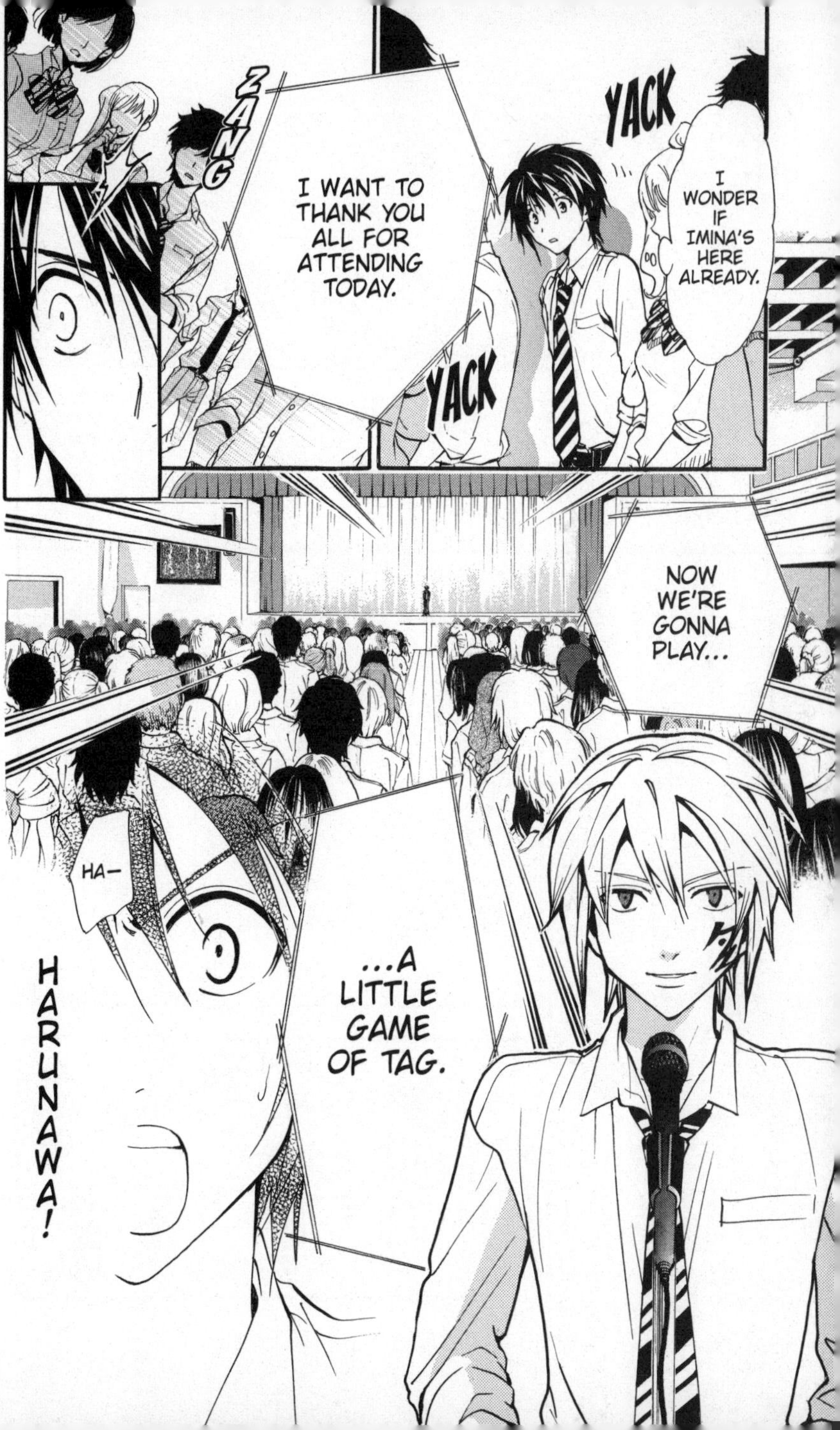
YACK
I WONDER IF IMINA'S HERE ALREADY.
YACK
I WANT TO THANK YOU ALL FOR ATTENDING TODAY.
ZANG
NOW WE'RE GONNA PLAY...
...A LITTLE GAME OF TAG.
HA—
HARUNAWA!

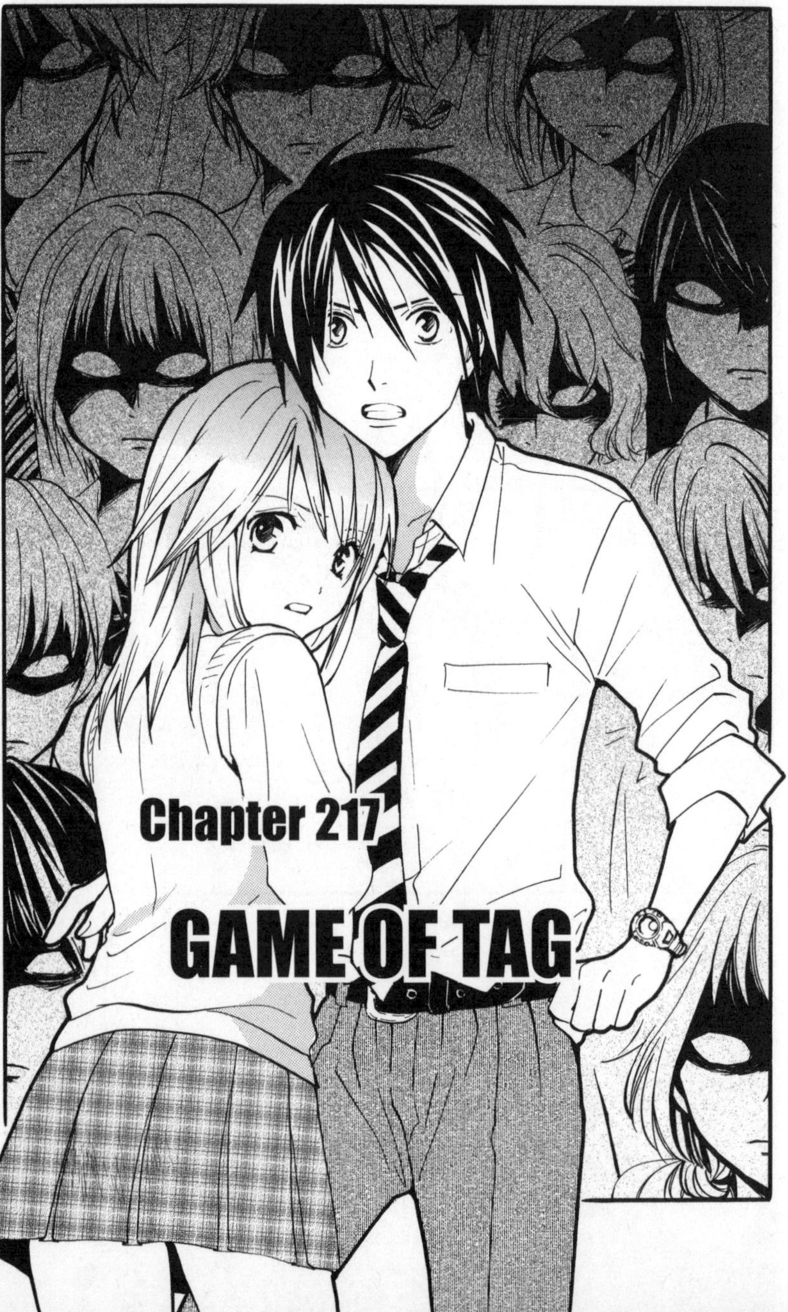
Chapter 217
GAME OF TAG

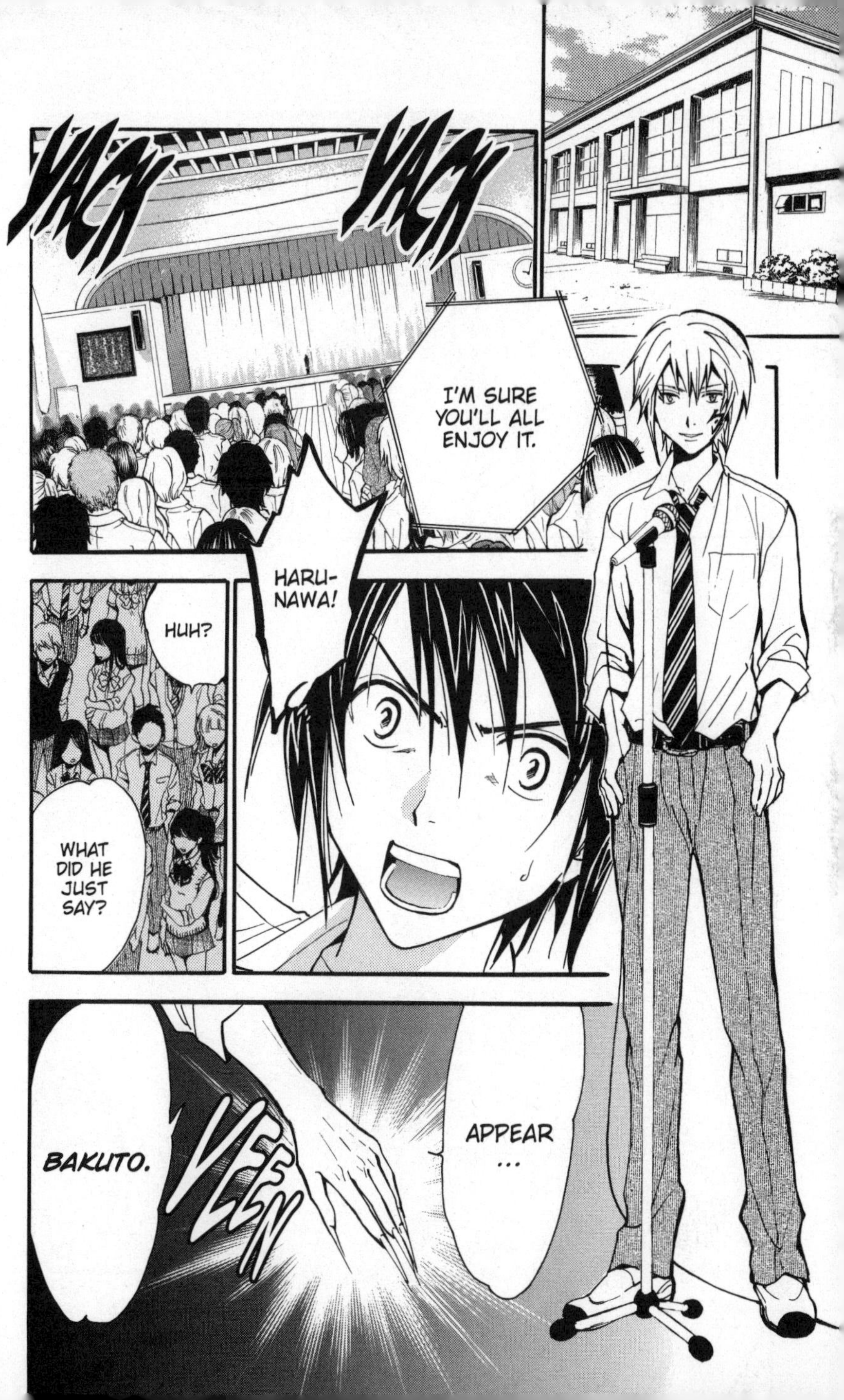
I'M SURE YOU'LL ALL ENJOY IT.
YACK YACK
HARU-NAWA!
HUH?
WHAT DID HE JUST SAY?
APPEAR ...
VEEN
BAKUTO.

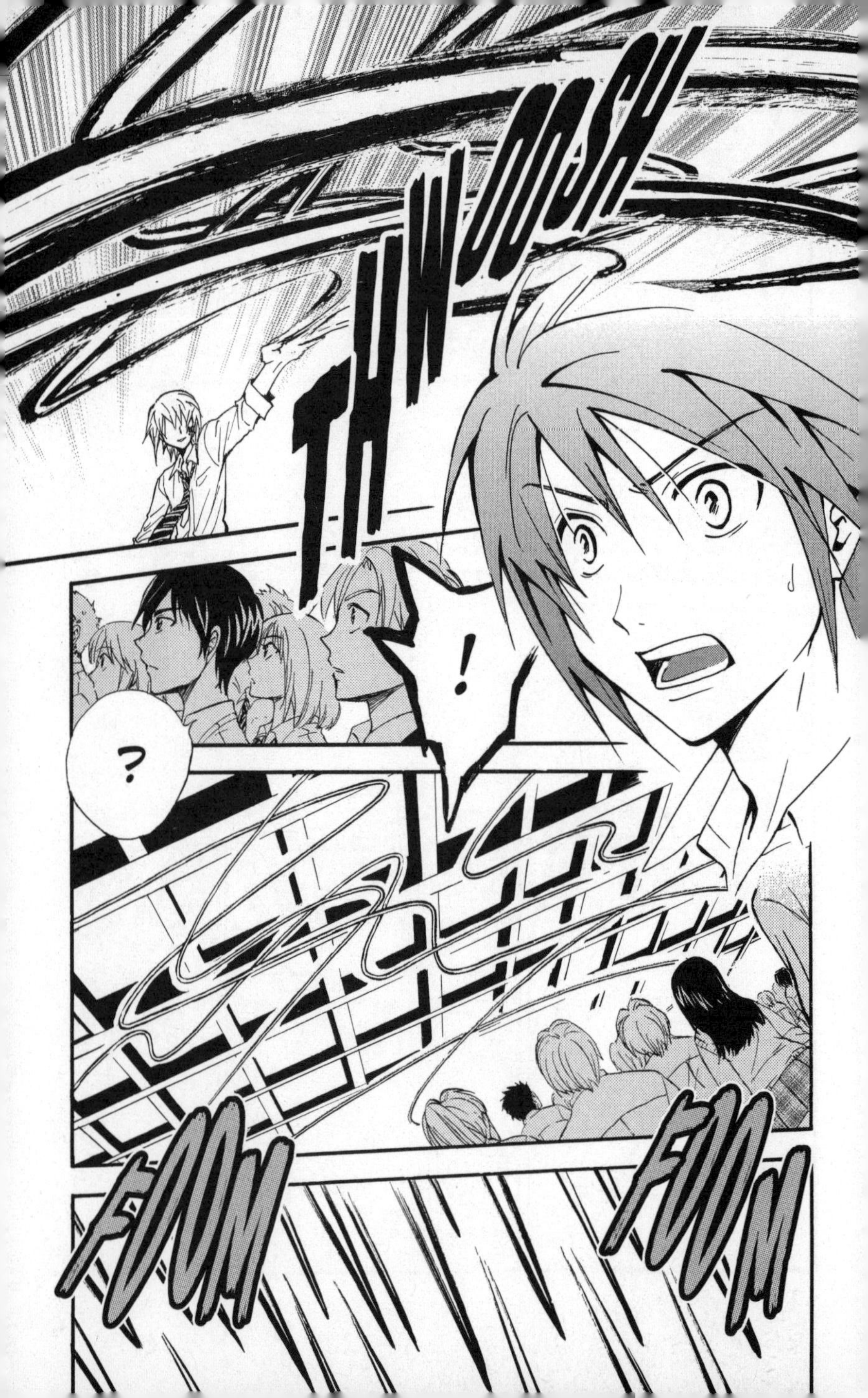
THWOOSH
!
?
FWOM
FWOM

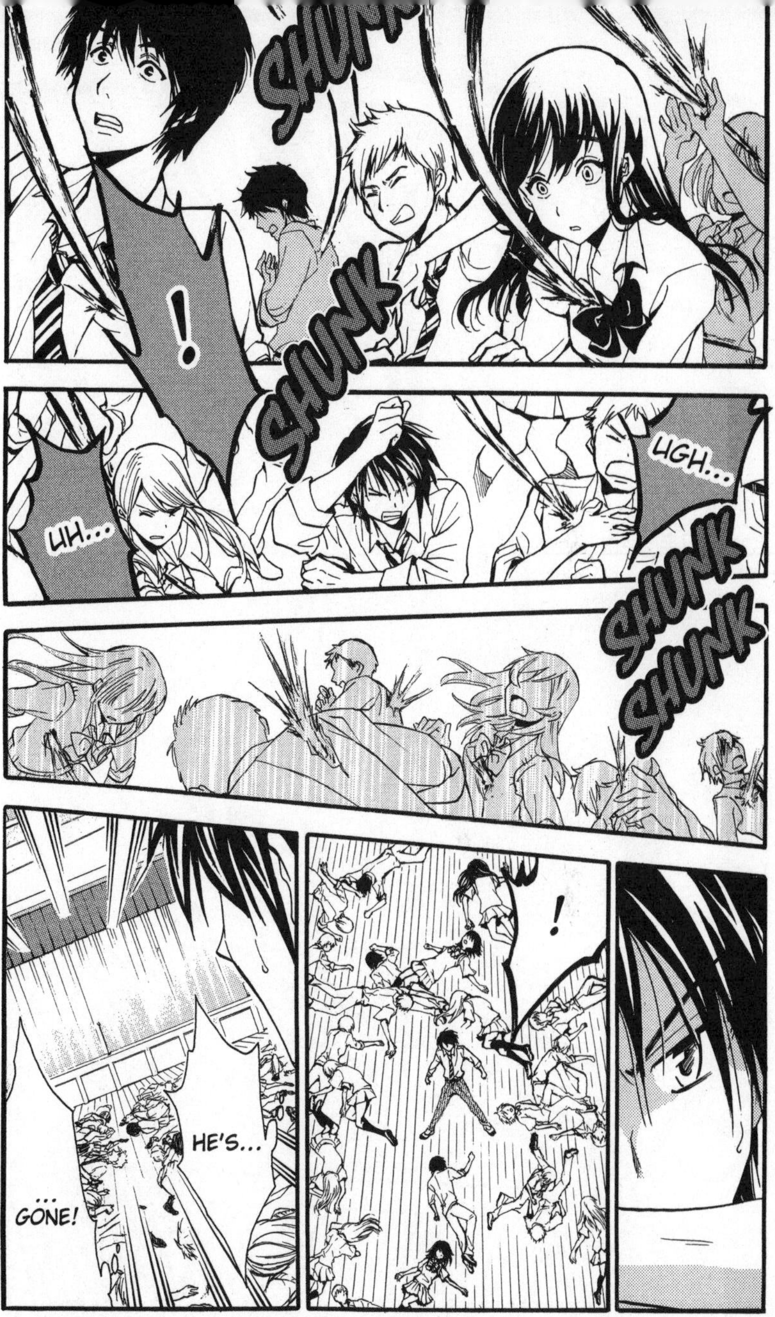
SHUNK
SHUNK
!
UGH...
UH...
SHUNK
SHUNK
!
HE'S...
...GONE!

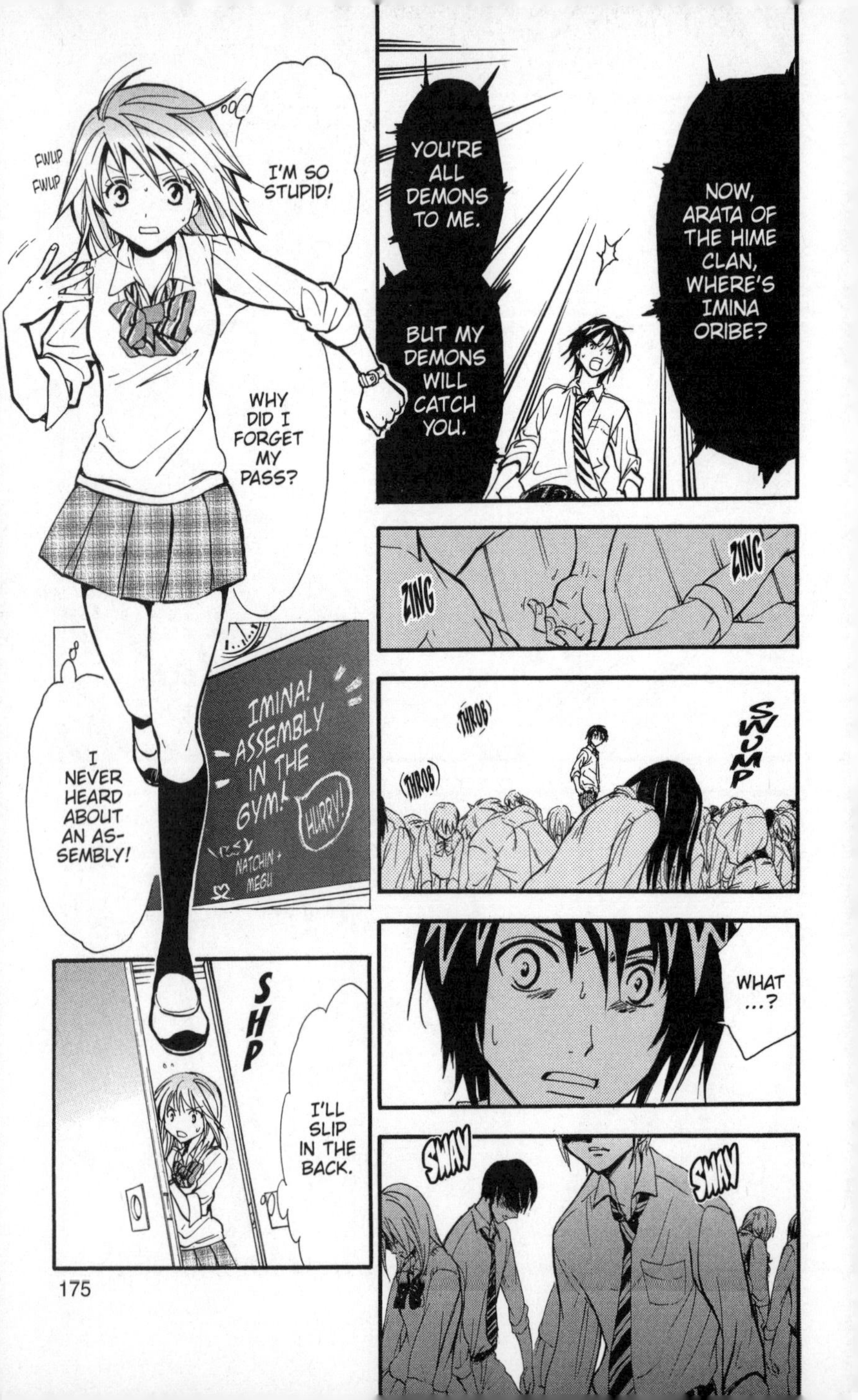
NOW, ARATA OF THE HIME CLAN, WHERE'S IMINA ORIBE?
YOU'RE ALL DEMONS TO ME.
BUT MY DEMONS WILL CATCH YOU.
ZING
ZING
SWUMP
THROB
THROB
WHAT ...?
SWAY
SWAY
FWUP FWUP
I'M SO STUPID!
WHY DID I FORGET MY PASS?
IMINA! ASSEMBLY IN THE GYM!
HURRY!!
NATCHIN + MEGU
I NEVER HEARD ABOUT AN ASSEMBLY!
SHP
I'LL SLIP IN THE BACK.

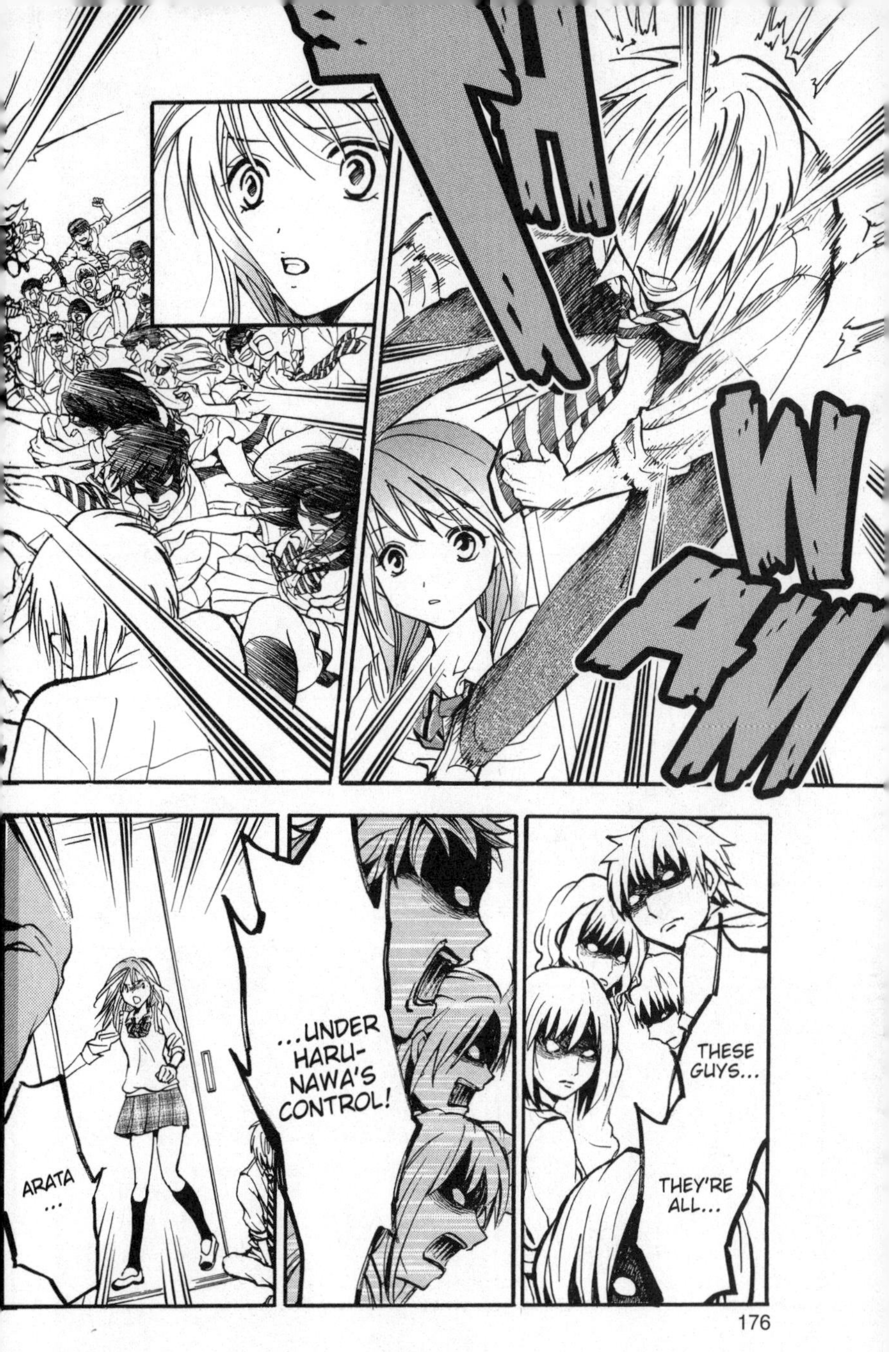
THESE GUYS...
THEY'RE ALL...
...UNDER HARU-NAWA'S CONTROL!
ARATA ...

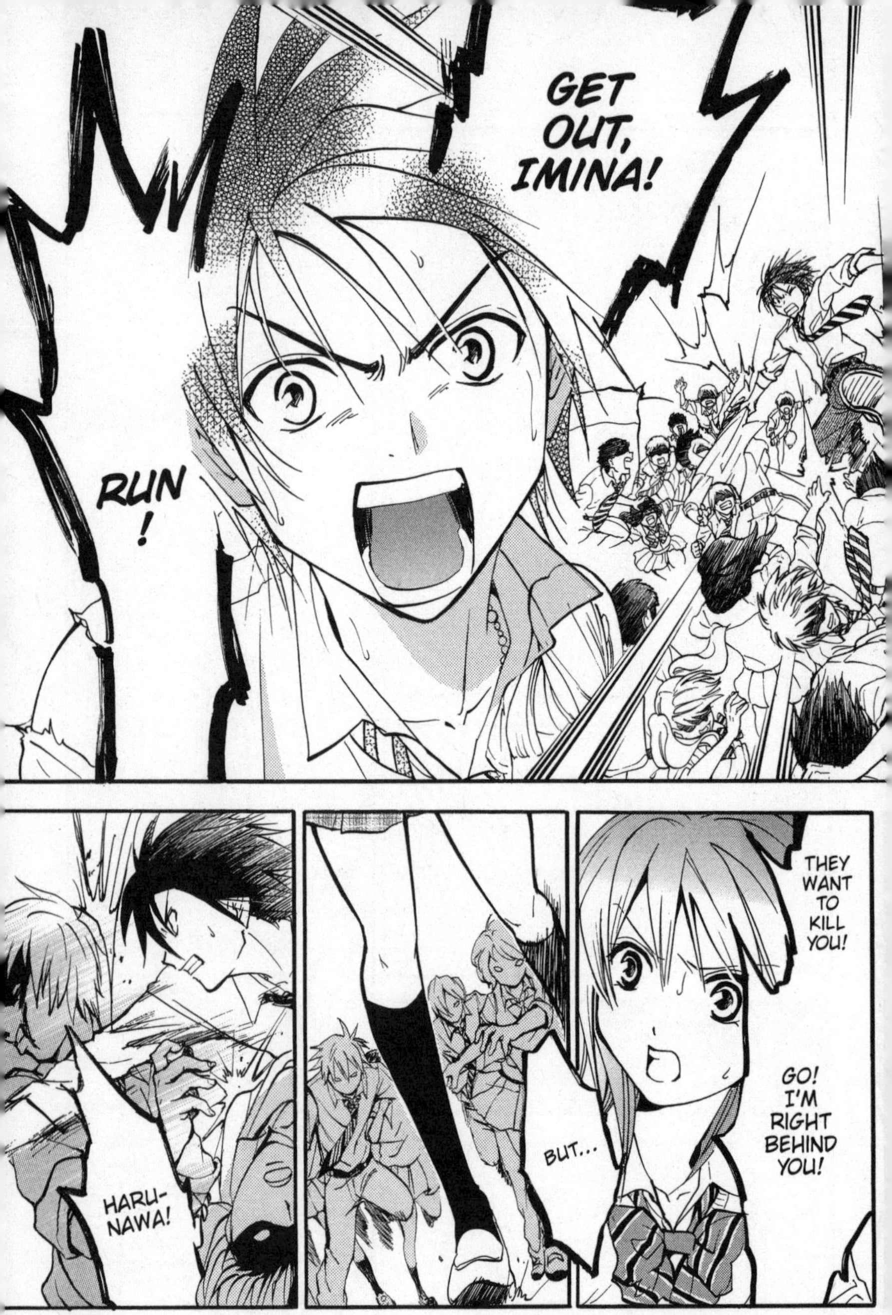
GET OUT, IMINA!
RUN!
THEY WANT TO KILL YOU!
GO! I'M RIGHT BEHIND YOU!
BUT...
HARU-NAWA!

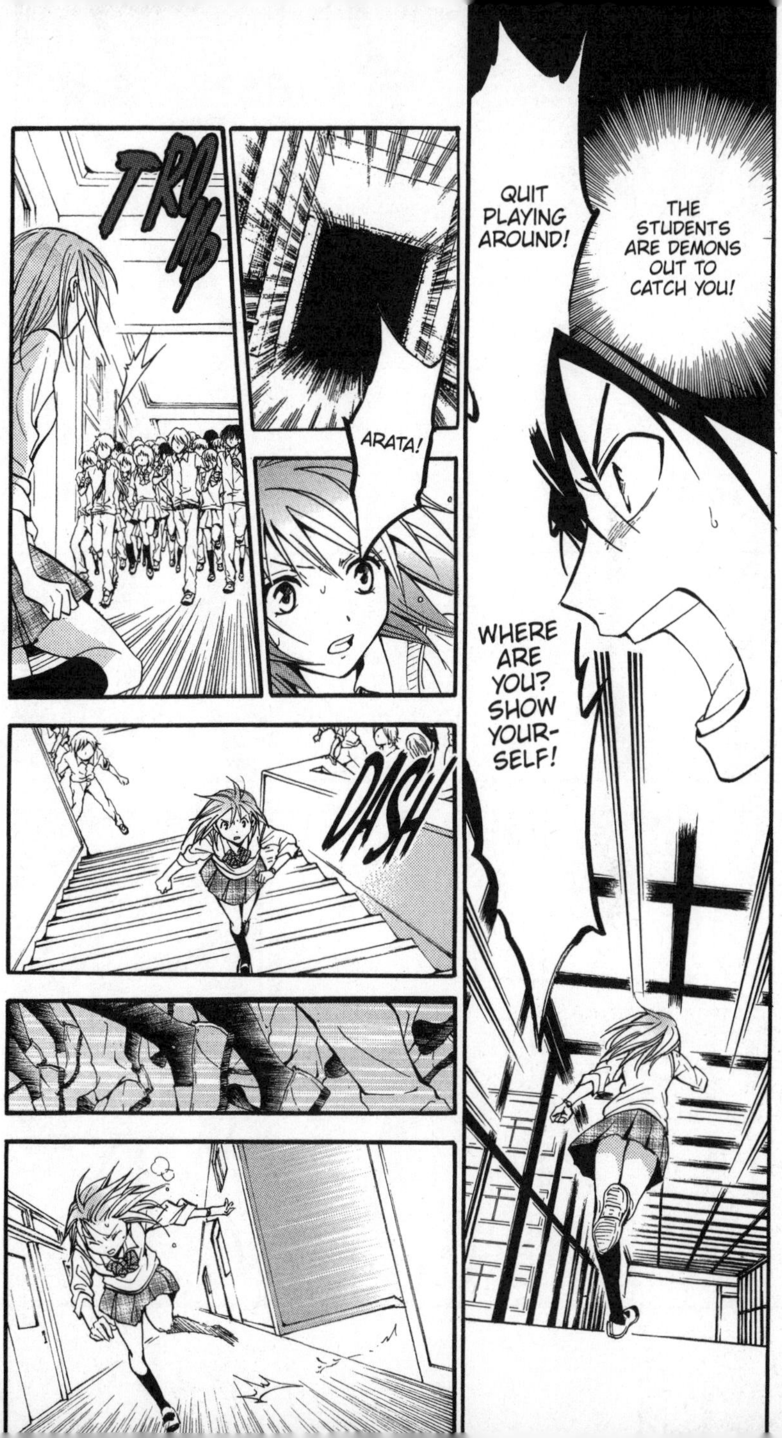
THE STUDENTS ARE DEMONS OUT TO CATCH YOU!
QUIT PLAYING AROUND!
WHERE ARE YOU? SHOW YOUR-SELF!
ARATA!
TROMP
DASH

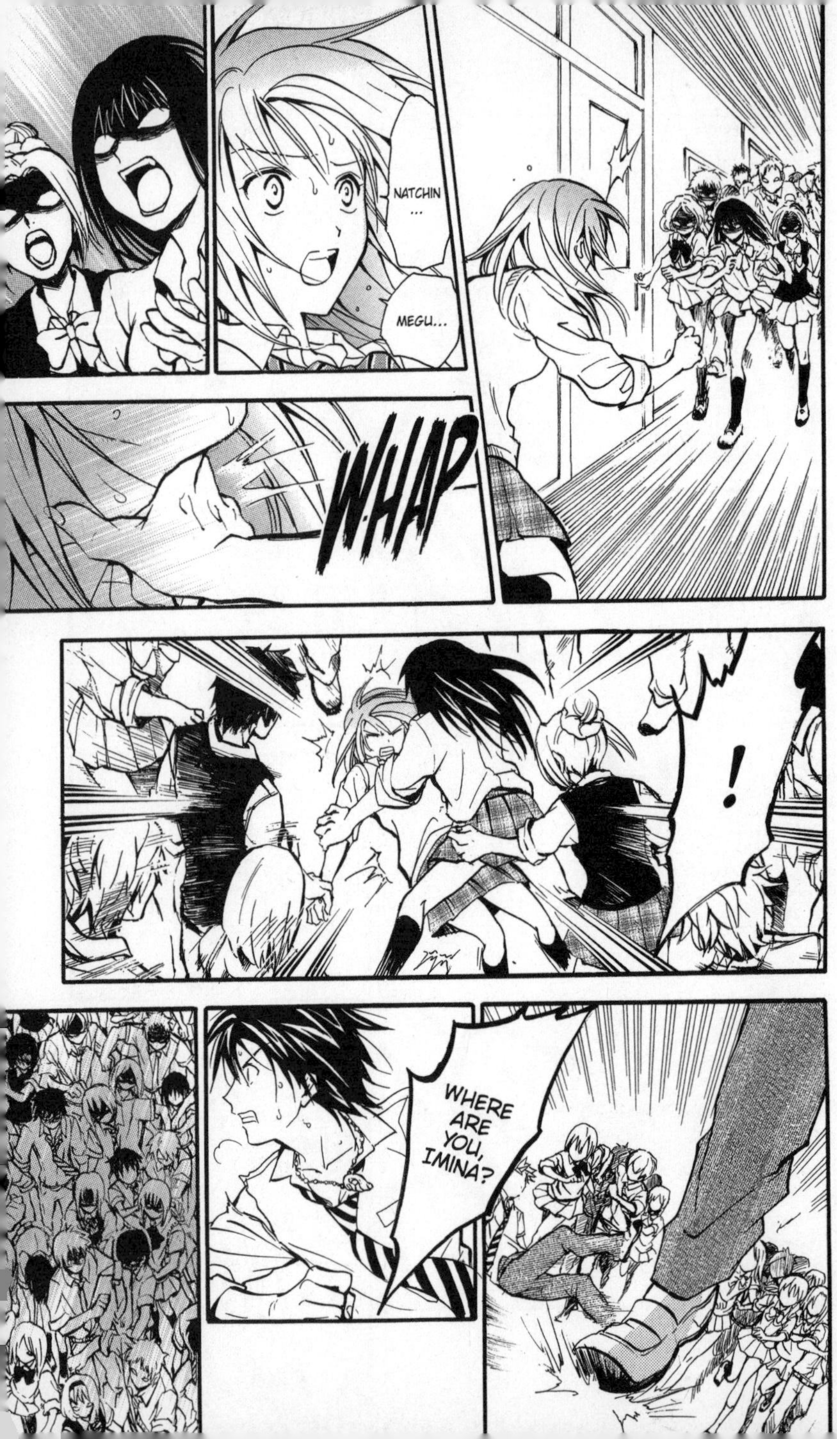
NATCHIN ...
MEGU...
WHAP
!
WHERE ARE YOU, IMINA?

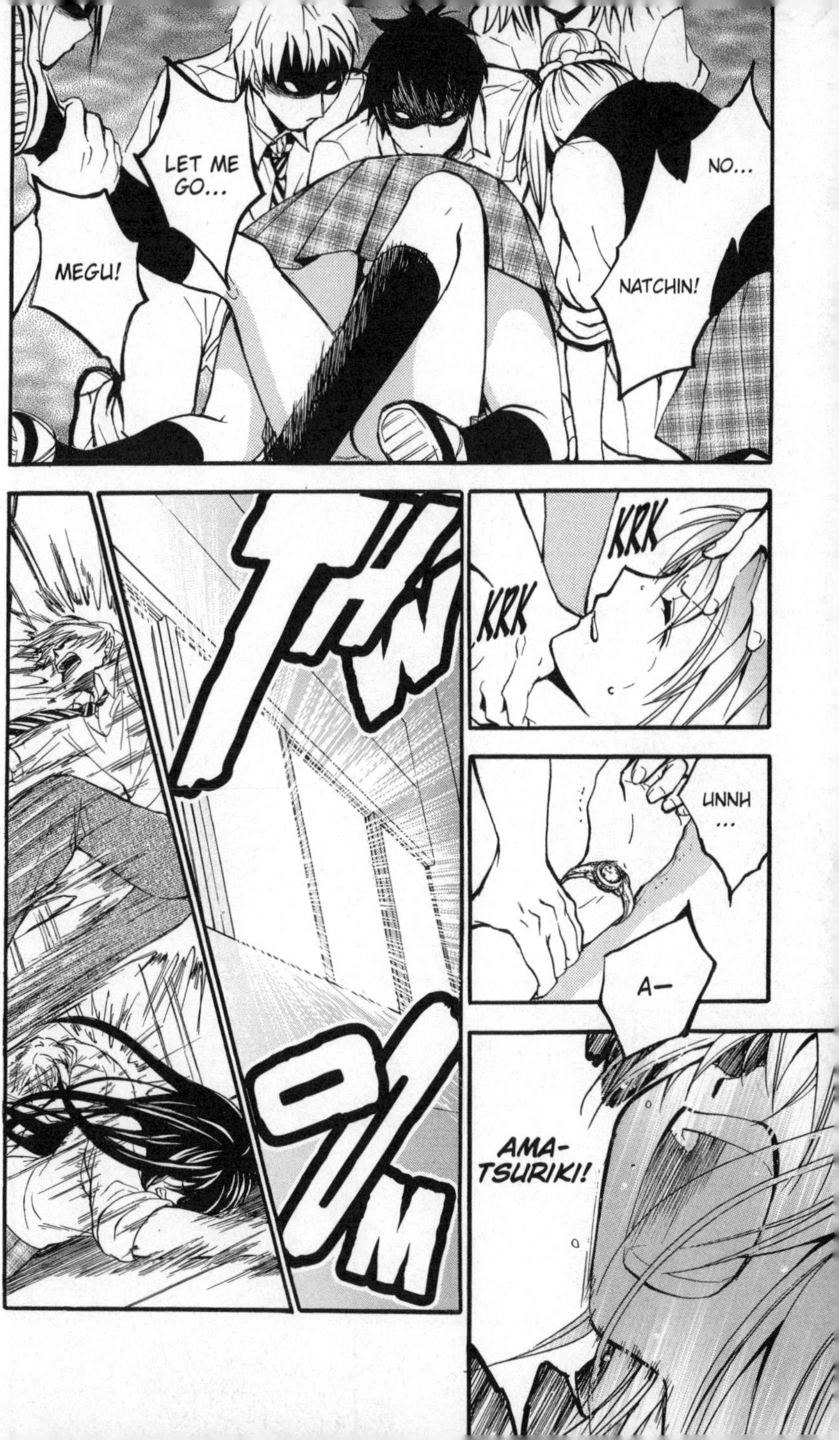
NO...
LET ME GO...
NATCHIN!
MEGU!
KRK
KRK
UNNH...
A—
AMA-TSURIKI!

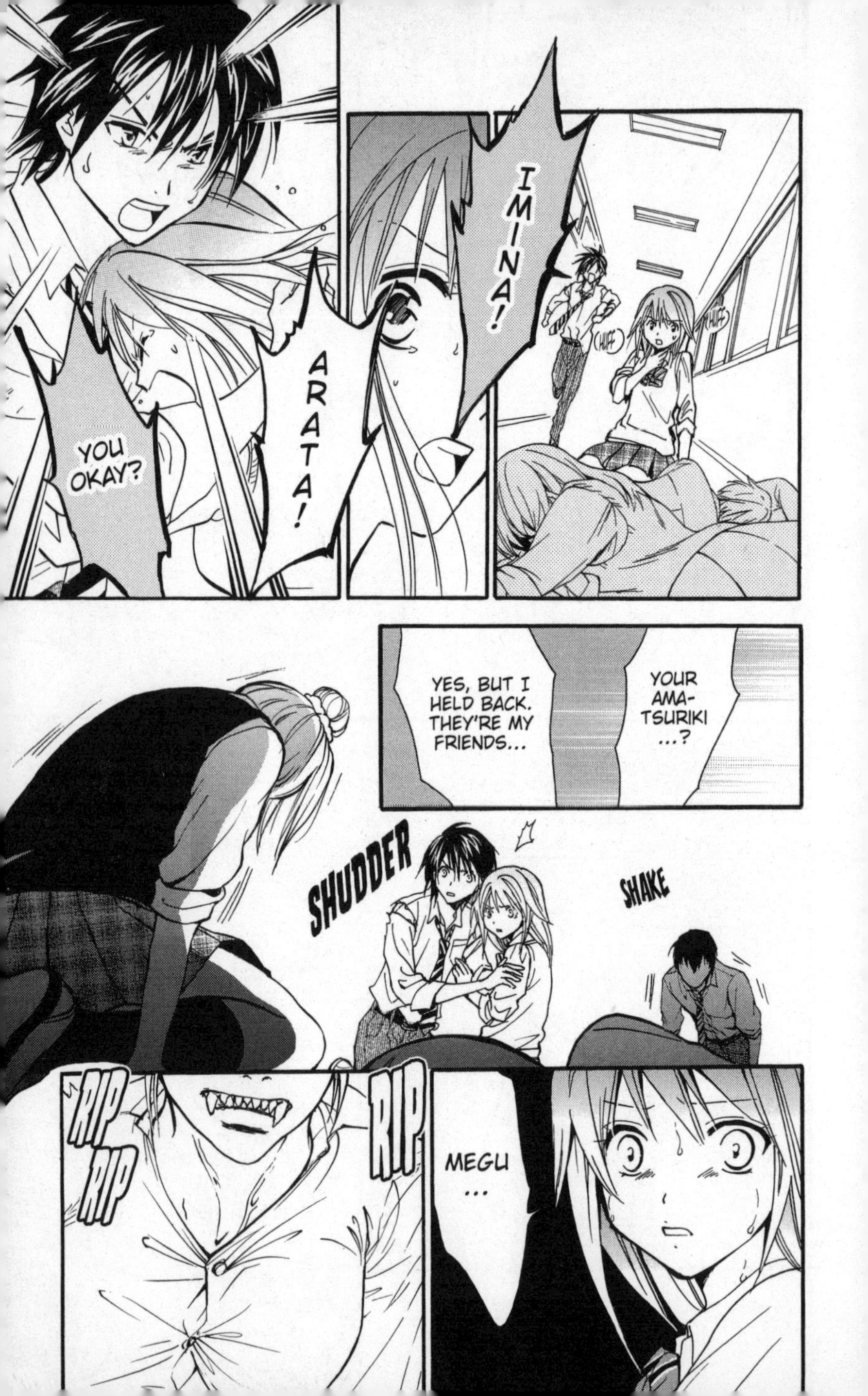
HUFF
HUFF
IMINA!
ARATA!
YOU OKAY?
YOUR AMA-TSURIKI...?
YES, BUT I HELD BACK. THEY'RE MY FRIENDS...
SHAKE
SHUDDER
MEGU...
RIP
RIP RIP

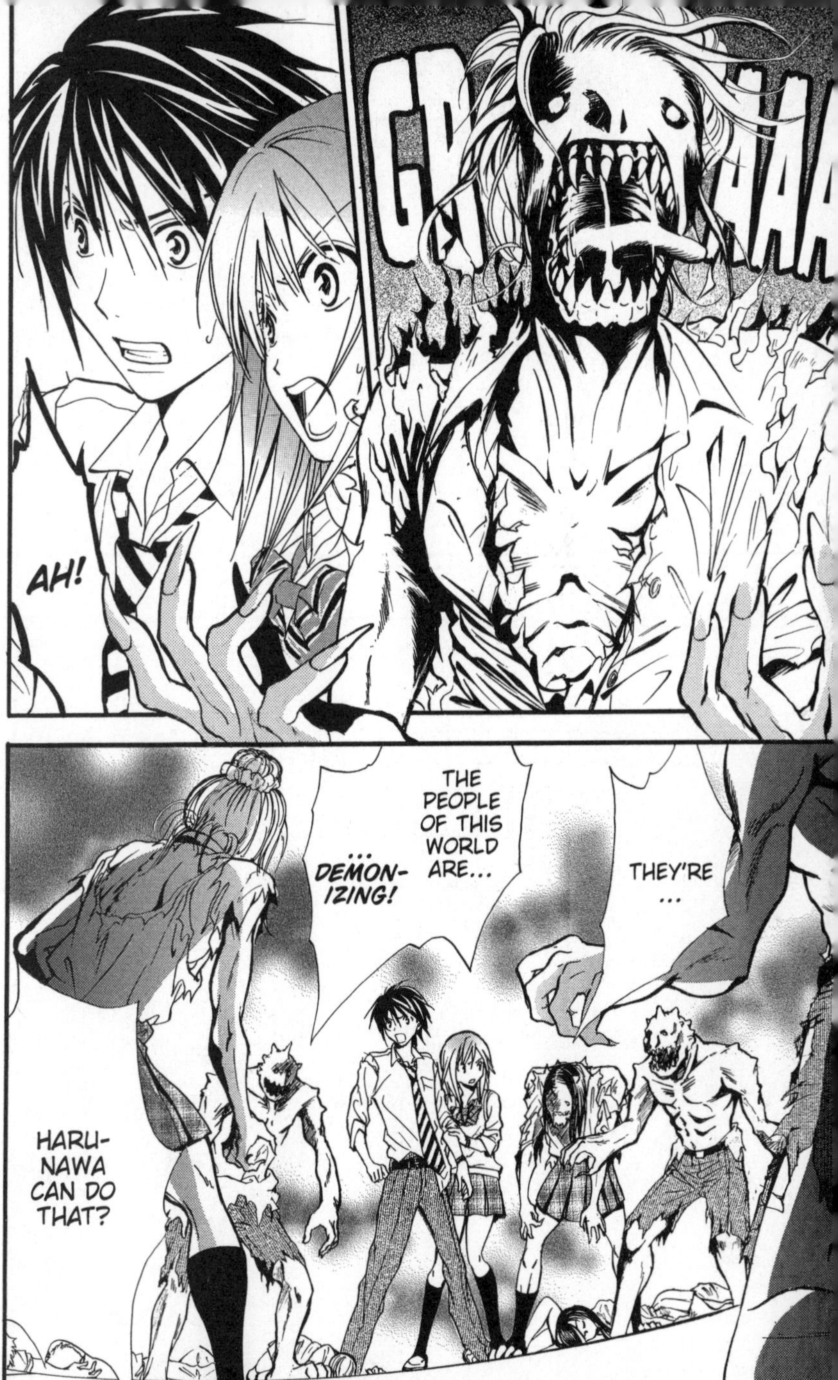
AH!
THEY'RE ...
THE PEOPLE OF THIS WORLD ARE...
...DEMON-IZING!
HARU-NAWA CAN DO THAT?

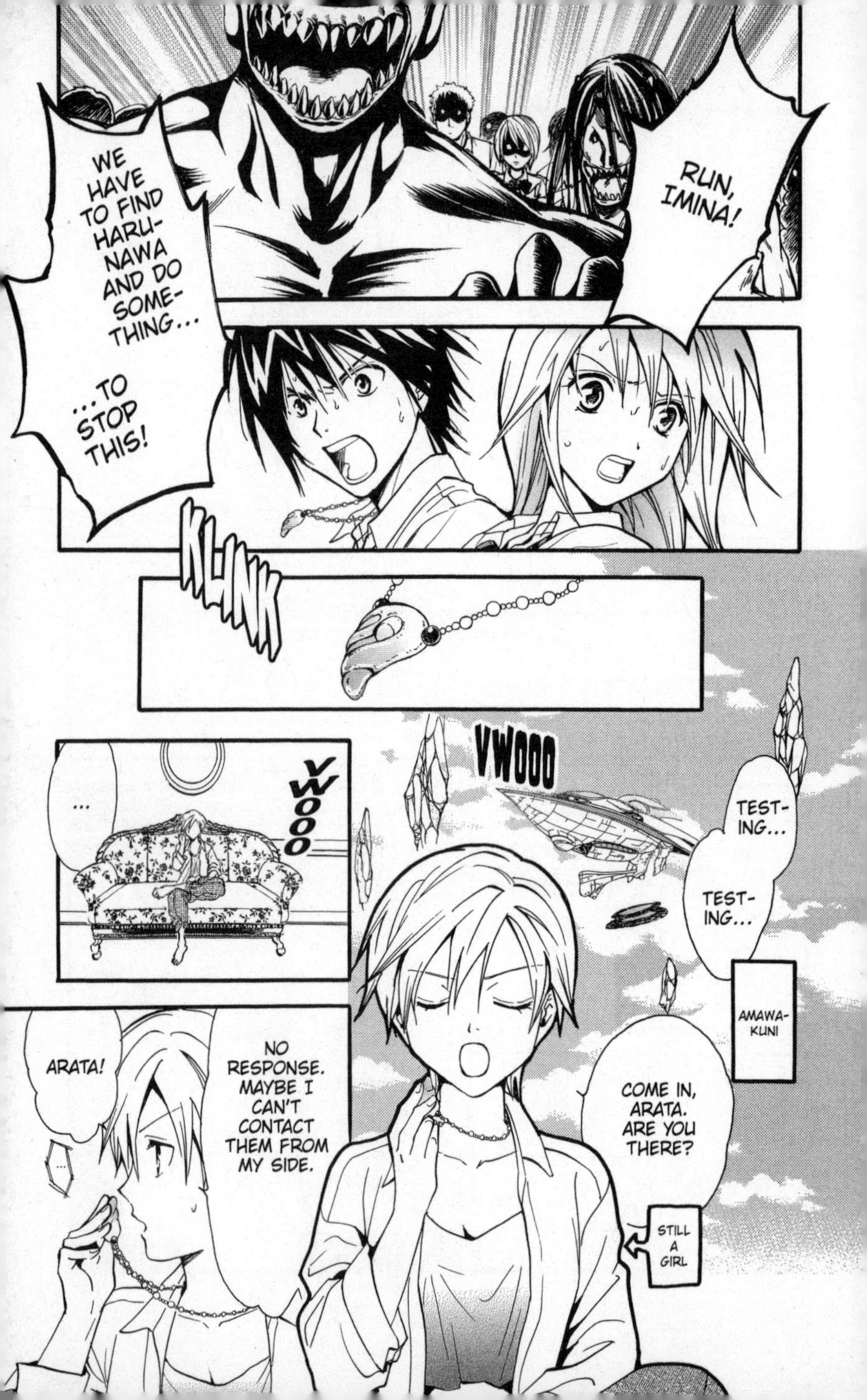
RUN, IMINA!
WE HAVE TO FIND HARU-NAWA AND DO SOME-THING...
...TO STOP THIS!
KLINK
VWOOO
TEST-ING...
TEST-ING...
AMAWA-KUNI
COME IN, ARATA. ARE YOU THERE?
STILL A GIRL
VWOOO
...
ARATA!
NO RESPONSE. MAYBE I CAN'T CONTACT THEM FROM MY SIDE.
...

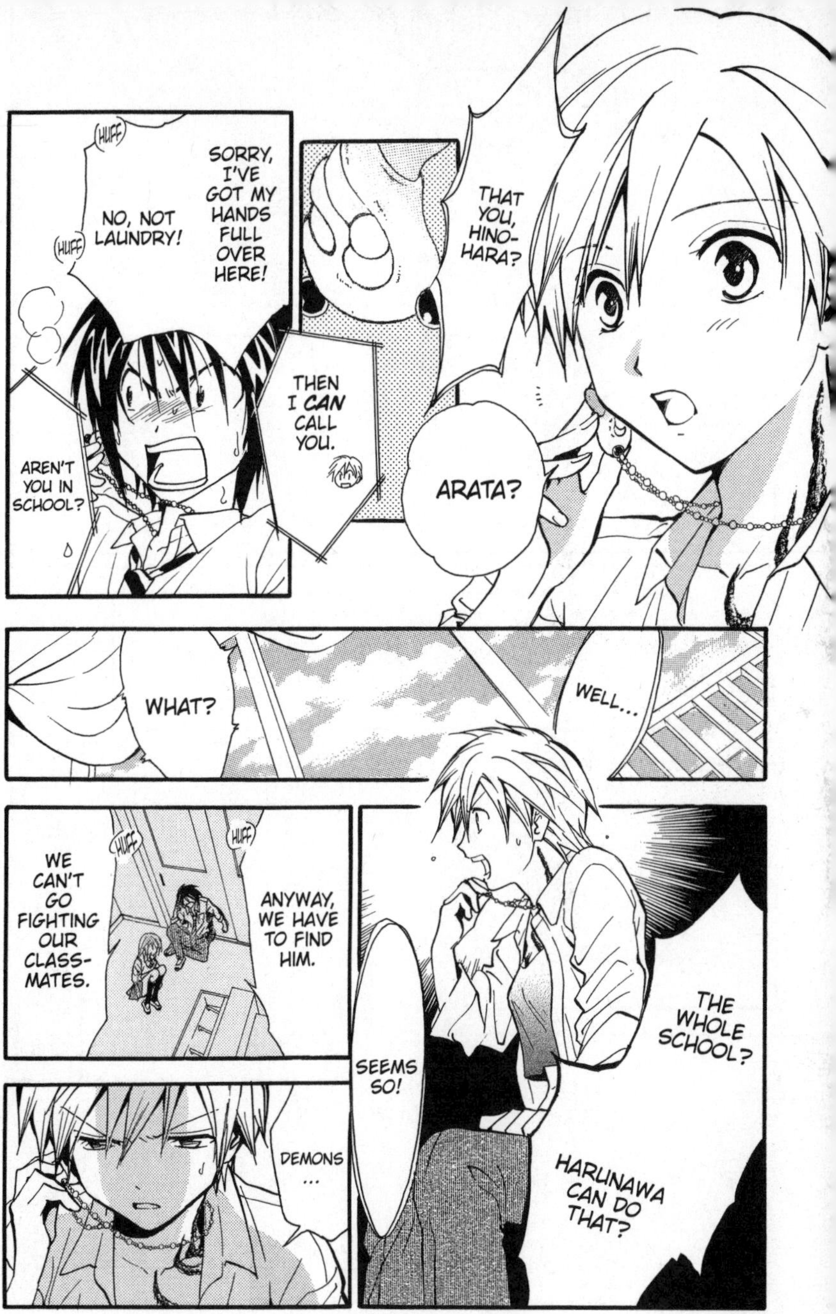
THAT YOU, HINO-HARA?
ARATA?
THEN I CAN CALL YOU.
SORRY, I'VE GOT MY HANDS FULL OVER HERE!
(HUFF)
NO, NOT LAUNDRY!
(HUFF)
AREN'T YOU IN SCHOOL?
WELL...
WHAT?
THE WHOLE SCHOOL?
SEEMS SO!
HARUNAWA CAN DO THAT?
(HUFF)
(HUFF)
ANYWAY, WE HAVE TO FIND HIM.
WE CAN'T GO FIGHTING OUR CLASS-MATES.
DEMONS...

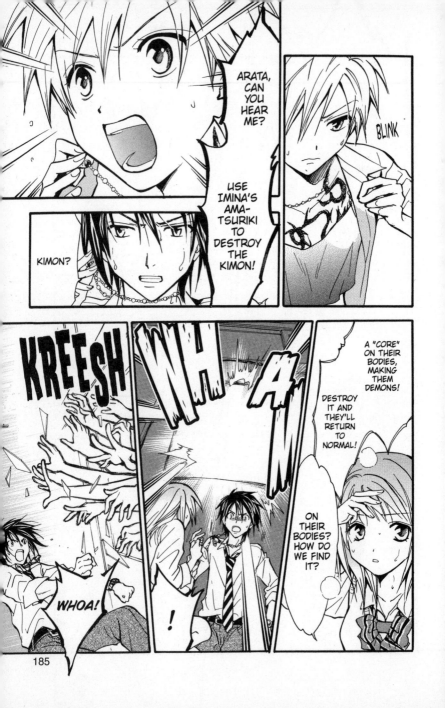

ARATA, CAN YOU HEAR ME?

BLINK

USE IMINA'S AMA-TSURIKI TO DESTROY THE KIMON!

KIMON?

KREESH

WHAM

A "CORE" ON THEIR BODIES, MAKING THEM DEMONS!

DESTROY IT AND THEY'LL RETURN TO NORMAL!

ON THEIR BODIES? HOW DO WE FIND IT?

WHOA!

!

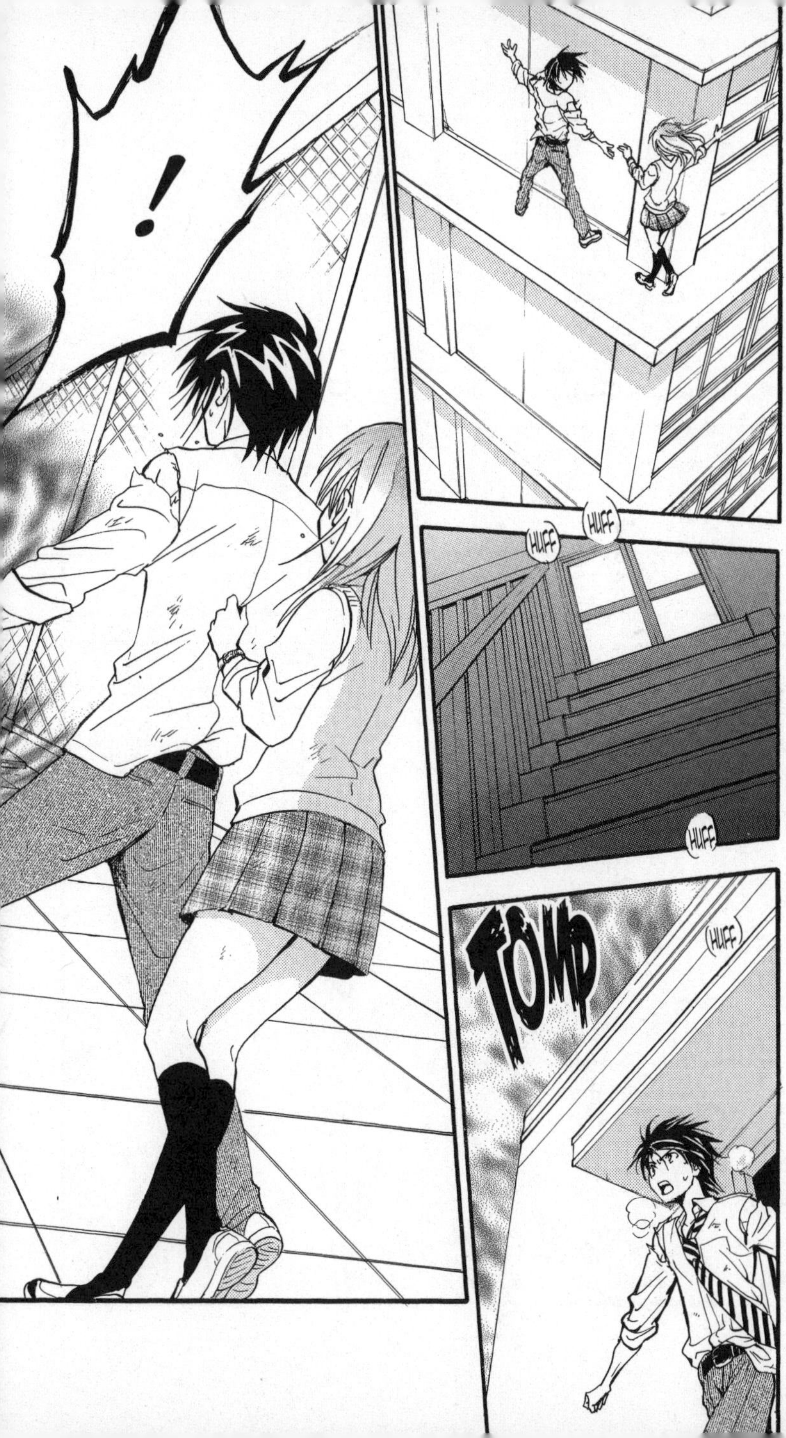
HUFF
HUFF
HUFF
HUFF
TOMP
!

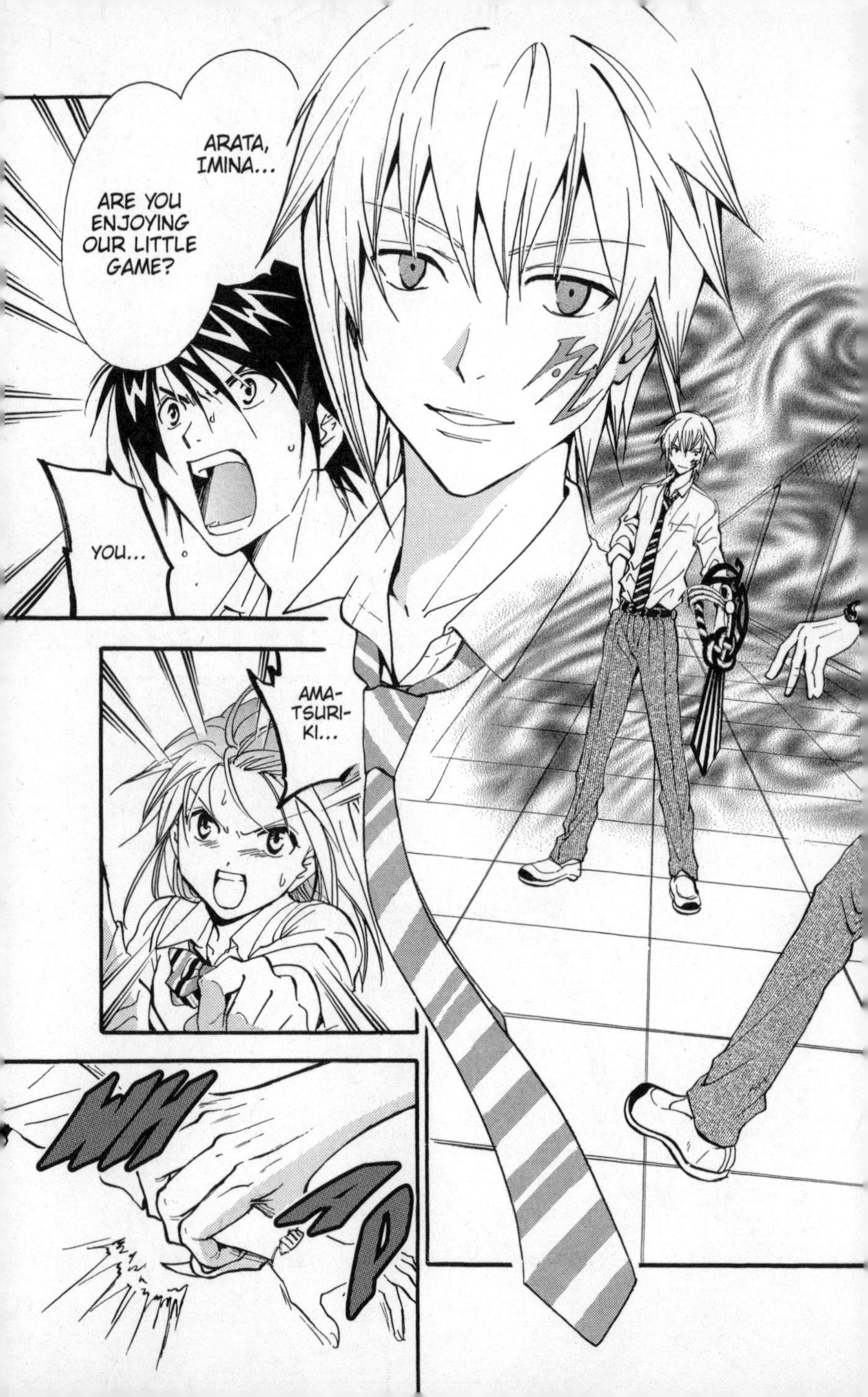
ARATA, IMINA...
ARE YOU ENJOYING OUR LITTLE GAME?
YOU...
AMATSURIKI...
WHAP

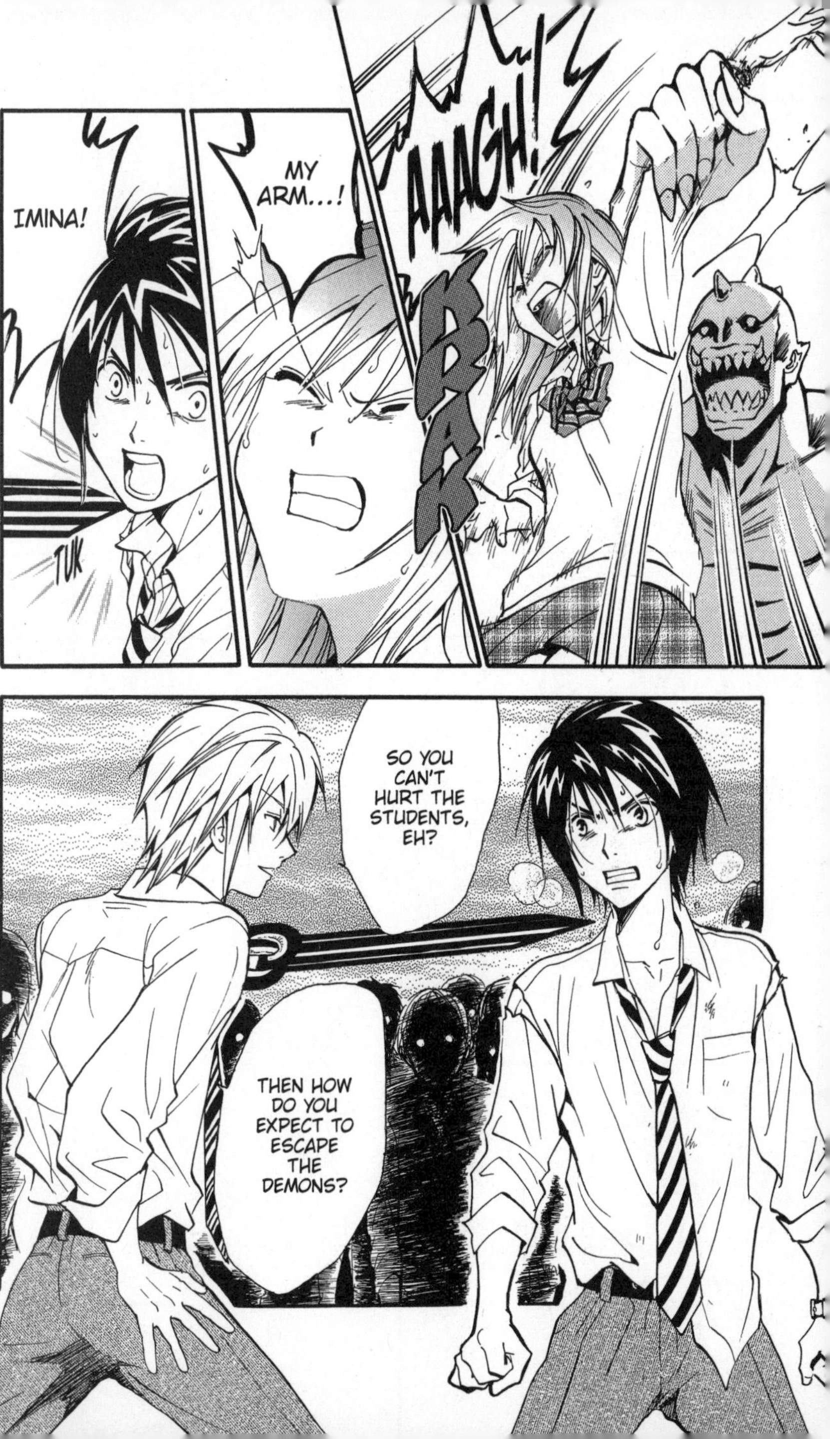
AAAGH!
BAK
MY ARM...!
IMINA!
TUK
SO YOU CAN'T HURT THE STUDENTS, EH?
THEN HOW DO YOU EXPECT TO ESCAPE THE DEMONS?

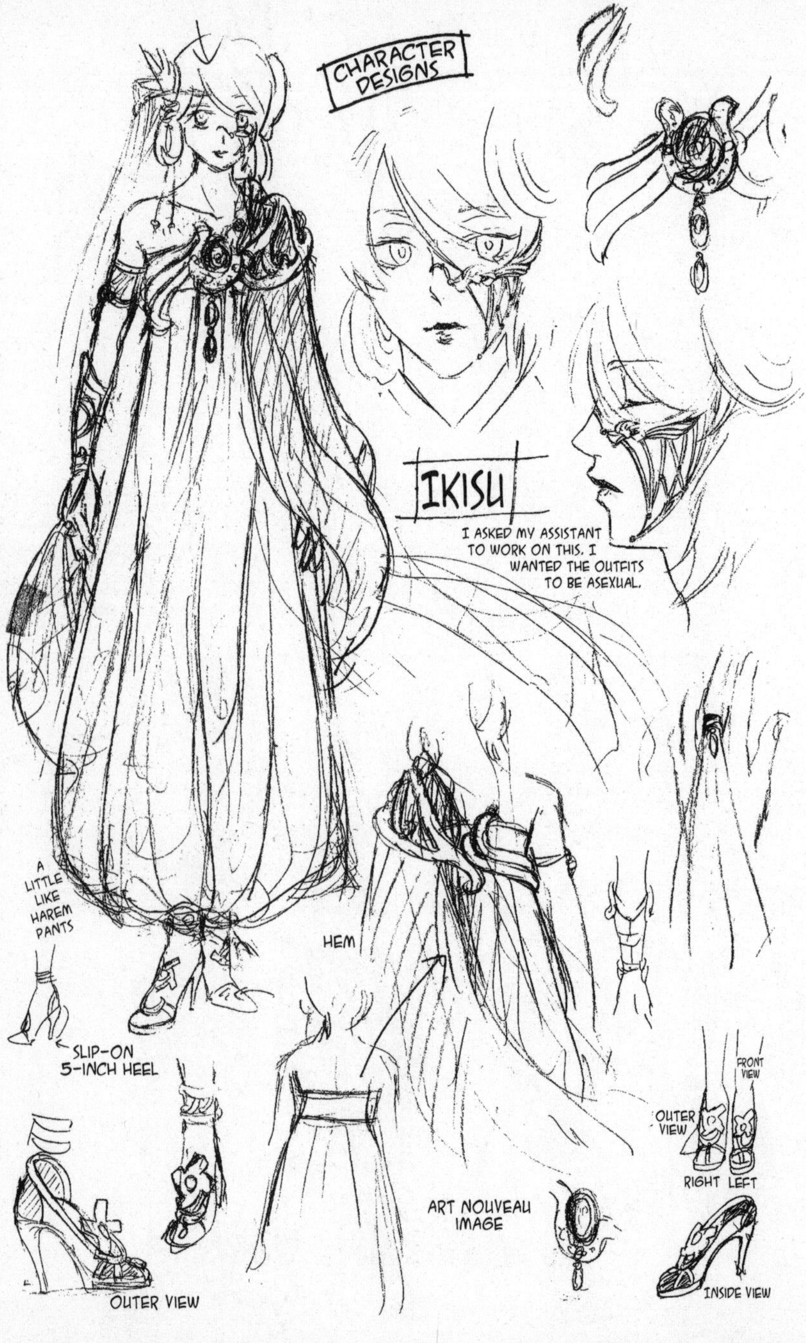
CHARACTER DESIGNS
IKISU
I ASKED MY ASSISTANT TO WORK ON THIS. I WANTED THE OUTFITS TO BE ASEXUAL.
A LITTLE LIKE HAREM PANTS
SLIP-ON 5-INCH HEEL
HEM
FRONT VIEW
OUTER VIEW
RIGHT LEFT
ART NOUVEAU IMAGE
OUTER VIEW
INSIDE VIEW

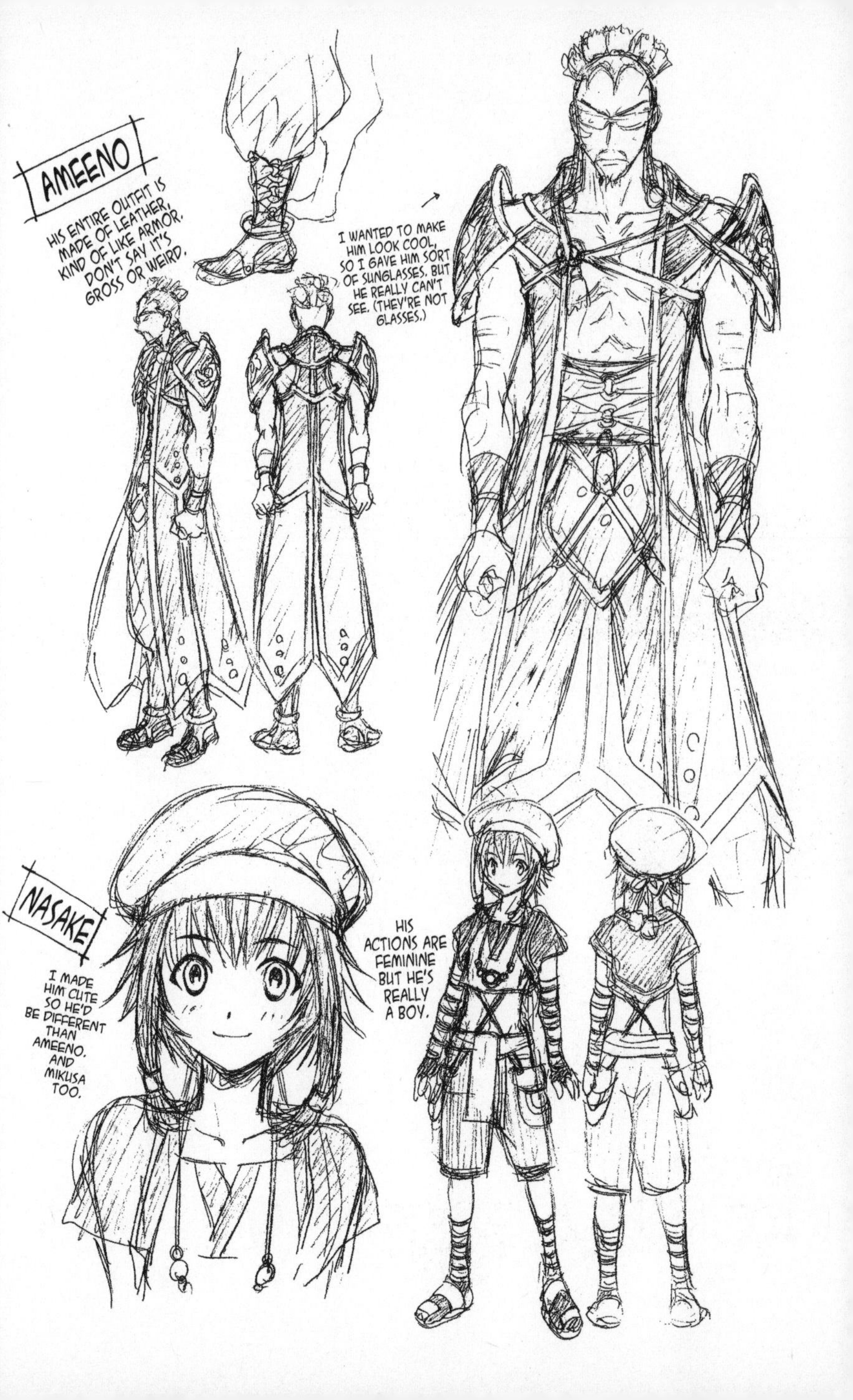
AMEENO
HIS ENTIRE OUTFIT IS MADE OF LEATHER, KIND OF LIKE ARMOR. DON'T SAY IT'S GROSS OR WEIRD.
I WANTED TO MAKE HIM LOOK COOL, SO I GAVE HIM SORT OF SUNGLASSES. BUT HE REALLY CAN'T SEE. (THEY'RE NOT GLASSES.)
NASAKE
I MADE HIM CUTE SO HE'D BE DIFFERENT THAN AMEENO. AND MIKUSA TOO.
HIS ACTIONS ARE FEMININE BUT HE'S REALLY A BOY.

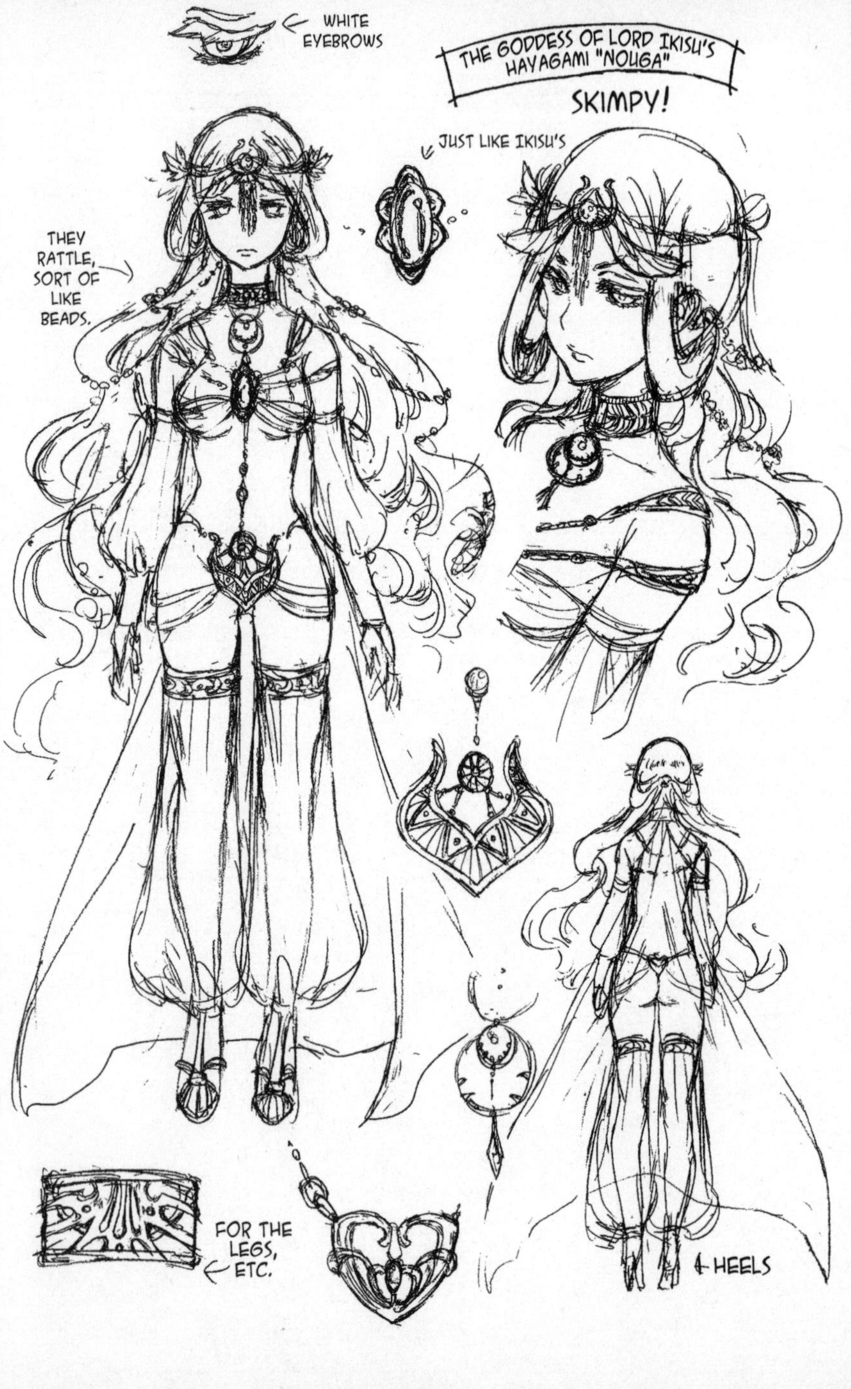
THE GODDESS OF LORD IKISU'S HAYAGAMI "NOUGA"
SKIMPY!
WHITE EYEBROWS
JUST LIKE IKISU'S
THEY RATTLE, SORT OF LIKE BEADS.
FOR THE LEGS, ETC.
HEELS

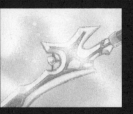

It's been a while since I was discharged from the hospital.

I had some trouble with my digestive tract, so lately I think about taking care of my intestines all the time. When I go to sleep, when I'm up, I'm always conscious of my intestines. This is just like love...!! (Not)

Anyway, acupressure seems to help, so I did a whole lot of research and became more and more familiar with it. I went out and bought "Sennenkyu" moxibustion plasters and even put it on my shoulders on my own when I felt an ache. I felt something hot, and lo and behold, the tank top I was wearing had come in contact with the plaster and gotten singed. Thank goodness it was silk—it didn't burn. If it had been a synthetic fabric, I'd have been burning hot and maybe even gone up in flames.

Just like love...!! (Not)

I will be extra, extra careful so that I can continue this series. (`д´;)

–YUU WATASE

AUTHOR BIO

Born March 5 in Osaka, Yuu Watase debuted in the *Shôjo Comic* manga anthology in 1989. She won the 43rd Shogakukan Manga Award with *Ceres: Celestial Legend*. One of her most famous works is *Fushigi Yûgi*, a series that has inspired the prequel *Fushigi Yûgi: Genbu Kaiden*. In 2008, *Arata: The Legend* started serialization in *Shonen Sunday*.

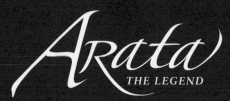

ARATA: THE LEGEND

Volume 22
Shonen Sunday Edition

Story and Art by YUU WATASE

ARATA KANGATARI Vol. 22
by Yuu WATASE
© 2009 Yuu WATASE
All rights reserved.
Original Japanese edition published by SHOGAKUKAN.
English translation rights in the United States of America, Canada, the United
Kingdom and Ireland arranged with SHOGAKUKAN.

English Adaptation: Lance Caselman
Translation: JN Productions
Touch-up Art & Lettering: Rina Mapa
Design: Veronica Casson
Editor: Gary Leach

Printed in the U.S.A.

Published by VIZ Media, LLC
P.O. Box 77010
San Francisco, CA 94107

10 9 8 7 6 5 4 3 2 1
First printing, June 2015

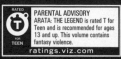

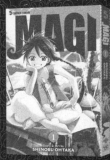

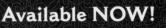

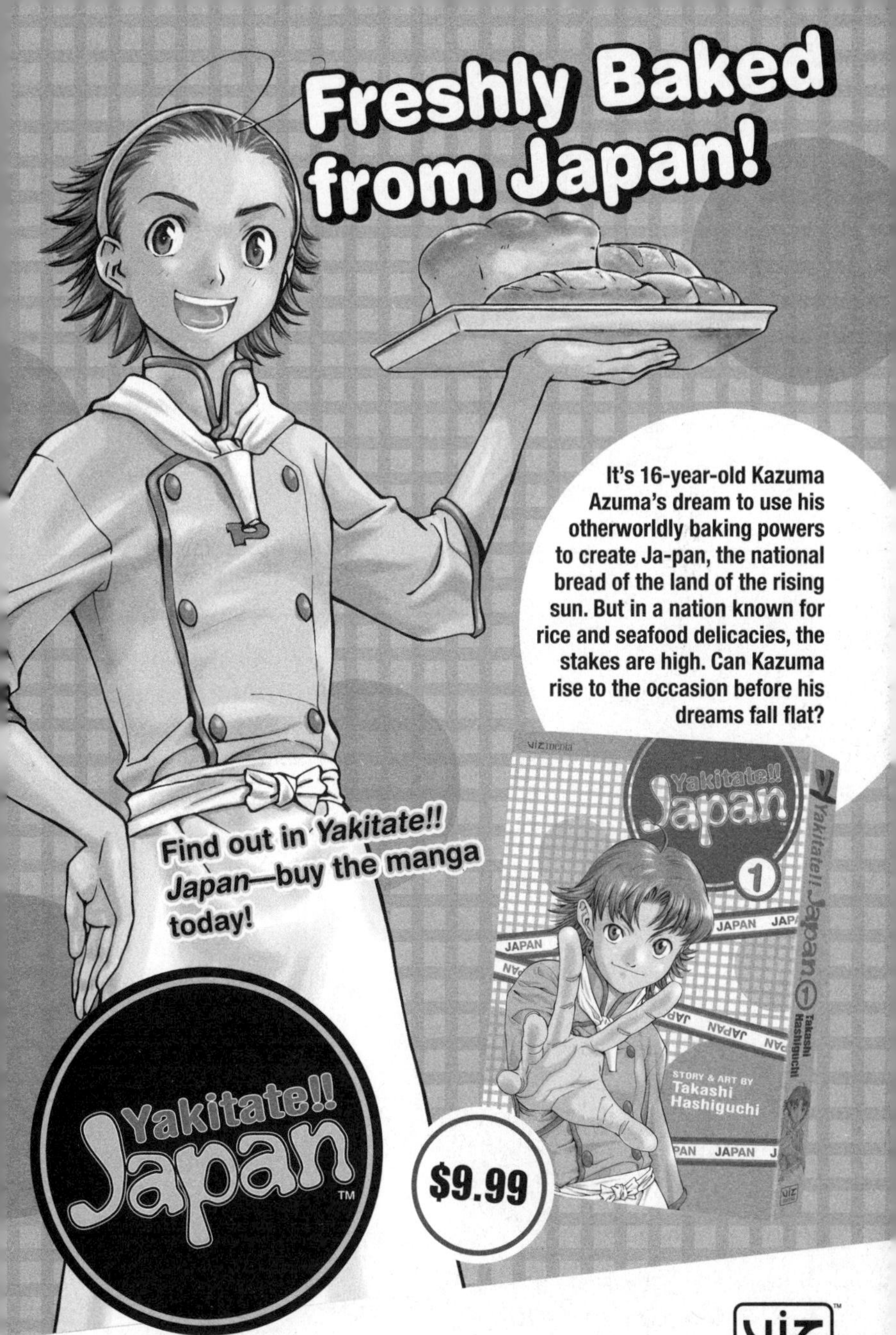
Freshly Baked from Japan!
It's 16-year-old Kazuma Azuma's dream to use his otherworldly baking powers to create Ja-pan, the national bread of the land of the rising sun. But in a nation known for rice and seafood delicacies, the stakes are high. Can Kazuma rise to the occasion before his dreams fall flat?
Find out in Yakitate!! Japan—buy the manga today!
Yakitate!! Japan™
$9.99
Yakitate!! Japan 1
STORY & ART BY Takashi Hashiguchi

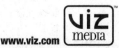

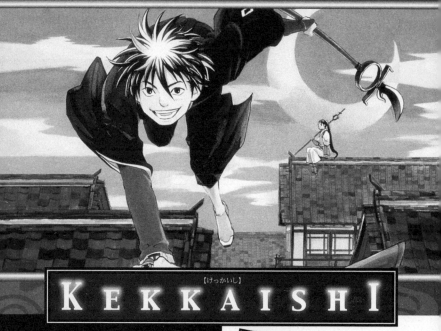
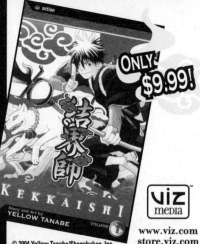

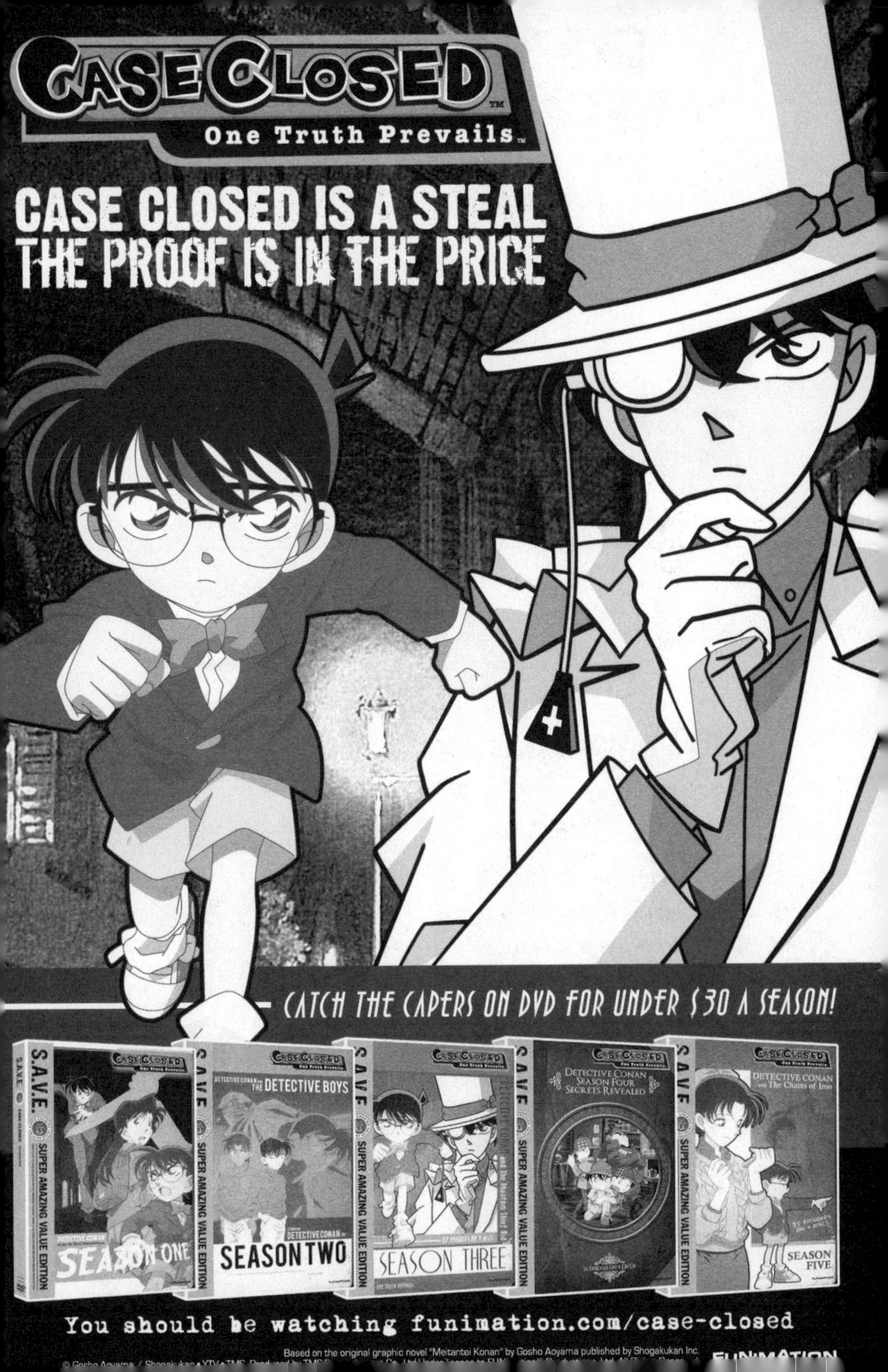

CASE CLOSED
One Truth Prevails
CASE CLOSED IS A STEAL
THE PROOF IS IN THE PRICE
CATCH THE CAPERS ON DVD FOR UNDER $30 A SEASON!
S.A.V.E.
SUPER AMAZING VALUE EDITION
SEASON ONE
DETECTIVE CONAN and THE DETECTIVE BOYS
SEASON TWO
SEASON THREE
DETECTIVE CONAN SEASON FOUR SECRETS REVEALED
DETECTIVE CONAN and The Chains of Iron
SEASON FIVE
You should be watching funimation.com/case-closed
Based on the original graphic novel "Meitantei Konan" by Gosho Aoyama published by Shogakukan Inc.
FUNIMATION

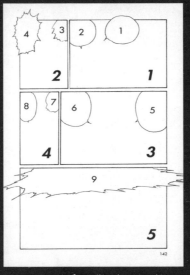

← Follow the action this way.

THIS IS THE LAST PAGE

Arata: The Legend has been printed in the original Japanese format in order to preserve the orientation of the original artwork.

Please turn it around and begin reading from right to left. Unlike English, Japanese is read right to left, so Japanese comics are read in reverse order from the way English comics are typically read. Have fun with it!